Behold Virginia:
THE FIFTH CROWN

VIRGINIA

EN DAT QUINTAM

GEORGE F. WILLISON

Behold Virginia:
THE FIFTH CROWN

Being the Trials, Adventures, & Disasters

of the First Families of Virginia,

the rise of the Grandees,

& the eventual Triumph

of the Common & Uncommon Sort

in the Revolution

New York: HARCOURT, BRACE AND COMPANY

1952

PRINTED IN THE UNITED STATES OF AMERICA
BY THE HADDON CRAFTSMEN, INC., SCRANTON, PA.

Preface

MUCH has been written about early Virginia. But its story, all too human with its comedies and tragedies, its follies and heroics, may bear telling again with particular attention to things as they were there, for they were seldom what they seemed and almost never as first reported.

While I have read the documents for myself, I owe a heavy debt, which I here happily and gratefully acknowledge, to the patient labors of many great Virginia scholars—among others and more especially, W. W. Hening, E. D. Neill, Alexander Brown, Philip Alexander Bruce, Edward Arber, Susan M. Kingsbury, and Thomas Jefferson Wertenbaker.

For much useful technical aid and assistance, my thanks go to Roel Wolfson, Charles Swick, Malcolm Willison, and T. H. W., who bore the load of preparing the manuscript for press, offering countless fruitful suggestions and catching many a slip and *gaucherie*.

Lastly, I wish to thank the New York State Library at Albany, the New York City Public Library, the Library of Congress, and others for many special services. Too few Americans realize that our great libraries are now among the best in the world, as rich as most in their collections, better than any in quickly guiding the student and giving him access to the treasures on their shelves.

GEORGE F. WILLISON

South Hill
August 7, 1951

Table of Contents

Behold Virginia:

THE FIFTH CROWN

Prologue

In the American mind the Old Dominion has long occupied a place apart, for Virginia, both early and late, has been a fertile field for romancers.

And there was romance, though of a very grim sort, from the start—and so much romanticizing that it is often difficult to distinguish fact from fiction.

To some, Virginia was "Earth's only Paradise." It was as pleasant a land "as ever the sunne shined on, temperate and full of all sorts of excellent viands," and infinitely rich, according to Seagull in *Eastward Ho!* (1605), a popular play of the day.

> I tell thee, golde is more plentifull there than copper is with us. . . . Why, man, all their dripping pans and chamber potts are pure golde, . . . and for rubies and diamonds, they goe forth on holy-dayes and gather 'em by the seashore to hang on their children's coates. . . .

To others, Virginia was "a miserie, a ruine, a death, a hell," which was somewhat nearer the mark. In the experience of the earlycomers it was a "slaughter-house" in which four out of five

3

perished, usually within a year, often within a few weeks of arrival.

Virginia grew up to be a great beauty, the mother of many distinguished men, but she was born an ugly duckling and had a childhood so terrible that at times it seems scarcely real.

No catastrophe in history, no war or plague—not even the Black Plague—took a higher rate of lives than the colony in its first decades.

The causes of Virginia's miseries were manifold—accidents, disease, incessant warfare with the Indians when peace could have been achieved, ignorance, inertia, want of judgment, egotism, broken promises, petty personal vanities and ambitions, greed, false hopes and conceptions, and the general character of the colonists.

That anyone at all survived early Virginia's unusual combination of ills is really a miracle, a monument to the durability of the human frame.

Virginia began as a business enterprise, yet nothing could have been more unbusinesslike. Though often at swords' points, the colonists and the directors of the enterprise at home had one thing in common—a rooted aversion to learning anything from experience.

They made the same mistakes over and over, each year adding new ones, always hoping to make water run uphill if they tried once more and just a little harder. No men ever clung more tenaciously to their prejudices and misconceptions. None were ever more blindly wedded to their *idées fixes*.

Were it not for the records, the story of early Virginia would be incredible. As it is, written by the actors themselves, it often passes beyond belief, at times reaching almost to the point of madness, as in Captain John Smith's account of his exploits and accomplishments in Virginia, which, so he came to believe, he had founded and sustained almost singlehandedly.

On the contrary, it was a fortunate day for the colony when Smith, after a disastrous year as commander-in-chief, was shipped home in disgrace. History provides few examples of greater follies than Smith's during his brief day of command, yet his fables still strongly color almost every picture drawn of early Jamestown.

The Virginians were not a dedicated people like the Pilgrims and Puritans of New England, which led to practical difficulties. There was a sad want of unity and common purpose. It was every man for himself, and the Devil take the hindmost—which the Devil did, in great numbers. There was no sense of community in early Jamestown, for the men who founded it had not come to stay. They had not brought along their families with the intention of building homes and fashioning a new way of life for themselves in the wilderness.

Rather, they had come, one and all, as soldiers of fortune, cherishing a single idea—to get rich as quickly as possible and return home to live at ease. Regarding themselves as transients temporarily on duty at an outpost of empire, they did not dig in and lay a sound footing upon which to build.

They had been promised and expected to receive supplies from home, which usually came in too little and too late. When hungry, which was perennially, they tried to live off the country, off the Indians, who ordinarily had just enough for themselves and felt under no obligation to feed men—unwelcome intruders, at that— who made no effort to feed themselves.

That frightful ordeal in the winter of 1609 and the spring of 1610, when nine out of ten died and the surviving "anatomies" could scarcely rise from their beds, was well named the Starving Time, but Virginia's first two decades were one long starving time, filled with agony, frustration, and death.

The history of the American frontier, strewn as it is with hardship and disaster, has no chapter as tragic and gruesome as the first one written here by men who scorned to learn the ways of the wilderness, who declined to adjust to the iron laws of their environment.

Generations later, their descendants, having mastered the ways of the wilderness, would play a major role in pushing the frontier rapidly westward to the Pacific. But their forebears, the English pioneers along the James, were probably the worst frontiersmen that the world has ever known. None ever took longer to learn that they had to be self-sustaining, that they were fools to depend upon any but themselves for their bread and their very lives.

Among those who founded the first families of Virginia were men from many lands—*vignerons* from France, glassmakers from Italy, woodworkers from Poland, carpenters from Germany, Negroes from the West Indies and the Gold Coast. But most were English and, with few exceptions, very poor.

Many of them—all too many—were Gentlemen. Always written with a capital "G," this was no mere courtesy title as it has since become. Rather, it was a badge of honor denoting rank in the rigidly stratified social structure, a troublesome relic from the past, and it bestowed special rights and privileges.

It was the very mark of a Gentleman that he did no manual labor and performed no useful chore. He did not plant corn or build himself a house, expecting that to be done by others. It was beneath him to handle an ax or a hoe even if he starved or froze to death in consequence, as many a one did at Jamestown. The Virginia gentleman (with a small "g"), a man of some industry and enterprise, proud of his practical skills and abilities, was a later breed, a native product.

In major part, however, the F.F.V. consisted of the "Common Sorte," as their "betters" styled them. A great many of these came as indentured servants, as bond slaves obliged to serve their masters without pay for a period of years.

Much fault was found with these poor unfortunates, who were denounced by many as the "very scum and offscouring" of England. Some came from the jails, it is true. Others were homeless children picked up on the streets of London, lewd women from the Bridewell and other houses of correction, "mayds" somehow gathered for sale as wives, and vagrants or unemployed, recruited among the "sturdy beggars" who had been swarming throughout England since Queen Elizabeth's day, displaced by rapid economic change.

Most of the early colonists, it appears, were city-bred, possessing few skills or trades of immediate use in Virginia, and those in command constantly complained of their "beastial slothfullnesse" and "intemperate idlenesse."

But it is doubtful that the "Common Sorte" deserved all of the obloquy and abuse heaped upon them. As a contemporary observed, they were, in general, no better and no worse than those who stayed at home. They represented a more or less average cross-section of the English people of the day, though a few elements were missing—most conspicuously, the sturdy English yeoman. For years, Virginia suffered from want of a few good farmers.

Whatever their origin or status, all suffered alike in the unpromising and mismanaged beginning of the Virginia venture, which more than once all but collapsed, barely escaping the fate of England's earlier attempts to gain a foothold in the New World. Even the most ambitious of these, Sir Walter Raleigh's in 1587, had ended in catastrophe and mystery, with the loss of all the colonists left on Roanoke Island, who vanished without leaving a trace.

After this disaster, almost twenty years passed before England again did anything about her desire to share the riches of the New World—riches that Spain had been monopolizing for more than a century to the envy of the world.

The "first mover" in the new enterprise was one of Raleigh's men, Captain Bartholomew Gosnold. Returning from a voyage to America in 1602, Gosnold spent several fruitless years trying to stir up interest in colonization. At length he got the ear of "certaine of the Nobilitie, Gentry, and Marchants," who in turn obtained support from some of the highest in the land—notably, the King's chief minister, Robert Cecil, Earl of Salisbury, and the Lord Chief Justice, John Popham, distinguished by the fact that he was probably the only chief justice in history who could boast, and openly did, of having been a highwayman and cutpurse in his youth.

Led by the "noble, good" Chief Justice, this group obtained a grant to "that part of America commonly called Virginia"—so named by Raleigh for Elizabeth, the Virgin Queen, whose favorite and perhaps lover he then was. As defined by the patent, Virginia was an immense tract embracing most of our country. In terms of modern geography, it extended from Cape Hatteras, in

North Carolina, to the northernmost coast of Maine, and west from those points to the Pacific.

The King divided the tract into two parts, North Virginia and South Virginia, to be governed by a single Royal Council, and for each part a company was formed "to begin a plantation and habitation in some fitt and convenient place."

While it was something to have such a generous patent, it was something else again to obtain sufficient funds to proceed—to hire ships, recruit colonists, and furnish them with all essential supplies. Months were spent in preparations, for England could ill afford another expensive defeat on the American coast.

Sponsored and supported by Popham, the North Virginia Company was the first in the field, dispatching a small ship in the summer of 1606, only to have it captured by the Spanish. A second ship took out a small company which established itself at Sagadahoc, near the mouth of the Kennebec, in what is now Maine. A few reinforcements arrived, but after a year, complaining of the severe cold, the colonists packed up and sailed for home, abandoning Sagadahoc where all of their "former high hopes had been frozen to death."

Nor would much better success attend the South Virginia Company, which had been forced to proceed more slowly.

In the business of colonization, it seemed, the English had no capacity at all.

I

Westward, the Star

To get the pearle and gold,
And ours to hold,
VIRGINIA,
Earth's only Paradise . . .

—MICHAEL DRAYTON

*W*ITH pennons flying, the ships were ready at last and lay in the river, off the stairs at Blackwall, in East London. Alongside a few lighters were tied up, putting on board the last of the stores for what all knew would be a long and dangerous voyage.

Though destiny rode with these ships, as time would tell, there was no great excitement, just the usual bustle and confusion on the eve of departure. Barges were plying out and back to the stairs on last-minute business. Along the quay a few were gathered to wave farewell to some loved one—to a husband perhaps, or a father, or son, or some beloved companion.

On board, crowding the rails for a last look at familiar scenes —and, unhappily, it was the last for most of them—stood a bright and strange motley of adventurers, altogether as unlikely a crew of Argonauts as ever hopefully sailed in quest of the Golden Fleece.

In the throng were many gallants in silks and satins, dissipated men of the world, still smelling of the stews and grog-shops of London in which they had spent their fortunes—a few sober

Gentlemen, also in silks and laces—standing apart, a younger son or two of the great nobility, who expected and received exceeding deference on that account—a number of grim and hard-bitten soldiers, eager to use their swords in carving out of the New World a fortune for themselves—all too few plain working people, artisans and laborers, also a group apart, prudently keeping out of the way of their "betters"—and at least half a dozen boys, wide-eyed and almost breathless with excitement.

More than 140 in all, none too many for their venture but far more than enough to overcrowd the narrow ships, they had visions, each of them, of finding the pot of gold at the end of the rainbow that now shone so bright in the western sky. Though they did not quite credit all of the tales they had heard about the fabulous wealth of Virginia, they could at least hope to find, if even half the stories were true, some of the golden *pots de chambre*, encrusted with jewels, which the Indians in Virginia were said to use. With luck, they could return triumphantly home with their spoils to live in ducal splendor for the rest of their days, as so many of the *Conquistadores* had done.

And yet, as the anchors came up, there must have come to all a sharp realization, like a knife in the heart, that they were staking their lives on a desperate gamble, with the odds heavily weighted against them. As they were well aware, they were not the first of the English to sail toward that luminous western star that had caught the eye of all Europe. Many other expeditions had been sent out, far larger and stronger than theirs, and all had ended in failure—some in such utter disaster that not a survivor was left to tell the tale. The mysterious fate of Raleigh's lost colony at Roanoke must have shadowed the hearts and minds of all.[1]

Nor was the start of their voyage auspicious. It was a cold and blustery day late in December, 1606—a Saturday, the 20th *—and some with a more knowing eye for the weather may have

---

[1] Small numbers refer to notes beginning on page 377.

* All dates, unless otherwise noted, are Old Style (in accordance with the Julian calendar which was used by England and her colonies till 1752). For current New Style (Gregorian calendar), add ten days.

doubted the wisdom of setting sail just then. But orders had been given and under lowering skies, with a storm obviously making up, the small fleet weighed anchor and dropped slowly down the Thames, led by the flagship, the *Sarah Constant* (100 tons). In her wake came a smaller ship, the *Goodspeed* (40 tons), trailed by a pinnace, the *Discovery* (20 tons). Rounding the headlands at Thanet, with a gale now blowing, the ships beat their way down the Channel past Dover and headed out to sea.

The admiral of the fleet and the commander of the *Sarah Constant* was one of Raleigh's men, Captain Christopher Newport, "a Marriner well practised for the westerne part of America." Now in his early forties, Newport had made a name and a fortune for himself while still a young man by capturing a great prize ship, the Portuguese carrack *Madre de Dios*, bringing her home with millions in gold and silver loot, "the most brilliant feat of privateering ever accomplished by Englishmen."

Whatever his prowess as a privateer, Newport proved to be something less than brilliant as Admiral of Virginia, making his first mistake here in taking his three small ships to sea in the teeth of a heavy winter gale. Breasting mountainous seas, making little or no headway, the ships had to turn back after two weeks of hard going. On January 5, sixteen days out of London, when they should have been well on their way to Virginia, they dropped anchor off the Kentish coast, in the Downs, within sight of the Thanet headlands—back almost to where they had started.[2]

Here, in the lea of the Goodwin sands, the ships rolled and rocked at anchor for almost a month, riding out many fierce storms but suffering "no great losse or danger," thanks to the "skilfulnesse" of Captain Newport. But the latter would have shown more skill and judgment if, after his initial blunder, he had put into port to replenish the stores consumed during this six weeks' delay—stores that were none too ample to begin with, seeing that the company might have to live on them for a year or more, as proved to be the case. Newport's "skilfulnesse" had already signed the death warrants of scores committed to his charge.

For weeks, with the ships dragging at anchor, tossing and pitching violently, the passengers had been sick and all were now quite out of temper. Distressed and discouraged, uneasy about their present danger and even more about the distant prospect, they fell to petty bickering and angry brawling among themselves, establishing a pattern that later raised havoc at Jamestown and soon became quite Virginian.

Nothing could have been more conducive to discord and confusion than the orders issued for the voyage by the Royal Council for Virginia. To prevent any conflict of authority while at sea, Newport had been given sole and absolute command of all on board. The names of those who were to govern in Virginia as members of the resident Council, the form and powers of their government, directives on policy and practice—all of these had been locked up in a box that was not to be opened until the company reached its destination, wherever that might be, and went ashore to settle.

Without leaders, with no concrete plans to consider and discuss, with nothing to center attention and create some unity of thought and purpose, the company fell apart into quarreling factions, each striving to advance itself by intrigue and maneuver, creating bitter personal antagonisms that almost wrecked the venture more than once and cost hundreds, even thousands, of lives. No doubt there was much sharp criticism of Newport and others responsible for their present plight and dangerous delay. And there were those who whispered in corners, or talked quite openly, about their ideas of what should be done—not only now, but when they got to Virginia. Indeed, as soon became evident, there were almost as many ideas about this as there were men on board.

One in the company must have known that he had been appointed to the Council in Virginia and that his name lay in the little wooden box—Edward-Maria Wingfield, one of the "Gentlemen and divers others" to whom the King had granted the Virginia patent. A man of fifty or more, a veteran of the wars in the Low Countries and in Ireland, proud of his name and aristocratic connections,[3] Wingfield took it upon himself to assert some authority from the start, which aroused much resentment, especially on the part of one young blade, Captain John Smith, who almost lost his head as a result.

The authorities in London, acting through Wingfield, had made a "right choice of a spirituall pastor" to minister to the company and remain in the colony. On the Archbishop of Canterbury's recommendation, they had selected an "honest, religious, and courageous Divine," the Reverend Robert Hunt, a graduate of Oxford, who was, said Wingfield, in no way "touched with the rebellious humors of a popish spirit, nor blemished with ye least suspition of a factious scismatick."

In the raging storms, with the ships in danger and the future growing darker day by day, Hunt did what he could to mediate with God and turn away His wrath, summoning the adventurers again and again to renounce their sins and pray for forgiveness. Hunt took his duties seriously—far too seriously, many complained, especially the gallants and men of fashion, who felt that they were called to prayers and services much too often. They were particularly incensed at being made the chief targets of Hunt's usually unflattering discourse, so that they were delighted when he had to take to his bunk, where he lay "so weake and sicke that few expected his recoverie."

And "some few, little better than Atheists, of the greatest ranke amongst us," took this occasion to slander Hunt and viciously attack him, hurling scandalous charges against him, hoping to drive him off the ship. But all this could "never force from him so much as a seeming desire to leave the busines," and he foiled his "godlesse foes, whose disasterous designes (could they have prevailed) had even then overthrowne the businesse, so many discontents did then arise." In the end, "with the water of patience and his godly exhortations," but chiefly by his good example, he "quenched those flames of envie and dissention." It would have been a godsend if he had quenched those flames, but he could not, and smoldering fires remained.

At length, having lost six precious weeks which should have seen them almost to Virginia, the ships tacked out of the Downs and again stood off to the southwest, heading for the Canary Islands, far down the African coast, for Newport had chosen to sail the usual long and roundabout southern route, ignoring a much more direct course charted just a few years before by one of his own captains, Bartholomew Gosnold, master of the *Good-speed* and vice-admiral of the fleet, a "most honest, worthy, and industrious Gentleman."

Another of Raleigh's men, perhaps the ablest of those on board and certainly the wisest and most humane, one of the few with any knowledge of the wilderness or any experience with colonization, Gosnold had brought out in 1602 a company which settled for a time on what is now known as Cuttyhunk, one of the Elizabeth Islands, lying near Martha's Vineyard off the southern coast of Cape Cod.

In his voyage to the Elizabeths, Gosnold had followed the usual course down the French and Spanish coasts to Portugal, where he had turned west and struck directly across the Atlantic by way of the Azores, saving 1,000 leagues (more than 3,000 miles) and two or three weeks of sailing. If Gosnold now proposed this much shorter course, as he surely must have done, his arguments made no impression on Admiral Newport, who proceeded to the Canaries, where he took on wood and water before picking up the steady trade winds that were to waft him across the high seas to the West Indies.

Cramped in narrow quarters for more than two months now, nowhere near their destination as they should have been, with scurvy and other diseases spreading among them, the passengers were more restless and irritable than ever. There was grumbling on all the ships, and one young "pistol" evidently did a great deal of talking about what was wrong and what should be done to correct it, letting all of the discontented know that they could depend upon his strong right arm.

Only twenty-seven, the son of a poor Lincolnshire farmer, Captain John Smith had early become a soldier of fortune and was already the hero, as he later told the story, of many brave encounters and fantastically wild adventures on land and sea—in France, in the Low Countries, in Scotland, in Italy, Austria, Hungary, Transylvania, Turkey, Russia, Bohemia, Spain, Morocco, and waters adjacent. After many hairbreadth escapes—and he would have many more—he had returned home in 1604, a captain in rank and with 1,000 ducats in his pocket, immediately turning his eyes toward America as a new field of exploit.

Much time and good paper have been wasted in arguing for and against the "historical accuracy" of *The True Travels, Adventures, and Observations of Captaine John Smith, in Europe, Asia, Africa, and America* (1630). It is not history at all, but a lively travel book, a very readable historical romance in the manner of the day, written with obvious literary elaborations. Yet there was probably some truth, a kernel of fact, in most of the incidents described, even in that which Smith most prized—his boastful prowess in slaying and cutting off the heads of three Turkish champions whom he had engaged, one after the other, in single-handed combat outside the walls of "Regal"—a town not found on any map, as Smith's critics never tire of pointing out.

And yet, as testimonial to his feat at non-existent "Regal," the Duke of Transylvania, his commander-in-chief, granted him the right to bear a coat of arms and in London many years later, in 1625, the College of Heralds accepted the Duke's testimonial and granted Smith a coat emblazoned with the three Turks' heads he had carried off in triumph so long before.

Smith was never one to hide his talents, or hold his tongue, and now as he swaggered up and down the deck talking of what he had done and what he would do, he was soon deep in the bad graces of many—of Wingfield particularly, for that blue-blooded gray-beard found the brash young upstart insufferable, soon leveling serious charges against him.

Late in March, having roughly followed the course taken by Columbus on his second voyage in 1493,* the ships made their landfall in the West Indies, at what is now Martinique, swinging around to the north to anchor off Dominica, "a very faire Iland . . . full of sweet and good smells," where the company refreshed itself for several days. Though now two months behind schedule, Newport began a leisurely and rather aimless cruise through the

---

* On that voyage more than a century before, Columbus had commanded a force ten times as strong as Newport's, having seventeen ships and 1,200 heavily armed fighting men.

Indies, exploring many islands, going ashore at Nevis to spend almost a week enjoying the hot baths there.

Here at Nevis a pair of gallows was erected. But as remarked by the man for whom they were intended, "Captain Smith . . . could not be persuaded to use them." Wingfield and "some of the chiefe (envying his repute)," so he said, had charged him with mutiny, saying that he "intended to usurpe the governement, murder the Councell, and make himselfe King," asserting that some of his confederates had confessed the plot and stood ready to "affirme it."

Probably there had been some loose talk, perhaps even a boastful threat or two of taking off a few heads, for Smith was quick to anger, vindictive, and notably indiscreet. But mutiny does not appear to have been intended, and Newport intervened to save Smith's life. He placed him under nominal arrest, however, and kept him there for several months, adding a new source of conflict and contention.

At length, after several more weeks of needless loitering, the ships "disimboged" out of the West Indies and headed north, crossing the Tropic of Cancer four days later. In another four days, Newport announced, they would be at their destination.

But the fourth day came and went, and then the fifth, sixth, and seventh, without any sign of land. All on board were "not a little discomforted, seeing the Marriners had three days passed their reckoning and found no land." Though he enjoyed the reputation of being an "excellent Navigator," Newport had made, as was evident to all, a gross and dangerous error in charting his course here. Even the masters of the ships were so concerned that Captain John Ratcliffe, in command of the *Discovery*, "rather desired to beare up the helme to returne to England than make further search."

That might well have been the decision, forced by Newport's repeated blunders. But the choice was not left to the befuddled Admiral and his bewildered captains, for suddenly, to add a sharp and instant peril, an "extream storme" struck the ships, raging all night "with winds, raine, and thunder in a terrible manner." The tempest scattered the fleet and with not a stitch of canvas flying, drifting under bare poles, the ships were driven far to the north and out to sea.

On the following day, after much beating up and down in search of one another, the ships were together again—and as lost as ever. More so, in fact, for Newport had been sailing by dead reckoning and it was quite impossible to determine how far they had drifted during the night. Throwing out the sounding line, they "could find no ground." The next day they sounded, and the next day, and the next, but "had no ground at a hundred fathoms."

It seemed useless to go on searching in this blind manner. But "God, the guider of all good actions," was at the helm, it appears, for at dawn the next day the lookouts spied a faint dark line along the western horizon. To the relief of all, they soon found it to be "their desired port, beyond all their expectations, for never any of them had seene that coast."

With a favoring breeze, the ships stood in and easily slipped between its protecting capes to enter the "Bay of Chesupioc * directly, without let or hinderance," dropping anchor in sheltered waters along its south shore. Having been twice as long in passage as expected, they were now more than two months overdue, a matter of fatal consequence, the effects of which lingered for years.

Nor was this the end of their voyage, as the weary and weather-beaten passengers soon learned to their dismay. They were still many miles from their destination and several weeks from being free at last from the foul holds of the ships.

* That is, the Chesapeake—from the Indian *K'tchisipik*, or Great Water, as it is indeed.

II

Jamestown Planted

*. . . a very fit place for the
erecting of a great cittie.*

—CAPTAIN JOHN SMITH

CLOTHED in all the bright splendor of spring, with trees and shrubs and fields in flower, Virginia must have seemed literally a paradise to the tired men on the ships as they gazed at it in wonder. All were passionately eager to go ashore, if only to stretch their legs along the beach and lie on the green earth for an hour or two.

But only a few, chiefly Gentlemen, were granted the pleasure of "recreating themselves on shore." Led by Captain Newport, they did a bit of exploring, but found "nothing worth the speaking of," they said (and one wonders what they expected to find), "but faire meadows and goodly tall Trees, with such Fresh waters running through the woods" that they were "almost ravished at the first sight thereof."

As they were returning to the beach, they had a sharp and bitter foretaste of trouble. Effecting a complete surprise, some of the local Chesapeake tribe came creeping through the woods "upon all fours, . . . like Beares, with their Bowes in their mouthes," and suddenly let fly at them, painfully wounding several before they were driven off—the opening skirmish in a long and bloody con-

18

flict waged treacherously and with revolting savagery on both sides.

On the flagship that night, in the presence of the "principall" Gentlemen, Captain Newport broke open the sealed box entrusted to him and read the orders and instructions drawn up to guide and govern the yet unborn colony. Seven men, it transpired, had been appointed to the Council in Virginia—Newport, Wingfield, Gosnold, John Smith, John Ratcliffe, John Martin, and George Kendall. These were to elect one of themselves to serve as president for a year, who, "with the Councell, should governe." Matters in the Council were decided by a majority vote, with the president enjoying a "double voice," casting two votes when he desired. But the members of the Council were not sworn in at this time, no doubt at Newport's insistence, for the company was still technically at sea and therefore under his sole command.

One of the papers in the box, the first of many such long and detailed documents that bedeviled affairs in Virginia for generations, was entitled "Instructions by way of Advice." Some of the advice, especially that of a general character, was sound enough. They should not teach the Indians to shoot and should never allow them to carry their arms because they might run off with them. When shooting a blunderbuss in the presence of the Indians, they should chose their best marksmen, for if the shots went wild, the Indians would "think the weapon not so terrible."

Quite as important, they should have "great care not to offend the naturals" and should establish a trade with them for corn and "all other lasting victuals." To avoid the danger of famine, this trade should be established "before they perceive that you mean to plant among them," for the Indians might become very hostile when they learned what was intended.

"Lastly and chiefly, the way to prosper and achieve good success is to make yourselves all of one mind, for the good of your country and your own." Whatever else was achieved in early Virginia, this never was.

All of this advice was good and if it had been followed, the colony would have been spared untold miseries and a long series of disasters. But the more detailed instructions telling them just

how to proceed were worse than useless, as might have been expected of directives written in London by men who had only the
vaguest notion of the lay of the land or what might be encountered
there. The elaborate instructions, when not irrelevant, were self-
contradictory, and yet it was these that the Council chose to obey
as commands, while the wiser and more general advice was simply
ignored or deliberately flouted.

First, which seemed logical and obvious enough, the colonists
should find the mouth of some large and navigable river. But they
were not to settle there, for they would be too exposed to attack if
the Spanish denounced them as trespassers and came to drive them
out, as was not unlikely. Rather, they should proceed up the river
as far as they could sail in a 50-ton vessel. If the river had more
than one large tributary and there was nothing much to choose between them, they should select that which "bendeth most toward
the North-West, for that way," they were informed, "you shall
soonest find the other sea"—the fabulous South Sea, which would
lead them to the riches of India, the Spice Islands, and Cathay.

They should not fail to determine whether their chosen river
had its source in the mountains, or in some lake. If in some lake,
those in London opined, "the passage to the other sea will be the
more easy and [it] is like enough that, out of the same lake, you
shall find some spring which runs the contrary way towards the
East India Sea, for the great and famous rivers of Volga, Tanis,
and Dwina have their heads near joyned, and yet the one falleth
into the Caspian Sea, the other into the Euxine Sea, and the third
into the Polonian Sea"—which could hardly be denied.

They should spend two months at this, led by Captains Newport
and Gosnold. These two should take forty men, a third of the
company, and when they did "espie any high lands or hills," Gosnold and twenty men should "cross over the lands and, carrying a
half dozen pickaxes, try if they can find any minerals"—mines, of
course, were always found on hills. Meantime, forty men should
be building a fort, while thirty should be assigned to felling trees,
clearing fields, and planting crops upon which the lives of all depended.

With the Gentlemen amusing themselves along the beach, finding "good store of Mussels and Oysters," some with "pearles," the "meaner sorte" were put to work assembling the shallop, or longboat, which had been brought over in sections between decks. When she was assembled three days later, a party set out in her to explore the southern shore of the bay, sounding from time to time and finding only shallow water, which put them "out of all hopes of getting any higher with our ships," a most disconcerting prospect. As they were returning late in the afternoon, they noted a point of land on the far shore and though it was perilously near dark, they decided to sail across a wide stretch of open water to view it. Here, close to shore, they found an excellent channel many fathoms deep, which gave them such "good comforte" that they named the point Cape Comfort—or Point Comfort, as it soon came to be known, a famous seamark since that day.

Having wasted another precious day,* Newport brought his ships across to Point Comfort, where a party went ashore, meeting some of the local Indians. The latter were very friendly and led them to their pleasant village, Kecoughtan, or Great Town, in what is now Newport News. The amiable Kecoughtan sat them down to a feast, danced for them, and offered them their first taste of Virginia tobacco, which they liked very well, smoking it— or rather, as the phrase always ran, "drincking" it—in long earthen pipes, which were much like theirs, they noted, "but far bigger, with the bowle fastened together with a piece of fine copper."

The Kecoughtan told the English something of the surrounding territory and of many great rivers that emptied into the Chesapeake—the Powhatan, the Pamunkey, the Rappahannock, the Potomac, and the Susquehanna. The last, they learned, lay some distance to the northwest and ran deep into the land, just such a river as those in London had recommended. But as the ships were lying at the mouth of the Powhatan, or Falling Waters, they decided to explore that broad river without delay, for another week had slipped by since they had made their landfall. As it was now May,

---

* They spent it building a huge cross and erecting it on the southern cape at the entrance of the Chesapeake, christening it Cape Henry for the King's elder son. The opposite point to the north was soon christened Cape Charles for the King's younger son, Charles I in later years.

there was not a day to lose if they were going to get a crop into the ground so that they might have a harvest to see them through the winter.

A few days later, having slowly sailed some fifty miles upstream, the English came ashore on the north bank of the river, in the country of the Paspahegh, who proved to be quite as friendly as the Kecoughtan. "Entertained with much welcome" by Wowinchapuncka, the local werowance, or chieftain, the English spent several days here exploring the neighborhood. They then turned about and dropped downstream to examine a likely spot noted by one of Gosnold's men, Captain Gabriel Archer. Both Gosnold and Archer wished to settle here, which would have been done "to all the Collonie's contentment," except that it was "disliked because the ships could not ride neere the shoare."

Leaving Archer's Hope,* as it has since been known, the ships were brought about and started upstream again, making for a peninsula nearby. Roughly square and a mile or two across, it was virtually an island, cut off from the mainland except for a narrow sandy neck, which offered an advantage from the point of view of defense. At the upper outside corner they found a channel so deep and close to shore that the ships could be brought alongside and "moored to the Trees" along the bank. This, too, was an important consideration, for no other good landing place had been found along the river.

Altogether, said Captain John Smith in his always confident manner, it was a "verie fit place for the erecting of a great cittie." More experienced in such matters, Captain Gosnold disagreed, not liking the site for many reasons, and quarreled with Wingfield about it.

As soon became all too apparent, the "island" had grievous disabilities. It was heavily wooded, having no open fields. To clear sufficient ground for a fort and gardens would require great labor. Their instructions had warned them to have a care about this and had cautioned them against settling "in a low or moist place," such as this was, with great swamps and marshes round about.

* A few miles up Archer's Hope Creek lies the historic town of Williamsburg, established many years later.

Quite as bad, it had no good source of fresh water—no brooks or springs—so that all would have to drink the murky waters of the river, which were salt at high tide and filled with muck at low.

Unhappily for him and for the colony, which almost perished as a result, Gosnold's objections were overruled. If the voyage had been made in two months, as anticipated, they could have taken time for further search. As it was, they had been on the ships almost five months now and all were restless and anxious to get off, no matter where—even here—and they could scarcely have made a worse choice. But necessity forced a decision and at last, on the 13th of May, 1607, "with their barge still coasting before them, as Virgil writeth Aeneas did, arriving in Latium upon the bankes of the River Tybur," the weary wayfarers came to their "seating place" to build, it might be, another Rome.

The Council of Virginia now took office, its members swearing upon the "holy Evangelists" to perform their duties faithfully— to be true and loyal subjects of the King—to allow no one to return home without their leave—to see that no letters were written about Virginia that might discourage others from coming—to keep all of their business a secret from the colonists, who were not to be informed of anything unless this was authorized by London. Subject only to the authority of the Council in England, the resident Council could rule almost as it pleased and from the start exercised its power in an arbitrary and high-handed manner though it had been ordered to govern as nearly in accord with the laws and customs of England as possible.

As he appears to have anticipated, Edward-Maria Wingfield was chosen as president, and an "oration made why Captaine Smith was not admitted to the Councell as the rest." Though still under nominal arrest, Smith was free to move about and soon had his revenge—such a revenge as few have ever enjoyed, for his scores of enemies, whether guilty or not of the scandalous charges he hurled at them, remain impaled to this day upon the point of his sharp and venomous pen. His scathing caricatures of them and the portrait he drew of his own accomplished self—always in the right, ever battling heroically against cowardice, sloth, stupidity, and vice—are reflected upon almost every page ever written about Jamestown and our American beginnings.

Having carried the supplies and their personal belongings ashore, all fell to work—or at least, those who were obliged to, the laborers and servants. The latter sweated under the supervision of the president, the Council, and the Gentlemen, who comprised at least half the company. There were so many superintendents that it was probably a good thing that some of the Gentlemen went wandering off into the woods, led by George Percy, the bluest of blue bloods among them, the only son of the great nobility in the company.

In his middle twenties at this time, an abler and more compassionate man than most, Percy was the brother of the Earl of Northumberland, then locked up in the Tower of London, having been sentenced to prison for life for his part in the celebrated Gunpowder Plot to blow up King James when he appeared before Parliament. As another Percy, Thomas, had sheltered the chief villain, Guy Fawkes, the whole Percy family was under a cloud, which probably explains why young George had come to Virginia as an ordinary Gentleman adventurer, without rank or honor.

In their wanderings through the woods, Percy and his friends found the "pleasantest suckles, the ground all flowing over with faire flowers, . . . many strawberries, . . . woods full of Cedar and Cypresse, . . . a garden of Tobacco, and other fruits and herbes," happily wending their "way in this Paradise" until they were tired and turned back to cast a critical eye at what their men had been doing in making a "place to pitch their Tents," felling trees, erecting fortifications, preparing ground for fields and gardens.

For the town, a small area was laid out in the form of an isosceles triangle. Its base extended some 400 feet along the river bank; its shorter sides met at a point several hundred feet back in the woods. At Wingfield's insistence, after a sharp clash with Captain Archer, it was fortified in a most primitive manner, with a simple barricade of logs and branches piled up shoulder-high. Altogether, the "barricado" enclosed less than an acre of ground—rather tight quarters into which to squeeze streets, a market place, gardens, a church, a storehouse, shelters, and living space for more than a hundred men.

Work on the fort had scarcely begun when Newport took a large number of men, the strongest and ablest in the company, and set out, as instructed, to find the headwaters of the river and discover the South Sea. Sailing in the shallop, they went ashore frequently and were "entertayned with much Courtesye in every place." Some eighty miles upstream, they came to a pleasant Indian village with gardens and great fields of corn about it, beautifully situated on a hill that sloped gently to the waterside. Powhatan's Tower they named it, for they mistook the brave-looking chieftain here for the Great Powhatan, of whom they had heard many tales, the "emperor" of the powerful Powhatan confederacy made up of more than thirty tribes inhabiting most of tidewater Virginia.

Always suave and tactful with the Indians, Newport paid the local chieftain the greatest deference, proposing a league of peace and friendship, which was accepted. All went well until Newport announced his intention of proceeding up the river and asked the werowance for guides. Offering many excuses, the latter refused, obviously fearing to stir up his enemies, the Monacan, a formidable people who came down almost every year "at the fall of the leaf" to ravage his country.*

Notwithstanding the chief's displeasure, the English went on, only to be stopped within a mile or two by "great craggystones in the midst of the river," where the water came tumbling down over rocky ledges with such violence that a boat could not get through. Though they did not know this, they had come to the Fall Line that sharply divides the coastal plains from the piedmont all along this part of the seaboard.

Before turning back, Newport had his men fashion a large cross, which was set up here at the Falls, in what is now Richmond. With elaborate ceremony, Newport renamed the river,

---

* The members of the Powhatan confederacy were of Algonkian stock. The Monacan and their neighbors and cousins, the Manahoac, were Siouan tribes which had pushed in from the west some time before the English arrived.

christening it the James, and formally took possession of all the surrounding territory in the name of the King, proclaiming "with a greate showte" that he had the "most right unto it." Standing nearby and frankly puzzled, an Indian from Powhatan's Tower inquired the meaning of all this.

"Your countriemen will lie much," Pocahontas once remarked to Captain John Smith after much experience with the English, and Newport was as glib and plausible as any. The two arms of the cross, he said, "signified King Powhatan and himselfe; the fastening of it in the myddest was their united league; and the showte, the reverence he did to Powhatan"—which "did exceedingly rejoyce" the chief and all his people when reported at Powhatan's Tower.

Dropping slowly down the James, Newport and his men visited here and there, enjoying many a feast, plying their hosts with "beere, Aquavite, and Sack," pouring so many "hott Drynckes" down the amiable chief at Arrohateck's Joy that he was unable to move the next morning, having such a hangover that he was convinced in his innocence that he was about to die. Loitering along, Newport began to suspect from several curious incidents that all was not well at the fort and hastened there, having been gone a week, to find that it had just received a rude shock and was nursing many wounds.

On the first night ashore there had been an alarm when some canoes shot by close to the ships. A few days later two Indians walked in to announce that the chief of the Paspahegh was coming to be "merrie" with them, "with a fat deare." Escorted by a hundred braves, who "garded him in a very warlike manner," Wowinchapuncka soon appeared, obviously to see what was going on here at Jamestown, having good reason to be curious and concerned. After all, this was his country, the home of his people for generations. What did these intruders intend? Was it true, as some said, that these strange palefaces had come from the underside of the world to take their lands from them and put them to the sword, that they were bent on conquest? No doubt the English assured the Paspahegh, as they did Powhatan later, that they did not intend to stay, having come up the river only to mend their ships and take on water.

Wowinchapuncka's visit went pleasantly enough until one of his braves was spied making off with a hatchet.* He was violently thrown to the ground, another brave ran to his defense, others joined the fray, and when the English reached for their guns, the chief "went suddenly away, with all of his company, in great anger." But there seemed to be no ground for apprehension, for he soon dispatched a messenger to say that he was sending some deer as a present. The venison soon arrived, "but the Sawse," as Percy observed, "came within a few dayes after."

The absence of Newport and his party had been noted, and the day before their return the Paspahegh suddenly struck in great force, catching many of the English while at work outside the barricade. Surprised in the open without arms, they fled in panic to the fort, with howling braves on their heels. The latter would have followed them through the gates but for a stout resistance hastily organized by President Wingfield, who stood in the front rank and "shewed himselfe a valiant Gentleman," miraculously escaping injury though an arrow was "shott cleane through his beard."

During the fight, which "indured hott about an hower," the Indians swarmed around the barricade, using it to protect themselves as they "shot through the Tents" and at men running frantically for cover. Had it not been for the cannon on the ships, all would have been destroyed. Though the cannon brought down nothing but the bough of a large tree, the boom of the big guns awed the Indians, as it continued to do for years, and at length they withdrew. They had killed a boy on the pinnace and wounded about a fifth of the company, almost a score, including four members of the Council.

* "These Salvages are naturally great theeves," the Reverend Samuel Purchas piously remarked in a marginal note opposite his report of this incident in his *Pilgrimes* (1625).

The English, when looting empires and stealing continents, as they were bent on doing here, always violently objected to the peccadilloes of the natives.

The war that began here was long and costly. More than any other single factor, it shaped events in Virginia for years, constituting a heavy drain upon the blood and treasure of the colony, keeping it so strained and exhausted that for a long time it remained in an almost chronic state of collapse. Perhaps the conflict was inevitable. Perhaps it could not have been averted or postponed. Perhaps no accommodation of conflicting interests could have been achieved, but at least an effort might have been made. It was Virginia's tragic fate that no sincere and honest attempt was ever made to work out a *modus vivendi*, as was later so successfully done by the Pilgrims at Plymouth, by Roger Williams in Rhode Island, by William Penn in Pennsylvania, and by others elsewhere.

After the Paspahegh attack, even the opinionated Wingfield was persuaded that Jamestown should be protected by something more substantial than "boughs of trees." Men were put to work cutting long poles, fifteen feet long, which were driven into the ground and laced together to form a high palisade. At each point of the triangular fort was built a strong bulwark in which to mount cannon that commanded the approaches to the fort. With the assistance of Newport's sailors, this task was rushed to completion within a few weeks, and none too soon, for "many were the assaults and Ambuscadoes of the Salvages."

Every day the Indians came, but no one ever saw them until it was too late. They lurked in the woods, or crept up to hide in the tall grass under the bulwarks, and the colonists, "by their disorderly straggling, were often hurt." One of the Gentlemen, while the palisade was going up, found nothing better to do than go for a stroll in the woods, unarmed. He soon came running into the fort, having six arrows through him, from which he died a few days later. Another, going out to answer a call of nature, was shot "in the somwhat, dangerously." When they could find no other targets, the Indians lofted arrows into the fort, scoring an occasional hit, or amused themselves by shooting the English dogs.

Jamestown had not the strength to retaliate. But it felt that it could defend itself at least if it were not starved out—a very worrisome "if." The overlong voyage had consumed a large part of the supplies. A little corn and a few English seeds had been carelessly planted and as carelessly tended, so that no crop could be expected. No attempt had been made to establish a corn trade with the Indians, and that was now out of the question. There was only one hope—supplies from home.

But supplies from home depended, in part, upon sending back in the ships some cargo of value to satisfy the merchant adventurers, if only as an earnest of better things to come. At great labor a little clapboard was cut and loaded. Newport's sailors gathered some sassafras, but at fearful cost to the colonists, for the sailors spoiled and lost precious, irreplaceable tools. Others had been digging here and there, all around Jamestown, and loading some mysterious stuff into a barrel, under the direction of one of the Council, Captain John Martin, son of a London goldsmith, Sir Richard Martin, Master of the Royal Mint.

Wingfield and his friends wanted to ship Smith home to answer charges of mutiny, saying that the authorities there might take a more lenient view of his "designes" and thus "not touch his life or utterly overthrowe his reputation." But Smith "scorned such charitie" and demeaned himself so well, he said, that "all the company did see his innocencie and his adversaries' malice," which "begat a generall hatred in the harts of the company against such unjust commanders."

Again Newport intervened and patched up a truce, with the aid of Parson Hunt. The charges against Smith were dropped, he was allowed to take his seat on the Council, and all in Jamestown swore to live together in peace and love, solemnizing the occasion by taking communion together in their rude outdoor chapel. Here, under an old sail stretched as an awning between the trees, the company sat on unhewn logs as "good Mr. Hunt" preached an appropriate sermon from behind a bar of wood nailed between two trees, which served as a pulpit.

With peace apparently established—within the fort, at least—Newport sailed for home early the next day, June 22, promising to be back with supplies as soon as he could, leaving behind in beleaguered Jamestown not more than a hundred men,[1] for already a third of the original company had perished.

As the ships vanished down the river, many must have wondered whether they would ever see Newport again. After all, he might go down at sea and the adventurers would not learn—at least, not in time—of Jamestown's desperate need for relief. Or he might be stayed in England or be shipwrecked on his return. Newport had promised to be back within twenty weeks at most, or by mid-November, and one may well believe that all, even the most irreverent, prayed fervently for his "good passage and safe retorne," meantime hoping that they could somehow manage to survive that long.

III

Dust, Death, and Garboile

*. . . we are falne upon a lande
that promises more than the lande
of Promisse.*

—SIR WALTER COPE

L ONG overdue, Newport reached England late in July after a
five weeks' passage. Putting in at Plymouth, he scratched
off a note and sent it posthaste to London, addressed to the Earl
of Salisbury, a principal Secretary of State and "ye Patron of the
most Christian and noble enterprise of Plantation," to inform
the latter of his arrival and let him be the first to know the
wonderful news, the "glad tidings" from Virginia.

"The countrie is excellent," wrote Newport, "and very rich
in gold and copper." He would not take time, he said, to detail the
"expectaunce and assurance we have of great wealth," for all
could soon determine that for themselves. He had brought home
a fair sample of the gold dust they had discovered at Jamestown, and he would be with Salisbury soon "to show it to his
Majesty and the rest of the Lords." The "dust" had been
gathered by Captain John Martin in his mysterious operations.

Though jealously guarded as a secret, this news quickly spread
and naturally created a sensation—not only among the merchant
adventurers, but at Court. In granting the patent, the Crown had
reserved for itself a fifth of all precious metals found. With visions

31

of another Mexico or Peru dancing before their eyes, all those with a stake in Virginia could scarcely contain themselves as Newport took his time in slowly sailing around from Plymouth to London, to be closeted there with the excited and almost breathless members of the Royal Council for Virginia. They were more than pleased with what they heard and saw, and one of them immediately dispatched a long and most exuberant letter to the Earl of Salisbury.

"If we maye beleve either in words or letters, we are falne upon a lande that promises more than the lande of Promisse. Instead of mylke, we fynde pearle—and golde, insteede of honye," wrote Sir Walter Cope in boundless rapture.

"There is but a barrell full of earth, but there seems a Kingdome full of the oare. You shall not be fedd by handfulls or hatfulls after the Tower measure, but the *Elzabeth Jonas* & the *Tryumpe* & all the ships of honour may have their bellyes full— for in all their fortyfycations, after two turfs of earth, this sparme or oare apearethe on every parte as a solid body, a Treasure endlesse proportioned by God accordinge to that Sufferaigne's harte that rewards everyone & knows not how to say nay."

An assay of the ore had been made at Jamestown and Sir Walter added in a postscript to his letter, piling extravagance upon extravagance, that this assay had been shown to one Beale of London, "an excellent tryer of minerals, who says the trial [at Jamestown] was ignorantly made, the earth not half tried—for if it had, it would have turned black and the gold run together in the bottom. That this holds £1,200 in the Tonn. That ther is more in the pot, and he verily thinks it will yield £2,000 [$100,000] * at the least in the Tonn."

The English, after many false starts in the New World, had struck it rich at last!

There was only one worry. The envious and "all-devouring Spaniard" would certainly pounce upon this new Golconda if he could. To prevent that, large reinforcements had to be dispatched

---

* Throughout, monetary sums have been roughly equated with the real value—that is, the purchasing power—of the pre-war 1940 dollar. For the current [9:37 a.m., August 1] 1951 dollar, add at least 30 per cent.

to Virginia at once. This meant raising money—a great deal of it—and that always presented thorny problems, but Cope had a ready solution.

As a group of London merchants had just subscribed £25,000 ($1,250,000) for a trading venture of the East India Company, Sir Walter suggested to Salisbury that the latter should go to them "in his Majestie's name" and persuade them to invest their money in Virginia instead. He had already discussed this with Sir Thomas Smythe, governor of the East India Company and a leader in the Virginia business, he said, and Smythe had agreed that this could easily be arranged to the immense profit of all.

But four days later, hoping that he had not made a complete fool of himself, Cope had to write Salisbury a very different letter.

"This other daye we sent you newes of golde, but this daye," he reported with obvious chagrin, "we cannot returne you so much as copper. . . . In the ende, all turned to vapore." *

Bitter and as credulous as ever, Cope angrily attributed this fiasco to the machinations of Captain John Martin, who, he said, had deceived not only "pore" Captain Newport, but the "King & State"—and "meant, as I heare, to have cozened his owne father," the goldsmith, hoping thus to obtain a large private shipment of supplies. Though thoroughly unscrupulous at times, Captain Martin was really quite innocent here and as gullible as any. The truth was that the Virginians, like millions of "greenhorns" before them and since, had been hopefully digging "fool's gold"—iron pyrites.

Nor was this the end of our first great gold boom. As to the colony in general, reports by Newport and others seemed to agree that Virginia had a pleasant and healthful climate and that the company there was well established at a likely spot along the James, "the famousest River in the world." And "we thincke," added the Council in Virginia, "that if more may be wished in a River [passage to the South Sea], it will be founde."

---

* Even if the dust from Jamestown had contained some gold—which it did not—the estimate of its value by the "excellent tryer of minerals" was fantastic, being far beyond the value of any ore ever found in North America —or anywhere else, for that matter.

Indeed, Virginia was "like that pleasant land described by Moses," rich and fertile, endowed with "gold-showing mountains" and abounding in natural resources that promised the quick and profitable production of all kinds of things: timber, naval stores, fish ("our fishing for sturgeon cannot be worth less than £1,000 a year"), furs, wine, drugs, soap ashes, silk, sugar, olives, tobacco ("after a year or two, £5,000 a year"), hemp, flax, fruits and berries, sassafras, dyestuffs, iron, copper, pearls—and gold!

Let no one doubt that there was gold in Virginia, Sir Thomas Smythe insisted. Newport had merely made an "error in not bringinge of the same ore of which the first tryall was made there," and the Captain felt so badly about it that he was resolved not to see the Earl of Salisbury again—which perhaps was just as well—until he had gone out and brought back that which he "confidentlie believed he had brought before."

But the ships, the merchant adventurers complained, had brought back nothing but a "taste" of clapboard and some sassafras, which did not begin to pay the cost of the voyage. They could see "no hope of any extraordinary consequence." And yet, so they said in the first of many propaganda tracts, they "freshly and cheerfully determined to send supplies to the colonists as soon as possible."

This was false, like so much else in their always highly glossed reports. The adventurers were split by bitter wrangling. Many now withdrew from the enterprise in disappointment and disgust. Others refused to invest any more money until some profit was assured. Only with the greatest difficulty could a few be persuaded to venture even trifling sums to relieve the desperate needs of the colonists.

All were well aware that Jamestown had been left with provisions for thirteen or fourteen weeks at most. That time had already elapsed, and yet no ships were on the way because of constant bickering and "some private ends" among the adventurers, as one of them complained, saying that if nothing else could touch their hearts, they might at least be moved by pity for "them that are there, gone upon promise of supply, or else exposed to a most unchristian and lamentable fortune."

The adventurers were not more callous or selfish than most men, it is reasonable to assume. No doubt many of them pitied the plight of the colonists, but pity was not a proper entry in a merchant's books, and this was a matter of business. Unless some profit were paid, it could not continue. In despair, one of the Council informed Salisbury that unless he gave "some personal and prompt attention to the action," there was "no way but apparent ruine."

Another month passed before two small vessels finally cleared from England, the *John and Francis* and a "nymble pinnace," the *Phoenix*, with a "hundred men and victualls"—little enough, to be sure. One wonders if the adventurers would have done anything at all if they had known the state of affairs at Jamestown, if they had had the slightest intimation of what had been going on there.

The gaunt specter of famine had been stalking the fort for months, almost since the day of Newport's departure. What could one expect, said Cape Merchant Thomas Studley, who was in charge of the common store, for "supposing to make our passage in two months with victuall to live and the advantage of springe to worke, we were at sea 5 months, where we both spent victuall and lost the opportunity of the time and season to plant."

While the ships stayed, the colonists augmented their meager rations with a little biscuit, which the sailors would "pilfer to sell, give, or exchange with us for money, Saxefras, furres, or love." With the ships gone, there remained only the "common kettell," which provided a mere half pint of wheat and barley for a man a day, and this, "having fryed some 26 weekes in the ship's hold, contained as many wormes as graines."

Their lodgings were "Castles in the ayre," for their tents were rotten and their "Cabbins worse than naught." Drinking the murky waters of the river brought on serious disorders. Malaria and burning fevers crept out of the swamps to strike down scores. Almost all lay prostrate, brought down by hunger and disease, and day by day the death toll mounted:

The sixth of August, there died John Asbie, of the bloudie Flixe [bloody flux, or dysentery].

The ninth day, died George Flowre, of the swelling.

The tenth day, died William Bruster, Gentleman, of a wound given by the Savages. . . .

The fourteenth day, Jerome Alikock, . . . of a wound; the same day, Francis Midwinter and Edward Moris, Corporall, died suddenly.

The fifteenth day, there died Edward Browne and Stephen Galthorpe.

The sixteenth day, . . . Thomas Gower, Gentleman.

The seventeenth day, . . . Thomas Mounslic.

The eighteenth . . . Robert Pennington and John Martine, Gentleman [Captain Martin's son].

At times the company could not muster five able-bodied men to man the bulwarks against the Indians, who continued to prowl around the fort and pick off stragglers. Even the sick had to be pressed into service. No matter how weak and ill, each man had to stand guard every third night, "lying on the bare cold ground what weather soever came," and then had to stand guard all the next day—"which brought our men to be most feeble wretches, . . . night and day groaning in every corner of the Fort, most pittifull to heare, . . . some departing out of the World, many times three or four in a night; in the morning, their bodies trailed out of their Cabines, like Dogges, to be buried."

Never, exclaimed George Percy, were "Englishmen left in a forreigne Countrey in such miseries as we were in this new discovered Virginia."

During that first awful summer—and worse summers would follow—those in command at Jamestown provided no leadership or inspiration of any kind, failing to take even the most elementary measures for survival. Interested only in themselves and their petty ambitions, the members of the Council spent their entire time in bickering, quarreling, and scheming against one another. They were worse than useless, for they bent all things to selfish aims. Eager for personal advantage, torn by mean and spiteful jealousies, they were prepared, as soon appeared, to cut each other's throats

for place and preferment. As for the "common sort" committed
to their charge, they were left to shift for themselves while the
Council hatched some new folly or outrage. For months—for
years—Jamestown was a scene of misery and disorder that has
seldom, if ever, been matched.

Ominous signs of trouble had flashed soon after the landing.
Among the Gentlemen, there had been a "murmur and a grudge
against certain preposterous proceedings and inconvenyent Courses,"
and a petition was presented "to the Councell for reformatyon."
It is not clear what the specific complaints were, but they were
obviously aimed at President Wingfield and his "audacious command." Perhaps he had ordered the Gentlemen to do some work
in the fields or on the palisades then going up, which they would
certainly have regarded as both "preposterous . . . and inconvenyent." A storm was averted when Newport intervened and
persuaded the Council to issue new orders defining the Gentlemen's rights and privileges.

But this truce soon dissolved in the bitterest kind of wrangling.
With the company growing weaker day by day, the fort rang
with strident clamor as reckless charges and countercharges flew
back and forth. As president, Wingfield took a high view of the
powers of his office, ignoring the majority decisions of the Council,
stubbornly going his arbitrary way, which led to more complaints
about his "audacious command" and "hard dealing."

He was partial, it was said, in distributing the rapidly dwindling
supplies in the storehouse. According to Cape Merchant Studley,
only the watery gruel in the common kettle was equally shared,
and there were those who charged that the president had engrossed and hidden for his own use the oatmeal, beef, oil, wine, and
"what not" in the store so that he and his favorites might feast
while others starved.

For spreading this damaging story, well calculated to inspire
serious trouble and even bloodshed, Wingfield called Captain
Smith to account and "tould him privately, in Master Gosnold's
tent," that he had given a little pork and a few things out of his
private stock to an old man who lay dying. If Smith "in his
malice" gave it out otherwise, he lied!—and, the haughty aristocrat

contemptuously added, it had been proved to Smith's face that he "had begged in Ireland like a rogue, without a lycence," [1] and to such, he said, "I would not my name should be a Companyon."

The truth was, according to Wingfield, that Smith and others on the Council had made these charges against him to cover their own selfishness and greed. It was they, led by Captain John Martin and Captain Gabriel Archer, who had gluttonous eyes on the storehouse and were demanding special allowances for themselves and their friends, some going so far as to say that if Wingfield would not "amend their allowance, they would be their own carvers." To have granted their demands would have left the rest to starve, said Wingfield, and he declined to join "in such an ignorant murder."

As it was, the prospect was bleak indeed. All that relieved the pressure upon the dwindling supplies was the rapidly rising death toll, which left fewer mouths to feed.

> The two and twentieth day of August, there died Captaine Bartholomew Gosnold, one of our Councell; he was honourably buried, having all the Ordnance in the Fort shot off, with many vollies of small shot.
> The foure and twentieth day, died Edward Harington and George Walker. . . .
> The six and twentieth day, . . . Kenelme Throgmortine.
> The seven and twentieth . . . William Roods.
> The eight and twentieth . . . Thomas Stoodie [Studley], Cape Merchant.

The death of Gosnold, "that worthy and religious gentleman," was a heavy blow, for upon his life, as Wingfield declared and all agreed, stood a great part of the hopes for the "good success and fortune of our government and Collony." Alone among the members of the Council, he seems to have had some regard for the common welfare, being not solely interested in self—and pelf. He kept free of the petty squabbles and mean-spirited intrigue around him. An able man, gentle in nature and conciliatory in spirit, he was liked and respected by all.

It is a singular fact—as remarkable as any in the records of early Virginia—that in all those records, filled as they are with malicious backbiting, foul slander, savage criticism, and small-minded carping, there is not a critical or unfriendly word about Gosnold, a wise and accomplished leader whose name, undeservedly, has been almost forgotten.

As he was highly competent at sea and one of the very few who had any knowledge of the ways of the wilderness, it would have been well if Gosnold, "the first mover of the Plantation," had been chosen to bring out the expedition and direct affairs at Jamestown. As it was, he did his best to mediate the constant strife and preserve some measure of good sense in the Council. With his restraining hand removed, there was an immediate explosion.

First, Captain George Kendall was removed from the Council and imprisoned on the pinnace because it "did manifestly appeare that he did practize to sowe discord betweene the President and the Councell." As all were doing this, Kendall's offense must have been something quite special. But his arrest did not end the "jangles," for the other members of the Council—Smith, Martin, and Ratcliffe—now turned on Wingfield.

Appearing at his tent one morning with a warrant signed by themselves, they announced that they thought him "very unworthy to be either President or of the Councell, and therefore discharged him of both." As Wingfield was very unpopular, resistance was obviously futile, and after a great deal of pointless argument he surrendered to the three who had usurped command—the Triumvirate, he dubbed them.

"Dispose of me as you will," he said, "without further garboile."

But the "garboile" was only beginning. The Triumvirate confined Wingfield on the pinnace, allowed Captain Kendall to come ashore, and elected Captain John Ratcliffe as president. To the sick and hungry at Jamestown, voiceless except for their moans and groans, it must have seemed that any change in command could be only for the better, but they had much to learn. The "disgustfull" brawls continued as affairs drifted from bad to worse and more perished:

The fourth day of September, died Thomas Jacob, Sergeant.

The fifth day, there died Benjamin Beast. Our men were destroyed with cruell diseases, as Swellings, Flixes, Burning Fevers, and by warres; and some departed suddenly, but for the most part they died of meere famine. . . .

The eighteenth day, died one Ellis Kinistone . . . of the cold. The same day, at night, died one Richard Simmons.

The nineteenth day, . . . one Thomas Mouton.

Many died in sheer despair, for Newport's return could not be expected for two months at least. All lived in constant terror of the Indians, "each houre expecting the fury of the Salvages," who could easily have wiped out the settlement with even a half-hearted attack, leaving no trace of it in the wilderness or on the pages of history except perhaps for a line or two. In this crisis the Triumvirate, each thirsting for personal revenge, could think of nothing better to do than bring Wingfield to trial, spending days in the most ridiculous proceedings.

As drawn up by his old enemy, Captain Gabriel Archer, a half-trained lawyer who was now Secretary-Recorder of the colony, the charges against Wingfield were, for the most part, frivolous and absurd, as the latter protested. It was charged that he was a Roman Catholic and in league with the Spanish to destroy the colony—that he had not brought a Bible with him [yes he had, said Wingfield, but it had been stolen from his trunk, along with his preserves, sweetmeats, and other tidbits]—that he did "much banquit and ryot" amid the groans of the dying—that he had denounced Captain John Martin as a slacker, declaring that he did nothing but tend his pot, spit, and oven—that he had starved Captain Martin's son to death—that he had called Smith a liar—that when Captain Ratcliffe was sick, he had denied him a chicken, a spoonful of beer, and had served him with "foule Corne" [Wingfield had a chicken-coop that was a source of great envy and much coveted]—that on several occasions he had "deprived" the company of hearing a sermon on Sundays—that he intended to seize the country and proclaim himself king.

"My mynde never swelled with such impossible mountebank humors," Wingfield replied, dismissing Archer's "pennworke" as nonsense. But he had to confess that he had removed from the storehouse and secretly buried some oil, vinegar, sack, and brandy— "two gallons of each, the sack [sherry] reserved for the Communion table, the rest for such extremities as might befall us." And "Lord!" he exclaimed, when the Triumvirate discovered this, "how they then longed to supp up that little remnant, for they had now emptied all their owne bottles and all others they could smell out."

Wingfield's secret removal of supplies was cause enough to mistrust his judgment and intentions. Worse was his admission that he did not know what had gone into the storehouse or what had been taken out, excusing himself by saying that Cape Merchant Studley, now in his grave, had never given him an inventory of the food, clothes, tools, trading articles, and other essentials upon which Jamestown's life depended.

"As occasion moved me," he said, "I expended them in trade or by gift among the Indians." Likewise, Newport had taken "what he thought good," with no check or record of what had been taken. "Only I was well assured," said Wingfield, "that I had never bestowed the valew of three penny whittles to my owne use, or to the private use of any other, for I never carried any favorite over with me nor intertayned any there."

Wingfield's assurance of his personal honesty may be accepted, but the appalling fact remained that no one knew what was in the storehouse and that various persons were dipping into it at their pleasure—which explains much about later quarrels and disasters, for the store was always badly managed, often with a want of concern, a carefree disregard of consequences, that seem almost incredible.

Sentenced to pay five times the value of all goods for which he could give no account, Wingfield was returned to confinement on the pinnace, only to be dragged off a few days later to stand trial again—this time, for slander. After more "garboile," he was ordered to pay Captain John Smith £200 for charging him with mutiny and John Robinson £100 for declaring that the latter had hatched a plot "to run away with the shallop to Newfoundland" and thus return home—which, if they could have managed, all would have been happy to attempt, including Wingfield himself, as soon became evident.

These petty persecutions brought the deposed president some sympathy and support, and the colonists "still grew mutinous" as the Triumvirate did little but waste time, stumbling from folly to folly. Coming on board the pinnace one day in line of duty, the blacksmith of the company managed to convey privately to Wingfield the "commendations" of Captain Kendall, George Percy, and others, who took this means of letting him know, he said, that they would be "glad to see me on shore."

Here was a veiled but unmistakable invitation for him to lead a revolt against the Triumvirate, which would certainly have meant bloodshed. Though he had ideas of his own, Wingfield was not prepared to go that far and sent back word to his friends that as they were "honest Gentlemen and had carried themselves very obediently to their governors," he hoped that they were not now thinking "of any ill thing unworthie of themselves."

Suspecting that something was afoot, President Ratcliffe questioned the blacksmith, James Read, about his visit to the pinnace. Getting little satisfaction, Ratcliffe began to abuse and belabor the blacksmith, who, in turn, "not only gave him bad language, but also offered to strike him with some of his tools." Such conduct by an "inferior" was intolerable. Tried for mutiny and convicted almost on the spot, Read was led to the gallows, "continuing very obstinate, as hoping upon a rescue." At the last moment, not wishing to be a scapegoat for his "superiors," he asked to have a word with Ratcliffe and saved himself by denouncing Captain George Kendall, who was seized and confined on the pinnace.

Kendall, Wingfield, and others, it appears, had been plotting to seize the pinnace and sail for home with a few of the "better sort," abandoning the rest to the "furie of the Salvages, famine, and all manner of mischiefs and inconveniencies," as Smith exclaimed in great indignation, and with cause, for he was one of those to be left behind, along with "good Mr. Hunt" and forty more.

Ordered to come ashore to be questioned about this, Wingfield defied the Triumvirate and refused to leave the pinnace—which, suddenly, to the utter dismay of everyone in Jamestown, was seen moving out into the river, headed for home, under the command of Wingfield and Kendall, who had "strengthened themselves with the sailors and other confederates." Those on shore recovered their wits in time to open fire with muskets and cannon, bringing the *Discovery* to a halt, forcing her "to stay or sinke in the river."

For this, as he deserved, Captain Kendall was stood up against the palisade and shot. Though he remained under arrest, no action was taken against Wingfield, no doubt because of his exalted station. Though daring much, the Triumvirate evidently thought better of shooting one of the first and most influential of the Virginia patentees, even for a treachery that threatened the lives of all and the collapse of the entire enterprise.

December had come—but not Newport—and none would now have been alive if it had not "pleased God, after a while," to send them aid from a quite unexpected quarter. None could have survived these tragic and wholly misspent months of "garboile" if the Indians, hitherto so hostile, had not brought them "Bread, Corne, Fish, and Flesh in great plentie"—without which, said Percy, "we had all perished." Nature had also provided some welcome relief, for great flocks of waterfowl had come into the river late in the year and they managed to bag some of these.

But these unexpected bounties provided only a temporary stay to the gnawing pains of hunger. The Indians could spare no more corn from their always scanty larders. The waterfowl had departed. Even if Newport did come eventually, it might be too late.

There was only one hope—"to search the country for trade"— which they might well have been doing for many months now.

IV

Weromocomoco

*Why have you and your friends
come to this country?*

—POWHATAN

SINCE the death of Thomas Studley in August, when hunger
had begun to pinch so sorely, the Cape Merchant had been
Captain John Smith. It was his vital responsibility—a matter of
life or death to the colony—to manage the dangerously depleted
supplies in the storehouse and to replenish them if at all possible.
But Smith had done nothing about this. He was so wrapped up
in "garboile," so determined to have revenge on Wingfield, that
it was not until late November, with the store reduced to a two
weeks' supply, that he was moved at length "to search the country for trade," pushing off in the shallop with a half dozen men.

Though he later represented that he had been the leader of the
company from the start, even that he had organized the expedition
and brought it out, this was Smith's first independent command,
and he brought to it his usual energy and resolution, rare qualities
among the leaders at Jamestown at any time. He also brought to it
his usual want of discretion, a compulsive need to assert himself
and have his own way at whatever cost, a boastful conceit that he
alone was right, and a firm faith in bluff, bluster, and violence,
being either unable or unwilling to foresee and accept the conse-

44

quences of his arbitrary acts. Nothing that he did was wrong; nothing that another did was right.

Blind to the need of some consistent and sensible policy toward the Indians, Smith improvised from moment to moment, often moved by sheer caprice—courting the Indians as friends one day, alienating them by some sudden unprovoked violence the next, setting a pattern that caused infinite trouble. It was unfortunate for the colony that it was he who largely conducted and decisively shaped its relations with the Indians for the next few years.

Dropping down the James "to trade for Corne and try the River for fishing," Smith and his men came ashore at the village of Kecoughtan, where the company had been so well received on entering the Chesapeake six months before. Again, the Indians were very friendly. But as they had little enough corn for themselves, seldom planting enough for their own needs, they were not disposed to trade it for a few trinkets until—as Smith phrased it in his *True Relation* (1608)—"God, the absolute dispenser of all hearts, altered their conceits."

In early Virginia, as elsewhere down the ages, God got credit for a lot of mischief, as here at Kecoughtan, for Smith was lying. When the Indians declined to trade, he dropped "curtesie," as he later confessed in his *Generall Historie* (1624), and "made bold to try such conclusions as necessitie inforced, though contrary to his Commission," thus shattering the precarious truce under which Jamestown just barely managed to survive.

Running the shallop ashore, Smith and his men leaped out and let fly with their muskets at the Indians who had gathered to meet them and resume their talks. Taken by surprise, not knowing what to make of this, the Indians ran for the woods, leaving behind several wounded and their Oke, "an Idoll made of skinnes, stuffed with mosse, all painted and hung with chaines and copper." After a skirmish or two, the Indians sent messengers to sue for peace and Smith dictated his terms. He would stop shooting and return their Oke if they would fill up the shallop with corn. This was done and so, said Smith, they "parted friends."

But the loot was little—some thirty bushels of corn, supply for two days at most. Mid-December had come, with Newport now a month overdue, and again there was talk of sending Ratcliffe or Archer home to bring back supplies. But as Smith and Martin objected to this, the Council decided to send a party "towards Powhatan for corne." Lots were drawn to determine who should lead this expedition, and the lot was Smith's.

After some preliminaries, during which he pursued his usual ruffling course, Smith took nine men in the shallop, a fourth of the surviving company and the larger part of those able to bear arms, and headed up the Chickahominy River, a large tributary coming down from the north to empty into the James a few miles above the fort. Proceeding as far as he could in the shallop, he left the vessel in a broad stretch of the river, hired a canoe with several Indians to paddle it, and went on upstream with two of his men—Thomas Emry, carpenter, and John Robinson, "Gent."

Upon this wholly irresponsible and foolhardy action rests most of Smith's popular fame. His course served no useful purpose whatever. There was no pretense that it would add anything to Jamestown's supply of corn. Even Smith admitted that "wise men" might tax him with "too much indiscretion," as many did. But he excused himself by saying that the Indians appeared to be friendly and there was the possibility—nay, the "probabilitie"—of finding a lake leading to the South Sea or something "of worth to incourage our adventurers in England." But these were rationalizations after the event, for his motive, as he inadvertently let slip at the time, was a petty and personal one—to win glory for himself and silence the "malicious tungs" of his critics.

Smith had no sooner disappeared upstream than those on the shallop, disobeying orders, came ashore to do some marauding. Indians surprised them, killed one, and chased the rest back to the vessel, which they almost boarded. Casting free at last, abandoning Smith and his two men to their fate, the crew hastened back to Jamestown to report the bad news.

When days passed without word of the missing men, Smith was given up as lost, which left only two on the Council, President Ratcliffe and Captain Martin. The former proposed that Captain Archer should be seated and, though Martin objected, the ambitious and always contentious Secretary-Recorder stepped up and took Smith's place—soon another cause of time-consuming conflict.

Presently, Smith sent word by Indian messengers that his two companions had been surprised and slain, and that he was a prisoner living in constant fear of death, having been captured by a large hunting party of the Pamunkey.

Proceeding far up the Chickahominy, Smith had left his two men guarding the canoe and set out alone through the woods, soon finding himself in the midst of an Indian deer drive with scores of braves all around him.* Defending himself with his pistol, killing two, he was finally forced to surrender when he slipped into a "bogmire," in White Oak Swamp apparently.

Brought before the great chief Opechancano, tall and powerful, grave of mien, a man of uncommon wit and skill as the English would many times learn to their cost, Smith was at his resourceful best. Presenting the chief with a compass set in a small ivory ball, he used this "globe-like Jewell" to illustrate his points as he rapidly discoursed on a great number of things— "the course of the sunne, moone, starres, and planets, . . . the greatnesse of the Land and Sea, the diversitie of Nations, varietie of complexions, . . . the roundnesse of the earth, and how we were to them Antipodes."

The chief and his men were astonished, as it was intended they should be, for they "imagined the world to be flat and round, like a trencher, and they in the middest." Awed by the "magic" of the compass,[1] impressed with Smith as a powerful medicine man, the Indians took him off to dinner and set before him more venison and bread "than would have served twentie men," as he noted, recalling the starvation rations at Jamestown. He was well treated and so well fed that he became uneasy that he was being fattened up as a sacrifice to the "Quiyoughquosicke"—"a superior power they worship," he explained, without explaining much, and "a more uglier thing cannot be described."

Taken here and there as the Pamunkey moved about in search of game, Smith kept protesting all the way that he had to see the

* There were "200 Salvages," Smith first reported, who later became "300 bowmen."

Great Powhatan. After a time, Opechancano agreed to conduct him to his brother, the big chief. Still under the impression that the latter was the young chieftain whom Newport had met at Powhatan's Tower near the Falls, Smith was much surprised when he was taken by a long roundabout trail to Weromocomoco, or House of the Werowance, on the far bank of another great river, the modern York, then known as the Pamunkey, which parallels the James about ten or twelve miles to the north.*

Here at Weromocomoco, near the head of the river, in a cove now known as Putin Bay,† Smith was met by several hundred scowling braves, all in their brightest paint and feathers, who stared at him as if he were a "monster." Leading him into the "palace," a long arbor-like structure, these "grim courtiers" introduced him with a great shout to Wahunsonacock, better known both then and now as the Great Powhatan, overlord of all these parts.

The "Emperor," Smith noted, was an older man of sixty perhaps, large and well proportioned, with gray hair and a "sowre look." Wrapped in a great coonskin coat, with strings of pearls gleaming at his throat, he was seated before a fire, resting on a low platform like a bedstead, cushioned with embroidered leather pillows and gaily colored mats. On either hand sat a "young wench of 16 or 18 yeares," and along the sides of the house, "two rowes of men and, behind them, as many women, with all their heads and shoulders painted red, their heads bedecked with the white downe of Birds," and with a "great chayne of white beads aboute their necks."

It was a "brave sight," Smith declared, and he was even more impressed when Powhatan, "with such a grave and Majesticall countenance" as hardly seemed possible "in a naked Salvage, . . .

---

* The Pamunkey was later renamed the Charles, and then the York, as it has since been known. To avoid needless complications, it will hereafter be referred to as the York. It has two main tributaries, known to the Indians as the Mattaponi and the Youghtimond. The former retains its name. In time, the latter came to be known as the Pamunkey, by transference from the main stream. Hereafter, it will be referred to as the modern Pamunkey.

† About ten miles below the present town of West Point. "Putin" is a corruption of "Poetan," which in turn is a corruption of "Powhatan."

did kindly welcome me with good wordes and great Platters of
sundrie Victuals, assuring me his friendship and my libertie within
four days."

In Opechancano's presence and using the "globe-like Jewell,"
Smith again discoursed on the roundness of the earth and the
course of the sun, moon, and stars, which "much delighted" Powhatan, who suddenly inquired:

"Why have you and your friends come to this country?"

"Because," said Smith, "being in a fight with the Spaniards,
our enemy, and being overpowered, near put to retreat, we were
by extreme weather put to this shore, where . . . at Kecoughtan
they kindly used us. We, by signs, demanded fresh water. They
described to us how up the river was all fresh water." The pinnace
being leaky, Smith concluded, "we are enforced to stay to mend
her till Captain Newport, my father, comes to conduct us away."

"Why, then," asked the chief, "did you go farther up the river
in your boat?"

"So that I might be able to talk about the Back Sea, that on the
other side of the main," said Smith, "where there is salt water."

Powhatan began talking of the peoples round about and the
many lands under his dominion. To put him in his place, Smith
began to describe the vast territories under King James, "the innumerable multitude of his ships, . . . the noyse of Trumpets,
and the terrible manner of fighting under Captain Newport."
Smith's ready wit created an imposing new title for Newport,
styling him "the Merowance," or King of all the Waters—and at
his greatness, as who would not, the big chief "admired."

Whenever the English and the Indians sat swapping lies, as they
often did, it is frequently difficult to decide which were the more
guileful and which the more gullible, for Powhatan now began
telling pleasant stories, later confessed to be false, about the "great
turning of salt water" not far above the Falls on the James, con-
firming what his brother Opechancano and others had said.

This could only be the South Sea, Smith concluded, later ex-
citedly reporting that some called it "five dayes, some sixe, some
eight," to the point where that sea "dashed amongst many stones

and rockes each storm, which caused oft times the head of the [James] River to be brackish," which indeed was news.

After more of such pleasantries, having treated his prisoner "with all the kindness he could devise," Powhatan allowed Smith to depart, sending four men to guide him to Jamestown and to bring back from there the presents which Smith had promised— two big guns and a grindstone.

Though this was the story that Smith first told a few months after his adventure, he told quite another many years later, changing the lines considerably and adding a scene about which there has been much romanticizing and much sharp controversy as well—both misplaced, for there would seem to be little good ground for either.

After he had been led into Powhatan's presence, there had been a long powwow, it appears, and the "conclusion was, two great stones were brought before Powhatan." Smith was seized, his head was laid upon the stones, and "being readie with their clubs to beate out his brains, Pocahontas, the King's dearest daughter, when no intreaty could prevaile, got his head in her arms and laid her owne upon his to save him from death." Upon these few lines has been built one of the great American sagas.

The chief's "dearest daughter" was a young girl of eleven or twelve. Her name was Matoaka, but as she was an attractive and lively minx, she was called Pocahontas, or Little Wanton. It may well be that Little Wanton, curious about the exotic-looking stranger, fascinated by his strange garb, pale face, blue eyes, and luxuriant whiskers, threw herself upon Smith and claimed his life, a right recognized by the Indians and exercised on many occasions.

In any case, whatever her interests or motives, Pocahontas had her way, according to Smith's story, and her father now invited him to come and live at Weromocomoco, offering him land along the river, saying that Smith could make hatchets and other tools for him, and bells, beads, and copper ornaments for Pocahontas. As Powhatan made his own "robes, shoes, bowes, arrowes, pots," and could "plant, hunt, or doe anything as well as the rest," he presumed that the Captain was a jack-of-all-trades like himself.

But Smith declined with thanks. This was no career for a dashing young blade who had traveled the world and burned with passion to scale the heights to fame and fortune. Insisting that he had to return to Jamestown, he was sent on his way a few days later—"with 12 guides," it seems, and not just four as he first reported.*

It was now January, more than six months since Newport's departure. As he had not returned, many doubted that he ever would. Those in the fort were in utter despair; almost thirty had died of hunger and cold in recent weeks. To the amazement of everyone, since they had long since given him up as dead, Smith suddenly appeared at the fort, where almost all welcomed him, he said, "with the truest signes of joy they could expresse"—all but President Ratcliffe, Captain Gabriel Archer, and their friends, who had decided to go to England for supplies. As the majority on the Council, Ratcliffe and Archer had made this decision some days before, but had been unable to depart, "so extreame was the weather and so great the frost." With a break in the weather, they were just sailing as Smith arrived. Outraged, having no desire to be left trapped in Jamestown with no means of escape, Council order or no Council order, Smith ran to the waterfront and "with the hazard of his life, with sacre, falcon, and musket shot," he again forced the pinnace "to stay or sinke in the river."

And it was at the hazard of his life, as he learned before the day was out.

* The Pocahontas story and Smith's general credibility on events in Virginia will be considered in due course.

V

Father Newport

. . . for which, and other worse
tricks, he had not escaped ye halter
but that Captain Newport interposed
his advice to the contrary.

—EDWARD-MARIA WINGFIELD

*I*N FORCING the *Discovery* to turn back, Smith had put his head
into a noose, signing his own death warrant, for Ratcliffe and
Archer turned on him in fury, charging him with responsibility
for the loss of the three men killed by the Indians on his reckless
expedition up the Chickahominy, saying the "fault was his that led
them to their ends," as it was in part. Digging into his scraps of
legal lore, Archer found a bit of Mosaic law, citing a passage from
Leviticus, and charged Smith with murder.

What an ironic homecoming after so many narrow escapes!
Smith was immediately tried, convicted, and sentenced to die, expecting his hanging the same day or the next, remarked Wingfield with a wry smile, "so speedie is our law there."

With Smith out of the way—and silenced forever, it seemed—
Archer proposed and President Ratcliffe adopted an idea that must
have been wildly acclaimed throughout the fort. For Jamestown,
used to the arbitrary decisions of the Council, it was a quite revolutionary idea. A "parliament" should be called—evidently of all
the freemen, though it may have been for Gentlemen only—to discuss what should be done.

Should they try to hold on? They were at the end of their resources. It was at least eight months till harvest.

Or should they flee the country?

There can be no question about what the decision would have
been if the "parliament" had met. But it did not, for at sunset
that day a white sail appeared down the river and the *John and
Francis* soon put in, bringing the long-awaited Newport and the
First Supply, two months overdue.

After costly delays in England, Newport had again chosen to
sail the long way round by way of the Canaries but, fortunately
for the starving at Jamestown, he had managed this passage in ten
weeks instead of eighteen. In the tropics, yellow fever and other
diseases had carried off many passengers—a score or more, a sixth
of the company—and in a heavy fog off the Virginia Capes the
"nymble pinnace" *Phoenix* had vanished with almost forty on
board.

The *John and Francis* landed some seventy colonists, about half
of whom were Gentlemen. After the tales they had been told at
home, they could scarcely believe their eyes at sight of the thirty-
eight gaunt and ragged survivors at Jamestown, less than a third
of the original company.

Even Newport was dismayed. Coming ashore, he found "all in
combustion"—with Gosnold dead, Kendall shot, Wingfield under
arrest, Smith sentenced to death, Ratcliffe sick, Martin still ailing,
and Archer virtually in command. The storehouse was empty, the
fort was falling down, and Archer was talking of calling a "parliament." As it was obvious what its decision would be, Newport
quickly put a stop to that.

Though happy in a way to see Newport, many of the colonists
must have suspected that their troubles had just begun and that
their last chance of escape was gone. But there were two in particular who were overjoyed to see Newport, whose arrival "saved
Master Smith's life and mine," said Wingfield, "to our unspeakable comfortes."

With Newport had come a new member appointed to the Council, Captain Matthew Scrivener, "a very wise, understanding
Gentleman," who brought to its deliberations some well-directed

energy and good sense, commending himself—for a time, at least —even to testy and jealous John Smith.

Supported by Scrivener, Newport persuaded the Council to free both Wingfield and Smith. The former was not restored to the Council, but the latter was, and he was no sooner seated than he turned on Archer, who had drawn his murder indictment, and deposed him—with Wingfield cheering on this attack against his old enemy who was always inclined "to look upon his little self with great-sighted spectacles, derrogating from other men's merits by spewing out his venomous libels and infamous chronicles upon them." For that and "worse tricks," said Wingfield, they would now have hanged Archer except that Newport "interposed his advice to the contrarye."

There was literal "combustion" as well. A few days after Newport's arrival, fire broke out and almost in a flash Jamestown was reduced to ashes. Flames consumed most of the ammunition, blankets, bedding, and wearing apparel of the colonists; a large part of the supplies brought by Newport; all but three houses, even the palisades. Parson Hunt lost his library and, like others, "all but the cloathes on his back," but "none did ever hear him repine at his losse."

Coming in "that extreame frost," which the first Virginians long remembered, the fire brought heavy and fatal hardships. Many of the weak and sick among the original company and many of the newcomers perished for want of shelter. There was a general want of all things, as a recent arrival complained in a letter home, begging his friends to send him their old clothes—"large or small garments, doublets, trousers, stockings, capes, or whatever may appear fit"—and paper and ink, or anything at all, for "everything is needed."

They might also use their influence, he added, to have him made a member of the Council—"as much for my honour," he explained, "as that I may be better able to pay my debts." Those on the Council "are no better than I," he modestly observed, "and understand State affairs as little as I do"—as acute an observation on Virginia as had yet been made.

It seems scarcely credible, but it was not until April, three months later, that Smith and Scrivener "divided betwixt them the rebuilding our towne, the repairing our Pallizadoes, . . . and to rebuild our Church and re-cover the Store house."

The church was a "homely thing like a barne," said Smith, "set upon Cratchets, covered with rafts, sedge, and earth," with walls made of the same materials. The best of the houses were "of a like curiosity," but most of them consisted merely of "punches sett in the ground and covered with Boardes," and of such bad workmanship that they scarcely kept out the wind and the rain. There were no half-timbered houses, no framed houses, and no log cabins. Neither here, nor at Plymouth, nor at Salem and Boston, did the first settlers build log cabins for the good reason that they did not know how. The log cabin, apparently so natively American, came from the Old World, brought to our shores by the Swedes and the Finns when they came to settle along the Delaware in the 1640s. While the new shelters at Jamestown left much to be desired, they were far better than the rotten tents, the cold and damp dugouts, and the ramshackle huts in which the men had lived—and died—before the fire.

Meantime, Jamestown had again been reduced to living on the bounty of the Indians. Once or twice a week, Powhatan sent braves, often with Pocahontas in their company, bringing venison, turkeys, squirrels, fish, and corn, which "saved many of their lives that else for all this had starved with hunger."

Smith took entire credit for this, for he had "so inchanted those pore soules (being their prisoner)" that they "admired him as a demi-God." Such confidence they had in him that they would not come near the fort until he came out to meet them and receive their presents—half for himself, half for "Father" Newport, who had come to be regarded as the Great White Chief from Smith's expansive account of his authority and prowess.

Powhatan's friendly aid and what few supplies Newport could spare from the ship's stores prevented famine, but Jamestown was nevertheless hungry. As always in early Virginia, some fared much better than others. Though the practice had been strictly forbidden, the officers and crew of the ship were carrying on a brisk private trade, presumably with their own private stock of goods and sup-

plies. But as ships never came with proper bills of lading, Jamestown early suspected, as was the case, that the seamen were help-
ing themselves to the general cargo and selling their pilferings to
the desperate colonists, forcing them to buy their own supplies "at
15 times the valew."

Virginia long continued to suffer from "such pilfering occasions,"
as Smith sharply complained, and from Newport's easy way in
telling pleasant tales about the "great plentie" in Virginia, which
led the adventurers to send out ships with inadequate supply.
"And had not Captaine Newport cried *Peccavi*," said Smith, they
would have taken him off his ship and made him stay a year in
the colony "to learne to speake of his owne experience."

Whether legitimate or not, a "damnable" private trade flourished. Those with "money, spare clothes, credit to give bills for
payment, gold rings, furres, or any such commodities" could obtain food and drink from the ships. George Percy, for one, drew
huge bills of exchange on his brother, the Earl of Northumberland, for the essentials and even the luxuries of life. But most men,
as one poor soldier complained, had only a "little meale and water,
. . . whereby, with the extreamity of the bitter cold aire, more
than halfe of us died" in that piercing winter.

Jamestown was still a charred ruin. Shelters were badly needed,
but Newport now decided to go visiting, taking forty men with
him, most of the able-bodied in the fort. He wished, he said, to
pay his respects to Powhatan, who had expressed a desire to see
him. Arriving at Weromocomoco, fearing some treachery by "that
politick Salvage," he sent Captain Smith ahead to announce his
coming and present the chief with a red coat, a white hound, and a
fancy hat.

Delighted with these "Jewells," Powhatan proclaimed his desire
for a "perpetuall league and friendship" with the English, who
were not to be regarded as strangers, he told his people, "nor as
Paspaheghans, but Powhatans," and free to enjoy the "Corne,
women, and Country." Indian maids were not the least of the at-
tractions that brought runaways from Jamestown.

The next day "Father" Newport came ashore "with a trumpet
before him," acting his most awesome and regal. But Powhatan

was far more impressive and easily stole the show, being an old hand at such things, sitting his throne "with such a Majestie as I cannot expresse," said Smith, never easily awed, "nor yet have often seene, either in Pagan or Christian."

As an assurance of his "love," Newport presented the chief with a youth whom he termed his "son." Aged thirteen, Thomas Savage by name, the boy had just arrived, doubtless as an indentured servant, so that his wishes in this matter did not have to be consulted. But it was not such a bad assignment as the boy may first have feared. It kept him out of Jamestown and its miseries much of the time, enabling him to survive for almost twenty years. During that time he performed many valuable services as guide, interpreter, and spy, enjoying great favor and prestige among the Indians, to whom he was always known as Thomas Newport.

Powhatan was so pleased that he, in turn, presented Newport with his "son and trustie servant," Namontack, "one of a shrewd subtill capacity." The latter soon accompanied Newport to England, making a second visit later, and the youth may actually have been one of the chief's numerous family, for the English now learned that by his various wives he had twenty sons, and that Pocahontas was one of a dozen daughters.

As Cape Merchant, Smith had brought along some hatchets, knives, bells, mirrors, beads, and the usual articles of trade, as well as some cloth, "very much moth-eaten," which Sir Thomas Smythe had bought of the East India Company for the Virginia trade. Laying out his wares, Smith asked the chief how much corn he would give for each of these.

Seeming to "despise the nature of a merchant," Powhatan declined to do business in this way and appealed to Newport, saying that it was not agreeable to his greatness to trade for trifles "in this piddling manner." Over Smith's objections, Newport agreed, "thinking to out-brave this Salvage in ostentation of greatnesse and so to bewitch him with his bountie as to have what he listed" —with the result, said Smith scornfully, that he did not obtain four bushels of corn for what should have brought twenty hogsheads.

But Smith, according to his account, saved the day. He would have preferred to flash his sword on Powhatan, but instead, "smothering his distaste," he brought out a few trifles and flashed them before the chief. Some blue beads took his eye, but the more he offered, the more Smith seemed to "affect them," saying they were "composed of a most rare substance of the colour of the skyes and not to be worne but by the greatest kings in the world." Naturally, the chief was "halfe madd to be the owner of such strange Jewells," and Smith was finally persuaded to part with a pound or two in exchange for several hundred bushels of corn.

Altogether, it was a pleasant visit and after a week of "feasting, dauncing, singing, and much mirth," the English departed, more impressed than ever with Powhatan, all agreeing that he had carried himself very well, "considering his education."

Proceeding up the river, they paid a visit to Opechancano, who received them "with a natural kind affection." After Smith had provided him with "blew" beads at exorbitant rates, Newport's party returned to Jamestown, bringing enough corn for three months at least. Newport's visit had turned out far better than any had reason to expect, and the history of Virginia would have been very different if the amity established at this time had not been wantonly destroyed by the English—by Captain John Smith, in particular.

As it was now spring, all should have been busy planting corn, but there was "no talke, no hope, no worke, but dig gold, wash gold, refine gold, loade gold." Convinced that Jamestown rested upon a foundation of almost pure gold, Newport and Captain John Martin were anxious to vindicate themselves by proving that here was a true El Dorado, that they had simply made an error in shipping home the wrong ore before. To prevent a similar error, the adventurers had sent out two refiners, two goldsmiths, and a jeweler,* and these "gilded refiners with their golden promises made all men their slaves in hope of recompense."

Many had their doubts about all this. Smith was heard to tell Captain Martin and his men that until they showed him a more

* And for good measure, six tailors and a perfumer!

substantial trial, he was "not inanmored with their durtie skill," and nothing did more torment him, said one of his devoted soldiers, "than to see all necessarie businesse neglected to fraught such a drunken ship with so much gilded durt."

At length, when the *John and Francis* could hold no more, Newport departed, doubtless convinced that his long stay had been well spent, confident that the merchant adventurers would agree when they saw the immense treasure stowed away in the hold. With him went two former members of the Council, sent home "to seeke some place of better imploiment"—the unhappy Wingfield, who never saw Virginia again, and his bitter enemy, the always troublesome Captain Archer, who would come back, stir up more "garboile," and perish wretchedly in the Starving Time. With his departure, Wingfield vanishes into the mists of history, probably retiring to private life in some restful and quiet spot where the noisy brawls and anguished cries at Jamestown were not even an echo.

Turning from mining after Newport's departure, the company began its spring planting, but abruptly broke off to welcome a most unexpected arrival—Newport's "nymble" pinnace, the *Phoenix*, long given up as lost. After vanishing in the fog off the Virginia Capes, unable to make way against strong head winds, she had turned back to the West Indies and spent the winter there. Her able skipper, Captain Francis Nelson, had put the interval to good use, keeping his men in health by having them gather the products of the islands, and the vessel now came in with her hold bulging with "victuall." What Nelson had, he "freely imparted," as an astonished Jamestowner noted, "which honest dealing (being a Marriner) caused us all to admire him. We could not have wished more than he did for us."

Deciding that the fort was now as well supplied as could be wished, "both with a competent number of men and also for all other needful provisions till a further supply should come," those in command let the spring planting go and turned to other things. It would take untold misery, catastrophe after catastrophe, to teach these English the simple truth that they could not safely depend upon any but themselves for supplies, that they were fools to entrust their very lives to the easy promises and uncertain performance of others. This would seem obvious, but it was twenty years before Virginia planted and harvested a crop that anywhere near met its needs.

The reasons for this, however, are not so simple and obvious. In large part, the early Virginians were Gentlemen of the sword, not men of the plow. They would not demean themselves by handling an ax or a hoe, they declined to perform any manual labor, or menial chore, even if that meant death as a consequence. "They would rather starve and rot with idleness," as Smith and others declared, "than be persuaded to do anything for their own relief."

As for the artisans and laborers—the "common sort," who were obliged to work—they were city folk, for the most part, knowing little and caring less about farming. They had no desire to undergo the heavy labor of chopping fields out of the forest and cultivating them without the aid of oxen or other work animals. Nothing reveals more about early Virginia than the astonishing fact that there was not a plow going in the entire country for almost ten years.

Those termed laborers, said Smith, were "footmen and such as they that were Adventurers brought to attend them, or such as they could persuade to goe with them, that never did know what a day's worke was, . . . poore Gentlemen, Tradesmen, Serving-men, libertines, and such like, ten times more fit to spoyle a Commonwealth than either begin one or helpe to maintaine one. For when neither the feare of God, nor the law, nor shame, nor displeasure of their friends could rule them here [in England], there was small hope ever to bring one in twentie of them ever to any good there [in Virginia]." Some of them, however, showed "better mindes and grew more industrious than was expected. Yet ten good workemen would have done more substantial worke in a day than ten of them in a weeke."

Requests for workers instead of idlers were ignored by the adventurers, who desired "but to packe over as many as they could," saying that good laborers were more useful in England and that the cost was the same whether they sent a "roarer" or a workman.

Furthermore, the colonists had been sent out, one and all, to work for the profit of the adventurers. In lieu of payment for their labor and services, they had been promised food, clothes, and other essentials.

Well, then, let those promises be kept! Why should they break their backs in the fields to relieve the adventurers of their responsibilities? Though prudence might have suggested a longer view, they were naturally averse to paying their own wages, so to speak.

Lastly, there were few, if any, in the company who had any permanent interest in Virginia and its progress. They had not come to make homes for themselves in the wilderness as did so many millions during the next three centuries. They had come in the hope of making a fortune and returning home as quickly as possible to enjoy the spoils—if only they could find something to spoil! They were transients, soldiers of fortune temporarily on duty at an outpost of empire on a remote frontier. If they could get supplies from home, or live off the Indians, why waste time planting? There were always so many more promising and exciting things to do—such as finding gold mines, or the South Sea, or "making discoveries."

After Nelson's "happy coming," the Council decided to send a large expedition, three fourths of those in the fort, to explore the James to its source and scour the country for "commodities." This force, under the command of Captain Smith, spent a week learning how "to march, fight, and scirmish in the woods." But the expedition was abandoned when Captain Nelson refused to aid and because many protested that no matter how profitable the voyage might be, they would be "taxed for the most indiscreete men in the world, besides the wrong we should doe to Captaine Newport," who held a special commission assigning "all discoveries" to him.

More time was wasted in a protracted quarrel between Martin and Smith on the cargo that the *Phoenix* should carry home. Martin wished to load her with more of his "phantasticall gold," but Smith won his point and the pinnace finally departed, after several weeks' delay, laden with cedar. On board was Captain

Martin, who had "made shift to be sicke near a year," said Smith
with savage malice, and "being always very sickly and unserviceable, and desirous to injoy the credit of his supposed Art in finding the golden mine, was most willingly admitted to returne for
England." And what a lecture he must have been read by his
father, the goldsmith, master of the Royal Mint!

Meantime, Newport had arrived in England. Perhaps he wrote
the Earl of Salisbury another letter to ask for an audience and
assure him that this time he had successfully accomplished his
mission. Perhaps Sir Walter Cope again snatched up his pen and
let his imagination soar. Unfortunately, most of the records are
missing, and the few that remain are pointedly silent about the
"gilded durt" on the *John and Francis*. After the first fiasco, the
adventurers had no desire to be embarrassed again and said nothing about the matter.

But their groans were audible, and there was a tempest of angry
criticism. They had invested thousands of pounds in Virginia and
what had they received? Nothing but tons of dross! And the
Phoenix had been lost, which would cost them dearly. Nor could
they find anything to encourage them in the reports that came
from Jamestown about the deadly "summer sickness," the recur-
ring state of famine, the precarious truce with the Indians, and
the brawls in which the leaders spent their entire time.

More adventurers withdrew from the enterprise, which was
soon "in the greatest straits for money that can be imagined," as
the Spanish ambassador gleefully reported to Madrid. Philip III
was interested, for he had looked upon Virginia with a jaundiced
eye from the start, claiming that it was a trespass upon his dominions, fearing that it had been established as a base for a flank attack
upon his rich empire in the West Indies and to the south—which,
to a degree, it had.[1]

Not long after, the gloom was somewhat relieved when the
Phoenix, written off as lost, suddenly appeared bearing Captain
Martin and some cedar clapboard. But the adventurers were far
less interested in either of these than in a manuscript and a chart
that she had brought along, both by Captain Smith. The latter
had somehow managed to find time in spite of his many exploits,

real or alleged, to write a rather extended account of all that had happened since the first ships sailed from Blackwall.

His account, entitled *A True Relation* (1608), was colored by his annoying penchant for self-glorification and was biased by his bitter personal animosities toward so many men. Yet, with all that, it was substantially true, as is evident from any careful study of contemporary documents. Smith's was a far more honest piece of reporting than any of the official tracts that followed. He painted life at Jamestown as it was, in all of its excitements and all of its agonies and abuses as well. The picture was not prettified for purposes of propaganda and promotion. It was not designed to beguile the naive or trap the unwary. More than any other, Smith had a passionate interest and faith in Virginia—a lifelong faith and interest that nothing could shake—but he never allowed phantasy to blind him to the facts of life there.

What is more, Smith had mastered a rough and vigorous style, a colorful Elizabethan prose that rushed along pell-mell, half out of breath to get things said, turning here and there to make a brilliant sally. Smith had wit, a sarcastic sense of humor, an eye for amusing and significant detail, and a hand for turning a graphic phrase. Above all, he knew from long practice the tricks of telling a good story, whether true or false.

But Smith's narrative, just because it was so grim in parts, interested the adventurers less than the chart which accompanied it. On his map of Virginia, Smith had incorporated the now "certain news" that the South Sea lay close by, and that a stretch of water not far to the north led to it. This created a sensation, of course, and hastened preparations for Newport's return.

But Smith's "certain news" had quite unexpected consequences. Ironically, it led to the founding of a rival colonial empire along the North Atlantic. Bearing the map and a letter from Smith, whom he knew, Captain Henry Hudson crossed from London to Amsterdam, where the Dutch hired him to find the South Sea passage. A few months later, unknown to those at Jamestown, Hudson was prowling along the Virginia coast in the *Half Moon,* turning north to explore the great river that now bears his name. Upon his voyage the Dutch based their claim to the rich Hudson

Valley and within a few years established a trading post at its mouth, on the island of Manhatta, where the town of New Amsterdam later flourished.

But Smith did not intend to have anyone anticipate him in making the great discovery, whether "all discoveries" belonged to Newport or not. On the very day the *Phoenix* departed, he embarked in the shallop with fourteen men, including seven "gallants," and headed up the broad waters of the Chesapeake, determined not only to find the South Sea but the source of a "glistering metal," presumed to be silver, which the Indians had shown them.

At the outset, the party made a great discovery, finding such "abundance of fish lying so thicke with their heads above the water" that, in want of nets, they tried to catch them in frying pans. None of them had ever seen better fish, or in greater variety and number, but a frying pan, they found, "was a bad instrument to catch fish with." The discovery of this fine fishery in the Bay was of first importance, but nothing was done about it for years.

Coming ashore here and there, Smith pursued his usual blustering course with the Indians and at all times "so incountered them and curbed their insolencies as they concluded, with presents, to purchase peace." Always venturesome, he pressed on until his men, "oft tired at their oares, their bread spoiled with wet so much that it was rotten," began to grumble. Smith turned back, discovering another great river on his way home, the Patawomeck (Potomac), up which he sailed to the head of navigation, to Great Falls as it is now known, about fifteen miles above Washington.

In Jamestown, after an absence of seven weeks, the party found the "last Supply all sicke" and most of the others ailing, "some lame, some bruised, all unable to do anything but complain of the pride and unreasonable needlesse crueltie of their sillie President." Ratcliffe, it appears, had "riotously consumed the store" and had the company at work building a "pallas in the woods"—for his personal use and pleasure, said Smith. Rather, it may have been planned as an official residence, a sort of Government House.

In any case, with so much else to be done, it was a silly business, and the company rose against Ratcliffe, demanding his removal, begging Smith to take his place. But the latter declined, substituting his "deare friend," Captain Matthew Scrivener, then very ill with fever, and as the company was weak and the weather was hot and no one was doing anything, he left them "to live at ease" and set out to finish his "great discovery."

On this voyage, with a crew of twelve, Smith reached the head of the Chesapeake and hopefully sailed up the Susquehanna River, only to be stopped shortly, blocked by the falls where a large power dam now stands at Conowingo. Again, the "certain" passage to the South Sea had eluded him. But in the neighborhood the party met some of the huge braves of the Susquehannock tribe, "a mightie people," cousins of the astute and formidable Iroquois.

From them Smith learned of the great waters beyond the mountains to the northwest and of the "river of Cannida," where they obtained hatchets and tools from the French.* The "great waters" were obviously the Great Lakes, as the French early learned, but the English could not be persuaded of this for years. More than a half-century later, they were still hopefully seeking the South Sea, believing that it lay just over the mountains.

On their return, Smith and his men spent more than a month coasting down the shores of the Chesapeake, exploring the Rappahannock and other larger rivers, clashing frequently with the Indians, striking them many a cruel and treacherous blow. Back in Jamestown after six weeks, they found "many dead, some sicke," and ex-President Ratcliffe under arrest for mutiny.

A few days later, in September, 1608, "by election of the Councell and the request of the company," Smith agreed to become president, and he noted immediate improvement. Ratcliffe's half-built "pallas" was abandoned, the church repaired, and work was started on new buildings to receive the supplies they expected. The fort was "reduced to a five-square forme"—that is, it was changed from a triangular to a five-pointed figure, which brought a little more ground within the palisade, perhaps a half acre or more. Every Saturday the company held military drill in a field

* Just at this time, in the summer of 1608, Quebec was founded by the French under Champlain.

outside the west bulwark. A new roof was placed on the storehouse —after the horse had been stolen, so to say.

Through the "honest diligence" of Captain Scrivener, their little harvest had been gathered and put away in the dilapidated storehouse which it was Smith's duty as Cape Merchant to keep in repair. He had failed to do so, and the corn was now found to be "so rotten with last somer's rain and eaten with rats and wormes as the Hogges would scarcely eat it." Smith always made much of his exploring voyages up the Chesapeake, boasting that he had sailed more than 3,000 miles. But he would have been much better employed nearer home in doing, for once, what he was supposed to do.

Jamestown again teetered on the edge of the abyss. The boats were hurriedly trimmed for trade and dispatched under the command of Captain George Percy. As they were slowly drifting down the James, bound nowhere in particular because no one knew where corn could be had, they met the *Mary and Margaret* coming in with the Second Supply and turned back, trusting that the ship was bulging with provisions.

VI

The Five-Peeced Boat

*. . . and as for any salt water beyond
the mountains, the relations you have
had from my people are false.*

—POWHATAN

OFF THE *Mary and Margaret,* doubling the population,* came
some seventy people, with the usual complement of Gentlemen, more than thirty in all. But there had also come, for the
first time, "many honest, wise, and painefull workemen of every
trade and profession," including eight "skillfull workemen from
forraine parts." Four "Polanders" had been sent over to make
glass. Of the four "Dutchmen," one was a Swiss and the others
were probably Germans from the Rhineland. These were to make
tar, turpentine, pitch, soap ashes, clapboard, wainscoting, masts,
and similar things. These foreign workers were not only to ply
their trades but instruct the colonists in their "mysteries" for the
immediate profit of the adventurers. A few good farmers willing
to work in the fields would have been rather more useful at the
moment, but the adventurers were not interested in farming.
They wanted "commodities" to ship home for sale there.

It is true that if the adventurers were to continue financing the
enterprise, they had to have some return on their investments.
It is equally true, and after a time it should have become obvious,

* Of those previously sent, three out of four had died.

67

that their demands for immediate profits were self-defeating, leading to fiasco after fiasco, each more costly than the last, both to themselves and the colony. But they persisted in their short-sighted course, stubbornly pursuing it until they were bankrupt.

The ship had brought two "ancient Souldiers and valiant Gentlemen" to be added to the Council, Captains Richard Waldo and Peter Winne—as well as a future governor of the colony, Captain Francis West, another self-centered and quarrelsome "gallant," a younger brother of Lord de La Warr.

But far more welcome and exciting to the lonesome men at Jamestown, unhappy celibates all, were two others, the first women to step ashore at Jamestown—Mistress Forrest, wife of a Gentleman on board, and her young maid, Anne Burras, or Burroughs, probably the daughter of one of the company's fourteen "Tradesmen," or craftsmen. Unattached and fancy free, Anne was a great prize, though she was only thirteen:

And the first white wedding held on Virginia ground
Will marry no courtly dame to a cavalier
But Anne Burras, lady's maid, to John Laydon, laborer,
After some six weeks' courtship—a Fall wedding
When the leaves were turning red and the wild air sweet.
And we know no more than that, but it sticks in the mind,
For they were serving-maid and laboring man . . .
They were half of the first families of Virginia.
Well, where do you start, when you start counting F.F.V.s? *

The Laydons lived happily together for many years—at least, they were living and still together in 1625, when they were two of a handful of early arrivals yet surviving, having had four daughters meanwhile.

Altogether, as several noted, the company on the *Mary and Margaret* was of "better qualitie" than any yet sent. But the hungry and hopeful at Jamestown were dismayed to learn that the ship had come "without victuall," that she had brought noth-

* From *Western Star* by Stephen Vincent Benét, published by Rinehart & Company, Inc. Copyright, 1943, by Rosemary Carr Benét.

ing for them, or for the newcomers either, which created an alarming situation.

To complicate matters and cause endless distractions, Newport had received strict instructions on just what should be done—instructions that could only be carried out by commanding almost the entire time and energies of everybody at Jamestown. Newport had been commanded, among other things, "not to returne without a lumpe of gold, a certaintie of the South Sea, or one of the lost company of Sir Walter Raleigh!"

And these instructions, the adventurers warned, were to be carried out to the letter, and without fail. They would accept no more excuses. They were tired, they said, of being put off with hopes and promises. Let the colonists get to work and send "some few proofes" of their industry and good intentions. The Council seemed to make a "mysterie of the business" and were "so set upon faction and idle conceits" that nothing was ever done. This could not go on.

More than £2,000 ($100,000) had been spent to send out the *Mary and Margaret*, the adventurers asserted, adding ominously that if the ship's return cargo did not defray this heavy charge, the colonists could expect nothing more from them and were "like to remain as banished men."

Newport had also brought along a number of presents for Powhatan, including a copper crown, and now proposed to go to Weromocomoco to place it on his brow. As president, pleased to assert his new authority, Smith strongly objected to all of Newport's projects, pointing to the absolute necessity of getting corn from the Indians, arguing that now was the time to get it while it was still to be had. And how, he asked, could any cargo be provided for the ship if most of the company went off to perform "this strange discovery but more strange coronation"?

While sound enough, Smith's arguments might have been more persuasive if he had not been away all summer on "strange" discoveries of his own. His recognition of Jamestown's peril came rather late. Still, his was good advice. But Newport won over the Council with the assurance that he would bring back ample supplies of corn both from Weromocomoco and from his South Sea expedition, "inferring that Smith's propositions were only devices to hinder his journey . . . [so that Smith might] effect it him- selfe, and that the crueltie Smith had used to the Salvages in his absence might occasion them to hinder his designes." [1]

Partly to save time, partly to clear himself of Newport's sus- picions, Smith offered to go to Powhatan and persuade him to come to Jamestown to receive his crown and conclude an alliance against his traditional enemies, the Monacan.

"If your King has sent me presents," Powhatan proudly re- plied, "I am also a King, and this is my land. Eight days will I stay to receive them. Your Father must come to me, not I to him, nor yet to your fort. I will not bite at such a bait."

Nor did he want their aid against the Monacan. "I can revenge my own injuries," he declared, and "as for any salt water beyond the mountains, the relations you have had from my people are false."

Though he failed in his mission, Smith had a pleasant surprise and with his men enjoyed a fascinating "anticke" which he, and doubtless the others, long remembered. While they were sitting in the open around a fire waiting for Powhatan to appear, there suddenly came from the woods a "hydeous noise and shreeking." Suspecting treachery, they snatched up their arms but quickly dropped them when "thirtie young women came naked out of the woods," their bodies all brightly painted, with Pocahontas in the lead wearing a "fayre paire of Buck's hornes on her head, an Otter's skinne at her girdle and another at her arme, a quiver of arrows at her backe, a bow and arrowes in her hand." Those be- hind were carrying swords, clubs, pot sticks, each with something in her hand and "all horned alike."

Rushing from the woods "with the most hellish shouts and cryes," they made a circle about the fire, "singing and dauncing with the most excellent ill varietie," now "falling into their in- fernall passions" and then resuming their solemn songs and dances. After an hour or more of this "maskarado," they darted back into the woods as they had come, laughing and shrieking, soon reap- pearing not quite so naked to invite the visitors to one of their lodges, where he and his men, said Smith, were "more tormented" than ever by "these Nimphes" who kept crowding and pressing upon them, "most tediously" crying:

"Love you not me? Love you not me?"

A feast was set, "fruit in baskets, fish and flesh in wooden platters, beans and peas," and every "salvage daintie their invention could devise." As some maids served, others sang and danced about the guests, who were pleased and quite impressed. After much mirth, the men were conducted to their lodgings for the night by singing nymphs who danced along "with firebrands (instead of torches)," lighting each man to his own as to a bridal chamber, which it no doubt was.[2]

Some days later, with fifty men on the pinnace, Newport arrived at Weromocomoco with his presents—a basin and ewer, bed and furniture, as well as a scarlet cloak and other bright apparel, which Powhatan was finally induced to put on after he had been persuaded that they would do him no harm.

But "fowle trouble" they had in getting him to kneel to receive his crown, "he neither knowing the majesty nor meaning of a Crowne, nor bending of the knee." Tired of trying to educate him, exasperated at his ignorance, they got hold of him by the shoulders, pushed him down, clapped on the crown, and at a signal the cannon on the ships in the river boomed.

In "horrible feare," Powhatan leaped to his feet and sent the copper crown flying. But seeing all was well, he "remembered" himself and gave Newport a few presents—his old shoes, a mantle, and a few bushels of corn. The English were anxious to buy more corn. But as the Indians had had a bad crop, they were disposed to sell very little, and Newport returned with only sixteen bushels, barely enough to feed Jamestown for a day or two.

The coronation took time, and now other men were detached to go on an equally fruitful mission. Proceeding far to the south, into what is now North Carolina, they returned at length to report "little hope and lesse certaintie of them that were left by Sir Walter Rawley."

But the main mission had yet to be accomplished. Taking two thirds of the company, Newport set out to find gold mines and the South Sea, feeling sure of success, basing his confidence upon

Smith's "certain news" that the Back Sea lay nearby. But Newport declined to take Smith along, which left the latter in a fury and, to improve the interval, he took a gang downstream to cut timber and make pitch, tar, turpentine, and clapboard as return cargo for the ship.

In the gang were two gallants of the Second Supply, Gabriel Beadell and John Russell, "both proper Gentlemen," and such heavy work was strange to them. "Yet lodging, eating, drinking, working, or playing, they but doing as the President did himselfe, all things were carried so pleasantly," said Smith, "as within a weeke they became masters, making it their delight to heare the trees thunder as they fell."

But the axes so blistered their "tender fingers" that at every third stroke they uttered a resounding oath—which inspired Smith's celebrated moral law, long a story-book favorite. Each oath was counted and at night, for his every curse, the culprit had a "Cann of water powred downe his sleeve." But the effect was not as salutary as might have been hoped, for Jamestown continued to curse and blaspheme so mightily that the death penalty was soon prescribed for chronic offenders.

"But let no man think that the President and the Gentlemen spent their time as common wood-hackers, at felling of trees and such like labours, or that they were pressed to anything as hirelings or common slaves," Smith hastily added in describing this scene of the happy wood-choppers. On the contrary, Gentlemen worked only if and when they pleased, "only as a pleasure and a recreation." Still, thirty or forty of such volunteers did more work in a day than a hundred of those who were driven to it. Even so, said Smith, "twentie good workmen had beene better than them all."

Meantime, Newport had proceeded to the Falls in the pinnace, carrying a boat that he had brought from England. This boat was central to his scheme, an essential of success, and he was proud of it. It had been made in five sections, a contraption born of an idea once tossed off by Powhatan in a casual conversation. It was Newport's plan to ship the sections up to the Falls, have his men carry them above the Falls and assemble them there, so that he might sail on up the river to its source and the "great turning of salt water," which evidently occurred along the very crest of the mountains. The boat seemed a feasible idea and much money had been spent on it. Unhappily, the sections had been made much too large and heavy. Sweat and toil as they would, the men could not get them above the Falls and they had to be abandoned there, a total loss.

Smith had ridiculed Newport's expedition from the start, particularly his "five-peeced boat." If he "had burnt her to ashes," Smith tartly remarked, "one man might have carried her in a bag. But as she is, five hundred cannot."

Newport was not too discouraged. Pressing on toward the South Sea, he and his men marched upstream some forty miles, where they stopped and spent two or three days wandering around in the wilderness. Turning back, they prospected for gold along the way, spending some time "in refining, having one William Callicut, a refiner, for that purpose." One piece of ore contained some silver, the latter assured them, and "better stuffe might be had for the digging." With nothing more than this, they started back, "halfe sicke, all complaining," and stumbled into the fort "neare famished," bringing not a grain of the corn that Newport had promised.

Supplies at Jamestown were so short that the *Mary and Margaret* could not depart, having insufficient provisions for the voyage home. As this had to be remedied, Captain Matthew Scrivener went around to Weromocomoco where he found the people, in spite of Newport's friendly visit and the imposing coronation, "more readie to fight than trade." They were very suspicious and much on their guard, for Smith had been on the rampage again, conducting several ill-advised and unprofitable raids in defiance of the Council, which had threatened to depose him as president for flouting its decisions.

Through Namontack, Powhatan's now-traveled son about to depart with Newport again for his second visit to England, the Indians finally agreed to sell Scrivener enough corn to see the *Mary and Margaret* home, and she sailed late in December, 1608, after a four months' stay, during which Newport had faithfully followed his instructions and accomplished absolutely nothing, leaving the colony weaker than before.

The ship was carrying a "taste" of pitch, tar, soap ashes, clapboard, and glass, as well as two barrels of iron ore collected by Smith.* As president, he had also sent the adventurers a blistering letter in reply to their criticism of affairs at Jamestown. Whatever his faults, Smith had none of the degrading and disgusting obsequiousness of most of his contemporaries.

"I humbly intreat your Pardons," Smith began, "if I offend you with my rude Answer." There was no "mystery" about the business, at least so far as he was concerned. Though he was not a scholar, yet he was past a schoolboy, "and I desire to know what either you there, or these here, doe know but what I have learned to tell you by the continual hazard of my life. I have not concealed from you anything I know. But I feare some cause you to believe much more than is true."

The tales they were told about the great natural plenty of everything in Virginia were false, "and Captaine Newport we much suspect to be the author of such inventions." To be sure, there were fish in the sea, fowl in the air, deer and other game in the woods, but their bounds were "so large, they so wilde, and we so weake and ignorant, we cannot much trouble them."

If £2,000 had been spent in sending out the *Mary and Margaret,* as the adventurers asserted, someone had been scandalously cheated, for the supplies received at Jamestown were not worth £20. Though the colonists had only a little meal and water—and not sufficient of that—the sailors and officers of the ships lived well enough, some of whom, it was said, "maintaine their families out of what you send us."

Hereafter, he pleaded, "let us know what we should receive and not stand to the Saylers' Courtesie to leave us what they please."

And in sending more people, "send but thirty carpenters, husbandmen, gardiners, fishermen, blacksmiths, masons, and diggers-up of tree roots, well provided, than a thousand of such as we

* The ore was sold to the East India Company for £68 ($3,400)—little enough, but the adventurers' first return on their investment, though nowhere near the £2,000 of cargo they expected on this ship.

have." It was a waste of money to recruit and send out skilled foreign workers, makers of glass and other things, until the colonists were able to sustain themselves and provide for such workers upon their arrival.

It was even more foolish to expect great quantities of tar, pitch, timber, and other commodities "till more necessary things be provided, for in overtoyling our weak and unskillfull bodies to satisfie this desire for present profit," said Smith, touching the root of the matter, "we can scarce ever recover ourselves from one Supply to another."

In time, better things might be expected, "but as yet you must not looke for any profitable returnes"—which must have left the merchant adventurers aghast.

One more of the original Council returned to England with Newport—the former president, hapless Captain Ratcliffe, "a poore counterfeited Imposture," wrote Smith. "I have sent you him home lest the company should cut his throat. If he and Archer return again, they are sufficient to keepe us always in factions."

Both would soon be back to join Smith in new "jangles."

VII

Smith, Dictator

Think you I am so simple . . .

—POWHATAN

FOR THREE months now, Smith had been president, but none too happy in playing a secondary role under the shadow of "Father" Newport. With the latter gone, Smith strode to the center of the stage and took command with his always great energy and with more than his usual abandon, ignoring hostile criticism and friendly counsel alike. Cost what it might, he was determined to do what he pleased, scorning the decisions of the Council, which now consisted of himself, Captain Scrivener, and the two new members, Captains Waldo and Winne. That Smith somehow survived his almost incredible follies of the next few months, which were his last in Virginia, is really the miracle of his life.

Casting all caution aside, Smith led foraging raids up and down the river. But these brought in very little corn, for the Indians, grown wary and suspicious, had fled from their villages and taken everything with them. Baffled here, enraged by the Indians' "duplicity," Smith proposed to risk all on one master stroke. With no thought of the league of peace and friendship so recently sworn at Weromocomoco, Smith decided "to surprise Powhatan and all his provision."

In an attempt to justify his treachery, Smith declared that it was Powhatan's policy to starve Jamestown—which for sheer impudence could scarcely be exceeded. The Indians were under no obligation to feed men—intruders, at that—who took no pains to feed themselves. And yet, as Smith saw, something had to be done to get corn. The alternative was unthinkable—to sit idly in the fort and slowly starve to death. He, for one, preferred to die by arrow or tomahawk.

At just this time, giving proof of his friendship, Powhatan sent word that he would fill up the pinnace with corn if Smith would give him a "grindstone, fifty swords, some peeces [guns], a cock and hen, with copper and beads." He also asked Smith to send him some men to build him a house. "Knowing there needed no better castle than that house to surprise Powhatan," Smith immediately dispatched two of the English and three Dutch carpenters, intending to follow with a large armed force at the proper time.

This course was "censured as very desperate" and had the support of only one member of the Council, Captain Ralph Waldo. The others, Scrivener and Winne, did their best to prevent it— "for some private reasons," said Smith, always ready to attribute opposition to the meanest and pettiest motives. Scrivener now ceased to be his "deare friend." Resolved to be "Caesar or nothing," the former was plotting "to ruine Captaine Smith," though it rather appeared, as events bore out, that the Captain was eagerly bent on doing that himself.

Commanding Captain Waldo to be ready to come to his rescue if necessary, Smith set sail with forty-six men in the pinnace. Bad weather held them up for almost a week at the mouth of the river. Chilled to the bone, they came ashore at the village of Kecoughtan, ruled by Pochins, one of Powhatan's many sons. Concealing their aims, they spent Christmas here and "were never more merrie," they said, "nor fed on more plentie of good oysters, fish, wild foule, and good bread, nor never had better fires in England than in the drie, warme, smokie houses at Kecoughtan."

At Weromocomoco, Smith and his lusties again enjoyed "plentie of bread, Turkies, and Venison." But Powhatan was plainly not pleased to see them, pointedly asking them the next day when they would be going. He had little corn himself, he said, and his people even less. Scorning the trifles offered in trade, he demanded a basket of copper for a basket of corn, saying he could "eate his corne but not the copper," finally refusing to trade for anything but swords and guns.

"Powhatan," said Smith, masking his fury, "though I had many courses to have made my provision, yet believing your promises to supply my wants, I neglected all to satisfy your desire. And to testify my love, I sent you my men for your building, neglecting my own."

And to requite such "love," the chief had engrossed all supplies and forbidden his people to trade, thinking to force the English to meet his "strange" demands for guns and swords. He had been told before that they had none of these to spare, and he might now learn to his cost that they well knew how to use what arms they had to keep themselves from want.

"Yet steal or wrong you I will not," Smith concluded, "nor dissolve that friendship we have mutually promised, except you constraine me by your bad usage." The chief was not deceived by this, for he had learned something of Smith's "grand design" and told him so.

"Some doubt that I have of your coming hither," he said, "makes me not so kindly seek to relieve you as I would, for many do inform me your coming hither is not for trade, but to invade my people and possess my country."

Smith was quite taken aback, suspecting that the carpenters from Jamestown had warned the chief that some mischief was on foot, as they had. Smith was particularly incensed against Faldoe, the Swiss, a man of "great spirit, judgment and resolution," whom he had sent to spy on Powhatan, "then little doubting his honestie, nor could ever be certaine of his villainy till neare half a year after."

The Indians, it is clear, could have overwhelmed the English and killed them to a man, and their forbearance is remarkable. But Powhatan declared that he did not want war, and the wise and wily old chieftain went on to speak more common sense, humane philosophy, and statecraft in a few sentences than Smith—and many another down to our day—ever learned in a lifetime.

"Captain Smith," he said, "you may understand that, having seen the death of all my people thrice, and not anyone living of those three generations but myself, I know the difference between peace and war better than any in my country. . . .

"Think you I am so simple as not to know it is better to eat good meat, lie well, and sleep quietly with my women and children, laugh and be merry with you, have copper, hatchets or what I want, being your friend, than be forced to fly from all, lie cold in the woods, feed upon acorns, roots, and such trash, . . . leaving my pleasures to such youths as you, who, through inadvisedness, may as quickly and miserably perish for want of that which you would never know where to find?"

Why take by force what could be obtained by friendly means? What could be gained by war? The Indians would fly to the woods and hide their provisions, leaving the English to starve. Why should Smith and his men be suspicious, seeing that the Indians were unarmed?

"Let this, therefore, assure you of our loves and every year our friendly trade shall furnish you with corn—and now, also, if you would come in friendly manner and not thus with your guns and swords as to invade your foes."

But to Smith, all of this was only "subtill discourse." At length, after more powwow, Powhatan was persuaded to trade for what corn he could spare, but he did not like what was offered.

"Captain Smith," he declared, accurately taking the measure of the man before him, "I never used any werowance as kindly as you. Yet from you I receive the least kindness of any. Captain Newport gave me swords, copper, clothes, a bed, towels, or what I desired, ever taking what I offered him, and would send away his guns when I entreated him. . . . Of you I can have nothing but what you regard not. And yet you will have whatsoever you demand. Captain Newport, you call father, and so you call me. But I see, for all us both, you will do what you list, and we must both seek to content you. But if you intend to be friendly as you

say, send hence your arms that I may believe you, for you see the
love I bear you doth cause me thus nakedly to forget myself."

Smith promised that he and his bodyguard of eight would come
ashore the next day unarmed. But at that very moment he flashed
a signal to the pinnace that the men there, his main force, should
immediately come ashore fully armed to seize the chief. But the
latter, like Smith, was "past a school-boye" and not to be taken
in such a clumsy snare. He adroitly slipped away and vanished as
hundreds of his braves gathered to defend themselves and their
town.

With a loud cry that he had been betrayed, Smith bounded to
his feet and ran out of the "pallas," followed by his guard, all
shooting wildly, wounding several. Through Powhatan's efforts
a truce was patched up and Smith departed, very disappointed but
still hopeful. He decided to leave the "Dutchmen" behind, instructing them "to give Powhatan all the content they could" and
entice him back to Weromocomoco where he might the more
easily be trapped.

Growing bolder, Smith sailed up the river "to try conclusions"
with his old friend, the chief of the Pamunkey, Opechancano, who
entertained the marauders "with feasting and much mirth" for
several days. When trading began, Smith picked a quarrel. Prepared for trouble, the Indians quickly assembled and one of Smith's
men whispered to him that "at least seven hundred Salvages, well
armed, had invironed the house and beset the fields."

The startled English were "dismaied with the thought of such
a multitude," as well they might have been. But Smith once again
rose to the occasion. As he pictured the scene, he calmly turned
to his men and delivered them a long speech, evidently in the
presence of Opechancano and his angry braves—who presumably
stood about leaning on their bows till Smith had finished.

"Worthy Countrymen," he began in a bombastic harangue that
smells, among other things, of midnight oil,* "were the mischiefs

---

* This speech was certainly written later and inserted in the record for
reasons apparent in the speech itself. That Smith, who never took advice,
ever actually asked for it, as he pretends here, is most unlikely. And even
here, he was not interested in the opinions of others or disposed to consider
them—"the time not permitting any argument," he said.

of my seeming friends no more than the dangers of these enemies, I should little care were they as many more if you dare do but as I.

"But this is my torment: that if I escape them, our malicious Council, with their open-mouthed minions, will make me such a peace-breaker (in their opinions in England) as will break my neck. I could wish those here that make these seem saints and me, an oppressor.

"But this is the worst of all, wherein, I pray you, aid me with your opinions.

"Should we begin with them and surprise their King, we cannot keep him and defend well ourselves. If we should each kill our man and so proceed with all in the house, then shall we get no more than the bodies that are slain, and so starve for victual.

"As for their fury, it is the least danger, for well you know, being alone assaulted by two or three hundred of them, I made them, by the help of God, compound to save my life. And we are sixteen, and they but seven hundred at the most.

"And assure yourselves, God will so assist us that if you dare stand but to discharge your pieces, the very smoke will be sufficient to affright them.

"Yet, howsoever, let us fight like men and not die like sheep.

"But first, I will deal with them to bring it to pass we may fight for something, and draw them to it by conditions. If you like this motion, promise me you will be valiant."

Perhaps his men brandished their guns and gave a great shout to assure him of their valiance before Smith turned back to pursue his quarrel with Opechancano, who may have been sleeping all this while—as perhaps the reader has.

First, Smith proposed to the chief that they repair to an island in the river and fight it out in singlehanded combat, "the conqueror take all," no doubt hoping to add another head to his trophies.* But not understanding chivalry, Opechancano declined and in a rage Smith grabbed the towering chieftain by the hair—

* If Opechancano had accepted and had killed Smith, it is interesting to speculate on what the adventurers, the Council for Virginia, and the Crown would have thought and done upon learning that the chief had won title to their colony in Virginia by rolling dice with Smith, as it were.

by the arm, so he first told the story—and holding a pistol at his breast, "led the trembling King, near dead with feare, amongst all of his people." The latter, it appears, were quickly persuaded to lay down their arms, "little dreaming any durst in that manner have used their King." Smith then laid down his ultimatum:

"You promised [which they had not] to freight my ships ere I departed and so you shall, or I mean to load her with your dead Carcasses! Yet if, as friends, you will come and trade, I once more promise not to trouble you—except you give me the first occasion."

There may have been some trouble at Matchcot, but it is highly doubtful if anything even faintly resembling this bombast occurred. In any event, Smith obtained a little corn and then went foraging in neighboring waters, forcing the Indians there to contribute part of their small supplies of corn to Jamestown's support, but "with such complaints and tears from the eyes of women and children," one tough soldier was impelled to remark, "as he had been too cruel to have beene a Christian that would not have been satisfied and moved with compassion."

Word came from Jamestown of a serious mishap there, which was most disturbing. Smith had appointed Scrivener to command the fort in his absence and carry out his instructions. But the latter, beginning "to decline in his affection to Captaine Smith . . . and willing to cross the surprising of Powhatan," went off to visit Hog Island a few miles downstream, no doubt hoping to get some porkers to relieve the growing hunger at Jamestown.

Scrivener set out with ten men in a skiff, taking along Captain Waldo, whom Smith had appointed "to be ready to second his occasions." It was the bitterest kind of weather with a gale blowing, and in "that extreame frozen time" the skiff went down, "but where, or how, none doth know, for they were all drowned," leaving the inexperienced Captain Winne as the only member of the Council at Jamestown.

Smith kept this "heavie news" from his men, for he was still bent on his "grand design," sending two men ahead to Weromocomoco to lay a sure trap this time. But these two found that the "damned Dutchmen" had spoiled everything by persuading

Powhatan "to abandon his new house and Weromocomoco, and to carry away all his corne and provision." His people were "so ill affected" that the two sent to lay the snare doubted for a time whether they could escape with their lives.

Furious to have been balked but judging the time inauspicious "to revenge their [the Indians'] abuses," Smith set sail, having been out six weeks, and soon arrived at Jamestown, where he put 279 bushels of corn into the storehouse.*

This was a stay to the colony—but obtained at what cost. The Indians never forgot and never forgave Smith's cold treacheries, his transparent lies, and the many humiliations heaped upon them—least of all, Opechancano, who in time would take a terrible revenge, not once but twice.

Smith now deliberately provoked trouble in the neighborhood. Falling suddenly upon the Paspahegh and the Chickahominy, he killed some, captured others, "burnt their houses, tooke their boats and their fishing weares [weirs], and planted them at James Towne for his owne use, and now resolved not to cease till he had revenged himselfe upon all that had injured him."

Yet Smith, for his part, had no misgivings, excusing himself for being so "charitable" to the Indians, who were quite undeserving, being "only an idle, improvident, scattered people, . . . careless of anything but from hand to mouth"—but not half so idle, careless, and hand-to-mouth as those at Jamestown, who looked to them for support.

Since Newport's departure, Smith had been virtually a dictator and now he was one in fact. The death of Captain Peter Winne left him the only member of the Council, the sole authority at Jamestown, and he was less disposed than ever to brook any criticism or entertain any gratuitous advice.

For months, nothing had been accomplished at Jamestown. Men were too weak to work even if they had wished to—which most of them did not. But with spring coming on and some corn in the storehouse, Smith divided the company into gangs of ten to fifteen and set them to work felling trees, clearing new fields,

* Grown in Smith's later report to 479 bushels of corn—and 200 pounds of deer suet.

planting corn, building houses, gathering "commodities" for the ships soon expected, and performing other useful chores.

There was nothing very arduous about this. Men worked only four hours a day * and spent the rest in "pastimes and merry exercises." Even so, there were many complaints, and the "unto-wardness of the greatest number" inspired Smith, so he recorded, to another long harangue.

"Countrymen," he declaimed, "the long experience of our late miseries, I hope, is sufficient to persuade every one to a present correction of himself. And think not that either my pains or the adventurers' purses will ever maintain you in idleness and sloth.

"I speak not this to all of you, for divers of you, I know, deserve honour and reward better than is yet here to be had, but the greater part must be more industrious or starve."

As there was no longer a Council to protect them, sluggards would now have to do what he had so often commanded. Here-after, life at Jamestown would be governed by this law, the second of Smith's celebrated edicts—"that he that will not work, shall not eat, except by sickness he be disabled. For the labours of thirty or forty honest and industrious men shall not be consumed to maintain a hundred and fifty idle varlets."

Things went rather better for a month or two. Whether less worried about tomorrow's breakfast or more frightened by the Dictator's scowl and unpredictable humor, the colonists cleared and planted more than thirty acres of corn, cut some timber, and made fifty barrels or more of pitch, tar, and soap ashes as cargo for the next ship to come. Indian prisoners instructed and aided them in making nets and weirs to catch sturgeon. They built a score of houses and put a new roof on the already dilapidated church. A blockhouse was erected on Hog Island, and another near James-town, at the neck of the peninsula, where a market was estab-lished for the Indian trade. They dug a new well, "of excellent sweete water, which till then was wanting," and began to con-struct a "fort for a retreat," across the river, on a bluff still

---

* Which Smith later changed to "sixe houres a day," no doubt to make the record look better.

known as Smith's Fort, "very hard to be assaulted and easie to be defended."

But the retreat was not half finished when it had to be abandoned, and all other work as well. Jamestown awoke one morning to find famine again stalking the streets, more grim and menacing than ever, loosed by the carelessness of Smith and the officers under him. The corn he had obtained in his marauding up the York and the Chickahominy had been placed in the storehouse, sealed in casks. When these were now opened, the corn was found to be "halfe rotten and the rest so consumed by the many thousand rats" that it did "drive us," said Smith, "to our wit's end"—which was becoming a chronic state at Jamestown.

Never had there been such a crisis as this under Dictator Smith—president, Council, and Cape Merchant in one. Its stock had often sunk low, but never before had the storehouse been quite empty, with not an edible in it. There was only one thing to do—virtually abandon Jamestown.

Sixty or more were sent downstream to live on the oyster banks. Under George Percy, others sailed to Point Comfort to fish. But they soon returned, having made no catch at all, for in six weeks they "could not agree once to cast their net." Still others went up to the Falls, where they found only a few acorns and berries, and were soon back in Jamestown, famished. Many desperate men ran away to the Indians, some going to Powhatan, who was hospitable and fed them in spite of Smith's outrageous follies.

Those at the fort—at least, the more sensible and industrious—fished the river for sturgeon or gathered "tochwogh" and other roots, digging enough in a day to keep them a week. But such was the "strange" condition of most of the company, "distracted lubberly gluttons," that if they had not been forced, *"nolens volens,* to gather and prepare their victuall, they would have starved and eaten one another."

Many of these lived by stealing kettles, guns, swords, hoes and other tools, and selling them to the Indians for a capful of corn or a handful of wild fruits and berries. If they could have managed, they would have sold the cannon, their houses, even Jamestown itself, said Smith, and used a thousand "exclamations, suggestions, and devises to force him . . . to abandon the Countrie."

Smith put up with their "exclaiming follies" till he found the agitator of them, one Dyer, "a most craftie knave and his ancient maligner, whom he worthily punished"—on the gallows, no doubt. He then assembled those at Jamestown for another long speech, his last in Virginia, assuming no responsibility himself for their present plight, laying the blame entirely upon them.*

"Dream no longer" of the vain hope of obtaining corn from the Indians, he told them, or "that I will forbear to force you from idleness and punish you if you rail.†

"You cannot deny that, by the hazard of my life, many a time I have saved yours when, might your own wills have prevailed, you would have starved—and will do still, whether I will or no."

But by God, he protested, since necessity could not force them to gather the fruits of the earth for themselves, he would force them to gather not only for themselves, but for the sick. "As yet, I never had more from the store than the worst of you, and all my English extraordinary [i.e., private] provision that I have, you shall see me divide among the sick. . . .

"The sick shall not starve, but equally share of all our labours, and everyone that gathereth not every day as much as I do, the next day shall be set beyond the river and forever be banished from the fort and live there or starve." ‡

This decree, which many murmured was "very cruell," caused "idle varlets" to bestir themselves, said Smith, with the result that

---

* Smith's basic theme is evident in the lines that follow. But the speech, as first reported in his *Proceedings* (1612), is obviously a later literary elaboration of that theme. It was further elaborated and embroidered some years later in his *Generall Historie* (1624), where a number of sentences were changed and others added, which was Smith's way of "writing" history.

† Later, a sentence was added here: ". . . But if I find any more runners for Newfoundland with the pinnace, let him assuredly look to arrive at the gallows."

‡ Smith later dropped the "forever" and toned down the sentence to read: ". . . and be banished from the fort as a drone till he amend his conditions or starve."

of two hundred men, except Scrivener and those that were drowned, there died "not past seven or eight"—which was a bald lie, as Smith's own pages demonstrate. Since Newport's departure and Smith's assumption of supreme power, more than half the company had perished, including "good Mr. Hunt," leaving only eighty wretched survivors.

But Smith was not sobered by any of this. He was still bent on his "grand design" of trapping Powhatan. But first, he had to get rid of those "damned Dutchmen" who had betrayed his plans and were now enjoying many a good laugh at his discomfiture. He appointed two men to go and "stab or shoot them." Before the assassins could depart, however, events took a sharp and quite unexpected turn.

Providentially, a small ship put in, sent out by some of the adventurers as a private speculation, under the command of young Captain Samuel Argall, "a good Marriner and a very civil Gentleman," later a governor at Jamestown. The ship had been sent to fish for sturgeon and, incidentally, seek a shorter route to Virginia, one safer and less expensive in money and lives than the long roundabout route by way of the Canaries. As Gosnold had charted such a short course by way of the Azores in 1602, and had been followed by Captain Martin Pring the next year and by Captain George Weymouth in 1605, why the adventurers felt the need of having the course charted again is a mystery, though simple ignorance may be the answer. In any case, Argall had come by way of the Azores and made his passage in good time, arriving in mid-July, 1609, to find the colonists dispersed along the oyster banks and elsewhere, all in rags and ravenous with hunger.

The ship was "well furnished with wine and bisket" and provisions of many kinds. Though these were not intended for Virginia, but for the Indian trade, Argall agreed to let Smith have them, which eased the latter's mind of many worries. But his pleasure was short-lived, for the ship had also brought news that left him aghast, speechless with impotent rage. Argall delivered letters from London that "much taxed the President for his hard dealing with the Salvages and not returning the ships fraughted."

Worse, bitter as gall, came word that he had been relieved of command.

New officers had been appointed to govern Virginia, Argall informed him, and were already on their way with the Third Supply.

VIII

Hurycano

*. . . no man would acknowledge a superior,
nor could from this headless and unbridled
multitude be anything expected but disorder
and riot.*

— *A True and Sincere Declaration*

T HOROUGHLY dissatisfied with the conduct of affairs both at
Jamestown and in London, the merchant adventurers had
decided to redress the "jarres and ill proceedings" by reorganiz-
ing the whole enterprise, obtaining from the Crown a new charter
granting them much enlarged privileges, powers, and territories.

Under the original patent, a single royal council had been
charged with responsibility for both South and North Virginia,
so called. As this council had a divided interest, as no member was
specifically charged with anything, there was great waste, in-
efficiency, and delay in the conduct of day-by-day business.

To correct this, those interested in Jamestown now separately
incorporated themselves as the "Treasurer and Company of Adventurers and Planters of the City of London for the first Colony
in Virginia." The Treasurer was the Company's chief officer,
managing its business affairs and serving as president, or governor.
The first Treasurer was to be appointed by the King. Thereafter,
he was to be elected annually at a general assembly of the adventurers.

Second, a new Royal Council was created to deal solely with

the affairs of South Virginia, being granted almost sovereign powers. The Council and the Treasurer formulated general policies, chose the chief officers at Jamestown, and laid down such "orders, laws, directions, instructions, forms, and ceremonies of government and magistracy" as, in their judgment, seemed fit.

Third, the bounds of Virginia were vastly enlarged. Originally, the adventurers had been granted 10,000 square miles, in the form of a 100-mile square centered on the point of settlement. Now they were granted all territory between a point 200 miles north of Point Comfort and a point the same distance to the south, which embraced all of what became Maryland and Delaware and most of North Carolina. In addition, this 400-mile strip extended from coast to coast, from the Atlantic to the "Other Sea." As the latter lay some 3,000 miles to the west, this enormous tract contained more than 1,200,000 square miles. The Company did not know this, however, and would have been shocked to be so informed, still being firmly convinced that the South Sea lay nearby, not more than a few hundred miles to the west at most.

Fourth, the charter made a drastic and basic change in the government at Jamestown. Instead of a president elected by the Council, the new chief officer was a governor appointed by the Royal Council at home. Granted almost absolute authority, he alone was to rule. The Council at Jamestown was retained, but it was reduced to a merely advisory body. It had no power of decision and not even the right to discuss and debate except at the governor's invitation. Virginia was to be governed even more arbitrarily than England under James I, who was more and more insistently asserting his claims to absolutism as he busily elaborated the doctrine of the divine right of kings.

As the first Treasurer of the new Virginia Company, the King chose Sir Thomas Smythe, one of the great merchant princes of the day, a chief architect of the far-flung British Empire of later years. Now in his early fifties, a member of Parliament, a man of vast and varied interests, a founder and for many years the governor of the powerful and enormously rich East India Company, Smythe had a finger in many succulent pies, being a leader and a large stockholder in the Turkey Company, the Muscovy Company, the French Company, and the Levant Company, among many others. He had been knighted in 1603 and sent as ambassador to Russia, returning two years later to devote himself more zealously than ever to trade and exploration.

With Smythe's appointment, a new vigor and purpose immediately became apparent in Virginia affairs, though his administration was later severely censured and even his personal integrity was questioned. At this time, however, his proved abilities and his great prestige restored a little hope among the glum adventurers. Now persuaded that nothing could be expected from the colony until a strong foundation had been laid, the Company announced that it was sending out "under the conduct of one *able* and *absolute* Governor," a large company of five hundred men, "with some number of families—of wives, children, and servants—to take fast holde and roote in the land."

Let no riffraff or "idle Gallants" apply, the Company warned. There had been too many of these on previous voyages. The Company wanted blacksmiths, carpenters, coopers, shipwrights, turners, "and such as know how to plant vineyards; hunters, fishermen, and all who work in any kind of metal, men who make bricks, architects, bakers, weavers, shoemakers, sawyers, and those who spin wool—and all others, men as well as women."

The interested were to sign up at Sir Thomas Smythe's great house in Philpot Lane. As lure, the Company promised each man a small sum to outfit himself for the journey. At Jamestown he would have a house, vegetable gardens and orchards, as well as food and clothing, and all would receive a share "in the division of the land" when that was declared.

To do this required large sums, obviously. As many were openly scoffing at Virginia, the adventurers answered with a barrage of tracts, "divine, human, historical, political, or call them as you please," said the Archbishop of York, who complained that he, for one, wished "no further intelligence" on that score.

The Deputy Treasurer of the Company, Robert Johnson, contributed *Nova Brittania*. A lengthy and tedious plea for support, it purported to be the speech of a formerly disgruntled adventurer who had seen the light and was now urging his fellow adventurers to invest their all in Virginia for the glory of God and King and Country, for they were now assured of a handsome profit on their "adventures, costs, and travaile in the end."

Eminent divines were enlisted to paint the beauties of Virginia, which they had never seen, and to press the point that everyone had a sacred duty to support the business as a matter of conscience, which shocked the Spanish ambassador.

"They have actually made the ministers in their sermons dwell upon the importance of filling the world with their religion," he wrote to Philip III in great indignation, "and demand that all make an effort to give what they have for such a grand enterprise." They had issued a book in which they declared that, "for the increase of their religion, and that it may extend over the whole world, it is right that all should support this Colony with their persons and their property. It would be a service rendered to God if Your Majesty would cut short a swindle and robbery like this," the almost apoplectic Zuniga concluded. *"I hope you will give orders to have these insolent people quickly annihilated"*—a rather naive view in a man of state perhaps, but still quite common, on both sides of the Iron Curtain.

All of the tracts, speeches, and sermons were stuffed with utter nonsense. Virginia was pictured as a "garden of Eden," a "most sweete and wholsome" spot. The voyage there was neither long nor tedious. It had been said "of the land of Canaan that Isaack sowed in that land and found in the same yere a hundred fold. . . . But here is a greater matter, . . . [for] this land giveth five hundred fold at one harvest . . ." In addition, there was "undoubted hope of finding Cochinell, the plant of rich Indigo, Graine-berries, Beaver hydes, Pearles, rich Treasure, and the South Sea leading to China, with many other benefits." All should support "this imployment for Virginia," for every opposition was "an opposition against God, the King, the Church, and the Commonwealth."

Not content to rest their hopes on "literature" alone, the adventurers dispatched letters to the officials of many cities and towns asking them to invest public funds—and their individual savings, too—in Company stock at £12 10s. ($625) a share. Taking their troubles to the Crown, they obtained the aid of the Privy Council, which was just then pondering the problem of ridding London and its suburbs of "swarms" of idle persons, "a continual cause of dearth and famine and the very originall cause of all the Plagues that happen in this Kingdome."

The Council "advised" the Lord Mayor and aldermen of London to raise money for the removal of these "unnecessary inmates" to Virginia. The Lord Mayor, in turn, wrote to the great merchant and craft guilds of the city and virtually commanded them to buy shares in the Company, which most of them did—the Mercers, Goldsmiths, Vintners, Fishmongers, Skinners, Merchant Tailors, and some fifty more. Subscribing £200 from its treasury, the Merchant Tailors noted that, as individuals, they had already invested £586 10s. 4d. ($29,500).

By one shift or another, the Company succeeded in raising a great deal of money in a surprisingly short time. By May, 1609, just when the starving at Jamestown were scattering to the oyster banks, a fleet of nine vessels was ready to sail under the command of Sir Thomas Gates, one of the original patentees, named to be Virginia's first governor.

In his late forties, a "grave expert soldier," Gates had been in America before, having been with Sir Francis Drake in 1586 when the latter rescued and carried home the first of the companies sent out to Raleigh's ill-fated colony at Roanoke. Knighted for gallantry in action at Cadiz in 1596, Gates had been serving in the Netherlands for the past five years as a captain of English mercenary troops recruited to aid the Dutch in their heroic and successful struggle to throw off the Spanish yoke and win their independence. On going to Holland, he had been introduced to the English ambassador at The Hague by Sir Henry Wotton, wit and poet, who wrote:

"I entreat you to love him and to love me, too, and to assure yourself that you cannot love two honester men." *

---

* It was Wotton who defined an ambassador, being one himself, as an "honest man sent abroad to lie for his country"—which highly incensed that humorless pedant, King James.

Second in command to "honest" Gates was an old Elizabethan sea dog, Sir George Somers, one of the most engaging figures in early Virginia, another of the original patentees. A man of means, he and his friends in the West of England had invested £940 ($47,000) in the enterprise. Now approaching sixty, but still hale and hearty after years spent in harassing the Spanish and capturing their ships in the Caribbean, Somers was a "Lion at sea but a Lamb ashore," being an amiable and generous soul. Singularly free of envy and malice, he was ever disposed to put the common welfare before private profit and advantage. Named to the new post of Admiral of Virginia, Somers had a Vice-Admiral as aide, "Father" Newport, who had been demoted and was now third in command.

Led by the flagship, the *Sea Venture,* the fleet of nine vessels proudly put to sea carrying some five hundred passengers, including perhaps fifty women and children, as well as "six Mares and two Horses," the first to be shipped to Virginia. Leaking badly, the pinnace *Virginia* had to turn back. Though explicitly instructed to avoid the long southern passage, Gates conferred with Newport and shaped his course for the Canaries. It was midsummer, and under the blazing sun of the tropics infection raged throughout the fleet, claiming many lives.

The Company had overcrowded the ships, which were so "pestered" and dirty, as a distressed passenger complained, that "betwixt decks there can hardlie a man fetch his breath by reason there ariseth such a funke in the night that causeth putrifaction of the blood and breedeth disease much like the plague. The more fall sick, the more they annoy and poyson their fellowes." At least eighty died, almost a fifth of the company, the plague being "somewhat hotte" on two of the ships, with scurvy and fever claiming victims on all.

As it cost £10 ($500) to outfit and transport each man, those who died en route represented quite literally a dead loss on which the Company could hope to recover nothing. Yet the Company, down to the last, went on "pestering" its ships, squandering its money, and sacrificing hundreds of lives.

But the worst of this wholly unfortunate voyage occurred off the Bahamas, late in July, when the fleet ran into a hurricane, one of those fearful twisters that come roaring out of the Indies every summer. The sky went black, mountainous seas rolled over the ships, as those below were knocked about during an "Egyptian night of three days' perpetual horror." The smallest of the vessels quickly foundered, a frail ketch, with twenty on board.

Badly battered and far off course, the *Blessing* fell in with the *Lion* and the *Falcon* about a week later, and then with the *Unity*, which was "sore distressed," with all of her seamen down but the captain and "one poore sailor." For just such a contingency, it had been arranged that the ships, if separated, should make their rendezvous at Bermuda. If this order had been obeyed, Virginia would have been spared a year of chaos and infinite misery that ended in almost complete catastrophe. But in the Virginia business, plans for cooperative and coordinated action were made, it would seem, only to be ignored, for the masters of the *Blessing* and her sister ships, finding the wind "large for Virginia," decided "to decline their commissions" and bore away for the Chesapeake. Later, the *Diamond* limped in, and finally the *Sparrow*, barely afloat.

But the *Sea Venture* did not appear. After months of anxious waiting, she was given up as lost, which was a double blow, for the flagship was carrying all of the new officers—Gates, Somers, and Newport. They had agreed to sail together after an acrimonious dispute about precedence which had held up the departure of the fleet, already too long delayed, and which had quite unforeseen and tragic consequences.

As drawn by the Company, their commissions stipulated that whichever of the three first reached Virginia should dissolve the former government and take command. But Gates, jealous of his authority, objected to this, perhaps fearing that if Somers or Newport arrived first and assumed command, there might be dispute and dissension later. It was therefore arranged that the three of them, their commissions, and all official orders and instructions should go on the *Sea Venture*, which was now missing.

Piling off the battered ships, still bruised in body and soul by the "hurycano," the newcomers found little to cheer them as they viewed Jamestown, which was so different from what they had been led to expect. There was no shelter for them. The sickly season had begun, and the fort rang with the groans of the dying. Their hair stood on end as the survivors at Jamestown told them tales of hunger and woe, of the miseries of life on the oyster banks, "which kind of feeding caused all their skins to peel off from head to foot."

Most of the provisions on the ships had been spoiled as high seas poured down the hatches during the hurricane. The newcomers came in so hungry that they swept into the fields and quickly devoured all of the corn, though it was still green—which was only one of a "thousand mischiefes" done by this "ill-conditioned" company.

No doubt the Company had tried to recruit "honest and painefull" workmen. But no good workman wished to place himself and his skill at the command of the Company for seven years. As a consequence, the adventurers had to take what men they could get, and all accounts agree that those in the Third Supply were "unhallowed creatures, . . . wicked Impes, . . . a factious crue, . . . a lewd company, wherein were many unruly gallants packed hither to escape ill destinies." Some were so bad, so utterly useless, that they were sent back with the ships.

But worse than any, according to Smith, were three leading Gentlemen, and how his eyes must have blazed as the ships tied up and all of his old enemies marched ashore—Archer, Ratcliffe, and Martin!

As they had been "troublesome at sea," he said, so they "beganne againe to marre all ashore, for, . . . graced with the title of *Captaines of the passengers*, seeing the admirall [flagship] wanting and the great probabilitie of her losse, they strengthened themselves with the newe companies, so railing and exclaiming against Captaine Smith that they [the newcomers] mortally hated him ere they saw his face."

These three were resolved, said Smith, "to rule all or ruine all," which was quite unfair, for it was Smith who had made that resolve, having no intention of sharing his rule with anyone until the *Sea Venture* arrived, if it ever did, or until another ship came with other officers or official orders deposing him. Martin and

Ratcliffe had been renamed to the Council. But as their commissions were on the *Sea Venture,* Smith refused to seat them and "would admit of no assistants."

With nothing in the storehouse and more than three hundred mouths to feed, almost twice as many as ever before, the more sober may have hoped for some sensible and concerted action to avert the disaster so plainly impending. Instead, there was nothing but riot and disorder. As Smith's presidency had still a month to run, his opponents agreed among themselves that he should be allowed to finish his one-year term, at which time George Percy should succeed him.

Meantime, Smith's pretensions to supreme authority were simply ignored. Virginia now had not one president, but half a dozen, and all at loggerheads—Smith, Percy, Martin, Ratcliffe, Archer, and Francis West—each going his own way, for "no man would acknowledge a superior," and "on earth was never more confusion and misery."

Again, the company had to disperse in search of food. Captain Ratcliffe took some men down to Point Comfort where they built a stockade and lived rather well—or at least, better than most. Martin and Percy led another party downstream, to the mouth of the Nansemond, where they were quickly in trouble, for the Indians there were still smarting from injuries suffered during Smith's bloody raids.

Foolishly dividing his force, Martin sent the larger part by land under Lieutenant Michael Sicklemore, "a very honest, valiant, and painefull soldier," taking the rest with him in the shallop. Failing to find Sicklemore and his men at the appointed rendezvous, he refused to go in search of them in spite of Percy's protests.

Instead, Martin demanded that the chief of the Nansemond sell him an island in the river in return for a few trinkets. As the island was the chief seat of the tribe and its sacred burying ground, the chief refused. Seizing the island, the English hunted down the Indians, "burned their howses, ransacked their Temples, tooke down the Corpses of their deade kings from off their Tombes, and carried away their pearles, copper, and Bracelets wherewith they doe decorate their Kings' funeralles."

Never noted for his courage, uneasy and apprehensive after his savage looting which had brought in little corn, Martin returned to Jamestown, abandoning Lieutenant Sicklemore and his men to their fate. Starving, some of the latter crowded into a small open boat, ostensibly to cross the James in the hope of obtaining corn from the friendly Indians at Kecoughtan. They were never heard of again. If they obeyed orders, they were either killed by the Indians or drowned in the river. But as the boat and their bodies were never found, it is quite as likely that, in sheer despair, they put to sea in their tiny craft and perished in a frantic effort to reach the Spanish settlements in Florida or one of the English fishing stations along the Maine coast.

Sicklemore and the others, twenty or more, were trapped and killed by the infuriated Nansemond, who knocked them on the head and, with grisly irony, stuffed their gaping mouths with bread.

A larger party of more than a hundred went up to the Falls and built a fort there, under the command of Captain Francis West. In the latter's absence, many of his "disorderlie company" went marauding on their own account, stealing the Indians' corn, robbing their gardens, breaking into their houses, taking prisoners for ransom, beating men, women, and children. Arrow and tomahawk cut down a number of these. Others fled for their lives and came stumbling into Jamestown seriously wounded.

Determined to assert his authority, Captain Smith went up to investigate, finding fault with all things, especially with the fort, which had been erected on low ground, subject to floods and "invironed with many intollerable inconveniences."

Without consulting anyone, Smith went to Powhatan's Tower a mile or two downstream and bought that pleasant hillside village from the "Little Powhatan," Parahunt, another of Powhatan's sons. It was his intention to place West's men in this "Salvage fort, readie built and prettily fortified with poles and barkes of trees," where there were "dry houses for lodgings and neere two hundred acres of ground readie to plant"—Nonesuch, Smith named it, for there was "no place so strong, so pleasant and delightfull in Virginia."

As part of the bargain, Smith had "sold" to Little Powhatan an English boy, young Henry Spelman, twelve years old, son of Sir Henry Spelman, a once renowned scholar whose bones lie in Westminster Abbey. Like so many early Virginians, young Henry seems to have been something of a scapegrace, even at so tender an age. "Being in displeasure of my friends," as he confessed, he had been sent away in the Third Supply, no doubt as an indentured servant.

Spelman had been in Jamestown only a few weeks when Smith took him off to the Falls where, "unknowne to me," the boy complained, "I was sold for a towne called Powhatan." But West's men were not interested in Smith's bargain and refused to move to Nonesuch. Persuaded that the way to fabulous gold mines and to the South Sea lay up the James, they intended to control and exploit that traffic by allowing none to pass their fort without paying toll.

For nine days, Smith tried "to reclaime them, shewing them how much they did abuse themselves with these great guilded hopes of the South Sea, mines, commodities . . ." But they scorned his "kind aide and authoritie" alike, threatened his life, and drove him and his five men away.

In reprisal, Smith ran off with their boats, including their pinnace, which had most of their provisions and ammunition on board, and anchored a few miles downstream. Perceiving this, Parahunt and his men came on board daily, said Smith, to complain of the depredations of West's men. They had endured much out of "love" for him, but they "desired pardon if hereafter they defended themselves." If he would lead them against West's men, they added, they would happily "fight for him against them." An attack by the exasperated Indians was obviously impending. Not only did Smith do nothing to prevent it. He seems actually to have encouraged—even inspired—it.

"Perceaving both his authority and person neglected," Smith "incensed and animated the salvages against Captain West and his company," according to George Percy, "reporting unto them that our men had no more powder than would serve for one volley of shot."

This reckless and quite indefensible betrayal of his own people has been blandly—or blindly—ignored by all historians of Virginia and all of Smith's biographers. The most serious charge ever brought against him, it was made not only by George Percy, but by young Henry Spelman, who was present. Moreover, treachery is implicit in Smith's own story.

Disgusted with West's "mutinous" men, he had no sooner left the fort, he said, than the Indians attacked, killing many and so frightening the others that they "submitted themselves upon any tearmes to the President's mercie." Why did he not go to the aid of those at the Falls? Perhaps because the Indians were carrying the terms of the "President's mercie."

In any case, Smith was still in the neighborhood—his boats had "run aground," he said—and after the slaughter, he rushed back to the Falls and "presently put by the heels sixe or seven of the chiefe offenders." Commanding the rest to follow him, he seated them "gallantlie" at Nonesuch.

But now Captain Francis West returned from Jamestown to precipitate "new turboiles." After bitter quarrels, he abandoned Nonesuch, moved his men back to the Falls, and Smith angrily "left them to their fortunes," running up sail for Jamestown. Along the way, while he was sleeping on deck, dreaming perhaps of some terrible revenge, a spark dropped into his powder bag, which went up in a great flash that burned him severely on the groin and thigh. "To quench the tormenting fire frying him in his cloaths," he plunged overboard "into the deepe river where, ere they could recover him, he was neere drowned."

Though "unable to stand and neere bereft of his senses by reason of his torment," Smith was not yet prepared to surrender his pretension to sole and absolute authority. He now charged Ratcliffe, Archer, and Martin with mutiny. While awaiting trial, according to the now psychopathic dictator, they "plotted to have him murdered in his bed." When that failed, they joined together "to usurp the government, thereby to escape their punishment."

None of this need be taken too literally. An attempt may have been made on Smith's life, for many would have been happy to be rid of him. As to usurping the government, the event was simple and obvious. Smith's term as president was about to expire, and Ratcliffe and Martin were determined, though their commissions had been lost, to take their seats on the Council as appointed and elect a new president. Wishing to avoid conflict, they asked Smith to surrender his commission, which he scornfully refused to do, saying that they might steal it from him, but "never would he give it to such as they." The latter then met, constituted themselves as the Council, deposed Smith, and elected George Percy as president.

This would be "blazoned a mutinie by such as retaine old malice," Archer wrote the Earl of Salisbury, "but Master West, Master Percie, and all the respected Gentlemen of worth in Virginia can and will testifie otherwise upon their oathes, for the King's patent we ratified, but refused to be governed by the President . . . after his time was expired."

There can be no doubt, as Smith declared, that if he had been well, he would have "quickly qualified the heat of these humors and factions." To add to its woes, Jamestown would have been a scene of frightful carnage, for Smith had a small, loyal, even fanatic following. Some of his "ould souldiers"—Anas Todkill, William Phettiplace, and Richard Pots, among others—begged to be allowed "to take off their heads that would resist his command," but Smith refrained from giving them the signal. Instead, he "sent for the Masters of the ships and tooke order with them for his returne to England."

Even yet Smith was not prepared to end the aimless vendetta. Refusing to recognize the Council or Percy's election, saying that he did not intend to leave the colony "without government and authority," he attempted in a final rash act to set up a rival regime by appointing his own successor. Except that we have Smith's word for this, it would be impossible to believe that he was ever so foolish, for there could have been only one certain result—open civil war, with one faction hunting the other up and down Virginia, as the Indians danced along the flanks leisurely slaughtering both.

Happily, no one in the fort was as fatuous as Smith, or so blindly embittered. His offer of the presidency went begging, for "none he

thought fit for it would accept it"—which spared Jamestown another and quite gratuitous horror, there being enough trouble as
it was.

Dispersed along the oyster banks during the spring and early
summer, the colonists had planted no crops. It was now harvest,
and corn might have been had from the Indians. But Percy and
the Council chose just this time to waste a month in drafting a
long indictment of Smith and finding witnesses to testify against
him. Many snatched at this opportunity to escape from the colony
and "got their passes by promising in England to say much about
him."

Smith was charged, among other things, with inciting the Indians against West's men at the Falls, with trying to poison the
"damned Dutchmen" with rat's bane, with starving the company
and forcing it to live on the oyster banks, with not showing "due
regard for Gentlemen," with planning to marry Pocahontas and
make himself "King of the country." [1]

Early in October, 1609, having been in Virginia little more than
two years, Smith departed, officially in disgrace and virtually a
prisoner. "This man is sent home," Ratcliffe informed the Earl
of Salisbury, "to answere some misdeameanors, whereof, I per-
swade me, he can scarcely clear himselfe from great imputation of
blame."

Smith always represented that his going was of his own choice,
that it was an unfortunate necessity imposed upon him—and the
colony—by his painful injuries which urgently required medical
attention. No doubt Smith did wish to go. It is quite clear, however, that Percy and the Council would have shipped him off in
any case.

As the still battered ships of the Third Supply dropped down
the river, Smith was already planning a speedy return to confound
his "oppressors," little dreaming at the moment that he would
never see Virginia again. Though nothing appears to have been
done about the charges against him, the Company never again
employed him in spite of his frequent and often pathetic pleas
to be put to some service. Though he was only thirty and at the
height of his powers, Smith had wrecked his career as a com-

mander in the field and as a leader in the councils of government. He had all but ended his days as a man of action, though he would later conduct an important exploration of the New England coast. But his years of fabulous exploit were over.

Though Smith always regretted it, it was probably just as well that he did not return to Jamestown. Unless he had radically mended his ways, which was quite unlikely as they were so in character, he most certainly would have come to a bad end under the dictators that followed him—Sir Thomas Dale, for one, would have brought him promptly to heel or hanged him out of hand.

A controversial figure in his day, Smith has remained one. Among his contemporaries, he was either fiercely loved or fiercely hated. Wingfield despised him. Gosnold distrusted him, fearing his "rash inadvisedness," as did Powhatan. George Percy dismissed him as an "ambityous, onworthy, and vayneglorious fellowe," who, in "aiming at Soveraigne Rule, . . . was justly deprived of all." Undoubtedly he was stubborn, opinionated, quarrelsome, and malicious, as Ratcliffe, Archer, and many others well knew.

But to others, to his "ould souldiers" especially, he was the "honest" Captain Smith—the bold, the confident, the reassuring, "ever emulous of vertue and honourable enterprises," a fearless commander who never sent them "where he would not lead them himselfe," a man "whose adventures were our lives and whose losse, our deaths."

Among Virginia scholars, opinion has equally been divided. To E. D. Neill, who first cast a critical eye on the old records, Smith's character and writings were "those of a gascon and a beggar," for he was "always in the attitude of one craving recognition or re-muneration for alleged services." In his works, Alexander Brown was even more critical, saying that *few men in any age have been more overrated than Captain John Smith.*

Yet the great English scholar, Edward Arber, who edited the Captain's complete works, concluded that Smith was "one of the best and bravest of Englishmen," that he was an "experienced and clear-headed practical man of business," that he bore an "unstained character as an English Gentleman and Officer." In addition, said Arber, "wherever we *can* check Smith, we find him both modest and accurate"—which is a most astonishing statement. Wherever "we *can* check Smith," he is both boastful and unreliable.

Still, Smith had his qualities. His resourcefulness, his personal courage, his skill in battle are beyond question. As for his accomplishments in Virginia, the record, largely written by him, speaks for itself. But this, above all, must be said for Smith—that almost alone of the early company, he loved Virginia, which remained his mistress to the end of his days. Almost alone, he regarded the colony as something more than a means to fortune, as an enforced and painful way-station on the road back to the stews or the more refined pleasures of London. In a real sense, he was the first Virginian.

Blocked in his passionate desire to contribute directly, Smith devoted most of his remaining years to aiding Virginia, gathering and publishing all information that he could find about it, ever brightening the luster of his own deeds and accomplishments there, yet always doing the best he could—which was a great deal—to advance the fortunes and the good name of the colony. Smith's pen served Virginia better than his sword, even though his pen often dripped venom or went slanting off in obvious bias and distortion.

With his offers to serve ignored, smarting under rebuffs and neglect, Smith later declared that he had never received "any content or satisfaction at all" for the five years and the more than £500 ($25,000) which he had spent in obtaining the original Virginia patent and in organizing a group in London "to be the meanes to raise a company to go with me to Virginia." This was as much as to say that he had initiated the venture, that he had brought out the first company, that he had been in command at Jamestown from the start, which was palpable nonsense.

Down the years, in fact, Smith did come to believe—or at least, to assert—that he had, almost singlehandedly, founded Virginia; that in its infancy the hard-pressed colony had been sustained by his efforts and wisdom alone; that it later almost fell into the grave in want of him to guard and nurse it—a conceit that became an enduring myth, long since an integral part of our American tradition.

IX

The Starving Time

*. . . All was fish that came to net
to satisfy crewell hunger.*

—GEORGE PERCY

EAGER to recoup its losses, the Company had been expecting much from the Third Supply, and now the battered remnants of Gates' once proud fleet came limping in, ship after ship, "laden with nothing but bad reports and letters of discouragement."

As the long tale of disaster was unfolded, the adventurers could scarcely believe their ears—the famine that had driven men to the oyster banks; the heavy mortality from plague and fever on the ships, and from the deadly "summer sickness" at Jamestown; the loss of the ketch during the hurricane and of the flagship as well, the *Sea Venture*, with Gates, Somers, Newport, and 150 more on board; the news that Jamestown stood in more desperate need of relief than ever before, with the Indians "as fast killing the settlers without the fort as famine and pestilence within."

Nor did this complete the tale of disaster. On their way home, two of the larger ships piled up on the rocky coast of Ushant, off the French coast, and went down with heavy loss, leaving a sole survivor to bring the news.

All of this struck the Company a stunning blow, made worse

by the fact that some of the "wicked Impes," sent out in the Third Supply and shipped back because they were "incorrigble," were running about telling the most horrendous tales about the miseries of life at Jamestown. Though somewhat embellished, the stories were essentially true, but the adventurers did not care about that. If their credit and that of Virginia were to be restored, they had to take steps.

As they had done before and would do so often again, the adventurers hurriedly published another tract, rushing through the press *A True and Sincere Declaration,* which belied its title on every page. Their "principall and maine" aim, as it had always been, was to spread the glad tidings of salvation among the Indians, to "recover out of the armes of the Divell a number of pore and miserable souls wrapt up unto death in almost *invincible ignorance.*" Though a formidable task, the adventurers were eager to undertake it, being anxious, they said, "to add our myte to the Treasury of Heaven." Incidentally, they might add more than a mite to the Company's treasury and that of the Crown, which was as it should be. They would "plant religion" and make some money—a just arrangement all around, even for the Indians. They would "buy of them the Pearles of Earth and sell to them the Pearles of Heaven."

Virginia offered "every appearance and assurance" of great wealth, promising almost immediately large profits from wine, pitch, tar, timber, glass, copper, dyes, cordage, pearls and gold—not to mention the "certaintie" of finding the South Sea. Corn and all else grew "with incredible usury" in the colony.

How was it possible that "such wise men" could so torment themselves and those in the colony "with such strange absurdities and impossibilities," John Smith later asked, "making religion their colour when all their aime was nothing but present profit, as most plainly appeared by sending us so many Refiners, Goldsmiths, Jewelers, Lapidaries, Stone-cutters, Tobacco pipemakers, Imbroiderers, Perfumers, Silkemen, . . . so doating on Mines of gold and the South Sea that all the world could not have devised better courses to bring us to ruine than they did themselves with many more such-like conceits? . . . Much they blamed us for not converting the Salvages when those they sent us were little better —if not worse."

With the last sentence at least, the adventurers would have agreed. All that Virginia lacked to bring it to perfection, they said, were some honest and industrious people—carpenters, smiths, bricklayers, gardeners, "Minerall men," brewers, vine dressers, sturgeon dressers, gun founders, fowlers, doctors, and "learned Divines to instruct the colonie and teach the Indians to worship the true God." Stating that it would not again accept "such an idle crue as did thrust themselves into the last voiage," the Company declared that it would no longer "suffer parents to disburden themselves of lascivious sonnes, masters of bad servants, and wives of ill husbands" at its expense.

While "unexpected tragedies" had cooled the zeal of many members, the Company declared its firm intention to proceed, announcing that one of the great nobles of the realm, Thomas West, Lord de La Warr, had been made Lord Governor and Captain General of Virginia for life, and that he would depart with a large company as soon as sufficient money came in. But money came in so slowly, unfortunately, that the Lord Governor's departure was long and almost fatally delayed.

In their plea for support, the adventurers admitted that there had been "some distress" along the James, occasioned by the "misgovernment of the commanders, by dissension and ambition among themselves," and even more by the "idleness and bestial sloth of the common sort." But all was now well, former faults had been remedied, the fear of famine had vanished, and the future was bright, for the "extremitie in which they were is now relieved."

This was a brazen and quite unprincipled lie, as the adventurers well knew from the reports that their ships had just brought in. But what a travesty of the truth it was, they had no idea. At the very moment their *True and Sincere Declaration* appeared, Virginia lay almost at last gasp, writhing in the agonies of the Starving Time.

Completing their long indictment of Smith, President Percy and the Council had belatedly turned to a problem that was quite familiar but that now bore a most terrifying aspect. There was less than two months' supply in the store, and it was at least ten months before they could reap a harvest, if any. No relief from home could be expected till late in the spring at least. No trade could be had with the Indians, who had been alienated by innumerable outrages perpetrated by Smith, Martin, West, and others. Hunger and tension at Jamestown were increased when Captain Francis West now brought his "disorderlie" company down from the Falls, having lost most of his boats and fifty men there, half of his company.

By his care and industry, the new Cape Merchant, Captain Daniel Tucker, stretched the supplies as far as he could, giving everyone a starvation ration of a half pint of corn a day. For once, the store was well managed. But this merely postponed the day when the humbler at Jamestown would again pay—and at frightful cost—for the follies of their masters, both at Jamestown and at home.

Winter had come, as bitterly cold as the first one at Jamestown that was so long remembered. Many of the weak and ailing, having pawned their clothes and their blankets for a capful of corn, froze to death in their beds. With the storehouse exhausted, all began to waste away. After they had eaten hogs, sheep, goats, and horses, devouring even their hides, they were "gladd to make shift with vermin, as doggs, catts, ratts, and myce." They ate boots, shoes, "or any other leather," said Percy, for "all was fish that came to net to satisfy crewell hunger."

When they had consumed everything eatable in the fort, men went into the woods "to feede upon Serpents and Snakes, and to digg for wylde and unknown Rootes." While they were foraging, many were cut down by the Indians. None could fish because all of the nets, under Smith's administration, had been allowed "to rot and spoile."

A ray of hope flashed in the darkening gloom when an offer of trade came from Powhatan. The latter had not been too unfriendly since Smith's "grand design" to trap him at Weromoco-moco, though he had taken the precaution of removing farther inland to the village of Orapaks, where he could be less easily surprised. By young Henry Spelman, the boy whom Smith had sold to the Indians for Nonesuch, the chief sent word that if a ship were sent with some copper, he would freight her home with corn, which was a godsend beyond the dreams of any.

Quickly dispatched with fifty men, Captain Ratcliffe came ashore at Orapaks, eager to trade, having most of his men with him. They were welcomed and feasted, but the next day there was trouble. Young Spelman, who was present, left two very different accounts of what happened.

According to the more probable, a quarrel developed when trading began, with each side complaining that it was being cheated, the Indians suspecting another of Smith's tricks with his "blew" beads. Someone struck a blow, again Powhatan quickly withdrew, and his exasperated braves fell upon the English, slaughtering them almost to a man—about thirty in all—only two escaping.

Among those who fell was the much-abused Ratcliffe, a man of no great ability, obviously, but certainly as able as his carping critics. His close friend and always ardent supporter, factious and contentious Captain Gabriel Archer, may have fallen at his side, for he died about this time in some unrecorded manner.

The Indians also attacked the pinnace, which caused great concern, for this was something which they had never dared before in fear of its cannon. But the vessel, though nearly captured, finally got away and returned to Jamestown with its small crew "neare starved," bringing none of the corn so prayerfully expected, nothing but news of the slaughter.

Another blow immediately followed, treacherously struck by one of their own, a member of the Council. Captain Francis West was sent in the *Swallow* to see what trade could be found in more distant waters, for men were now dying by the scores. The remaining pinnaces, the *Discovery* and the *Virginia*, were sent down to Point Comfort to fish. With a crew of almost forty, recruited largely among the "unhallowed creatures" brought over in the Third Supply, West sailed up the Potomac, where the Indians proved to be friendly and ready to trade. But they valued their corn at more than the few trinkets they were offered. Enraged, West turned his ruffians loose on the Indians, killing many, wounding more, plundering and burning their villages, making "implacable enemies" of the friendly Potomac.

On her way back, well loaded with corn and other loot, the *Swallow* stopped at Point Comfort, where a small fort had recently been built at Percy's orders.* The commander there informed West and his men of Jamestown's desperate need, urging them, said Percy, "to make with all the speed they could to releave us." Instead, the ruffians ran up sail and put to sea, abandoning the poor wretches at Jamestown to a horrible fate, leaving them without a large vessel and therefore with no means of trade or escape.

Eager for more and better loot, dreaming of "mountaines of gold and happie robberies," the runaways became "professed pirates." Nothing was heard of them until six months later when the *Swallow* crept into a small English port, having lost many of her crew from hunger, for she had not prospered under the Jolly Roger. If any of lesser "qualitie" had run away with a desperately needed vessel and turned pirate, he would have been shot or hanged forthwith—and good riddance. But Captain Francis West, younger brother of Lord de La Warr, soon returned to Jamestown to retake his seat on the Council there—and become, in time, a governor.

The flight of the *Swallow* reduced Jamestown to the ultimate horrors of the Starving Time. Nothing was "spared to maintaine Life and to doe those things which seem incredible," as Percy recalled almost twenty years later, still haunted by memories of those days when hunger drove men "to digge up dead corpses out of their graves and to eate them, . . . boyled and stewed with roots and herbes." Others "licked upp the bloode which had fallen from their weak fellowes." As one exclaimed, "It were too vile and scarce to be believed what we endured."

His mind unhinged, one man killed his wife, "powdered [salted] her, and had eaten of her before it was known," for which

---

* Algernon Fort, named for William (Algernoune, or "Redbeard") de Perci, one of William the Conqueror's captains and founder of the powerful House of Percy, for generations almost a sovereign power in the North of England.

he was executed. "Now whether she was better roasted, boyled, or carbonado'd, I know not," remarked Captain Smith, always ready with a quip, "but such a dish as powdered wife I never heard of."

Two out of three of those alive six months before were now in their graves. Quite hopeless, unable to escape, having only a small rowboat and an Indian canoe, the trapped survivors at Jamestown would have killed and eaten one another, according to Percy, but for the extraordinary pains and energy of the new Cape Merchant, Captain Daniel Tucker. Almost unaided, the latter succeeded in building a large shallop, which offered some slight hope of trade and of escape if aid did not come soon.

Putting the new shallop to immediate use, Percy went down to Point Comfort, to Algernon Fort, to learn the fate of the small garrison there, as nothing had been heard of it for weeks. Though a few had died, most of the men there were hale and hearty, enjoying the fresh breezes that blew in from the sea and the abundance of shellfish to be found along the shore. The crabs these men fed their hogs "would have been a great relefe unto us and saved many of our Lyfes," Percy indignantly noted. But Captain James Davies and his men had "concealed their plentie" from those at Jamestown because they planned to keep alive "some of the better sorte" and embark for home on the two pinnaces lazily riding at anchor in the roads, the *Virginia* and the *Discovery*, sent down to fish the Bay, which they had not done.

Half of the starving at Jamestown were going to be brought to the Point for relief, Percy announced. When these had recovered some strength, the other half would be brought down. If this did not suffice, he would bring down everybody and abandon Jamestown, for "another towne or forte might be erected or builded, but men's lives, once loste, could never be recovered"— a platitude the Company might well have pondered.

It would have been well if Jamestown had now been abandoned, as it ultimately had to be. But as happened so often in Virginia— and seldom for the better—Chance intervened. While Percy was at the Point, all were startled when two strange vessels appeared in the Bay late one afternoon. Fearing that these were hostile craft, perhaps Spanish, they kept close watch all night, only to discover in the morning that they were friendly vessels and carrying—of all people!—Sir Thomas Gates, Sir George Somers, "Father" Newport, and almost all of the company on the long-lost *Sea Venture,* which had vanished in the "hurycano" almost a year before.

Though shipwrecked, those on the *Sea Venture* had escaped without loss of life after a remarkable adventure, one that would bring a new distraction into Company business. The ship had almost gone down in the hurricane. After working with pumps and buckets for four days and nights in an effort to clear the hold of the ship, which was ten feet deep in water, all had given up in despair, breaking out bottles of brandy and "other good and comfortable waters" to drink to their reunion in another world. In the midst of that "hell of darkness," during which Somers was constantly at the helm, something suddenly loomed up in the murk, and Somers rightly guessed it to be the "dreadful coast" of the Bermudas, "said and supposed to be inchanted and inhabited with witches and devills, . . . [and] so wunderous daungerous of Rockes" that none could approach it without "unspeakable hazard of shippe wrack."

Rather than founder at sea, Somers decided to take a desperate chance and try to run ashore anywhere at all. While still a halfmile out, the ship crashed into a rock, then into another. Though badly shaken, she did not go down, for she was so tightly wedged between the rocks that she was held upright, almost as if standing in the stocks. Favored by low tide, all of the bruised and battered company were soon safe on shore.

Far from being bewitched, the haunts of fiends and demons, a bedeviled land of "monstruous Thunderstorms and Tempests," Bermuda proved to be a delightful place—altogether, a fairyland.* All of their supplies had been lost in the shipwreck, but here they found fish, fowl, fruits and berries, and the woods were full of

* The marvels of the islands, the wreck of the *Sea Venture,* and the "hurycano," as described by Sylvestre Jourdan, one of the shipwrecked company, inspired Shakespeare to a great play, *The Tempest.*

wild black hogs, fat and sweet, the descendants of swine off some Spanish shipwreck.

As the *Sea Venture* could not be freed from her rocky cradle, one of her boats was fitted up with a deck, and a Captain Raven, "a very sufficient Mariner," volunteered to take her to Virginia. He was to have ships sent from Jamestown for their rescue and, pending Gates' arrival, Virginia was to be governed by Captain Peter Winne, who had been in his grave for many months. The sea evidently swallowed Captain Raven and his men, for they were never seen again—and for Jamestown, it was perhaps just as well. Gates' order about the supreme command would only have made confusion worse confounded, for this was the time of the "tur-boiles" between Dictator Smith and those resolved to depose him.

At length, after anxiously awaiting some word of Raven's mission, Gates ordered that some vessels be built to carry the company on to Virginia, which aroused great resentment. A great many were quite content to stay where they were, saying that if forced to go on to Virginia, they "might well feare to be detained in that countrie by the authority of the Commander thereof, and their whole life to serve the turnes of the Adventurers with their travailes and labours."

Open rebellion developed when a humble clerk in the suite of Gates' chaplain, the Reverend Richard Buck, began "to advance substantial arguments, both civill and divine (the Scriptures falsely quoted), that it was no breach of honesty, conscience, nor Religion to decline from the obediance of the Governor or to refuse to go further, . . . since the authority ceased when the wracke was committed, and with it they were then freed from the government of any man."

The humble "clarke" and his lieutenants in these "divellish disquiets" were tried for mutiny and rebellion. All were convicted and sentenced to die, and all were executed with the signal exception of the chief rebel, who made "so much moane" that he was finally pardoned.

The name of the rebellious, Scripture-quoting, loud-bemoaning "clarke" was Stephen Hopkins, thus providentially saved to become in time one of our Pilgrim Fathers, being a passenger on the celebrated *Mayflower* that sailed ten years later, ostensibly bound for Virginia.*

In spite of murmuring and mutiny, notwithstanding quarrels between Gates and Somers, the company finally succeeded in accomplishing under Somers' direction the seemingly impossible task of fashioning out of the wreckage of the *Sea Venture* and whatever was at hand not only one vessel, but two—a large pinnace, the *Deliverance* (70 tons), and a smaller one, the *Patience* (30 tons).

Early in May, 1610, after nine pleasant months on the islands, with all in good health, Gates ordered the company on board. For the most part, it was reluctant to go and a few braver spirits, determined to remain, ran away and hid in the woods. Though they could easily have been well loaded, the ships were carrying only sufficient supplies for their voyage, for Gates assumed that he would find plenty of everything at Jamestown. Meeting Percy at Point Comfort, he was quickly disillusioned.

With no breeze stirring, the ships "plyed it sadly" up the river and finally reached Jamestown, which seemed rather the "ruins of some auncient fortification than that any people living might now inhabit it." It presented a grim and ghastly sight with the "pallisadoes downe, the ports open, the gates from the hinges, the church ruined and unfrequented." The houses of the dead had been torn down and used as firewood, for none dared to go into the woods for fear of the "watching, subtile, and offended Indian."

Of the three hundred people in the colony nine months before, there were only sixty "most miserable and poore creatures," all so emaciated that they "looked like anatomies." As the ships tied up, they ran naked out of their beds and fell upon the newcomers, crying and moaning:

"We are starved! We are starved!"

Having lost his mind, as had others, one Hugh Price came into the market place in a "furious, distracted mood," cursing and shouting that there was no God, for God would never have allowed his creatures to endure such agonies. In a frenzy, poor Price

---

* The curious connection between the mutiny in Bermuda and the famed Mayflower Compact is developed at some length in my *Saints & Strangers*.

dashed out of the fort later that day and the Indians quickly put an end to his miseries, killing two more men a few days later.

Finding all things so contrary to his expectations, "so full of miserie and misgovernment," Gates first assembled the company to hear a "zealous and sorrowfull prayer" by the Reverend Richard Buck. Then calling in Somers, Newport, Percy, Martin, and others, he asked their advice on what should be done, for what most grieved the "much grieved" Governor was that he could see nothing to do to repair the calamitous situation.

Gates had arrived with the usual elaborate set of instructions from home, full of misconceptions, contradictions, and what should have been recognized by now to be self-evident nonsense. He should make friends with the Indians. At the same time, he should force them to pay tribute, drive them from all the territory between Jamestown and the sea, seize their priests, and kill them if necessary. This would be neither "crueltie nor a breache of Charity," for until those "murtherers of Soules" were out of the way, the Company and the colony could make no progress in their "glorious worke" of converting the Indians, "the most pious and noble end of the Plantation."

As the spot was swampy and unwholesome, Jamestown should be abandoned as the chief settlement. Holding it merely as a port, Gates should build two new towns—one, above the Falls; the other, four days' journey to the south, near the mouth of the Chowan River, which should be their "principall and chiefe seate," for here they would find, said the Company, rich copper mines and "four of the English alive, left by Sir Walter Rawley." The latter would be of the greatest assistance in opening up the "wombe and bowels of the Countrey."

While doing all of this, Gates was to make quite sure that his men were producing plenty of tar, pitch, wine, iron, steel, pipe staves, and soap ashes, and that the ships were sent back heavily laden not only with these things but hemp, flax, silk grass, cod, sturgeon, caviar, pearls, and "other good commodity."

And lastly, let him not neglect the discovery of the "southe sea or Royall mines."

Dubious at best, the instructions were quite irrelevant as matters stood. The supplies brought from Bermuda would last only two weeks, and there were none to be had in the country. As the situation was obviously hopeless, all of the leaders, with the exception of Captain John Martin, agreed that there was only one thing to do "to preserve and save all from starvation." That was to abandon the colony and sail for home by way of Newfoundland, in the hope of meeting there with some English fishing vessels from which they might obtain supplies, for theirs would not see them across the Atlantic.

When Gates announced this, one may well believe that it was greeted "with general acclamation and a shoute of joy," especially by the still tottering survivors of the Starving Time. Forced to stay in the colony whether they wished to remain or not, they saw the prison gates opening at last. Many dreadful uncertainties remained —their small vessels might go down at sea, or they might perish from hunger along the way. But at least there was a ray of hope.

Personal belongings and the few precious stores were carried on board. As there was no space to carry them, the cannon were buried within the gates. Word was dispatched to inform the men at Point Comfort and order them to stand by until the ships came down from Jamestown in a day or two.

Hating Jamestown and all that it represented in their tortured lives, many wished to destroy the fort, threatening to burn it. But Gates objected, knowing that there was going to be trouble enough in satisfying the adventurers on his reasons for abandoning the country, which meant the wreck of all their hopes and the certain loss of their entire investment.

"My Masters," said Gates, "let the town stand. We know not but that as honest men as ourselves may come and inhabit here."

On June 7, 1610, two weeks after his arrival, three years after the first landing, Gates "commanded every man, at the beating of a Drum, to repair aboard"—and here was one command at least, perhaps the only one at Jamestown, that was obeyed with alacrity and without any grumbling. Gates remained on shore to the last to prevent any attempt at arson and finally, at noon, the pinnaces moved out from the bank and started down the river, "giving a farewell with a peal of small shot."

The wilderness had routed another proud and presumptuous intruder. Virginia had fallen a victim to ignorance, greed, sloth, petty personal ambitions, envy and malice, a want of foresight or even ordinary care, many untoward accidents, the rigors of a caste system which ruled that no Gentleman should work, all the ills of absentee management, and a really quite extraordinary incapacity to learn anything from experience. No company had ever spent three years learning less about the ways of the wilderness than these men at Jamestown.

If they had been favored with a good breeze, the pinnaces could have cleared from Point Comfort and been well out to sea before nightfall. As it was, having no breeze at all, they drifted slowly with the tide and anchored that night off Hog Island only a few miles downstream. But all on board were content. With any luck, they would be well away to sea by noon the next day. Though disappointed with their slow start, they were happier than they had ever been before in Virginia—or ever would be again.

X

La Warr

Brachium Domini: *This was the
arme of the Lord of Hosts.*
—*A True and Sincere Declaration*

*I*N NAMING him as Lord Governor and Captain General of Virginia, the Company had announced that Lord de La Warr—or "Baron de la Warte," as the Spanish ambassador called him—would soon depart with a thousand men. After the return of the ships of the Third Supply with their bad news about the "hurycano" and the sad state of affairs under Dictator Smith, the Company declared that La Warr would sail immediately with supplies and three hundred men to relieve the hard-pressed colony. But such a "coldness" had been bred among the adventurers that four months elapsed before La Warr was dispatched at last—with only 150 men and very scanty provisions.

On the eve of his departure, the Company had ordered a sermon by the Reverend William Crashaw, later published and widely distributed. "God is our friend," the learned Doctor declared, and everyone had a duty to assist La Warr's voyage "in four things: Countenance, Person, Purse, and Prayer." The adventurers were doubtless a little startled to hear that private profit was the "least and last end aimed at in this voyage." But they were pleased with the assurance that the colony would be "assuredly profitable in a short time." No one should believe the ill reports of Virginia spread by the "vulgar and viler sort." All was now well there.

Many contended that nothing could be expected of the colony because the people there were the scourings of the streets of London, the refuse of England, "a number of disordered men unfit to bring to passe any good action." Defending the character of the colonists, Crashaw declared that, for the most part, "they be such as offer themselves voluntarily, for none are pressed, none are compelled; and are like (for aught that I see) to those that are left behind—even of all sorts, better and worse." They were, in short, a representative cross-section of the English people, which was doubtless true. But that did not speed the building of Virginia, which required more than run-of-the-mill people. It required men of some purpose and dedication.

"Remember," Crashaw concluded, turning to La Warr, "thou art a General of Englishmen—nay, a General of Christian men. Therefore, principally look to religion. You go to commend it to the heathen. Then practice it yourselves. Make the name of Christ honorable, not hateful, unto them."

The company on La Warr's three ships was the usual motley—from the point of view of Virginia's immediate needs, the least likely yet sent out. His Lordship had brought along a military guard of honor and a large number of retainers and personal servants, all in scarlet liveries. In addition, at least half of the company consisted of Gentlemen of fashion. There were a few skilled workers—among them, several French *vignerons* sent over to cultivate the wild grape of Virginia. The rest La Warr dismissed as "debauched hands."

Fortunately for Virginia, La Warr did not sail the long southern course but the shorter route charted by Captain Argall the year before. In good time—and just in time—he arrived at Point Comfort, where he met "with such cold comforte that if it had not binne accompanied with the most happie newes of Sir Thomas Gates' arrival," he said, "it had binne sufficient to have brooke my hart."

After their night off Hog Island, the two pinnaces with all of the happy Jamestowners on board were making good speed down the river when a skiff suddenly appeared, sent by La Warr to inform Gates of his arrival. All hope of escape vanished as the voyage abruptly ended. Bringing his ships around, as La Warr had ordered, Gates started back up the river to the groans, curses, and "great grief of all . . . except only Captain Martin."

Once again, Jamestown had been saved by a miracle—or rather, by a series of miracles, all within a few weeks. It was the Company's opinion, though not shared by the Jamestowners, that "never had any people more just cause to cast themselves at the foot-stoole of God and to reverence his mercy than our distressed Colony."

Certainly, there had been an extraordinary concatenation of circumstance, "for if God had not sent Sir Thomas Gates from the Bermudas, within foure dayes they had all beene famished. If God had not directed the heart of that worthy Knight to save the fort from fire at their shipping, they had been destitute of a present harbor and succor. If they had abandoned the fort any longer time and had not so soon returned, questionless the Indians would have destroyed the fort. If they had set sail sooner and had launched into the vast ocean, who could have promised that they would encounter the fleet of the Lord Laware, especially when they made for the New Found Land, a course contrary to our Navy's approaching? If the Lord Laware had not brought with him a year's provision [which he had not] what comfort could those souls have received to have been relanded to a second destruction? *Brachium Domini*: this was the arme of the Lord of Hosts."

Landing at Jamestown, La Warr knelt in prayer and then ostentatiously marched to the church between his soldiers drawn up in file as a guard of honor, with the Gentlemen and his scarlet-liveried flunkies marching in rank behind him. Jamestown had often seen a show of authority, but never any with the pomp and circumstance of this. The surviving "anatomies" of the Starving Time must have rubbed their eyes in blank amazement. But if they were well advised, they kept their thoughts to themselves, for the Lord Governor was never one to take himself and his authority lightly.

Laying "just blame upon them for their haughtie vanities and sluggish idlenesse," he commanded them to amend their "desperate follies lest he should be compelled to draw the sword of Justice and cut off such delinquents." Then, ratifying a proclamation made by Gates, he put Virginia under martial law and "exemplified" that law in a series of thirty-seven articles detailing the punishment for particular offenses—as savage and barbarous a code as any in Christendom.

For speaking disrespectfully of the Lord Governor, the penalty was death. Similarly, for speaking disrespectfully of the King, or of any member of the royal family, or of the Virginia Company, or of "any book published by its authority"—such as the *True and Sincere Declaration,* which scores of disgruntled adventurers had ridiculed for the obvious nonsense it contained.

Death, too, was the penalty for speaking or doing anything "against the known articles of the Christian faith"—for blasphemy—for refusing to be catechized—for engaging in private trade with the Indians, or with incoming ships—for running away to the Indians, or trying to make off with a ship or boat—for adultery—for rape or sodomy—for mutiny, murder, or arson—or for any theft at all, no matter how small.

Other punishments fitted this atrocious pattern. If a baker, cook, or fisherman were caught cheating, he was to have his ears cut off. For a second offense, he was to serve the colony for a year as a "slave in the Galleys"; for a third offense, three years in the galleys. Anyone uttering "unlawful oathes" was, for his first offense, to receive a severe lashing; for the second, to have a "bodkin thrust his tongue"; for the third, to be hanged.

A third unexcused absence from the Sunday services also meant death. Lastly, it was ordered that every Sunday, before beginning the catechism or expounding the gentle teachings of Jesus, the minister should read from the pulpit these "Civill and Politique Lawes," from the first sanguinary article to the last, on pain of going hungry for a week.

Small wonder that there were loud complaints about this "Egyptian slavery and Scythian cruelty." Under martial law, as a prominent settler later protested, "many pore people in Virginia were deprived of their lives and goods, & many were brought into a condemnation & slavery." The governor's power was sole and absolute, and his every word was law.

The original patent had granted the colonists the rights and privileges of all Englishmen, and the Company later admitted that it had no authority to reduce them to virtual slavery under martial law. But for almost a decade La Warr's savage code, later broadened, was enforced with the utmost vigor.

Dividing the men into gangs, appointing officers to command them, La Warr allotted "every man his particular place, to watch vigilantly and worke painefully." Each was to perform his task "with alacritie"—or at least without resistance, if he valued life and limb. Nor should men fear that their strength would be sapped "for other men's profits," La Warr remarked from his easy chair, for really very little was expected of them—only six hours of toil on every day but Sunday.

At six in the morning, the work gangs were lined up and marched out to their several jobs, with the Gentlemen superintending as usual, contributing the influence of their "breeding and qualitie." This may have helped somewhat; at least, it kept the Gentlemen out of mischief and off their bunks, in the fresh air. At ten o'clock, the gangs were marched back and into the church for prayers, after which they were fed their dinner at midday, five or six men to a mess. In the afternoon, they were marched out at two and back at four, and into the church again for more prayers. If there were supplies enough, they then had supper.

Upon his arrival, La Warr had assured the hungry that his ships were heavily laden with provisions. While the Company might live on lies, the colonists could not, as his Lordship realized, hurriedly calling in Gates, Somers, Newport, Percy, and others to consider what could be done to avert another Starving Time, for his ships could scarcely provide for those on board. There were no crops in the ground. All of the livestock had been slaughtered. Trade with the Indians was cut off. Relief from home could not be expected until the following spring. There seemed nowhere to turn.

In their dilemma, "that worthie Captain," Sir George Somers, proposed a voyage to the Bermudas to obtain provisions there. Ever regarding the "generall good more than his owne ends," an attitude always worthy of remark at Jamestown, he offered to go himself and show the way, for it might be difficult for any but a "man of good skill in all passages by sea" to find the low-lying islands. A week after La Warr's arrival, the "good old Gentleman" sailed in his own Bermuda-built pinnace, the *Patience*, trailing the *Discovery* under the command of Captain Samuel Argall, promising to be back within a few weeks with pork, fish, fowl, and some live hogs for breeding.

To provide immediate relief, a crew went down to fish the Chesapeake, but in two weeks' time caught scarcely enough to feed itself. With the sturgeon running in the river, those at Jamestown were busily hauling their nets, "sometimes a dozen times, one after the other," but with little success.

La Warr could now think of nothing better to do than infuriate friendly Indians. Though nowhere explicitly stated, it is evident from the records and the course of events that La Warr, as instructed from home, had decided to drive the Indians from the country along the James. Whatever the justification, it was a most hazardous undertaking with the forces in hand.

Gates led a strong party down the river and landed at Kecoughtan, where the people had always been very helpful. It was here that Captain John Smith and his men, on their way to surprise Powhatan, had spent Christmas two years before and never been "more merrie." The Kecoughtan again welcomed the English, who came ashore with every show of friendship. One was carrying a tabor (a small drum), and Gates ordered him "to play and dawnse," said Percy, "thereby to allure the Indians to come unto him, the which prevayled."

Suddenly, at a signal, evidently sounded on the tabor, Gates and his men attacked, put five to the sword, wounded many more, routed the rest, and seized their pleasant village, which stood on a hill in "wholsome ayre," with gardens and fields of corn about it, "a delicate and necessary seat for a Citty or chief fortification."

Here Gates began to erect two small redoubts, Fort Henry and Fort Charles, on the banks of a little stream which was now named the Southampton River,* for the brilliant and somewhat erratic Henry Wriothesley, Earl of Southampton, Shakespeare's friend and patron, a leader and later the Treasurer of the Virginia Company. Brought down from Jamestown, the French *vignerons* were put to work here on the wild grape, promising to have excellent wine for export within a year or two—a project that was to delude the Company and the colony for years.

Unprovoked attacks were launched against the Indians all along the James. George Percy was ordered to drive the Paspahegh from their homelands around Jamestown. Advancing stealthily, he and his men attacked at night, taking the sleeping village by surprise, burning it and killing many. Chief Wowinchapuncka managed to escape with most of his people, but his wife and small children were captured and brutally slain. As the boats were returning to Jamestown, the children were tossed overboard and shot as they struggled in the water. Their mother was later put to the sword after Percy had refused to burn her at La Warr's suggestion, saying that he had seen enough bloodshed for one day.

Nor did the Paspahegh chief long survive his wife and children. He was ambushed and killed near Jamestown, and some of his braves were dispatched "to accompanye their master to the other world."

But all of this put nothing into the common store, which was growing leaner, and La Warr sent Gates and Newport home to inform the adventurers of the dreadful state of affairs after the Starving Time and to plead for large and immediate relief.

"To delude and mock this bewsiness no longer," wrote La Warr, no colonists should be sent out without at least a year's supply. And let the adventurers provide some honest workmen, "paines-taking men of the artes and practises," and not such people as they had recruited for his ships, men of such "distempered bodies and infected minds" that neither good example nor threats of shameful death could deter them from their "habitual impieties." Also, let them send doctors and medicine, in plenty, for

---

* It later lost a syllable and became the Hampton River, which empties into famed Hampton Roads.

all had been afflicted with "strange fluxes and agues," so acutely that half of those in the colony were sick and scores had died.

Finding Jamestown "very noysome and unholsome," quite insufferable in the hot and sickly summer season, La Warr had taken his flagship down to Point Comfort to enjoy the cool breezes there—a respite that all would have been pleased to share. But there was no rest for those at Jamestown. By the time of his Lordship's return, they had repaired the palisades, erected a new church, and built a number of houses.

Though still makeshift, the new houses were a great improvement, modeled on the arbor-like long houses of the Indians. They were covered on the outside with bark, "as durable and as good proofe against stormes and winter weather as the best Tyle, defending likewise the piercing Sunbeames of Summer and keeping the inner lodgings cool enough, which before in sultry weather would be like Stoves whilst they were, as at first, pargetted and plastered with bitumen or tough clay."

Inside, the houses were covered with Indian mats, and though wanting "Arras, Hangings, Tapestry, Gilded Venetian Corduvan and more spruce household garniture, and wanton City ornaments," they pleased everyone, even the Gentlemen, as one of them declared.

But if the houses were plain and nondescript, adding nothing to the "fashion and beauty of the Street," the church was quite elaborate, especially in the light of other needs. It reflected his Lordship's concern about the ecclesiastical proprieties and the externals of faith. Like most men of his class and so many of the professional soldiery, both before him and since, he found no difficulty in reconciling his worldly practices with his pious professions. Though conventionally devout, he was quite blind to the teachings of Christ. Any serious talk of the brotherhood of man—any slightest suggestion that if men were equal before God, they should be equal before the law—would have been anathema to him and have led straight to the gallows.

Some sixty feet long and about half as wide, the church was built entirely of cedar, as were the pews, the chancel, the pulpit, and the font, "hewen hollow like a canoe." A communion table was fashioned from black walnut. The church had "faire broad windows" to let the light in, and La Warr had it kept "passing sweet, and trimmed up with divers flowers, with a Sexton belonging to it."

Two bells were hung in the west end to summon the faithful, and woe betide any who did not come, faithful or unfaithful. There were two services every weekday for the work gangs, and two sermons every Sunday, morning and afternoon, and attendance at all was compulsory—death, as before noted, being the penalty for the third unexcused absence. The Pilgrims and the Puritans of the Massachusetts Bay Colony, long known for the frequency of their observances and the rigors of their "Holy Discipline," never knew anything like this regimen of compulsory prayers and services under the shadow of the whip and the hangman's noose.[1]

La Warr made a great occasion of the Sunday morning service. With a "guard of halberdiers in his Lordship's livery, faire red cloakes, to the number of fifty, both on each side and behind him," he marched to church, followed by the members of the Council, other officers, "and all the Gentlemen." Inside, with his subordinates arranged in rank on either side of him, he took his seat in the "Quier, in a greene velvet chaire," having a "velvet cushion spread on the Table before him, on which he kneeleth." The service ended, he was "waited on to his house in the same manner."

Many of the first prayers must have been for the speedy return from Bermuda of Somers and Argall, who were long overdue, having been gone several months now. Shortly, Argall put in alone, with the disconcerting news that he had been nowhere near Bermuda, through no fault of his own, and that Somers apparently had gone down at sea. Contrary winds had driven them off course, far to the north. Parting company in a heavy fog along the coast of Cape Cod, they had agreed to meet at Sagadahoc, near the mouth of the Kennebec, far up the Maine coast, but Somers failed to appear. After waiting some time, not knowing the way to Bermuda, Argall started back, fishing along the way, and now came in with little or nothing on board. Instead of a hold filled with the bounties of Bermuda, he had brought back only a "taste of cod and Hollybuts." [2]

Though his fate was not known for some time, Sir George Somers was lost to Virginia, and it was a great loss. Somehow missing Argall at Sagadahoc, he had "stirred away" for the Bermudas, where he immediately began gathering supplies "with extraordinary care, paines, and industry." But a week later he suddenly collapsed, dying "of a surfeit in eating of a pig." Though he had urged his men from his deathbed to finish loading the vessel and return with all speed to Jamestown, they were in no hurry, enjoying the peace and plenty of the islands. And when they did sail, it was not for Jamestown, "fearing to be stayed there," but for home, like another *Swallow*.*

Disappointing their hopes of relief, the Bermuda misadventure aroused grave anxiety in the minds of all. Percy, Argall, and others were sent out to buy or seize what corn they could from the Indians. Most of the able-bodied, however, were employed in what La Warr regarded as more important business.

One of Smith's "damned Dutchmen," William Faldoe, "the Helvetian," had gone to England, probably as a witness against Smith, and had persuaded the Company that he had finally wormed out of the Indians one of their most jealously guarded secrets—just where to find gold. Only too eager to believe, the adventurers had sent him back with La Warr to direct operations.

It was his Lordship's plan to sail up the river to the Falls with "most of his Choysest men," leave his boats there, march inland "to the foote of certain mountaines," and there build a fort in which to winter his men, who could "every day digg at those mynes." To muster a sufficient force for this, all work in Jamestown was abandoned, and men had to be recalled from Forts Henry and Charles, the two half-finished redoubts at Kecoughtan.

Some expressed their doubts about this, but La Warr was adamant. As one of his captains explained, if the mines "prove not according to our expectations, yet we have lost nothing but our

---

* Somers' heart was buried where he died, at a spot where the town of St. George now stands, founded a few years later and named in honor of the "ever worthy to be reverenced" Sir George, first Admiral of Virginia.

labour." And there would be this advantage, "that we shall have
a redoubt & some of our men in it against the next Spring when
his Lordship intendeth to march that way, something more
southerly, for the finding out the South Sea."

It was dangerously late in the year to be embarking upon such
an ambitious and hazardous project. But early in December, with
winter fast approaching, an advance party started up the James,
evidently foraging along the way. At the mouth of the Appomattox, twenty came ashore, all well armed, with one of them playing
a tabor. Suspecting mischief, the "queen" of the Appomattox
invited them to a feast, trapped and slaughtered them.

The only man to escape was James Dowse, the "taborer"—
which the Indians must have sincerely regretted, for the "Salvages
be not soe simple as many imagine who are not acquainted with
their Subtellties," Percy observed, "for they had not forgotten
how the Kecoughtan Indians had been allured and destroyed by
Sir Thomas Gates and that same Taborer."

The slaughter threw the whole project awry, for the victims
included Faldoe and "all the chief men skillfull in finding out
mines." As a consequence, the expedition did not proceed above
the Falls, stopping to build a small fort there, perhaps recon-
structing the fort built and abandoned by Captain Francis West's
"disorderlie" company two years before at the time of the trouble
about Nonesuch.

With his company of halberdiers, resplendent in their red cloaks,
La Warr came up from Jamestown to see that all was arranged
so that he could "proceed upon the discovery of mineralls the
next Springe." Nothing was accomplished, however, and more than
a hundred men spent a miserable and quite useless winter here,
"doing little and enduring much," as they complained, being constantly harassed by the now thoroughly aroused Indians, who
captured several and killed more—including La Warr's nephew,
Captain William West.

After a few months of this, his Lordship suddenly returned
to Jamestown and ordered his flagship made ready for sea. He
had been ailing, he said, and was now going to the West Indies,
to the island of Nevis, to take the hot baths there. He would be

back soon, and in his absence George Percy was to be governor, "a Gentleman of honour and resolution and of no small experience in that place."

In 1611, late in March, the *De La Warr* sailed with a suspiciously large number of Gentlemen on board, fifty-five altogether, his Lordship's friends and cronies for the most part, all presumably going to take the baths at Nevis.

Meantime, sent home to plead the necessity of the colony, Gates and Newport had arrived in London with the first news from Virginia in almost a year. And what terrible news it was, as they related the agonies and summed up the losses of the Starving Time.

The adventurers were horrified. To think that they had spent more than £20,000 ($1,000,000) and that what remained in Virginia was not worth "twenty hundred groats" ($160)! They "stood in state of Marchants that had adventured much and lost all," they wailed. If they dropped a passing tear for the dead and dying in Virginia, it left no trace in the records.

Again they debated whether "to enter into a new contribution . . . or abandon the action." At length, calling "honest" Gates before them, they begged him to deal plainly with them and "make a true relation of those things which were presently to be had or hereafter to be hoped for in Virginia."

Though he had been only a month or two in the colony, Gates assured them that "all things before reported were true." Virginia was "one of the goodliest countries under the sunne." It had a healthful climate and would soon be shipping home all kinds of "good commodities." To the iron, wine, timber, tar, and other items usually recited, Gates now added oranges, lemons, sugar cane, almonds, and rice, basing his confident prediction upon the fact that a few orange trees transplanted to Jamestown had weathered their first winter. Also, the colony had "innumerable white mulberry trees." Once silkworms were introduced, it would produce "in a short time" more silk of better quality than Italy or Persia—the first suggestion of another new venture that would waste time and energy for years.

But what interested the adventurers far more than this was

what Gates and Newport told them privately about the resources of Bermuda and its strong strategic position. This lightened their gloom and spurred them on, for here they might possibly recoup their losses, perhaps even turn a profit, as proved to be the case.

But first, they had to get possession of the islands. Though they had recently obtained a new charter, they now sought and obtained another which stretched Virginia's boundaries 900 miles to sea, sufficient to embrace Bermuda.[3]

Even so, it was not easy to raise money for what had to be done. Newport was giving out "great hopes for Virginia," as usual, but no one took him very seriously, especially now, for the report of the Starving Time had leaked out in spite of the Company's earnest efforts to suppress it. As this had to be counteracted, the adventurers again turned to the printing press.

Their *True and Sincere Declaration,* with its extravagant nonsense about the great prosperity of the colony, had appeared just at the worst of the Starving Time and was now a source of acute embarrassment. Their new publication was merely *A True Declaration,* designed to renew interest in Virginia by confuting such "scandalous" reports as had tended "to the Disgrace of so worthy an Enterprise." Let no one doubt that it was a rich and fertile land, beyond the conception of any. There had been some distress there, to be sure, occasioned by the colonists' "intemperate idleness," but all of that had long since been corrected by the "noble & worthie" La Warr.

Enclosing copies of the *True Declaration,* the Company wrote to "persons of worth" throughout the realm inviting them "to partnership in the great action of Virginia." If raised within two years, a sum of £30,000 ($1,500,000) would be sufficient to lay a "strong foundation for the annexing of another kingdome unto this Crown," the adventurers declared. And please, they said, send in money immediately, for one great cause of previous failure had been their "want of means to imploie good men . . . & to set forth our supplies in due season"—their first and rather belated admission that the tragedies in Virginia had not been entirely the fault of the "shiftless" colonists.

With the money received, three ships soon sailed under Sir

Thomas Dale with several hundred on board. Preparations were under way to send out a much larger fleet under Sir Thomas Gates. These large companies would immeasurably strengthen Virginia and, as the Company stressed time and again in its propaganda, they would certainly be put to excellent use by the "conscientious" La Warr, now that he had had a year's experience in the colony.

But just at this time, who should appear but the "conscientious" Lord Governor himself!

Flabbergasted, the Company asked him what brought him home at this time, without warning. Why should he so embarrass them? Well, said La Warr, he had been ill. First, "a hote and violent Ague"; then, the flux; followed by the "Crampe, . . . afterwards the Gout"; and finally, the scurvy—which was not with him, he hastened to add, a "sicknesse of slothfulnesse," as it was with others, but an "effect of weaknesse." Having spent a large part of his time "refreshing" himself at Point Comfort, well aware that half of the colony—almost two hundred people—had perished during his brief command in Virginia, he had the effrontery to say that he had suffered "beyond any other of that plantation."

None should mistake or misconstrue the reason for his return, which had been "accidental," he said. Sailing for Nevis, his ship had been driven to the Azores, where he and his friends had arrived "neare sicke to death of the scurvie, callenture, and other diseases." Oranges and other fresh fruit had soon cured that, and he would have returned to Virginia but for his friends, who had persuaded him not to do so, he said, "before I had perfectly recovered my strength . . . in the naturall ayre of my countrey, and so I came for England"—which, it would seem, was his intention from the start. He was just another "runnygate," like his younger brother before him.

As for Virginia, it was "wonderfull fertile and very rich," he declared, and he was prepared to give "full satisfaction to every doubt and scandall that lyeth upon that country."

Feeling that they had satisfactorily taken care of that in the *True Declaration*, the adventurers invited La Warr to address the Council for Virginia and a general meeting of the Company on his "unexpected returne home," an address published and circulated to silence many doubts and criticisms.

"Being now by accident returned," said his Lordship, he would soon go back, for Virginia was never more promising, justifying "whatsoever heretofore hath been reported of it." He had left there "upward of two hundred, the most in health," having "at least tenne months' victuals in the storehouse," * Some were making his return the "colour of their needlesse backwardness and unjust protraction." As for himself, he was so far from being discouraged that he was willing and ready, he declared, "to lay all I am worth upon the adventure." Cost what it might, he would return to the colony with "all convenient expedition."

But Virginia had seen the last of its "painefull" Lord Governor.

* He had left not more than 125 people at most and supply not for ten months, but for ten weeks, as Sir Thomas Dale soon angrily reported.

XI

The Marshal

*Not many give testimonie, besides their
names, that they are Christians.*

—SIR THOMAS DALE

WHATEVER his destination may have been, whether Nevis or
not, La Warr's sudden flight left affairs in disorder and
Acting Governor Percy had to extricate the colony as best he
could from his Lordship's follies.

The latter had left his party of gold-hunters stranded at the
Falls. Leaderless, hungry, and harassed by the Indians, they had
to be rescued by Percy, who brought them back to Jamestown,
abandoning the fort they had built, the end of another ill-con-
sidered project which had been a total waste of time and effort.

The return of those at the Falls brought on a crisis at Jamestown, which had been living on short rations for months. Unable
to feed all of the reunited company, Percy took a large number
down to Point Comfort, always the "most plentifullest place for
food." Percy and his men were still there several months later,
early in May, 1611, when three ships put in under the command of Sir Thomas Dale, who immediately took the reins of
government into his strong and ruthless hands, guiding Virginia
and fiercely spurring her on for a number of years.

Vigorous and imperious, a veteran soldier in his middle forties,

Dale had been trained in "that universitie of the warres," the Netherlands, which sent so many hard-bitten graduates to Virginia. After seven years of service there, Dale had crossed to Scotland in 1595 to join the retinue and household of young Prince Henry, infant son of James VI of Scotland. When that pretentious and ridiculous monarch, "the wisest fool in Christendom," came south to be crowned James I of England in 1603, Dale left the Court and returned to the Netherlands. But Prince Henry remained his friend and patron, and it was doubtless through the Prince's favor that he was knighted as Sir Thomas Dale of Surrey in 1606, at which time he was commanding English mercenary troops at the town of Oudewater, in South Holland, along with his friend, Sir Thomas Gates.

With the signing of the Dutch-Spanish truce in 1609, the mercenaries in Holland were left with little to do, and a large number sought adventure and employment elsewhere, many in Virginia. Dale was one of these, probably influenced in his choice by Gates. On the Earl of Southampton's recommendation that he was a "worthy and experienced souldier," one with "ability of body as well as mind," the Company had made him Marshal of Virginia, a post outranked only by that of Captain General La Warr and of Lieutenant General Gates.

Obtaining a three years' leave of absence from the Dutch, Dale crossed to London to discuss his mission and drive a bargain with the Company. He had already adventured £25 in the business, but now he was going to adventure his person, and Sir Thomas was never one to underestimate that. Finally, no doubt at Prince Henry's prodding, the Company agreed to "rate" his person at £700 ($35,000), or 56 shares, which made him one of the largest stockholders.[1] That done, he married Elizabeth Throckmorton, kissed his bride good-by a few weeks later, and—ever a man of duty—sailed for Virginia, not to return to her for more than five years.

Carrying 250 passengers, twelve cows (the first to be shipped), twenty goats, many dogs, "besides Conies, Pigeons, and Pullens," Dale's fleet came in with the *Star* flying the flag of "Father" Newport, Admiral of Virginia since Somers' death. Once more, scorning the shorter route charted by Gosnold and again by Argall, he had come the long way round, and the tropics had taken a heavy toll among the passengers, for the ships as usual were grossly overcrowded and "pestered by that meanes."

They were carrying so much cargo both on deck and below, as Dale protested in sharp criticism of the Company's practice, that there was "noe room for our men to be accommodated," and "their owne Aires and the uncleanliness of the ships, doggs, &c., gave some infection amongst us and was the cause of the loss of well more than a dozen men." *

After the glowing reports of Newport and others on its "well-doing," Virginia came as a great shock to the newcomers. Dale exploded with rage. Seizing Newport by the beard, he threatened to hang him for his pleasant stories—in particular for affirming the Company's "relation [its recently published *True Declaration*] to be true, demanding of him whether it were meant that the people here in Virginia should feed upon trees."

Coming ashore at Point Comfort, the outraged Marshal noted "omissions of necessary duties" on every hand. Though it was the middle of May, no corn had been planted, and there was none in the store. Moving up the river to Jamestown, he found the men there "at their daily and usuall workes, bowling in the streets." The fort was in a sad state of neglect and disrepair, with the storehouse, the church, and even the blockhouse tumbling down, and with the colonists' houses "ready to fall on their heads." Here, too, there was "no corne sett" and only "some fewe seedes put into a private garden or two."

As famine approached, Acting Governor Percy, it would seem, had been doing little but entertain his cronies. Others might be hungry, but Percy always managed to have plenty of supplies, procuring them by continuing to draw bills of exchange on his brother, the Earl of Northumberland. Just before the Starving Time, which doubtless explains why he was one of the few to survive that terrible year, he had drawn bills upon his brother for

---

* As figures were used in the Virginia enterprise, "well more than a dozen" might mean anything from twenty to a hundred. Here, it appears to have been about fifty, a sixth of those on board.

more than £430 ($21,500) of supplies. He had recently replenished his stores in a generous manner, admitting to his brother that he had been "not a little chardgable." But he had not been prodigal, he hastened to add, for the "place which I hold in this Colonie (the store affording no other meanes than a pound of meale) cannot be defraied with small expense, it standing upon my reputation (being Governor of James Towne) to keepe a continuall and dayly Table for Gentlemen of fashion aboute me."

Whatever his faults—and they were grave—Dale did something more than entertain Gentlemen of fashion. To his task he brought purpose, energy, a sense of order, and some feeling of responsibility for the people in his charge. Though a hard driver, a strict and often savage disciplinarian, he brought a ray of hope to hundreds of poor wretches who could see nothing ahead but more misery and almost certain death from the follies and cold indifference of their masters.

The stern Marshal soon had all at work planting corn, repairing the town, building barns, and digging a well to replace the old one that had spread so much contagion. Newport and his sailors built a "bridge," or wharf, to facilitate the landing of supplies, for much provision had been spoiled and lost in getting wet as it was carried ashore.

To insure "good order," Dale confirmed the system of martial law already in force and enlarged it by adding thirty-two new articles, all drawn from the barbaric military code used among the mercenary troops in the Netherlands. Every able-bodied man was now a soldier, enrolled in one of the trained bands, and Dale laid down the law on what a good soldier was, and just what he should and should not do.

First—and this must have seemed a deliberate mockery—he should "not set his minde overgreedily upon his belly and continuall overfeeding." He should not curse or indulge in "dicing, carding, and Idle gaming." He should avoid "that detestable vice of drunkenesse." And chastity, the Marshal primly observed, was a "vertue much commended in a souldier"—a virtue widely, if involuntarily, practiced in Virginia for some time. No matter how desperate his need, a good soldier should "not be hasty of his pay," and he would be well advised "to keepe his fidelity unspotted to his Prince and his General" even when his sufferings were "intolerable and infinite."

The Captain of the Watch was ordered to prevent "untimely sitting up late in usual assemblies, whether in private assemblies, publike tap-houses, or such like places." He was to command such "disordered persons" to go home and extinguish their fires and candles. "Night-walkers or unruly persons" met on the streets should be sent to their lodgings or to the Provost Marshal for punishment.

Dale had ideas about any number of things and laid down minute instructions about them. Every bed should be at least three feet above the ground. In the belief that soap somehow spread the plague, he threatened whipping and other meet punishment for anyone who washed clothes and threw out the suds "in the open streete within the Pallizadoes, or within forty foote of the same." Likewise, for any who cleaned a kettle, pot, pan, or any other vessel within twenty feet of the old well or the new pump. The whip also awaited those who dared "to doe the necessities of nature" without going at least a quarter-mile outside the palisades, where all must have been highly nervous to be in such an exposed position when any moment an arrow might come singing through the woods.

Workers continued to be marched to and from their chores under military guard, and into the church twice a day for prayers, a routine which Dale more strictly enforced. A half hour before morning and evening prayers, the Captain of the Watch closed the gates of the fort and placed sentinels, or "rounders." After the bell had tolled the last time, the "rounders" searched the houses and commanded everyone, "of what qualitie soever (the sick and hurt excepted)," to repair to the church as speedily as might be. After the last had entered, the Captain of the Watch locked the doors and laid the keys before the Marshal, who then called the roll—and woe to him who was absent without excuse!

As conventionally devout as La Warr, Dale ordered more religious exercises, composing a long prayer to be read at the guardhouse twice a day, morning and evening, at the changing of the

Watch. In course of the prayer that droned on through three thousand words, the soldiers first confessed that they had "sinned wonderously" in every conceivable way—through "blindness of mind, prophanenesse of spirit, hardnesse of heart, selfe-love, worldlinesse, carnall lusts, hypocrisie, pride, vanitie, unthankfulnesse, infidelitie, and other native corruptions," which had defiled them "even from the wombe and unto this day."

They then hurled imprecations at Satan—"We know, O Lord, we have the Divell and all the gates of Hell against us, but if thou, O Lord, be on our side, we care not who be against us." Finally, they asked that blessings be showered upon the King, the Queen, and the "royall seede," and upon the merchant adventurers, praying God to reward their "noble endeavours" by granting them a dividend on their investment.

"Yea," they exclaimed, doubtless with tongue in cheek, "reward it seven-fold unto their bosomes with better blessings."

Like Gates and La Warr before him, Dale had been instructed to find a suitable site on which to build a new settlement to supplant Jamestown as the chief in the colony. Having explored other parts,[2] the Marshal sailed up to the Falls and back down some twenty miles to a stretch where the river winds about in a series of great horseshoes. Here, in what was named the Curles, Dale came ashore on the north bank, at Arrohateck's Joy, where there was much high ground, many open fields, and a number of springs with fresh sweet water. It had "good aire, wholesome and cleere (unlike the marish seate at James Towne)." As the river almost encircled it, it could easily be defended.

Altogether, it seemed a "convenient, strong, healthie, and sweet seate," and Dale decided to build here, christening his new town Henrico in honor of his patron, young Henry, now Prince of Wales.

Under Dale's sharp eye, "the spade men fell to digging; the brick men burnt their bricks; the company cut down wood; the Carpenters fell to squaring out; the Sawyers, to sawing; the souldiers, to fortifying; and every man, to somewhat." Timbers cut at Jamestown were erected as a palisades across the neck joining the peninsula to the mainland. Outside the palisade, a deep ditch was dug across the narrow neck, which, filling up with water from the river, served as a moat and made Henrico "like an Ile." *

The "Ile" contained seven acres and provided far more living space than the narrow fort at Jamestown. Dale built watchtowers, storehouses, a "faire and handsome" church, and three streets of "competent and decent houses, the first storie all of bricks," evidently the first of the kind in Virginia. Spaced along the river front and occupied by the "honester kind of people," stood five blockhouses to guard the town against surprise from the waterside. As the Company was pleased to learn, there was more purposeful and constructive activity here, and more was accomplished in a few months, than in the four years since the landing.

But work was suddenly interrupted by an alarm that aroused serious apprehensions both in Virginia and in London for some time. A strange ship entered the Chesapeake one day, put a boat over the side, and three men came ashore near Point Comfort, unaware of the fort there. Surprised and captured, they proved to be Spanish. Saying that they were looking for a lost ammunition ship, they asked for a pilot to bring their carvel to safe anchorage nearer shore. An officer in Dale's fleet, John Clarke, who later played a friendly and helpful part in the Pilgrim story as first mate of the *Mayflower*, was sent out. No sooner had he stepped on board than, at a signal from the prisoners ashore, the carvel weighed anchor and put to sea, which convinced everybody that it had been sent ahead to reconnoiter the defenses of the Bay, that it was part of a war fleet advancing against the colony.

There was reason to be apprehensive, as Dale and others well knew, for Spain had taken a belligerent attitude toward Virginia from the start, protesting that it was part of His Catholic Majesty's domain, that it lay within the bounds of Florida. Madrid was persuaded that England wanted Virginia only as a "haven for pirates," planning to make it a "new Algiers," an armed base from which to loot the West Indies and prey upon the great plate fleets that were carrying back large quantities of silver, gold, and other loot from

---

* It has since become one and is known as Farrar's Island. The cut across the sandy neck was named Dutch Gap, apparently because the moat reminded Dale of the canals in Holland.

the New World. Time and again the Spanish ambassadors in London urged Philip III to attack Virginia and "drive those villains out from there, hanging them in time, which is short for the purpose."

Soon after the landing at Jamestown, such an order had been issued to a small war fleet stationed at the Windward Islands. But that fleet, it was found, was in no condition to undertake the task. Two years later, in 1609, when the colonists were living dispersed along the oyster banks, a ship had come north from Florida to reconnoiter and test the strength of the colony. Approaching the Chesapeake, the lookout spied a vessel under sail in the Bay—Captain Argall's, fishing to feed the hungry. The Spanish mistook it for a man-of-war guarding the coast and, not having been observed, turned back, all but foundering in that same "hurycano" which had battered the ships of the Third Supply and piled up the *Sea Venture* on the rocks at Bermuda.

Still concerned about Virginia, more anxious than ever to put an end to that "nuisance," Philip III had called in three trusted agents to undertake a secret mission. Sailing in one of his ships, they were to pretend to be searching for a lost ammunition ship. Actually, they were to prowl about Virginia and learn everything they could about it. If anything went wrong, they were to make out that they were simple sailors merely obeying royal orders. Under all circumstances, they were to hide their identity and the nature of their mission.

To lead this mission, the King had chosen Don Diego de Molina, a grandee of Spain, who had as his aide Ensign Marco Antonio Perez. The third spy was Francis Lembri, or Lymbry, a skilled and experienced English seaman long in the service of Spain, having been chief pilot of the ill-starred Grand Armada launched against England in 1588. These were the three who had come ashore at Point Comfort and been captured there. When they were brought to Jamestown, Dale threatened to hang them. But they begged off by successfully masquerading as simple sailors under orders to find a lost ship, which deceived Jamestown for a time.

Nevertheless alarmed by the strange incident of the Spanish carvel, Dale hastened to inform London of this and of other dangers threatening the colonists, who were "so few, so weake, and unfortified." Reinforcements had to be sent immediately if "this so pious, so heroicke enterprise" were not to collapse.

"My right noble Lord, . . . right excellent Lord, . . . thrice honored Lord, . . . right worthie to be most famous Lord," wrote Dale to the Earl of Salisbury in his most courtly and obsequious manner, it was folly "to strive any longer to settle a handfull of wretched people" in Virginia with the expectation that immediate profits might be had from their labors. It was even more foolish to expect sudden wealth from "secrett commodities and ritches" to be found in the colony. There were none. Even if there were, it was as impossible under the circumstances to find and possess them as "to poise and weigh the mountains."

Nothing could ever be accomplished so long as the Company sent out men and supplies in small driblets—and always too late—so that by the time they arrived, the colony was "worne and spent" and barely alive. What was needed was one huge supply, one "great disbursement," so that a broad and firm base could be laid upon which to build to some purpose. Only thus could Virginia prosper and cease to live a precarious hand-to-mouth existence that precluded substantial improvement of any kind.

Specifically, Dale asked for 2,000 men, to be recruited immediately so that they might be in Virginia by early spring, in time for the planting season. Given such a force, he could repulse the Spanish if they appeared, force the Indians to pay tribute in corn and other things, and "overmaster the subtle, mischievous Great Powhatan." He would force the chief either to abandon the country or come to some agreement about it. There would then be no scarcity of food, "the greatest enemie unto the speedy peopling of the Colonie," for men could till their fields in peace.

To recruit such a large force in so short a time might be rather difficult, Dale admitted, offering a suggestion later adopted to add to Virginia's bad repute. Colonists might be obtained in large numbers "out of the common Gaoles." Instead of being executed, felons under the death sentence should be banished for life to Virginia. If the King would decree that for a period of three years all such criminals should be transported, this would be a "readie way to furnish us with men," Dale argued, "and not allwayes with the worst kinde of men either for birth, spiritts, or Bodie." At least, they would not always be grumbling and wishing themselves in England again. With a halter awaiting their return, they would be only too happy to stay in Virginia and plant there with "all diligence, cheerfulness, and Comfort."

In any case, they could not be any worse than most of those already in Virginia—"so prophane, so riotous, so full of Mutinie and treasonable Intendments," according to Dale, that "not many give testimonie, besides their names, that they are Christians." Hastily recruited in "lasie and infected places," they were so weak and diseased that they were of little use. Of the several hundred men on his ships, not three score could be "imploied upon any labour or service," and everyone without exception "laments himself of being here and murmurs at his present state."

If he were sent the reinforcements he desperately needed, all would be well. He would stake his life that within two years Virginia would be prosperous and self-supporting. If large reinforcements were sent, he hastily added, let them be dispatched with a full six months' supply. Otherwise, they might as well stay at home.

But the adventurers, still upset by La Warr's "accidental" return, were in no mood for "one great disbursement," glumly observing that Dale had sent his ships back with nothing but "dolefull letters." As these "cast a great damp of coldness into the hearts of all," Dale's plea and ambitious plans were impatiently tossed into the basket. All that the merchant adventurers could agree to do, after many bitter quarrels and more withdrawals from the Company, was to dispatch several small ships with a few men and supplies that might be of some aid if the Spanish attacked.

Not long after the mysterious incident at the Point, the worst fears of the colony seemed to be realized when a large fleet was sighted off the coast making for the Chesapeake. As its six vessels included three carvels, Dale hurriedly called a council of war, proposing that he should concentrate his forces at Jamestown and make a stand in the fort there.

But Percy was skeptical about this, having little faith in either the courage or the loyalty of the colonists, doubtless fearing that many would welcome any who came to take them away from Virginia and break the chains of their bondage. It was "dowtfull," Percy argued, "whether our men would stand unto it ashore and abide the Brunte." But if placed on the ships and ordered to fight, "they must, for there was noe runninge away."

XII

This Religious Warfare

Are not these miserable people here better than hawkes,
hounds, whores, and the like?

—THE REVEREND ALEXANDER WHITAKER

*W*ITH Jamestown in great alarm, having his own doubts
about their loyalty and courage, Dale piled his men into
the ships and started down the river to meet the enemy, only to
discover to his immense relief that it was Sir Thomas Gates coming in by way of the West Indies after a passage "more long
than usual."

The latter's ships were carrying cattle, hogs, provisions, some
arms and ammunition, and three hundred of the "choicest" persons—among them, about twenty women, including Gates' three
daughters. His wife had also embarked with him, for Gates had
obtained a long leave of absence from the Dutch and evidently
planned to settle in Virginia more or less permanently, being the
first of the leaders to bring his family with him. But his wife had
died along the way, in the West Indies, and Gates sent his daughters home by the next ship—"a peece of prognostication," as was
shrewdly remarked, that he meant "not to tarry long after."

On his arrival a few months before, Dale had found about 150
people, all that remained of more than 1,000 that had been sent
out. A few had returned home, but at least 800 had died. To the

survivors at Jamestown Dale had added 250 people, and now Gates added 300 more, bringing the population to approximately 700, more than three times what it had ever been before. It now seemed that a firm foundation could soon be laid.

As Dale's superior, Gates took command and the Marshal returned to his work at Henrico. The Indians were very troublesome there, wounding many by lofting arrows into the town, killing all they caught at work outside the palisade. Provoked by these attacks, anxious to secure as much territory as possible, Dale seized other necks of land in the Curles and erected palisades to protect new settlements—Hope in Faith, Coxendale, and Mount Malado, "a high seat and wholsome aire," where he talked of building a guest house, or hospital, which would be provided with eighty beds "for the sicke and lame, with keepers to attend them for their comfort and recovery."

Such an institution was badly needed and would have saved thousands of lives, both by care of the sick and by checking the spread of infection. Everyone recognized the need of a hospital and there was constant talk of building one. But, in the Virginia pattern, nothing was done about it for years.

Nearby, on a large and fertile tract where the Appomattox empties into the James, Dale started still another settlement. Naming it Bermuda for the "strength of its situation," he laid out its many miles of fields and woodlands in the form of hundreds.* Here, at the Nether Hundred, Dale established the first settlement in Virginia that was to be more than a garrison town with a transient population. This was to be a stable and self-supporting community of permanent residents. To attract settlers, Dale offered them special rights and privileges, taking a tentative but important first step in changing the unproductive land and labor system.

At the end of three years, settlers at the Nether Hundred were to be released from bondage. They were then to be free to work for themselves. Their labor was no longer to be at the command

* A political subdivision of an English shire, the hundred was so named because it contained approximately a hundred families and could provide a hundred fighting men. Each hundred was entitled to its own local court.

of the colony or the Company. Meantime, each was to have a house rent-free, a garden, and supplies for a year, but every man had "to provide for himselfe and his family ever after."

Gates had been busy improving Jamestown and giving it a "handsome forme." He had built new and stronger palisades, "two faire rowes of howses, all of framed timber, two stories and an upper Garret or corne-loft high, besides three large and sub-stantiall Storehouses joyned together in length." Jamestown now felt sufficiently strong and secure to expand, building some "very pleasant and beautifull howses" outside the palisades.

All of this helped to make life in Virginia somewhat less trying. Subsequent events made plain, however, that Dale's and Gates' accomplishments were much exaggerated, especially as described by the Secretary of the colony, Captain Ralph Hamor, who was always given to extravagance. He could declare at just this time that Jamestown was now as "healthfull as any other place in the world," and that, contrary to what anyone might say, there was "plentie of corn."

Certainly, as all now knew, corn would grow in great abundance. But, as in previous years, little had been planted and that little had been neglected. Trade with the Indians was uncertain, though some friendly braves had been coming to Jamestown "bringing victuall with them." But Gates soon put a stop to that, cutting off one more source of supply. Saying that these Indians came rather as spies than "out of any good affection," he suddenly seized and executed them "for a terrour unto the reste, to cause them to desiste from their subtell practises."

Hunger again stalked the land. Many died during the winter. Death claimed Marco Antonio Perez, one of the Spanish prisoners, and his master De Molina almost shared his fate. In the spring, with rations short and getting shorter, Gates sent the *Trial* to fish the Chesapeake.

Late in April, 1612, the pinnace cleared from Jamestown with a crew of ten under the command of "that noble and well-deserving Gentleman," George Percy, twice a governor. Two years before, during the Starving Time, he had vehemently denounced the treachery of Captain Francis West and his men in running off with the *Swallow*. Now Percy and his crew, having made a good catch, decided not to return to Jamestown to relieve the hungry there, but "to give them the slip and run away," arriving in London several months later to "fill the towne with ill reports," as the Company loudly complained. However "disordered" many may have been, none in early Virginia put on a shabbier show than scions of the great nobility.

Angrily, the authorities took steps to have Percy and his "runny-gates" apprehended so that they might be punished "or at least sent back again." Whether any were sent back or otherwise punished does not appear. But nothing was done about Percy, who went undisturbed on his undistinguished way to his death twenty years later, having served for a time as a captain of troops in the Netherlands.

But other "runnygates," lacking the shield of the West or Percy name, suffered all manner of hideous torture and death for their attempts to escape from chronic hunger and disease, from servitude and savage martial law. Though some collapsed and died of sheer despair, bolder spirits were resolved to get away at any cost. Many fled to the Indians and were seen no more. Those unlucky enough to be caught were executed "in a most severe manner." Dale had some hanged; "some, burned; some, to be broken upon the wheel; others, to be staked; and some, to be shott to death; . . . and some who robbed the store, he caused to be bound faste unto trees and so starved them to deathe."

Unable to endure any more of this, five men fled south through the wilderness in the hope of reaching the Spanish settlements in Florida. They were tracked down and killed by Indians hired by Dale. A larger group conspired to steal away in a barge and a shallop, "therein to adventure their lives for their native country." Well aware that it was almost suicide to attempt this in such frail craft, they were deterred only by Dale's discovery of their plot. All were executed, including their leader, Jeffrey Abbot, a Gentleman who had been in Jamestown from the start.

"Here I entreat your patience for an Apologie, though not a pardon," wrote Captain John Smith in a passage that casts much light upon what was wrong in early Virginia. Abbot had long served as a soldier in Ireland and the Netherlands, and at Jamestown, said Smith, "he was a sargeant of my Companie, and I never saw in Virginia a more sufficient souldier, lesse turbulent, a better wit, more hardy or industrious. . . . How ingratefully those deserts might have been rewarded, envied, or neglected, or his far inferiours preferred to overtop him, I know not. But such occasions might move a Saint, much more a man, to unadvised passionate impatience. But, however, it seems he hath been punished for his offenses that was never rewarded for his deserts."

Nothing is a more pointed commentary on the management of Virginia affairs than the fact that the Company not only approved of the barbaric code inflicted upon the colony, but even proudly published it to the world under the title of *Lawes Divine, Morall, and Martiall*—with the aim of encouraging migration!

Naturally, it did nothing of the sort. Few with any choice in the matter would go to Virginia to endure a brutal and capricious reign of terror in addition to the ordinary hazards of life on a wild frontier. Martial law merely added to the Company's difficulties and the colony's bad repute, for, as the adventurers complained, there was "no common speech nor publike name of anything this day, except it be the name of God, which is more wildly depraved, traduced, and derided by such unhallowed lips than the name of Virginia."

With Virginia an "object of ridicule (a laughing stock, a shame)," the Company was driven to desperate expedients to keep afloat. Collections were £15,000 ($750,000) in arrears. When the Company brought suit, those who had signed subscriptions replied that their pledges had been obtained under false pretenses. They had been promised an immediate profit and now they were told that they could expect nothing for twenty years.

Others complained that the business had been carelessly managed, that huge sums had been wasted or injudiciously spent, as was true. Also, a few favored adventurers had made fortunes by "juggling" with the Company in the sale of supplies for the ships and the colony. "All the trash they could get in London was sent to us in Virginia," the colonists protested, objecting again and again to paying exorbitant prices for very inferior goods.

Men with money preferred to invest it in the lucrative ventures of the East India and the Muscovy companies, both of which were paying fabulous profits, often as much as 100 per cent a voyage. As its ships came in, one after the other, all "well and richly laden," the East India Company easily raised at just this time a sum of £400,000 ($20,000,000) in less than two weeks, twice as much as the Virginia Company ever managed to raise in its almost twenty years of existence.

At this time, too, with the incorporation of the Irish Society, Virginia lost the support of the rich merchant and craft guilds of London, which had invested considerable sums at the virtual command of the Privy Council. Henceforth, they interested themselves in the huge tracts of land they had been granted in the north of Ireland, in the county of Derry, soon called Londonderry, as it is still known.

Other ventures diverted money and attention from Virginia. The discovery of Hudson Bay convinced many that the long-sought passage to the South Sea lay that way. Composed largely of Virginia adventurers, with Sir Thomas Smythe as governor, a North West Passage Company was formed and immediately dispatched a ship under the command of Captain Francis Nelson, the able and generous skipper who had succored Jamestown after its first dreadful winter and was gratefully remembered by the colonists as the one "honest Marriner" they had known.*

Bermuda was an even more serious distraction, for the Company began to turn its hopes in that direction, especially after the finding there of a large amount of ambergris, worth almost its weight in gold. To Dale's plea for reinforcements and one "great disbursement," it turned a deaf ear, pleading poverty. Yet it found the means at this time to send out a sizable company in the *Plough* to take possession of Bermuda, for the latter seemed to offer many advantages. It was fertile and could easily be defended; the climate was temperate and wholesome; there were no Indians

---

* Deservedly, the kindly and accomplished skipper has a memorial on our shores—not in Virginia, as would be fitting, but in Canada—in the great Nelson River that empties into Hudson Bay.

there to dispute possession. Above all, it promised "commodities" —now, and not in some vague and distant future.

In their need for money, the adventurers turned to a device commonly used elsewhere but seldom in England, announcing a Great Lottery that would pay £5,000 ($250,000) in prizes. Everyone should buy a ticket. Besides the chance of winning a prize, one would be pleasing God in "forwarding that wholesome, profitable, and pleasant work of planting" to which the Lord had "set the first man and most excellent creature, Adam."

Moreover, everybody had a duty to the "common sorte" in Virginia. They had gone there on promise of supply. Were they to be abandoned and left to perish?

Anxious to promote a brisk sale of lottery tickets, perturbed by the "jests of prophane players and other sycophants, and the flouts and mocks of some who, by their age and profession, should be no mockers," the Company hurried through the press two more publications. One was *The New Life of Virginia*, written by Deputy Treasurer Johnson, who professed to be telling the truth about the "former successe and present estate of that plantation." [1]

What "with their planting and sowing of corne," the colonists were now enjoying not merely one but "two harvests in a summer." And the "plentifull fishing there, the store of fowles and fruits of the earth, their present provision sent from hence at every shipping, together with the speedy increase of those sundrie sorts of tame Poultry, Conies, Goats, Swine, and Kine landed there above a year ago with Sir Thomas Dale and since again by Sir Thomas Gates" assured continued plenty. In her new life Virginia was really to be envied.

While elaborating a somewhat different theme, *Good Newes from Virginia* sounded the same note. All had a duty to support Virginia and, incidentally, the Company. The dutiful would be well rewarded not only in this world but the next, they were assured by the Reverend Alexander Whitaker, the minister at Henrico, for the building of the colony was God's work. Though they could heartily agree with that, the adventurers must have been more than a little abashed as Whitaker continued.

"O, let us not then be weary of well-doing," he exclaimed, urging the Company to continue pouring money into Virginia "without hope of present profit," finding grave fault with the "covetous hearts of many backsliding adventurers at home." They should have a thought not only for the colonists but for the Indians, those "naked slaves of the Divell." Whether a penny resulted or not, these poor benighted heathen had to be brought into the fold.

"Wherefore, you wealthy men of the world, whose bellies God hath filled with hidden treasure, . . . [be] ready to distribute and communicate," he said. "How shamefully do most of you either miserably detaine or wickedly misspend God's goods whereof he made you his stewards."

Why, some of them spent a hundred pounds a year—or two, three, or five hundred, or even more—"about dogs, hawkes, hounds, and such sports." Others lost £2,000 or £3,000 a night at dice or cards. Yea, many were only too eager to "hire gardens at great rates and build stately houses for their whores."

Let these wastrels take heed and give some thought to the needs of those in Virginia.

"Are not these miserable people here better than hawkes, hounds, whores, and the like?"

To the question so framed, the answer was no!

There was no pleasure in spending money on Virginia. Nor was it a matter of charity. The colony was a business enterprise, and profits were needed to keep it going. As none had been paid, as there had been only heavy losses, men declined to risk more money on the venture. Even the Great Lottery was affected by the growing want of confidence in the Company and the management of its affairs. The sale of lottery tickets was so slow that the drawing had to be postponed several times.

In the end, after organized soliciting throughout the realm, the Company managed to sell only a part of its tickets. These brought it some £8,000, which was a bitter disappointment, for at least £25,000 ($1,250,000) had been expected. Desperate for funds, the Company sold Bermuda to Deputy Treasurer Johnson and ten of the adventurers for £2,000 ($100,000).

Bleak enough already, the prospects of Virginia darkened after

the sudden and unexpected deaths of its two most exalted patrons
—the Earl of Salisbury, the Lord Treasurer and virtually the
prime minister of the realm, who had dipped into the royal treasury more than once to aid the colony; and young Henry, Prince
of Wales. The latter's death was a heavy blow to the "constant"
adventurers, for the future of the colony and the "light of the
Court seemed to them much obscured by the setting of that bright
Star."

Again, there was serious talk of abandoning the colony. Most
of the adventurers had turned away, having been "long since
beaten out as from a hopeless action." Under the circumstances,
"worthie" La Warr was not disposed to hurry back to his post in
the wilderness. Returning from his fifth and last voyage to Virginia, "Father" Newport resigned as Admiral of Virginia, "seeing
the necessary yearly supplies for that plantation not to proceed
as was requisite for so honorable an action." Entering the employ
of the East India Company, he died of fever at the port of Bantam,
in Java, in 1617.

As ship after ship returned from Jamestown laden with "nothing but discomfort," many became convinced that Virginia would
soon "fall to the ground of itself," a view shared by the Spanish
ambassador, who kept himself remarkably well informed about
Virginia from the many English spies secretly on his payroll—
at least one, and possibly more, being on the Royal Council for
Virginia.

The colony had been suffering "great extremitie and miserie,"
Zuniga reported to Madrid, and in their discouragement and aversion to investing any more of their own money, the adventurers
had turned to a "general kind of begging, . . . by way of a
lottery." As such "uncertain shifts . . . could last but a year or
two," the colony was bound to "sink of itself." If His Catholic
Majesty would command the people in Virginia to get out of there
immediately, they would think it "most courteously done."

Such a command, it seemed, had been issued, for secret dispatches now poured in from Madrid and neighboring capitals that
Philip III was outfitting a large fleet "to attempt Virginia." Stung
into action, the Company took steps to warn and strengthen the

colony, but in its usual dilatory and inefficient way. One of its Bermuda ships was ordered to proceed on to Jamestown, where it finally arrived months later carrying no men and only a few supplies, though it brought many gloomy letters from home, which greatly alarmed and further discouraged those in the colony.

The rumor soon ran that the Spanish had attacked Virginia and put all to the sword. The story seemed so well authenticated, it was told in such minute and convincing detail, that the *Mercure Françoise* of Paris published the news of the massacre to the world. While London did not wholly credit the report, it did not seem too unlikely. There had been no word from Virginia in almost a year, and the fear grew that the colony had been destroyed—if not by the Spanish, then by the Indians or by famine— and this was the darkest hour "in all that time of three years' disaster."

But it was not as bad as feared. A ship came in at last, late in 1613, bringing "newes of their well-doing," which infused "some life into that action that before was almost at the last cast."

"Be not gulled with the clamorous reports of base people," wrote Dale, alarmed by intimations that the Company was seriously thinking of abandoning Virginia.[2]

"Believe Caleb [Gates?] and Joshua [Dale?]," he declared. "I have seen the best countries in Europe, and I protest unto you before the living God, put them all together, this country will be equivalent unto them if it be inhabitant with good people."

Reviving an old hope, he reported that they had captured the daughter of their greatest enemy who, for her ransom, offered to be their friend and show them where "to meet with gold mines."

But the ship, the adventurers sourly noted, "brought no commodities from thence, but only these fayre tales and hopes," and the crew of the *Elizabeth* was telling other tales, as the Spanish ambassador was pleased to report.

Some three hundred people remained in Virginia, which meant that more than half had perished since Dale's arrival two years before. Many of the survivors were sick, and all felt aggrieved, complaining that they had nothing to eat but a little corn and fish, and nothing to drink but water—a regimen which was, as the ambassador observed, "contrary to the nature of the English," who were known throughout Europe for their "large tabling and belly cheer." There can be no doubt, as the ambassador remarked, that all there would have returned long since "if they had been at liberty."

Though discouraged, the Company continued to stagger along from crisis to crisis. Disappointed with the return from the Great Lottery, it established a "little running Lottery" with tickets priced at 1s. and 2s. 6d. ($6.25) each, hoping that these could be readily sold and built up into a considerable sum.

Casting about for any means of support, the Company turned to the Parliament. Requesting aid, it presented a petition to the House of Commons, which was sympathetic, in part because a great many of the adventurers were members, more than a hundred in all. The House agreed to hear the Company's case for using public funds to support a private venture—the sort of raid on the taxpayer's purse that has been so popular down the ages, never more so than in our day.

Unfortunately, the Company's judgment here was no better than elsewhere. The spokesman it selected, the solicitor of the Company, Richard Martin, made a complete fool of himself, departing from his subject to lecture the House on how to conduct its business, addressing its members as if they were schoolboys. Angry and outraged, the House called him back and forced him to make an apology at the bar. Before anything more could be done, the King quarreled with the House about other matters and dissolved the Parliament, not calling another for seven years, leaving the Company with no hope of aid from that quarter.

The Company succeeded, however, in persuading the august Privy Council to lend its name and great influence to promoting the sale of lottery tickets. Though the adventurers complained of the "slow coming in of their money," some money did come in, and this saved the venture.

Seven years had now passed since the landing at Jamestown. The adventurers had spent £46,000 ($2,300,000) and received next to nothing in return. But things seemed rather more hopeful at last, for Dale, Whitaker, Hamor, and others reported that

Virginia was on a "better footing," that it could now support itself and would soon be shipping home "good commodity"—and
about time, the adventurers remarked.

But this was another castle in the air, one more illusion, for
Gates now appeared in London, "quite out of hart," to warn that
if aid were not immediately dispatched, the colony would "fall
to the ground." Like Newport and others, Gates had had his
fill of life in the wilderness. It was too primitive and strenuous
for one of his condition. Crossing the Channel to rejoin his
troops in the Netherlands, he died there eight years later, in 1622.

Dale, too, was anxious to return, disappointed with the Company's weak support of his labors in the vineyard of the Lord,
whose church, he said, "with greedy appetite I desire to erect."
He had been profoundly disturbed by the death of his patron,
young Prince Henry, who would have "ennamelled with his
favours the labours I undertake for God's cause and his immortal
honour." The Prince was the "great Captaine of our Israell" and
with his death, observed Dale, "I think the whole frame of this
business fell into his grave, for most men's forward (at least seeming so) desires are quenched, and Virginia stands in desperate
hazard."

He had been thinking of his wife, he added, and though "that
sallat [salad] give an appetite to cawse me to returne," he would
stay on a while and prosecute his "religious warfare." He would
remain "till harvest be got in, . . . so that this action of such
price, such excellency and assured profit (to mine own knowledge),
should not die."

XIII

Pocahontas

*Her education hath bin rude; her
manners, barbarous; her generation,
accursed. . . .*

—JOHN ROLFE

DALE's "religious warfare" had taken some curious and nefari-
ous turns and had brought in several unexpected prizes,
one being the inspiration of a renowned romance.

Two years earlier, in the summer of 1612, when the Company
professed to have no money to aid the colony, a ship had been
sent out secretly commissioned to undertake a very dubious and
dangerous mission of no interest or advantage whatever to the
hard-pressed colonists. Under the command of that "ingenious,
active, and forward young Gentleman," Captain Samuel Argall,
now rapidly rising to power and influence, the *Treasurer* came in
carrying fourteen cannon and sixty musketeers, all "trained to sea
service, to board a ship over the side, and forward and aft."

Stretching his authority, Dale commandeered the services of
Argall and his soldiers to relieve the acute distress along the
James, taking them down to the Nansemond where they spent six
weeks chasing the Indians up and down that river for their corn.
As the loot was small, Argall took his ship into the rivers to the
north to obtain what he could by trade or pillage. Hearing that
Pocahontas was visiting along the Potomac, he hastened there.

Nothing had been seen of Little Wanton for three years or more, not since the days of Captain John Smith when she used to come to Jamestown with gifts and, to the delight of all, would "get the boyes forth with her into the markett place and make them wheele, falling on their hands, turning their heels upwards, whom she would follow and wheele so herself, naked as she was, all the fort over."

Now a girl of eighteen and perhaps somewhat more sedate, but still gay and personable, the "Numparell" of Virginia was a desirable prize, and one that Argall intended to seize, being resolved, he said, "to possesse myselfe of her by any stratagem that I could use."

Approaching an old acquaintance, Japazaws, brother of the Potomac chief, he asked him to betray Pocahontas into his hands. If he did not, they could no longer be friends and that might have very unpleasant consequences. Fearing Powhatan's wrath, Japazaws hesitated but finally lured the girl on board the *Treasurer* on the promise of a copper kettle and a few trinkets, for which he "would have betraied his owne father," said Argall.

"To supper they went, merrie on all hands, especially Japazaws and his wife, who, to express their joy, would ever be treading on Captain Argall's foot, as who should say: *'tis done; she is your own.* Supper ended, Pocahontas was lodged in the Gunner's room."

Restless and apprehensive, she was up early next morning and anxious to go ashore, urging her friends to fly with her. Awakened, Argall coolly informed her that Japazaws and his wife might leave, but that she might not. He would "reserve" her until a peace was negotiated with her father, whereupon Pocahontas became "exceeding pensive and discontented." Making a great show of anger and protest, the villainous Japazaws and his squaw departed.

An Indian messenger was dispatched to inform Powhatan of this and the terms upon which he might ransom his daughter. He should return all the English he had with him, whether they had been captured or had taken refuge with him. He should restore all the "swords, peeces, & other tooles" that his braves had stolen or otherwise acquired. Last but not least—indeed, the most important—he should supply a "great quantitie of corne for the Colonie's reliefe."

This "unhandsome treachery" caused Powhatan much grief and concern, "partly for the love he bare his daughter and partly for the love he bare to our men, his prisoners." Many were not prisoners at all, but runaways from Jamestown, and all were quite content to stay where they were. They worked hard for Powhatan, perhaps because they enjoyed some freedom and intelligent direction under him, and he found them very useful, "though with us," as Secretary Hamor naively remarked, "they were unapt for any imployment."

Even so, the chief agreed to return these men, whether they wished to return or not. He accepted the other ransom terms and informed Argall that if he would bring his ship up the York, he would load it with corn.

But this seemed much too easy, and Argall now changed his mind. If Powhatan had readily granted so much, no doubt he could be forced to grant more. Instead of proceeding to Powhatan, Argall sailed for Jamestown "with all speed" to let those in command there exploit the kidnaping and dictate their own terms, delivering his still pensive prisoner into the hands of Dale, "that worthie and religious Knight," who undertook to instruct her in the principles of the Christian ethic and faith—which, under the circumstances, no doubt required some explaining.

Anxious for her safety, eager to free his daughter and have her with him, Powhatan was furious at Argall's second double-dealing. Nevertheless, he sent to Jamestown all of the English who were with him, a generous supply of corn, and a large number of guns, swords, and tools.

But this was not enough, Dale informed him. What he had sent would be accepted as part payment of the ransom, but what about the rest of the arms and tools they had lost? Until all were returned, they would "by no meanes deliver his daughter." From long experience Powhatan saw such tricks for what they were, and Jamestown "heard no more from him for a long time after."

Though the capture of Pocahontas proved to be very profitable in a strange way, Argall had not been sent out for that. Hastily putting the *Treasurer* in trim, he cleared from Point Comfort late in May, 1613, asking his friends to pray God to bless his "fishing voyage."

But Argall was not going fishing. He was going to hunt— Frenchmen.

By his secret commission, he was to drive out any "interlopers" found within the limits of the original Virginia grant, which stretched far to the north, to the St. Croix River, now the boundary between Maine and Canada. England suspected that the French were trying to establish themselves along the northern Atlantic seaboard, as indeed they were, feeling that they had quite as much right to settle there as the English, especially as they had been the first to build settlements in the region and take actual possession there.

In 1603, three years before the Virginia grant, a huge tract of land styled Acadia, extending roughly from the mouth of the Hudson River to the Gulf of St. Lawrence, had been granted to Sieur de Monts and his associates, who had erected a fort near the mouth of the St. Croix in 1604 and had since built other outposts along the coast.[1]

But the French were trespassers in English eyes and had to be routed. The London (or South) Virginia Company had no direct interest in this, and the hungry men along the James had even less. But the Crown was interested in empire-building and probably paid part of the expense of Argall's expedition. As England and France were at peace and James could ill afford to disturb it, the expedition had been sent out under false colors, flying the Company's flag, to lessen the possibilities of serious trouble. As it was, there were complications enough.

Heading north from the Chesapeake, Argall learned that the French had recently established an outpost and a Jesuit mission off the Maine coast, on the island of Mount Desert, near the present Bar Harbor. Without warning, offering no opportunity for a parley, Argall brought the *Treasurer* in with her guns blazing, killing a half dozen men, so taking the French by surprise that the fort and several vessels in the harbor were easily captured. Fifteen men escaped in a small boat and eventually reached France to report the attack, which inspired sharp and angry protests from Paris.

After plundering and destroying St. Sauveur, Argall placed half of his prisoners, about fifteen in all, in a small sloop and told them that they might go where they pleased—"a noble favor indeed," as one of them exclaimed. The rest he brought to Jamestown—among them Sieur de la Motte and two Jesuit friars, Pierre Biard and Jacques Quentin, who were assured by Argall that they would be well received by the Marshal, as the latter was a "great friend of the French."

But when they were brought before "this fine Marshal," he talked of "nothing but ropes and gallows," threatening to hang all of them, "especially the Jesuits." But Argall, who had promised them their lives, interceded and saved them from the gallows.

Emboldened by his easy victory, Argall sailed back to loot and destroy all French settlements along the northern coast, whether they lay within the limits of the Virginia patent or not. With the *Treasurer* and two captured French vessels, having the two Jesuit fathers on board, he stopped at St. Sauveur to complete its destruction. He then went on to the fort at St. Croix, which was soon reduced to ashes. Crossing the Bay of Fundy, he and his crew fell upon Port Royal and secured a "good deal of booty which they had not expected." Taking everything they could carry, "down to planks, latches, locks, and nails," they set fire to the fort—"a very pitiable thing," as Father Biard observed, "for thus in an hour or two were reduced to ashes the work and expenditure of many years." * If the Spanish had served them a like turn at Jamestown, the English would have wailed to high heaven, and we should never have heard the last of it.

But Argall's luck no longer held. Filled with loot, his own ship and the two captured French vessels headed for Jamestown but ran into a heavy winter gale that scattered the fleet. The smaller French vessel went down with all on board. The other, driven to the Azores, made for England, where it arrived early

* Port Royal was soon rebuilt. Again captured by the English in 1713, it was renamed Annapolis, as it has since been known. It lies on the lower western coast of Nova Scotia, well beyond the limits of the Virginia grant.

in 1614, laden with booty and having the two Jesuit fathers locked up in the hold, a source of acute embarrassment both to the Company and the Crown.

In the teeth of icy gales, it took Argall almost a month to beat his way down the coast to Jamestown, where the *Treasurer* landed what remained of his spoils—"much wheat, clothing, horses, and working tools." But as this did not begin to relieve the general scarcity, Gates was sent home to plead the necessity of the colony while Dale set out to extract what he could from the Indians, having a ready instrument at hand—Pocahontas.

Under the Marshal's ministrations, Little Wanton had renounced her "idolatry and openly confessed her Christian faith." In the dilapidated Jamestown church she was baptized with fitting ceremony and christened Rebecca—"and were it but the gayning of this one soule," Dale declared, "I think my time, toile, and present stay well spent."

While it was something to have made a Christian convert, the first in seven years, there still remained a most important consideration. Rebecca's ransom had not yet been paid. As nothing had been heard from Powhatan in months, Dale decided to stir him up and bring the matter to decision.

Mustering a large force, the "religious and valiant" Marshal sailed up the York, taking Pocahontas with him to bait Powhatan and his braves. He would force them to meet his demands or provoke them "to fight for her, if such were their courage and boldnesse."

Since his last ultimatum, Dale had increased his demands. Most of the men sent back to Jamestown had again escaped and returned to Powhatan. For each of these, Dale now demanded 500 bushels of corn because he had been "put to the trouble to fetch them," as if Powhatan were responsible for policing Jamestown, to keep the hungry and unhappy there.

As the English sailed up the York, the Indians made a "great bravado all the way," being rightly suspicious, wanting to know what was intended.

"I have come," said Dale, "to bring Powhatan his daughter, on condition that he will render all the arms, tools, swords, and men that have run away, . . . and give me a shipful of corn for the wrong he has done us." Otherwise, he would ravage the country and slaughter all that he met.

"If you are come to fight, you are welcome," the Indians replied, advising the whites to turn back if they valued their lives— "bragging, as well they might," said Hamor, "that we had ever had the worst of them in that river, instancing Captain Ratcliffe (not worthy remembering but to his dishonour), who, with most of his company, they betrayed and murthered."

At the suggestion of the Indians, Dale agreed to a brief truce, till noon the next day, so that messengers might be sent to Powhatan to learn his pleasure. When they failed to return on time, Dale and his men came ashore, "killed some, hurt others, marched into the land, burnt their houses, tooke the corne," and made "freeboote and pillage" of all that they found.

Pushing on into the Pamunkey, they dropped anchor off Matchcot, now Powhatan's chief village, where some four hundred braves were assembled along the shore, "well appointed with their bowes and arrows." Boldly, Dale and his freebooters came ashore. Quite as boldly, the Indians met them, walking among them, as the English uneasily noted, "with no shew of fear," demanding to "conferre with our Captaine on his comming in this manner."

Disappointingly, Powhatan was not at Matchcot, having gained a healthy respect for the stratagems and treacheries of the English. But Dale and his men were well received by the chief's brother, Opechancano, who promised to do what he could about payment of the ransom. And with that assurance, according to Dale's own account, he and his men departed, their demands unsatisfied, saying that as it was now April, they had to hurry "home to prepare ground and set corne."

To be sure, they should have been home preparing ground and planting corn. It is quite clear, however, that the Indians' bold stand and display of force had given them pause and persuaded Dale not to try "conclusions" just then. But he would be back after harvest, he thundered, and if the ransom were not paid then, he would "take away all their corne, burne all the houses upon that river, leave not a fishing weir standing, nor a Canoa in any creek thereabout, and destroy and kill as many as he could."

But here, as at Weromocomoco during Smith's captivity and dramatic rescue there, the second version of the story is far more interesting. The reason why the Marshal had been "so milde" at Matchcot was a very curious one—an avowal of burning passion, proclaimed under the most dramatic circumstances in one of the strangest love letters ever penned, if we can trust the word of the Secretary of the colony, Captain Ralph Hamor, one of the Marshal's chief aides.

While Dale was still "in parlee" with the Indians, threatening death and destruction, Hamor had whipped a letter out of his pocket, it seems, and handed it to the spluttering Marshal, who stopped then and there to read it. Signed by John Rolfe, it ran on page after page after page.

"An honest and discreet English Gentleman," one of the *Sea Venture* group wrecked in Bermuda, Rolfe had there lost his wife and newborn child. In Jamestown, he had been using his leisure and making a name for himself in experimenting with the coarse Indian tobacco plant, trying to improve its quality for his own taste and enjoyment, unwittingly laying the base of an economy that would sustain Virginia for generations, though this was not yet apparent and the very idea of it would be bitterly fought for years, for decades.

But while smoking his pipe—or "drincking tobacco," as the phrase always ran—the lonesome young widower, now almost thirty, had been thinking of other things than ways to improve the strain of *pissimore*, or *apooke*, as the Indians called the "noisome weed." He had fallen in love and here at Matchcot now announced it in a most unusual way, the start of the first great American romance, long a copybook favorite. While the story is familiar enough in a general way, the circumstances and the manner of love's avowal are not so well known.

Rolfe, it appears, had written a long letter asking the Marshal's "advice and furtherance of his love, if so it seemed fit for him." As Rolfe was at Matchcot, it is not clear why he chose to present his passionate and intimate feelings in a letter. It is still less clear why, if he had a letter, he did not present it himself instead of allowing

Hamor to do so, as the latter reported. In any case, so the record reads, the letter was presented in the midst of the powwow with the Indians—and it worked magic, to the surprise and delight of all.

When the Marshal was at leisure to peruse his "few lines," Rolfe began, "I trust in God the beginning will not strike you into greater admiration than the end will give you good content." It involved a "matter of no small moment" and arose "from an unspotted conscience," said Rolfe, "being well assured in my perswasion (by the often trial and proving of myself in my holiest meditations and prayers) that I am called hereunto by the spirit of God." But for this, he assured Dale, "I should not dare to offer to your view and approved judgment these passions of my troubled soule."

With the Marshal's consent, he wished to marry, not out of any "unbridled desire of carnall affection, but for the good of this Plantation, for the honour of our countrie, for the glory of God, for my owne salvation, and for the converting to the true knowledge of God and Jesus Christ an unbeleeving creature, Pokahuntas." *

The "vulgar sort," of course, would misinterpret his motives and fail to appreciate his "godly labour." But "let them know it is not any hungry appetite to gorge myself with incontinency; sure, if I would and were so sensuously inclined, I might satisfie such desire, though not without a seared conscience, yet with Christians more pleasing to the eye"—a most ungallant remark about his beloved, a quite gratuitous slap at the gay and comely Little Wanton, a Christian now herself.

Nor was he in such a desperate state that he cared not what became of him. He hoped to return to England one day, and there he could doubtless make a better match. But still, he had a "dutie to God."

Pocahontas' education had been rude, it was true. Her manners were "barbarous, her generation accursed." Altogether, she was "so discrepant in all nurtriture from myselfe that oftentimes, with

* But she had already been converted by Dale and christened Rebecca.

fear and trembling, I have ended my private controversie with this: Surely, these are wicked instigations, hatched by him who seeketh and delighteth in man's destruction. . . . Nor am I ignorant of the heavie displeasure which almightie God conceived against the sonnes of Levi and Israel for marrying strange wives."

But his conscience kept pulling him "by the ear and crying, Why dost thou not indevor to make her a Christian?" Why not, indeed, for it seemed a hopeful project, what "with her appearance of love to me, her desire to be taught and instructed in the knowledge of God, her capablenesse of understanding, her aptnesse and willingnesse to receive anie good impression."

Should he refuse to lead the blind into the right way? Should he refuse to feed the hungry and clothe the naked? Should he refuse "to actuate these pious duties of a Christian? . . . God forbid!"

If the Marshal approved, he would marry the poor girl, he said, "and perform the godly task appointed me." [2]

This letter, if written by Rolfe and so presented, must have struck the Marshal with "admiration," as the passionate lover had hoped, though Dale may not have been too pleased with the remarks about the girl's abysmal ignorance of God, for he had instructed her and converted her himself. Still, as the scene was drawn by Hamor, he quickly approved of Rolfe's proposal and even blessed his pious chore. Nor was Pocahontas averse when told of it. Being nearby on one of the ships, she came ashore to inform her brothers of what was intended. Messengers dashed off to tell Powhatan the news, and the English withdrew peacefully, "who otherwise," said Hamor, "would not have departed their river without other conditions."

Whatever the preliminaries, Rolfe and Rebecca were soon man and wife. Pocahontas had a husband already, it seems, having been married four years before to a brave named Kocoum. But this was deemed no impediment and in April, 1614, the marriage rites were performed at Jamestown, presumably by the Reverend Richard Buck and in the presence of a curiously cosmopolitan throng—a grandee of Spain, Don Diego de Molina, and his aide Lymbry; a French knight, Sieur de la Motte, and other French prisoners from St. Sauveur; a few "Polanders" and "damned Dutchmen," all eager to go home; many Indians in brave array; and several hundred ragged English of high and low degree.

Powhatan had been invited to attend. But in spite of much urging, that "subtle owlde foxe" declined to come to the wedding, suspecting another ruse, sending one of his brothers to give the bride away and "two of his sonnes to see the marriage solemnized."

It was a gala occasion, and there were many who envied Rolfe's good luck and evident bliss. Among others, Dale was lonesome. Though he had just written the Company to say that he had been thinking of his wife and "that sallat" tempted him to come home, his eye, it seems, was on another "sallat," for he now sent Hamor to Powhatan on a singular mission.

Pleased to see Hamor, the chief first wanted to know all about Pocahontas and her "welfare, her mariage, his unknowne sonne, and how they liked, lived, and loved together."

She was very well, he was assured, and so content that she would not think of coming home to live with him, at which Powhatan threw back his head and laughed, saying,

"I am very glad of it."

After an exchange of gifts, Hamor circled around to the point, praising the "exquisite perfection" of the chief's youngest daughter, his "darling and delight," saying that reports of her glowing beauty and many graces had fired the heart of Sir Thomas Dale. The latter asked in "brotherly friendship" that she be sent to live with him as a token of "perpetuall friendship," for the Marshal intended, said Hamor, as glib a liar as any of his countrymen, "to dwell in this country as long as he liveth."

But the girl was no longer with him, Powhatan replied. She had departed a few days before to become the wife of a neighboring werowance, being "sold" to him for two bushels of roanoke, or wampum.

But that arrangement could easily be broken by returning the wampum, Hamor argued, especially as the girl was "not full twelve years old and therefore not marriageable." Besides, Dale was so anxious to have her that he would happily pay three times as much for her in "beades, Copper, Hatchets, and many other things," for he wished to make her "his neerest companion, wife, and bedfellow"! *

But Powhatan was not to be bribed with beads, copper, and hatchets, saying that he had many children but delighted "in none so much as her." He would die if he could not see her from time to time, which would be impossible if she were at Jamestown, for he had long since decided "upon no termes whatsoever to put himselfe into our hands and come amongst us."

Besides, there was no need of another pledge of friendship, for "King" Dale already had one of his daughters. So long as Pocahontas lived, that should be a sufficient pledge of peace—as, in the event, it proved to be.

Even if Dale had no pledge at all, he had no reason to fear any injury, Powhatan concluded. Too many men on both sides had been killed and "by my occasion," he said, "there shall never be more. No, not though I should have just occasion offered, for I am now old and would gladly end my days in peace. So that if the English offer me injury, my country is large enough to remove myself farther from you. This much will satisfy my brother. . . . If it does not, I will go three days' journey farther from him and never see Englishmen more."

This, as things turned out, was the last the English ever saw of the great Powhatan, one of the towering figures in early Virginia. Passionately fond of his children, surprisingly humane and sympathetic in most of his dealings, sharp of mind, strong of body, stout of heart, he was a master of all the Indian arts of policy and government. In every respect he stood head and shoulders above any of the English who tried to match wits with him. As Smith, Ratcliffe, Dale, and others had learned, it was as hard to deceive him as it was to escape his stratagems and snares when he chose to lay them. As remarked before, his forbearance in regard to the English and their provocations was indeed remarkable, for he could easily have destroyed the colony on many occasions—during

* Hamor also published this letter, which must have come as something of a shock and humiliation to imperious Lady Dale, the Marshal's almost virginal wife.

that first awful winter, at the time of Smith's attempt to surprise him at Weromocomoco, or during the Starving Time, to cite a few obvious instances.

Now approaching seventy, but still hale and hearty, his grave countenance framed by long gray hair flowing down around his shoulders, Powhatan was as majestic as ever, more the "emperor" than he had ever been before. But he was growing tired of power, always preferring the simple joys of life, being most content when living quietly with his many wives and children, though he never missed an opportunity to be "merrie." Within a year or two he surrendered his powers and spent the remainder of his days at ease, visiting his married children and friends here and there in neighboring tribes, dying peacefully among his people early in 1618.

If Virginia survived its feeble and sickly infancy, it was thanks largely to Powhatan. It was not merely what he refrained from doing under severe provocation. Rather, it was what he did, for as Percy and others testified, if he had not kindly sent supplies to Jamestown on several critical occasions, they "had all perished."

Pocahontas' marriage, said Rolfe with some exaggeration, became the "ground-worke of their thrift and happiness." Yet it did bring years of peace, as Powhatan had promised, and the long truce enabled the pinched and weary colonists to turn to something more productive than incessant warfare.

In addition, and quite as important, Dale had made what was for him a surprising and remarkable discovery. No matter how brutally enforced, martial law did not grow corn. It served little or no purpose to march men into the fields and drive them like dumb beasts. He therefore took another hesitant step toward establishing a more fruitful land and labor system. Though the change did not work quite as well as expected, it helped to remedy much of what was so disastrously amiss. The remedy was as simple and obvious as giving the "shiftless" colonists some sense of responsibility and an incentive to work.

Three acres of cleared ground "in the nature of Farmes" were given to each man for present use, but not for permanent possession. On his acres he had to produce enough to feed himself and his family, if he had one. To tend his crops, he was allowed the equivalent of a month a year. His remaining time, as before, was at the disposal of the colony and the Company. In return, he was entitled—and it was often a merely theoretical right—to draw upon the store for whatever he needed except food.

The first of these "Farmers"—the first Virginia planter properly so called—was William Spence, "an honest, valiant, and industrious man," another of the few survivors of that ill-led company which had founded Jamestown and been decimated there.

Under the new order, those willing to work had a reasonable hope of being able to survive. They were no longer wholly dependent upon what their masters chose to do or failed to do. They were freed of the necessity of sweating out their lives to feed idle men of "qualitie." As a consequence, they now took more pains in a day than they had in a week, growing ten times more corn than before. Dale's reform, his one contribution, brought considerable improvement. But even greater was required, for the gaunt specter of famine was not yet laid. Virginia still faced years of hardship and almost incredible loss of life.

By 1616, after five years in the colony, Dale had grown weary of his labors for the Lord, especially in so unpromising a corner of the vineyard. Seeking more profitable employment, "having settled all things in good order . . . to his thinking," he sailed for home, never to return. As Newport had done, he entered the service of the East India Company, dying three years later in the Far East, a victim of tropical fever, efficient and brutal and self-righteous to the last.

As he had not much else to offer the adventurers for all of the money they had spent, the Marshal decided that they might be pleased if he brought back from Jamestown an Indian "princess" for their view. He had therefore embarked with Pocahontas and John Rolfe and their infant son, Thomas, who had been named for him as the child's godfather.

The ship also had on board Don Diego de Molina and his aide, Francis Lymbry, the English-born pilot. Held as prisoners since 1611 in spite of many shrill protests from Madrid, they were happy that the violent and summary Marshal had spared their lives and that they would soon be free again. But within sight of England, in a characteristic act, Dale suddenly turned upon Lymbry and hanged him from the yards, apparently just to assure himself that he still knew the ropes.

XIV

An Ingenious Young Man

*Thus what one officer doth, another undoth,
only aiming at their owne ends . . .*

—CAPTAIN JOHN SMITH

From first to last, the governors of colonial Virginia were an
imaginative lot in one respect at least. They let their fancy
free in describing their own accomplishments, though in elaborating that theme they all tiresomely said much the same thing.

Upon their arrival, they always found the colony in frightful
disorder and a sad state of decay. They always left it in a most
hopeful state, with all "defailments" corrected.

So, thanks to Dale and "contrary of many men's expectations,"
Virginia was now enjoying "great prosperytye & pease." Still,
half of the colony had died in the past few years, since the arrival
of his fleet and Gates' in 1611. Altogether, the Marshal left behind some 350 people—men, women, and children, now living
in six widely scattered and dangerously isolated communities.

At Henrico, near the Falls, were 38 men and boys, 22 of whom
were "farmers." A few miles below, at the Bermuda Nether
Hundred, was the largest settlement, with 119 people, including
17 farmers. Nearby, the West and Sherley Hundred had 25
men "imploied only in planting and curing tobacco, with the
profit thereof to clothe themselves and all those who labour about

the general business." There were only 50 men at Jamestown, including 31 farmers. Of the 20 at Kecoughtan, 11 were farmers.

Across the Chesapeake, at the tip of the upper peninsula guarding the Bay, was a more recent settlement, Dale's Gift. Here on the Eastern Shore, as it was then named and is still known, were 17 men engaged in fishing and making salt, all "fedd and maintayned by the colony."

In summary, there were 205 officers and laborers, and only 81 free farmers, who, of all the company, lived "most at ease." There were 65 women and children, perhaps an approximately equal number of each. This meant that there were ten men for every woman in the colony, a cause of restlessness and discontent that did not conduce to stability.

Repeating himself, Dale again assured the Company that Virginia was "one of the goodlyest & rychest kingdoms in the world," adding that as a token of better things to come he had brought home some "exceeding good tobacco, sassafras, pitch, potashes, Sturgeon & caviar, & other such Lyke commodytes."

"But yett no profitt is returned," the disappointed adventurers remarked. The things brought back were of no great value, and never would be unless they could be had in greater quantity and nearer home, for they did not even pay the costs of shipping.

The passage of time now forced the Company to wrestle with a new problem. Under the terms of its 1609 charter, the plantation was to be conducted on a joint stock basis for seven years. During that period there was to be no private trade, no private enterprise, and no private property of any kind, a system provisionally modified by Dale in part. At the end of the period, the Company was to declare a dividend in land to shareholders and to every freeman, whether a shareholder or not, who had "adventured" his person.

Henceforth, freemen were to be freemen in fact, and no longer the bond slaves of the colony and the Company. They were to be free to cultivate their dividends of land for their own profit and advantage. In addition, they were to be free to leave the colony and return home if they wished, and even to write letters without having them censored.

Though the seven years had elapsed, the Company could not carry out its promise without adding a new proviso, a mean joker. Now dependent largely upon the small running lotteries, it had no money for surveying and laying out the dividends of land, not to speak of providing a new governor and the supplies the planters so urgently needed. It therefore declared that only those who bought another £12 10s. ($625) share would receive their lands at this time—fifty acres a share, for the present, with more to follow. As few had any desire to buy another share, months passed before the Company found the means to dispatch a surveyor, a new governor, and the necessary supplies.

In their dilemma, the adventurers thought up two new schemes for breathing some life into Virginia. Both helped somewhat, at least keeping the colony alive, though they caused no end of complications later.

Eager for a large migration, far beyond what it could finance with its own meager resources, the Company began to issue extensive sub-patents to those adventurers who would transport large numbers of people to Virginia at their own expense and establish them there on unoccupied ground. These "particular" plantations were to be run solely for the profit of the adventurers involved, being virtually independent sub-colonies. For every person so transported, the "undertakers" were to receive a share in the Company and a hundred acres of land in the colony.

The first of these patents went to the always troublesome Captain John Martin, the "refiner," who was granted quite extraordinary privileges and immunities, soon a matter of fierce dispute. Another was given to Captain Samuel Argall and five associates, who received 2,400 acres on their promise to transport and settle twenty-four persons at their own charge.

Second, unable to supply the colony as amply as required, the Company turned that business over to a sub-company made up of those adventurers willing to risk their money in establishing a "magazine." This was a profit-making venture, though it never made a profit, a fruitful source of conflict for many years. The partners in the Magazine Company shipped goods to Virginia and traded them there for tobacco and other produce, sharing whatever profits or losses resulted. The Virginia Company was not involved except as it was an investor, having risked £800 ($40,000) in the venture, which it had to write off ultimately as a complete loss.

As he had spent five years recovering his "perfect health" in his "native ayre," the Company hoped that La Warr would now return to his post at Jamestown, but his Lordship did not yet find it convenient. As Deputy Governor to rule in his stead, the Company chose Captain Argall, that "ingenious, active, and forward young Gentleman" who had so well acquitted himself in kidnaping Pocahontas and burning out the French. To serve as his chief aide, the Company chose John Rolfe as Secretary of the colony, perhaps less for his merits than to honor his wife.

For a century or more, Indians had been seen occasionally in England. But never a "Princess," the daughter of a "King," and Pocahontas—or rather, Lady Rebecca—was honored and feted as royalty. Indeed, that harebrained pedant, King James, seriously questioned the presumption of a commoner like Rolfe marrying a "princess" without the Crown's consent. As such an offense was high treason, he ordered the Privy Council to ponder the matter.

As befitted her now Royal Highness, Lady Rebecca had brought along a large retinue, including a number of Indian maids and her brother-in-law, Uttamòtomakkin, more simply known as Tomakin. The latter was the chief of the party, the head of Pocahontas' household, having been sent along by Powhatan to discover all that he could about the English—how many of them there were, and what they lived on.

From the colonists' "continuall want and eagerness after corne," from their heavy labors to ship clapboard and similar products, Powhatan was convinced that England was a sparsely settled land with little food and few trees. "An understanding fellow," Tomakin came ashore with a knife and a stick upon which to notch the number of people he saw, but he soon gave that up.

Learning of Pocahontas' arrival, Captain John Smith snatched up his pen and wrote Queen Anne a letter to introduce the "Nonparella of Virginia." In this letter he related for the first time how that "tender Virgin" had thrown herself upon him and saved his life at Weromocomoco when Powhatan was on the point of beating out his brains, and how his life had again been saved when, at midnight, she came creeping "through the irksome woods" to warn him against surprise by Powhatan, who "had surely slaine her" if he had known.

"Jamestown, with her wild traine, she as freely frequented as her father's habitation," wrote Smith in handsome tribute, "and during the time of two or three years, she, next to God, was still the instrument to preserve the Colonie from death, famine, and utter confusion." [1]

In the houses of the great nobles, in the palaces of the highest churchmen, and even at Court, Lady Rebecca was paid every deference and entertained with pomp and circumstance. On Twelfth Night, she went to Whitehall to enjoy a masque written by the great Ben Jonson. She seemed pleased and made quite an impression, even upon critical professional courtiers, who generally agreed that they had seen "many English ladies worse favored, proportioned, and behaviored."

In a hat and elaborate ruff, toying with a fan, heavily clothed in stiff brocades, she sat for her portrait. Engraved by Simon de Passe, it was soon to be seen in many places.* This portrait of herself sitting in very solemn state as a great lady must have amused her, and how she must have laughed if she retained any of the high spirits and infectious gaiety of those days just a few years back when she was merely Little Wanton and used to gather up the boys and do cartwheels, naked, through the streets of Jamestown.

Still, she played her new role very well, with grace and style and remarkable poise, though the setting was strange and she was only twenty-one, carrying herself "as the Daughter of a King, and was accordingly respected not only by the great Virginia Company . . . but by divers particular persons of Honour." The Lord Bishop of London entertained her with "festival, state, and pompe" beyond anything he had ever offered other great ladies,

---

* The portrait bore the legend, "*Matoaka als Rebecka Filia Potentiss Princ: Powhatani Imp.* [Emperor] *Virginiae.*

according to the Reverend Samuel Purchas, who had met and liked her.

Presented at Court, Pocahontas was "graciously used" by the King, who was so taken with her "godly conversation" that he ordered the bishops to collect money in every parish "for the erecting of some churches and schools for ye education of ye children of those Barbarians in Virginia." Whether the once-so-condescending Rolfe shared these honors does not appear. But as a humble commoner, though married to royalty, he probably did not.

With its strange sights, sounds, and smells, and its even stranger rites and ceremonials, London evidently fascinated Pocahontas, and she wished to remain. But it was decided, "sore against her will," that she should return home, sailing with Governor Argall on his ships which, long delayed, were ready to depart at last, nine months after Dale's arrival.

Before the ships left the Thames, however, Pocahontas was suddenly stricken, dying within a day or two, probably of pneumonia. If the English found the climate of Virginia "searching," the Indians found that of England no less so, especially during the dark and dreary winter. Within a few months four of Pocahontas' Indian maids died, and all in her retinue had been ailing. Choked by the smoke and fog of London, she had retired up the river to Brentford, where she was when Captain Smith came to visit and talk with her for the last time.[2]

Sincerely mourned by him and many more, the Princess—or Lady Rebecca, or Mrs. John Rolfe, or Matoaka, or Pocahontas—was laid to rest with simple ceremony in the church at Gravesend, bringing "not more sorrow for her unexpected death than joy to the beholders to heare and see her make so religious and godly an end."

His "godly task" performed, Rolfe hurriedly wrote the Company to ask about the large pension it had bestowed upon Pocahontas, being anxious that "so liberall a stipend may not die with my wife but continue for her childe's advancement." He also asked the leaders of the Company to remember him "for some place of command and some estate of land to be confirmed to me and my childe."

Fearing that his infant son would not survive the passage, Rolfe left him in England, with Sir Lewis Stukley, cousin of Sir Walter Raleigh, whom Stukley villainously betrayed to his death. Soon marrying for the third time and raising another family, Rolfe never again saw the son born to him by Pocahontas, so far forgetting him, it appears, that he failed to mention him in his will.

Always venturesome, Argall tried a new and far shorter course to Virginia. Coming the northern route by way of Newfoundland and Cape Cod, he had a "speedy and prosperous passage," landing "all his men in good health," having lost only one of a hundred passengers along the way.

Since Dale's departure more than a year before, Virginia had been governed by Captain George Yeardley, one of the *Sea Venture* group and another graduate of "that universitie of the warres," the Netherlands, where he had served under Gates. Interested in tobacco himself, being the first in authority to appreciate that it was the best "commoditie they could devise for a present gaine," he had turned his own and other men's energies in that direction. With the result, said some, that Virginia was enjoying "peace and the best plenty that ever it had till that time."

But Argall was not impressed, finding everything "in ruinous condition." The colonists had "scarce ragges to cover their naked bodyes." The boats upon which the scattered settlements depended for trade, communication, and security in time of danger had been allowed to rot, being "out of repair" and "much spoyled." At Jamestown, where everybody was busily growing tobacco, even in the streets, Argall found "but five or six houses, the Churche downe, the Palizadoes broken, the Bridge [wharf] in pieces, the Well of fresh water spoiled . . . yea, the very Courts of Guard built by Sir Thomas Dale were ready to fall, and the Palizadoes not sufficiente to keepe out Hogs."

The Indians were "as frequent in their houses as themselves" and had become expert in the use of firearms, having many in their custody and possession. For one, Yeardley kept several braves to hunt for him, but all of this aroused no particular concern at this time. Powhatan's successor, Opechancano, had confirmed the league of peace and friendship, and Yeardley had recently concluded a treaty with the only formidable neighboring tribe, the Chickahominy, who in return for a few gifts to the chief and members of his council had agreed to become loyal subjects of His Majesty King James and pay an annual tribute of corn.

But the Indians were too poor to pay their debts and promised tribute, and Argall was worried, for the colonists had planted little corn. There was only one plow going in the entire country, for though they now had many oxen, the animals stood idle and useless as there was no one skilled in breaking them to harness. The fields were "wore out with maize," Argall noted, and could hold out for only a year or two. He could not clear new fields because he had no tools. It was all very discouraging, and Argall had no sooner landed than he asked to be relieved as governor.

Lest all starve, he immediately decreed that the colonists should plant at least two acres of corn for every acre of tobacco. But this edict was quietly ignored, for tobacco offered the sole means of procuring clothes, shoes, blankets, tools, and other necessaries. To regulate the trade, Argall ordered that no one was to sell tobacco at more—or less—than 3s. ($7.50) a pound, on pain of serving the colony as a slave for three years. As tobacco was bringing as much as 10s. ($25) a pound in England, the planters groaned at the little they were offered, but there was no help for that. Thanks to Yeardley's enterprise, the *George* soon departed with 20,000 pounds of tobacco on board—good, bad, but mostly indifferent, the adventurers complained. However, if sold at an average price of 5s a pound, the shipment was worth some £5,000 ($250,000), the first return of any consequence from Virginia, though most of the profits undoubtedly went to the partners in the magazine which supplied the goods that were traded for tobacco.

Like all the governors since Gates' day, Argall had been ordered to abandon Jamestown with its pestilential swamps and build a chief settlement elsewhere. Probably at Dale's suggestion, the Company had proposed the Bermuda Nether Hundred where there was now a small settlement named Charles City. But with all its faults, Argall preferred Jamestown and decided to put it in repair. Little was accomplished during the first summer, however, for disease again racked the fort and spread to other settlements. There was heavy mortality among the colonists, "far greater among the Indians, and a morrain [murrain, or pestilence] among the deer."

Even so, Argall reported to the Company that he had "improved almost everything." Still, he wished to be relieved of command. Everybody would be pleased to see La Warr "return to his Government." Meantime, he would do what he could, and on his efforts and decisions he hoped the adventurers would put "ye best construction." Little did they realize what a strain that was going to be!

Now that the joint stock was ended, Argall may have been honestly confused about what the Company intended and what course he should pursue under the circumstances. He may have assumed that all Company property was to be divided and broken up. In any case, that is how he chose to read his instructions. As it was now every man for himself, he did not intend to be the hindmost. Resolved to make a fortune for himself, he used his office for his own ends, for "many will make hay whilst the sunne doth shine, however it may fare with the generality."

A multiplicity of governors "is a great damage to any State," remarked Captain Smith with an eye on these years. "Thus what one officer doth, another undoth, only aiming at their owne ends, thinking all the world derides his dignity who cannot fill his Coffers, being in authority with anything. . . . And when they are fed fat, then in cometh others as leane as they were," and quite as determined to wax fat on the spoils of the land.

The Company had always admired the zeal of young Argall, that "everworthy Gentleman," and his zeal here was unmatched. He sold some of the Company servants to private planters for the term of their indentures, pocketing the proceeds. He removed the rest from Company lands and put them to work on his own "particular" plantation, at Argall Town, up the river a few miles from Jamestown. He sold the Company's livestock for his own account, though he asserted that he had been forced to do this to pay the wages which the Company had promised and never paid to the carpenters and other craftsmen. He forbade any trade with the Indians so that he might monopolize it for his own ends, seizing every opportunity to enrich himself both as Governor and as Admiral of Virginia.

Three Spanish vessels laden with hides had been captured by a ship in the employ of the Somers Island Company, which had been incorporated in 1615, at which time Virginia and Bermuda were divorced.[3] Suspecting piracy, the governor of Bermuda had sent the captain of the ship home to answer before the Board of Admiralty. Though the Somers Island Company denounced the piracy and disavowed any responsibility for the captain's acts, its statements were not entirely convincing, it seems, for the Admiralty and the Spanish ambassador continued to press the matter. Finally, to hush things up, the Bermuda adventurers agreed to pay £400 ($20,000) for the hides and took steps to recoup their loss.

Spreading the story that the hides had been spoiled and destroyed in an attempt to tan them, the governor of Bermuda secretly shipped them to Virginia where they were to be sold for the adventurers' account.* As contraband, they came into the hands of Argall as Admiral of Virginia. Sitting as his own Admiralty Board, he quickly handed down a decision, awarding the hides— to himself!

As rumors of this and other matters reached London, the Company did what it could to hasten La Warr's return to Jamestown. After seven years, he was now willing to go back "to make good the Plantation," having built himself a "very faire ship," the *Neptune,* on which he sailed early in 1618.

With him went some two hundred passengers—for the most part, servants in scarlet livery to wait upon his Lordship. Half of the others were Gentlemen of fashion, La Warr's friends and cronies. To have a "small number of adventurous Gentlemen to make discoveries and lie in garrison" might have been useful, "but to have more to wait and play than worke, and more com-

---

* As all members of the Somers Island Company were also members of the Virginia Company, the interests of the two sets of adventurers were always interlocked and often identical, as here.

manders and officers than industrious labourers, was not so neces-sarie," as Smith observed.

La Warr had no sooner departed than another letter came from Argall, quite insolent in tone and very disturbing. The adventurers were putting it very mildly and diplomatically when they in-formed him that it gave them "no pleasure."

Argall was offended that the Company had sent its letters to him through "so meane a man as the Cape Merchant," Captain Abraham Piersey, later a wealthy planter. He was highly incensed that Piersey had been joined with him "in equal trust." There was another thing the Company should know, and never forget!— he was not to be addressed as Deputy Governor, "he disdayning to be Deputy to any man."

He had told them before, he said, that the colonists needed clothes and had "to tend old ground for wante of tools." Why had such things not been sent? And "skilled husbandmen and meanes to set their Ploughs on worke"? With one plow, they had managed to plant thirty or forty acres of corn. But it "stood so long on the ground before it was reaped, it was most shaken." What little was harvested had been spoiled by the rats and cattle in the barn. To give Argall his due, he was a realist and did not entertain the Company with fairy tales.

"And you won't be overburdened with Tobacco," he sarcastically remarked, "nor with any other Commodity, because Tobacco is low and your goods high priced. And if the people fall upon hemp or other Commodity, it will be even as with Tobacco. You have wholly discouraged them."

Blandly announcing that he had sold all of the Company's live-stock for tobacco, Argall explained that he had hoped to dispose of the tobacco at 3s. a pound. But as it was not of the best quality, he had been forced to take much less for it, using the proceeds to pay the Company's debts in the colony. He was pleased to have been relieved of any responsibility for "ye magazine business," which was a fraud. As for the contraband hides, he knew quite well, being an Admiral, "how to dispose of unlawfull purchase."

Even Sir Thomas Smythe, related to Argall and a close friend, exploded at this. Many of the adventurers wished to carry the matter to Court, to make a formal complaint against Argall and "procure his Majestie's command to fetch him home." But others feared that this might set a dangerous precedent for the State to meddle in Company affairs and "give room to much publick Scandal and Reflection." Smythe and the Company officers therefore decided to proceed in a "milder and less clamorous way," sitting down to write Argall a blistering letter.

They had taken him to be an "honest Gentleman," they said, and "it is very strange to us to see you so changed."

What did he mean by encouraging the planters' "unjust accusations" against the magazine, "nourishing thereby, instead of pacifying, ye malcontented humors of such as seek to bring all to confusion?"

What was he hinting at in reporting that Opechancano and his braves had "given their country to Mr. Rolfe's child"? This could only be some sly "device" of his own.

As he very well knew if he had read his instructions, he had no authority to sell the Company's livestock. He had no authority to engross the Indian trade for himself and use the colony's boats for his own purposes. He had no right to detain the contraband hides, being well aware of "what trouble we had with the Lord Admirall and the Spanish ambassador, and how dearly they cost us."

By what right, they asked, "do you take the ancient Planters of the Colony who ought to be free, and likewise those from the Common Garden, to sett them upon your own imployments?"

What did he mean by using the store corn to feed his own men, "as if ye Plantation were only intended to serve your turne"?

As it had been planned to serve their turn, Smythe and the adventurers spluttered with rage. "Either you must think highly of yourselfe or very meanly of us in that, being our substitute, you will presume to offer us these wrongs and to suppose that you may doe what you list in such a publique cause without being called to accompt."

La Warr had already received orders to proceed against Argall, but the adventurers now sent a letter after him, amplifying his orders and urging him to proceed even more vigorously. His

Lordship should seize all of Argall's lands and goods, "as Tobacco and Furs, whereof it is reported he hath gotten together great store to the Colonie's prejudice." He should also seize Argall himself and ship him home "to satisfy the adventurers by answering everything as shall be laid to his chardge."

This letter was dispatched on a magazine ship, the *William and Thomas*, which sailed late in 1618 on what was to be a frightful voyage. The vessel ran into heavy wintry gales that drove her far off course. Supplies of food and water ran short, "ye fluxe" broke out, the captain and all officers died, leaving none with any skill in navigation. Of some two hundred colonists crowded on board, less than fifty survived the dreadful passage—a tragedy that sent cold chills down the spines of a poor and obscure company of English exiles in Holland, the original Pilgrim band, who had turned their eyes toward Virginia and were just then negotiating with the Company in the hope of obtaining free transportation.

Confident that La Warr had safely arrived at Jamestown and was restoring some semblance of order, having no doubt that their last letter would be delivered into his hands in good time, the adventurers turned to their constant concern, want of money.

What was their consternation a few weeks later when they learned indirectly, by way of a fishing vessel from New England, that La Warr had not reached Virginia, and never would!

His Lordship had died at sea, which meant that Argall could go on looting for months in his cool and contemptuous way, that their instructions and subsequent letter to La Warr would fall into his hands, that they could not stop his depredations until a new governor had been appointed and shipped out. The adventurers wrung their hands in impotent rage.

At the Azores, La Warr and many of his gallants had gone ashore to be wined and dined. Proceeding, the *Neptune* met with strong head winds and was driven slowly to the north. Many fell sick and almost fifty died, including the Lord Governor and many Gentlemen of fashion, whose bodies went over the side.

Though some suspected that they had been poisoned at the Azores, that seems unlikely, for the usual infection was raging on the "pestered" ship. Reaching New England and accidentally speaking the fishing vessel that brought the news of disaster to London, the *Neptune* slowly beat her way down the coast and finally dropped anchor at Jamestown after four months at sea, landing about 150 passengers. All weak and weatherbeaten, they brought ashore a "most pestilent disease (called the Bloody flux), which infected almost all the whole colonie"—"a disease never known before amongst us," said one ignorant of the afflictions of earlier years.

Not only was the *Neptune* carrying insufficient supplies for the people on board, but it brought the news that "great multitudes were a-preparing in England to be sent and relied much upon that victuall they should find there." Argall had twice warned about "what great miserie would insue" if large companies were sent out without ample provisions, but he now felt that this was no concern of his. Well aware that his days were numbered, for La Warr's instructions and the subsequent letter from the Company had fallen into his hands, no colonial governor was ever busier than he was during the next few months.

At this time, the notorious *Treasurer* put in, loaded with food, arms, and ammunition, having been chartered by Argall and his partners. The leader of the group was a powerful noble, Lord Robert Rich, soon to be Earl of Warwick, "a most designing, interested, and factious" member of the Company. It was Rich who had been instrumental in placing Virginia under the command of Argall, one of his "fastest friends and favourites."

As the colony was very short of food and ammunition, the supplies on the *Treasurer* would have been of great help. Far from putting anything into the store, the ship took corn from the dwindling supply at Argall's orders and put to sea, "manned with the ablest men in the colony"—ostensibly, to obtain salt and goats from the Azores; really, to make a "roving voyage on the Spanish dominions in the West Indies" under an old letter of marque issued by the King of Savoy. As this was plain piracy, the ship was to take refuge in the James in case of trouble, which gave some point to what the Spanish had long feared.

While the *Treasurer* was on the prowl, Argall gathered up whatever booty was close at hand, putting his spoils "under other

men's names and into the hands of great and powerful persons,"
like Lord Rich, so that the plunder could not be seized if anything
went wrong. Growing more daring and defiant, he even took the
servants off La Warr's plantation and placed them upon his own.

Serious conflict resulted when his Lordship's steward, Captain
Edward Brewster, vehemently protested. Now drunk with power
and enraged by any opposition—"a distemper very incident to our
American viceroys," as one of the colony's better historians, a
colonial Virginian himself, once remarked—Argall charged Brewster with mutiny and sentenced him to death. This was so outrageous that all of the ministers in the colony intervened and
Brewster was sent home in irons to have his "crime" reviewed
there.

Yet Argall, it is plain, was not half as unpopular in the colony
as he was at home. For one thing, he restricted his plundering
largely to Company property, and the planters could not work up
much sympathy for the adventurers after all they had suffered at
their hands. Second, he supported the planters' many just complaints about the Company's many broken promises, the delay in
laying out dividends of land, its failure to ship tools and other
essentials, the inefficient management of the magazine. Though
the Magazine Company had been granted a monopoly in the
tobacco and sassafras trade, he winked at private trade in these
and other articles, to the planters' advantage.

Though he was not responsible, many gave Argall credit for
the fact that under his regime they had been freed from bondage
and acquired lands of their own to cultivate. Lastly, he had not
been disposed to execute "in all severity" the savage martial law
laid down by La Warr and Dale. He freely pardoned many whose
offenses would have brought them to the gallows or the stake
under his righteous predecessors.

As has been well said of Argall, he "seems at least to have
understood the principle of Tiberias, that a shepherd should shear
his sheep, not flay them."

But the Company felt that it should do the shearing, and here
it was being fleeced. As soon as it learned of La Warr's death, it

appointed a new governor and ordered him to proceed to Virginia with all speed to seize Argall and his plunder.

Argall's partners, however, had anticipated this. Not wishing to lose their share of the loot, anxious about the piratical *Treasurer* business which might cost them their ship and their entire estates, Lord Rich and his partners hurriedly arranged to rescue Argall and carry away his spoils before the new governor arrived.

Quite unexpectedly, the *Elinor* dropped anchor at Jamestown early in April, 1619. Within two weeks, loaded with swag, she was at sea again—and just in time!

XV

The Burgesses

. . . we are not the veriest beggars in the world . . .
—JOHN PORY

As DISASTER piled upon disaster, an increasing number in the Company became sharply critical of Sir Thomas Smythe's administration. La Warr's untoward death and Argall's bold rapacity brought discontent to a head, leading to a change of management—which led, in turn, to more bitter quarrels as the adventurers cursed and clashed on questions of policy and on purely personal matters.

But whatever their views, no matter how discordant, the adventurers were agreed on one thing. They had to appoint a governor and send him out as quickly as possible to depose Argall and seize him before he made off with everything of value in Virginia. They would not have been surprised to hear that he had sold the colony itself.

Captain George Yeardley, Argall's predecessor, happened to be in London, having sailed home with some tobacco and his bride, Temperance Flowerdieu, who had been at Jamestown since 1609, arriving on the battered ships of the Third Supply. Now in his late thirties, an active and sensible man, a large and successful planter himself, he obviously had some knowledge of the country and its needs. In addition, he had already served as governor for more than a year. The Company therefore chose Yeardley on his promise "to proceed with all rigor" against Argall.

As a "reward" for his services, in the past and to come, the Company granted him 2,200 acres of land. And "to grace him the more," the King knighted him and he was now proudly Sir George, no longer one of the "common sorte." But some of his self-styled "betters"—in particular, Captain Francis West, the "runnygate"—still regarded him as a "mean fellowe," holding it against him that he had been a tailor in London before going off to the wars in the Low Countries and that his brother Ralph was in trade, keeping an apothecary shop at the "Signe of ye Hartychoke" in Wood Street. Yeardley's knighthood had gone to his head and had set him up so high, they complained, "that he flaunts it up and down the street in extraordinary bravery, with fourteen or fifteen liveries after him."

Indeed, so the gossip ran, he had spent £3,000 ($150,000) to outfit himself and his party for the return journey. If so, Yeardley's was the first considerable fortune to be made in Virginia, largely from tobacco and in less than ten years, for the Captain had arrived with nothing but his sword and buckler.

Late in April, 1619, after a "sore passage" that cost many lives, Yeardley reached Jamestown—just too late, for Argall had skipped on the *Elinor* about a week before. Perhaps Sir George was not too unhappy about this. Having already quarreled with Argall, knowing the latter's bold and daring ways, he had reason to fear serious trouble if he tried to arrest him and seize his plunder, for Argall had friends in the colony, having won them with his "good Licour and fayre protestations." With their help he had managed to escape with most of his loot, all of his "chiefest goods," leaving behind only his cattle and "some other things arising to no great valew."

To line his pocket, Argall had sold the common garden, most of the Company's servants, even the soldiers of the color guard provided for the governors. There was not a cow on any of the Company tracts. In short, all Company property was "utterly laid waste, . . . gone and consumed," as the adventurers wailed upon reading Yeardley's report, "there being not lefte at this time to the Company either the land aforesaid, or any Tennant, Servant, Rent or Tribute Corne, Cowe, or Saltworke." Nothing remained "but six Goates, . . . without one penny yielded to the Company for their so great losse."

All else was in ruins, too. Jamestown was in its usual state of near collapse, "with only those [brick] houses that Sir Thomas Gates built." At Henrico, once so promising, there were "three old houses, a poor ruinated church, with some few poore buildings." Several hundred people, almost half of the colony, had died within the year, largely from the pestilence brought on the *Neptune*. Everywhere, there was "great scarcitie of corne." With "fear of famine" acute, Yeardley immediately dispatched ships to obtain corn from the Indians and sent others as far as New England and Newfoundland for fish.

Discouraged from the start, Sir George found himself in unexpected difficulties when he tried to recover some of Argall's loot. The planters had bought the Company's servants, lands, and livestock in good faith and now refused to surrender them unless they got back what they had paid for them, which left Yeardley in a quandary. If he proceeded against the planters, there would be great commotion, loud cries of tyranny and injustice, and the planters were his friends. If he did not proceed against them, he would be in trouble at home. Also, there were those in the colony, some of influence, even members of the Council, who had been more or less involved in Argall's larcenies and opposed Yeardley at every turn. There were still others who had spoken untruths and signed fraudulent papers at Argall's instigation or dictation and were "now unwilling to give themselves the lie."

One of those unwilling to give themselves the lie was John Rolfe, who, as Secretary of the colony, had signed most of Argall's papers—deeds, titles, bills of sale, and other instruments by which the latter had defrauded the Company. Though he protested that his name was "unjustly joynted" with Argall's, he was prepared to defend whatever had been done, complaining that the charges against him and Argall had been made by "dishonest and faithless" men.

In all his years in the colony, he declared, "I never, amongst so few, have seene so many false-harted, envious, and malicious people (yes, amongst some who march in the better ranck). Nor shall you ever heare of any the justest Governor there who shall live free from their scandalles and shamelesse exclamations if way be given to their reportes."

But the Company was not interested in Rolfe's protest about his own innocence or his defense of the "justest Governor." He was in high disfavor and, though allowed to retain his seat on the Council, the Company displaced him as Secretary-Recorder, giving that lucrative post to one of the more interesting men of his day, John Pory, an indefatigable gossip whose long, breezy, amusing, and informative letters may still be read with pleasure.

Showing much promise as a youth, Pory had become a protégé of the great Richard Hakluyt, who had instructed him in "cosmographie and foreign histories." In 1600, he had published *A Geographical Historie of Africa,* a superior work that was well received. Entering Parliament, serving five or six years in the Commons, Pory then crossed to the Continent where he lived for some time, traveling widely and becoming something of a problem to his host of friends, many of whom occupied the most exalted positions in the realm.

Even in that day of Gargantuan appetites, Pory had made a name for himself as a trencherman and a tosspot, and his friends were constantly called upon to rescue him from some dire predicament or other, from a debtor's prison or worse. On one occasion when he was "in pawn" in Italy, a crony wrote his other friends to say that he needed meat and money, "for drink he will find out for himself if it be above ground or no deeper than the cellar."

Back in England in 1618 and penniless as usual, Pory was offered Rolfe's post, which he approached with great caution. Yeardley "infinitely desires my company," he told his friends, but when he inquired of the adventurers what they would allow him for his voyage and what he might expect to receive at Jamestown, they were as "dry as Pumystones, which is the reason I mean not to adventure my carcase in so dangerous a business for nothing."

When Yeardley promised to make his post worth at least £200

($10,000) a year, Pory accepted, provided Yeardley would lend him £50 ($2,500) to outfit himself for the voyage and his stay in Virginia.

A cultivated man of the world, one who had frequented the gayest and most intelligent circles in many lands, Pory brought charm and wit and sensibility to Virginia for almost the first time. Though Captain Smith and Argall sparked at times, the rest had been, for the most part, a dull and pretentious lot, solemn and self-righteous, entertaining an absurdly high opinion of themselves, never letting their eyes stray from the main chance.

Upon his arrival at Jamestown, Pory was first rather shocked by the "solitary uncouthness of the place." For one thing, he had to drink water. Not that he minded, he said, for "among these Christall rivers & odoriferous woods, I doe escape much expense, envye, contempte, vanity, and vexation of mind."

But uncouth as Jamestown was, "we are not the veriest beggars in the world," he added, for of a Sunday the local cowkeeper [Yeardley?] appeared in "fresh flaming silke," while the wife of one who at home "professed the black art, not of a scholar but of a collier at Croyden, wears her rough beaver hatt, with a faire pearl hatband, and a silken suit thereto correspondent."

Still, Jamestown provided no amusing gossip, no interesting talk, and no good company, "the soule of this life," said Pory, so he would keep his pen close at hand to write his friends and have "some good book always in store, being in solitude the best and choisest company."

What Virginia most needed, he observed, was the "English plough, Vineyards, and Cattle." If skilled men were sent out to cultivate the wild grape, the colony would soon "lade all ye ships that come with as rich wines as France and Spaine doth yield." But "of this subject enough," he said, after expatiating on it at some length, "for I thank God I drinke water here with as much (if not more) pleasure and content as I drank wine in other parts." Let the Company send out "husbandmen truly bred . . . both to manage ye Plough and breake our oxen and horses to that business."

At present, the colony's chief wealth lay in tobacco—or rather, as he shrewdly remarked, "in servants." It was they who grew the tobacco that made their masters rich. A planter with six servants could clear £1,000 ($50,000) a year, as some already had done. A planter without servants could hope to make £200 ($5,000) a year by his own labors.

Though assured that his fees would yield him at least £200 a year, Pory was still penniless, having obtained nothing as yet, he declared, "save only (if I may speak without boasting) a general reputation of integrity for having spoken freely to all matters according to my conscience and, as neare as I could discerne, done every man right."

Pory was being somewhat disingenuous here. A cousin of Yeardley's wife, he publicly attributed his appointment to that fact. The truth was that he had been appointed through the machinations of the Earl of Warwick and was now in his pay, as Yeardley soon discovered in intercepting his secret letters to Warwick on the Argall and *Treasurer* business.

Learning that Yeardley had discovered this clandestine correspondence, Warwick was furious, spreading the story to all in Virginia, even the Indians, that he was coming over soon to be governor, "with Captain Argall as his pilot, and that he would then call Sir George Yeardley severely into question for his government and take a full and sharp revenge."

This story gravely undermined Yeardley's prestige and authority in all quarters, and for telling it to the Indians, Captain Henry Spelman, now in his early twenties, was sentenced to be a slave to the colony for seven years.

Yeardley now clashed with Captain Francis West, objecting to the free and easy and over-generous manner in which the Captain was laying out lands for his late brother, the "thrice noble" La Warr. West went home in a huff, "whose help," snapped Yeardley, "may well be spared." In London, West got Warwick, Argall, and others to join him in demanding the appointment of a new governor, one with "personall Aucthoritye & greatness answerable to ye Action." It was impossible for a "vulgar and servile" spirit to govern a "vulgar and servile" people. The required obedience could never be commanded by "one no better than selected out of their own Ranke."

Let the Company send out some great nobleman, and then "many of ye Chiefe" in the colony, "now ready to revolt & looke home, would settle themselves with firmer Alacritye." Unless this were done, the petitioners threatened to "abandon and qwitt the Countrye & Action forever"—and it would have been well if they had.

With such powerful forces arrayed against him, meeting opposition on every side, Yeardley decided, being a "man of meek and gentle nature," that it was all too much for him, informing the Company that he wished to resign, for "I find it most fitt for me to live a retired life that I may not be wronged in that which is my deu and Right—I meane, my land of Weyanoke." Here, some miles above Jamestown, he had laid out his "reward" of 2,200 acres. His enemies now claimed that these lands lay within the bounds of Smythe's Hundred, a huge tract of 80,000 acres. Yeardley stoutly denied this, saying that he could write no more, "my harte being full of greyfe . . . that I am so unkindly and hardly dealt with."

Though worried and unhappy, Yeardley proceeded with vigor to institute, as instructed, a number of changes in the colony. All were for the better, and one was of the greatest consequence. Nothing in early Virginia can have been as widely and wildly acclaimed as Yeardley's proclamation that martial law was at an end, that Virginia was now to be governed "by those free laws which his Majestie's subjects live under in Englande," that "ancient Adventurers and Planters" were free of all service to the colony except for such duties as normally devolved upon members of any free community.

Every freeman who had been in the colony at the time of Dale's departure in 1616 was given a hundred acres of land, rent free, and as many more for each share he owned in the Company. Servants who had arrived before 1616 were also given a hundred acres, but they had to pay a quitrent of 2s. ($5.00) a year. Freemen arriving after 1616 were entitled to fifty acres each, at a quitrent of 1s. a year. Company servants were placed upon the public lands as tenants, being entitled to half of what they produced.

The system of public lands, too, was drastically transformed, entailing other basic changes. Given no specific remuneration, all officers had been charging the colonists extortionate fees for various services, being "carvers" of their own salaries, which naturally led to many gross abuses. The size of fees should be strictly limited, the Company commanded, especially those "of the Provost Marshalls and Jaylors, whereof we have dayly great Complaints."

To remove all temptation for oppression and corruption, "to ease all the inhabitants of Virginia forever from all taxes and public burthens"—what a laudable and ever-worthy-to-be-emulated policy!—the Company set aside 3,000 acres near Jamestown to be known as the Governor's Lands. In lieu of salary and other emoluments of office, the governor was to enjoy the produce and profits of these lands, and the Company promised to supply a hundred servants to work them, estimating with its usual optimism that the return from the lands would soon be worth £1,000 ($50,000) a year.

Similarly, tracts of 3,000 acres with a hundred servants attached were set aside in each of the four "corporations"—Jamestown, Henrico, Charles City, and Kecoughtan—for the "entertainment" of the members of the Council and other general officers. Smaller tracts of 1,500 acres with fifty servants each were provided for the support of borough magistrates and other local officers.

Every borough was ordered to lay out a hundred acres of glebe land for a minister and provide him with the equivalent of £200 a year. The Company had long professed interest in settling "godly, learned, and painful Ministers" in the colony, but had done little about it. There were only three ordained parsons in all of Virginia, one being Gates's chaplain, the Reverend Robert Buck, who had suffered much from the Company's many broken promises.[1]

As Virginia was now to enjoy the relative freedom of English law, the Company agreed in a momentous decision that the planters should have a "hand in the governing of themselves." They were granted the right to a General Assembly, which was to meet once a year "& no oftener but for very extraordinarie & Important occasions."

To guide the colonists in this unprecedented step, a charter defining the rights, powers, and privileges of the Assembly had been drawn up, largely the work of Sir Edwin Sandys, long an active member of the Company, having been Assistant Treasurer for several years now.

A libertarian in his political and religious views, Sandys had served in the Church for many years. Though he never took orders, he was given the lucrative post of prebend at York by his father, the Archbishop, who used the Church and its revenues to take excellent care of his many children. Resigning his sinecure after twenty years, during which he did little but collect his stipend and travel widely on the Continent, Sandys entered the service of the King, who knighted him in 1603 and bestowed upon him several large estates in Kent.

During his travels, Sandys had visited Calvinist Geneva and other centers of "heresy" on the Continent, visiting a number of Roman Catholic countries as well. Out of his observations he wrote *Europae Speculum,* an essay on the "State of Religion in the Westerne Parts of the World." It was a measured plea for tolerance and understanding of all Christian creeds, an argument against narrow and violent bigotry. Published in 1605, it so shocked the bishops that it was burned before St. Paul's Cathedral by order of the dread Court of High Commission, which was simply the Court of the Holy Inquisition sitting in Anglican vestments.*

Though once in royal favor, Sandys had since fallen from grace, partly because of his religious views but more because of his opposition in the House of Commons to the King's arbitrary acts, to his abuse of the royal prerogative as he busily and witlessly went on elaborating the doctrine of the divine right of kings. In 1614, Sandys had barely escaped being committed to the Tower of London for joining the great Sir Francis Bacon in a remonstrance against James's claims to absolutism and his encroachments upon the time-honored rights and privileges of the House.

* Not written for publication, Sandys' essay appeared without his consent, printed from a stolen copy, but Sandys never disavowed his views.

Some years later an enemy noted that he had been told by a friend of Sandys that there was "not any man in the world that carried a more *malitious* hart to the Government of a Monarchie than Sir Edwin Sandys did." He had been heard to say that if God had had a hand in framing any form of government, it was that of republican Geneva, and that in Virginia he "aymed at nothing more than to make a free popular state there," with himself and his "assured" friends as leaders.

Perhaps so, but no such views were reflected in the Virginia charter. It contained no radical proposals. It established a traditional and accepted form of representative government. It was notable only because it brought this traditional form to America for the first time.

Under the Great Charter, the General Assembly consisted of the governor and the members of the Council *ex officio*, and of "two Burgesses from each Plantation to be elected by the inhabitants thereof." Ten boroughs were authorized to send delegates to the Assembly, which is all we know, unfortunately, about the first election on our shores.

Who was entitled to vote? Probably all freemen of twenty-one or more. Bond slaves, the indentured servants, did not vote, of course. Nor did women, being the legal chattels of their lords and masters—indentured for life, so to speak.

How were candidates chosen? Were there local campaigns for rival slates? Was an Argall party opposed to a Yeardley party? Were candidates nominated by the people at large or picked by those in power?

A number of them, it is plain, were hand-picked or even self-chosen. Captain Ward's plantation was represented by the Captain himself and his chief lieutenant, and Lawne's plantation by Captain Lawne and his chief aide. Flowerdieu Hundred was represented by Lady (Temperance Flowerdieu) Yeardley's nephew.

But there were ordinary independent planters among them. One of the Burgesses from Henrico had arrived on the first ship as a laborer and had since come up in the world—Thomas Dowse, "the Taborer," who had lured the Indians at Kecoughtan to their doom and almost lost his life in stupidly trying the same ruse on the Appomattox.

On July 30, 1619, a day worth remembering, the Burgesses, twenty in all, assembled in Jamestown to exercise their wisdoms on behalf of Virginia, finding no better place to sit than the "Quire" of the church where La Warr had sat in ducal splendor with his green velvet cushion before him on which to kneel. After the Reverend Buck had led them in prayer, the Burgesses withdrew to the body of the church to make a bow to King James, "their most gratious and dread Soveraigne," being called in turn to take the Oath of Supremacy, "none staggering at it." * Returning to the choir, they took their seats alongside the Governor and the Council, who did not sit apart but with the elected representatives in the manner of the Scottish Parliament.

Two of the delegations were challenged. The Burgesses from Captain Ward's Plantation were soon seated, but serious complications arose in the case of those from Martin's Brandon, a "particular" plantation established some miles up the James by that irascible "refiner," Captain John Martin, as uncooperative as ever.

To its regret, the Company had granted Martin his lands "in as lardge and ample manner, to all intentes and purposes, as any lord of any manour in England doth holde his grounde." The Burgesses protested that they did not know what this meant, saying that it was impossible "to knowe the Prerogatives of all the manors in England." In the division of lands, Martin was demanding five hundred acres a share, five times what other "Ancient Planters" were receiving. Worse, he had been given the right to govern his plantation as he pleased, "free from any command of the Colonye," except for such aid and assistance as might be requested against a "forren or domestical enemy."

Martin's Brandon was virtually an independent principality

---

* Those taking this compulsory oath acknowledged the supremacy of the English Crown in spiritual affairs and renounced papal authority in ecclesiastical and civil matters. No good Roman Catholic could take this oath, and many of the left-wing Puritans objected to it, as did the Separatists (such groups as the Pilgrims and others) who had broken away from the Anglican Church.

within the colony, a quite impossible arrangement, and Martin had been exploiting his special privileges and immunities to attract settlers from other plantations.

It was notorious, the Assembly declared, that his plantation sheltered "divers bankrupt and indebted persons, with others of evill fame." Martin protected these "against the authoritie of the publique officers of this Collony and would not suffer them to be arrested for their debtes," commanding such officers "to departe his territorie, threatening them otherwise to lay them neck and heeles."

In addition, some of his men on a trading expedition to the Eastern Shore had committed numerous outrages against the Indians, a course likely "to breede danger and loss of life to others," for a sharp complaint about this, together with an ominous warning, had come from Opechancano.

Appearing before the Burgesses, Martin agreed to post security "for the good behaviour of his people towardes the Indians," for they had been indulging in a great deal of private marauding. But he absolutely refused to surrender his extraordinary rights and privileges.

"I hold my patent for my service done," he haughtily observed, "which no new or later comer can merit or challenge."

But the Assembly was of a different mind. It was not right for those at Martin's Brandon to make laws and then "chuse whether they would obey or not." On Yeardley's motion, the Assembly refused to seat its delegates, saying they were "spies rather than loyal Burgesses." In great anger Martin went home to join West, Warwick, Argall, and other troublemakers clamoring for Yeardley's recall.

In the stifling heat and dread miasma of Jamestown in midsummer, the Assembly gathered in the church each morning an hour after sunrise, at the third beating of a drum. As in the House of Commons, all sat with their hats on. When one was recognized by the Chair, he arose and stood uncovered while he spoke. And no one was to interrupt him until he had "finished his discourse, upon penalty of 100 pounds of tobacco."

Skilled in parliamentary matters from his years in the House of Commons, Secretary John Pory was chosen as Speaker and first read the "Great Charter, or commission of privileges, orders, and laws," which Yeardley had brought from London. Experienced in such proceedings, Pory introduced a "readie method" for studying and examining the Charter, dividing it into four "books," or sections, appointing a committee to consider each. The Assembly in general and the Burgesses in particular intended to have a good look at what was offered them.

Not that they would presume to correct what the "Council and Company in England had already resolved to be perfect," they said, but just in case they found something "not perfectly squaring with the state of this Colony or any lawe which did presse or bind too harde." In that case, they could then petition to have it changed, seeing that "this Great Charter is to bind us and our heyers forever."

Under the new order, the governor and the members of the Council were appointed by the Company as before. The governor had an absolute veto over the acts of the Assembly. Even those acts approved by him were not valid until they had also received the approval of the Company at one of its great quarter courts. The Assembly was both a legislative and a judicial body, being the only court of justice in the land.

Put to a vote, the Great Charter received "both the general assent and the applause of the whole Assembly." Still, its members had some suggestions to make and drew up a petition to the Company. Among other things, it pointed out the impossibility of the planters' paying taxes, rent, and other charges in coin, "whereof we have none at all." Rather, the Company should appoint a Sub-Treasurer to reside in the colony and collect the "true value" of rent and other obligations in tobacco and commodities—a sensible suggestion soon adopted.

Also, as no act of the Assembly was valid until approved by a quarter court of the Company, so the Assembly should have the "power to allowe or disallowe of their orders of Court"—a sensible suggestion summarily rejected.

Having quickly disposed of the Charter and related matters, the Assembly turned with the bright-eyed zeal of a novice to

perform what it regarded as its first duty, the reform of prac-
tically everything, establishing a pattern that has long since become typically American. Addressing itself to all kinds of problems—moral, religious, social, political, and economic—it passed
any number of measures that one would expect to find only in
Puritan New England.

All had to attend the two Sunday services, morning and afternoon, and bring their "peaces, swordes, poulder, and shotte" with
them, on pain of a fine of 3s. ($7.50) for every unexcused ab-
sence. This may have seemed rather rigorous to some, but they
were no longer threatened with death for their third unexcused
absence. On Sunday afternoons, after the service, ministers were
to catechize those "not yet ripe to come to the Communion" on
pain of "severe" censure. At all times, the ministers and church
wardens were to nose out all "ungodly disorders" and such
"skandalous offences as suspicions of whordomes, dishonest keeping with weomen, and such like." If suspension from the church
or excommunication did not induce reform, such sinners were to
be locked up and have their estates confiscated.

For every oath or curse, a freeman paid 5s. ($12.50), while a
servant paid with his hide, receiving a sound lashing. For being
drunk, one was first "reprooved privately by the minister"; for a
second offense, reproved publicly; for the third, "to lye in boltes
12 howers in the house of the Provost Marshall and pay his fees";
for the fourth, to suffer whatever punishment seemed good to the
magistrates.

To curb "excesse in apparell," about which the Company had
begun to complain, it was decreed that a man should be taxed
by what he wore. If he were unmarried, he should pay according
to his own apparel; if married, "according to his owne or his wife's,
or either of their apparell." If and when caught, those "gaming
at dice or Cardes" were to pay 10s. ($25) and have their win-
nings confiscated; both their winnings and their fines were to be
applied to "charitable and pious uses."

The Assembly's pronouncements on economic matters were
equally arbitrary and naive. Tobacco was to be sold at no more—
and no less—than 3s. a pound for the best leaf, and half that

amount for the second grade. Four "tasters" of tobacco were appointed to establish the grade, having authority to burn all inferior stuff before the eyes of the planters who grew it, to put them to shame.

Planters had to provide for every member of their households, including indentured servants, "one spare barrell of corne." They each had to plant ten wild grape vines a year, a hundred flax plants, and six mulberry trees so that they might raise silkworms.

No one was to trade with the Indians, or fish in the James or the Chesapeake, without a license. Official authorization had to be obtained to slaughter "any neat cattle whatsoever, young or olde," on pain of "forfeiting the valew of the beast so killed." With cows selling at £15 ($850) a head, the penalty was onerous.

No one was to sell to the Indians any hoes, or "any English dog of quality, as a mastive, greyhound, bloodhounde, land or water spaniel, or any other dog or bitche whatsoever of the English race." There was a 5s. fine for this, while the hangman awaited those who sold them "any piece, shott, poulder, or any other arms, offensive or defensive."

As recommended by the Company, the Assembly decreed that new plantations should be spaced at least ten miles apart, though Governor Yeardley and others voiced the fear, more than justified by events, that "in these troubled times" it was dangerous to have the colony so widely dispersed.

On August 4, the fifth day of the session, Yeardley adjourned the Assembly "by reason of the extream heat, both past and likely to ensue," announcing that he would call it again in the spring. Most of the Burgesses were ill. One had died. Yeardley had been ailing, and Speaker Pory was "extreame sickly and therefore not able to passe through long harangues."

As its last act, the Assembly instructed Pory to report its proceedings to London, which he did, and "to present their humble excuses to the Treasurer, Counsell, and Company in England for being constrained by the intemperance of the weather and the falling sick of diverse of the Burgesses to breake up so abruptly."

They were sorry, they said, not to have brought matters to "more perfection, being for the present enforced to send home titles rather than lawes, propositions rather than resolutions, attempts than achievements." They hoped that those in London would accept their "poor endevour" and be "ready to supporte the weakness of this little flocke."

The Burgesses, the Council, and the Governor need not have been so apologetic. Their decisions were certainly as sound and sensible as any yet taken in or about Virginia, and when Sir Edwin Sandys came to review them, he found them, "in their greatest parte, to be very well and judicially carryed & performed."

None of their particular acts was of any moment, to be sure. But even if the Burgesses had done nothing, they had made history by meeting and discussing problems that were the common concern of all. The planters of Virginia had acquired a measure of self-government, an instrument of freedom, that would stand them in good stead and provide them with a rudder to steer an ultimately safe course, however unsteady, through many severe storms.

The stormiest years lay just ahead as all of Virginia's old enemies gathered to attack her—hunger, disease, Indians, and stubborn folly on the part of those at home, now actuated by great good will and the best of motives, but still willfully blind to the necessities of the colony and stone deaf to any advice.

XVI

Under New Management

Choose the Devil if you will, but not
Sir Edwin Sandys!

—JAMES I

UNKNOWN to those in Virginia, a change had been made in
the command at home. The Company was under new management, news that would have eased Yeardley's worries and made
him somewhat less disconsolate.

In May, 1619, having been Treasurer for ten years, Sir Thomas
Smythe decided to retire and asked the Company to "elect some
worthy man in his place." He was getting old, he said, and as he
had recently been appointed a commissioner of the Royal Navy,
he could no longer give the business the "good attention" it required. He had, he told the adventurers, only two requests to
make—"their good report, according as he hath deserved," and a
speedy auditing of his accounts so that he might have, before he
died, his "*Quietus est* under the Companie's seale." He was given
a good report as the formalities required, but never his *Quietus est*,
for his books were found to be in great disorder.

Smythe's resignation, it appears, was not as voluntary as he made
out. One of the great merchant princes of his day, Smythe had
irons in many fires—in far too many for him to give the business
the "good attention" it required. His subordinates were rightly

suspected not only of "negligence in their Office" but of "collusion and unfair Dealing." More and more adventurers found fault with his administration. They did not, for the most part, have any criticism to make of the brutal martial law he had allowed in Virginia, or of the endless foolish directives that had distracted the colony and dissipated its energies for years, or of the Company's many broken promises to the usually desperate men along the James. But they were concerned that after spending so much money, they had received no dividend at all, not so much as a penny.

Effecting a temporary alliance, two very different and soon implacably hostile groups united to unseat Smythe, or at least force his withdrawal. The leaders of the first and larger group were the Earl of Southampton and Sir Edwin Sandys, both of whom in national affairs stood with the Parliament in its resistance to the pretensions of Stuart absolutism as expounded by James and the Court. The other group, composed of the Lords and Gentlemen in the Company, was led by the Earl of Warwick and his kinsman, Sir Nathaniel Rich. Warwick had taken violent exception to the strong measures which Smythe had aimed at Argall, measures that directly touched Warwick's interests and reputation as an honest man.

Sandys was chosen as Treasurer, defeating the candidate of the Court party, Deputy Treasurer Robert Johnson, now an alderman of London. Johnson hoped at least to succeed himself as Deputy Treasurer, but was defeated by Sandys' close friend, John Ferrar, a merchant of London, son of a wealthy skinner. As a "gratification," the Company voted Smythe twenty shares of "Old Adventure." Pointedly, and in a petty spirit that all had cause to regret, Deputy Treasurer Johnson was not given so much as a vote of thanks for his ten years of service, which created more ill will and personal rancor.*

---

* An effort was made at this time to unseat Smythe as Treasurer of the Somers Island Company. Sandys stood against him, but Smythe was re-elected. At this time, too, he was re-elected as governor of the East India Company. As he continued to be active in many other companies, his new royal commissionership cannot have taken up too much of his time, energy, and "good attention."

The new administration began well enough, arousing high hopes on both sides of the Atlantic. Though not particularly a man of business, Sandys was sincerely devoted to Virginia and had a disinterested zeal that promised much. Both he and Deputy Treasurer Ferrar were full of ideas and eager to carry them out. Though some had been tried before, they were determined to try them again, convinced that if undertaken with energy and on a sufficiently large scale, they could be made to work for the profit of all.

They agreed with Dale on the necessity of a great disbursement. Nothing could ever be accomplished by piecemeal commitments of men and money. They could not build to any purpose until a broad base had been laid. Their principles were sound enough, but their specific plans and practices left much to be desired, proving to be as calamitous as any.

The "inordinate excessive plantinge of Tobacco," upon which Virginia solely depended for trade, her one successful enterprise, should be stopped. It was extremely displeasing "to the Kinge and scandalous unto the Plantation and unto the whole Company" that so many years and so much money had been spent with nothing to show for them but "that smokie weed of Tobacco." Men could never be induced to invest their money in the Company and the colony if they were "to be paid in smoke."

Rather, the authorities at Jamestown should bend the planters' energies toward better things—iron works, wine works, glass works, salt works, silk houses, sawmills, shipyards, fishing fleets, tar plants, pitch plants, turpentine distilleries, and the growing of hemp, flax, silkgrass, and other "more solid commodities." But first, Virginia had to have more people. Of the 2,500 sent out, only 600 remained, far too few to accomplish anything of consequence, least of all the ambitious projects that they had in mind. Migration had to be encouraged or forced by every means at hand.

As it had done before, the Company turned to the printing press to confute all "scandalous" reports about the colony. Sitting down with a London physician, one Dr. Winston, who knew nothing about Virginia, Sandys penned another tract about that "earthly Paradise," with its "very healthful" climate, "goodliest woodes, . . . excellent fish, Fowle in very great store and variety," and its assurance of the richest commodities, everything from pearls and silk to almonds and olives. Due to the machinations of the Devil, "the great enemy of all good Actions," the colony had suffered somewhat, but the planters had finally won the favor of God by "better attending the Divine worship and more carefully observing his Holy and just lawes."

Though Yeardley had reported "great scarcitie of corne" and a fearful epidemic along the James, where hundreds had died and all had been "sore shaken with burning fevers," the Company asserted that Virginia had grown, "on a sodaine, . . . to double that height, strength, plenty, and prosperity which it had at other times attained." Any who said otherwise were "false and malicious," and the Company threatened criminal action against these "turbulent spirits," suspending some of its own members for "scandalizing" Sandys' *Declaration* by challenging its preposterous statements.

In 1619, the Company succeeded in recruiting and shipping to Virginia more than 1,200 people. During the year, almost 1,000 died on the ships or in the colony, "to the consumption of divers Hundreds and almost the utter destruction of some particular Plantations." Saying that they were sorry to hear this, Sandys and Ferrar advised the planters to pray harder as they pushed ahead with more ambitious plans for the next year.

One of Virginia's greatest needs, they decided, was a proper seal in the form of a coat-of-arms. As the Virginia "cote" first appeared, engraved by William Hole, official "sculptor of the iron for money," the escutcheon was quartered with the arms of England, Ireland, Scotland, and France.* Above, as a crest, appeared a native queen, an Indian princess, wearing a many-pointed oriental crown and looking something like a mermaid with her long hair flowing down over her shoulders to conceal her arms, but revealing her naked breasts, well pointed and placed almost on top of one another. At the sides, leaning on the escutcheon and rather drunkenly supporting it, were two bowlegged knights in plumed

* The arms of France had appeared on the royal escutcheon since 1337, when Edward III asserted his claim to the French throne. They were not removed till 1915, during the First World War.

helmets, beavers open, each holding an upturned lance. Below, ran the Latin legend: *En dat Virginia quintam.*[1]

Behold, Virginia gives the Fifth Crown!

Though a pretty conceit, it was of no particular help at the moment as the Company scoured the highways and the byways for more people. As Dale had first suggested, the Crown now ordered that certain convicted felons should be delivered to the Company and transported to Virginia, there to be banished for life.

As the savage law of the day made felonies of and prescribed the death penalty for some three hundred offenses, down to such minor misdemeanors as stealing anything worth more than a shilling, many of these so-called felons were merely poor hapless wretches who, in their distress, had tried to make off with a few loaves of bread perhaps, or a coat, or a pair of shoes. But there were hardened criminals among them no doubt, and it added to Virginia's disrepute that it was now to be peopled from the jails.[2]

Virginia's repute was bad enough already, even among felons. When two convicted thieves were offered their lives if they would go to the colony, they answered "at once, decidedly, and with one accord," that they preferred to die quickly on the gallows than by slow degrees along the James.

There were other poor wretches—and not convicts, either—who were offered no choice in the matter. For some time, since early in Elizabeth's reign, England had swarmed with "vagrants" and "sturdy beggars," thrown out of employment or off their small farms by rapid economic change, and now as the King and Court traveled about the country, they were trailed by a hungry crowd, "divers idle young people," who hoped to pick up a few crumbs from the royal table or earn a sixpence perhaps by running an errand for some courtier.

Their presence annoyed the King, who issued orders that these "dissolute" youths should be seized and shipped to Virginia, there to be reformed and taught some industrious way of life. The unfortunate young people were sent to London and as no ship was ready to sail, had to be locked up in the Bridewell, which was not the best place to begin their reform, for the notorious Bridewell, one of the foulest of the universally foul prisons in the land, was always filled to overflowing with the wildest and lewdest women of the town.

To dragoon more youths, even mere children, the Company evolved an ingenious idea of its own. It suggested that the London authorities should pick some of the "vagrant Boys and Girls that lie and beg in the streets" and deliver them for shipment to Virginia, where they would be put to work by the planters and trained in "some industrious courses."

The Lord Mayor and Council were delighted, apprehending a hundred children, both girls and boys, aged eight to sixteen. They were even persuaded to pay the cost of feeding, clothing, and transporting them, estimated at £5 ($250) a head. As the Company planned to sell the children for much more, it anticipated a sizable immediate gain, not to speak of the long-term profit to be reaped from having more hands at work in the fields along the James.

The boys were to serve their masters for a long period of years, till they were twenty-four. Girls were to serve until they were twenty-one, or married. When their indentures had expired, each was to have fifty acres of land.

But the children, the ungrateful wretches, wept and cried out against these "very beneficial conditions," refusing to go to Virginia where, "under severe masters," they might be "brought to some goodness." This created a difficult problem, for the Lord Mayor had no authority to deliver them or the Company to transport them without their consent. But the law was nicely evaded by obtaining a special warrant from the Privy Council, and the London waifs were shipped on the *Duty,* together with the "dissolute" youths from the Bridewell.

All of this cargo, human livestock, was quickly sold to the planters at £10 a head, paid in tobacco rated at 3s. a pound. But when the tobacco came to be sold, it brought less than 2s. a pound, and the adventurers commanded the planters to make up the difference and save the Company from "losse." As the Company had invested nothing, it had lost nothing. Whatever it received—more than £600 ($30,000)—was net gain, thanks to the taxpayers of London who had paid all costs. Nevertheless, the Company kept pressing the masters of the "Duty boys" to pay their "debts," which they were not disposed to do.

Even so, the adventurers were happy about this business and soon asked the London authorities to supply more children "upon reasonable Termes." Expanding the idea, Sandys wrote to justices of the peace throughout the realm asking them to seize and deliver to him "all such younge youths of 15 years and upward as they shall find burthensome to the Parish where they live," together with £5 each to pay shipping and other costs.

Growing more enthused about this ready method for having the public contribute men and money at the same time, Sandys suggested to Parliament the enactment of a law compelling every borough, town, and city to contribute "to the sending of their poore with whom they are pestered into Virginia." Though the proposal was greeted in the Commons "with a verie great and gratefull applause," nothing came of it, which was disappointing, as was the want of response to the letter sent to the justices of the peace.

Just when Sandys and Ferrar hoped to do so much, the Company's resources had never been so low. In resigning, Sir Thomas Smythe had cheered the adventurers with the report that he was leaving £4,000 ($200,000) in the treasury. But this was a verbalism, as Sandys soon discovered, for he had also left behind a stack of unpaid bills, some running back more than ten years, and these totaled more than £4,000.

Moreover, Smythe's accounts had been badly kept. Many adventurers who had invested large sums now discovered that they were not registered as stockholders. In the case of other adventurers, there were no receipts to show whether they had actually paid in their money or not. There were no warrants for many large sums allegedly spent. After wrestling with the books for months, the auditors declared that they could make nothing of them.

Plainly, those hired to conduct the Company's business had been careless and incompetent, even corrupt, as Smythe acknowledged in promising to make good "what damage appeareth hath been done to the Company by such officers as he trusted." In spite of this promise and his professed desire to have his accounts speedily cleared, Smythe procrastinated and obstructed, as Sandys complained, pointing out the Company's desperate need to know just where it stood financially and what money was owed it.

"I had thought," he remarked, "that no man carrying the face of an honest man could be displeased with being called to an Account, being the only justification & discharge of a true man. But it has fallen out otherwise. Instead of thanks for my labors, I have reaped a mass of malignitie."

Sandys was even more roundly abused when he sought to untangle the complicated affairs of the Magazine Company, which was deeply in debt and the object of constant criticism by the planters. Even its agent at Jamestown, Cape Merchant Peirsey, objected to the "aboundance of needless Comodities" foisted upon him in place of the "Ploughes and other necessaries" he had so frequently requested. Eager to recover the money which the Company had put into the venture, Sandys asked the manager of the magazine, Alderman Johnson, for an accounting. Johnson promised to bring in his books, but never did.

The Company, after much wrangling, decided to abolish the magazine. Hereafter, trade was to be "free and open to all men." But a proviso was added that the magazine's stock of goods at Jamestown, valued at £5,000 ($250,000), had to be sold before other goods would be admitted. This, too, was never settled, keeping the witches' cauldron boiling.

As there had been next to no return on an investment of £80,000 ($4,000,000), it proved to be quite impossible to persuade anyone to buy Company shares. During 1619, in spite of every effort, Sandys succeeded in raising only £37 10s. ($1,875) of "new adventure." Many who had made pledges now refused to honor them. Some money continued to come in from the small running lotteries, but this source was drying up. And now, upon the complaint of the House of Commons, the King abolished the lotteries as a public nuisance, leaving the Company with a large quantity of silver plate and other prizes to be disposed of at a loss.

Had it not been for large personal advances made by Sandys

and others, as much as £400 ($20,000) at a time, the Company would have foundered.

As if there were not confusion and contention enough, Argall had returned and now appeared with his mocking and scornful smile. Taking shelter behind the Earl of Warwick and other powerful protectors, he fended off all attempts to bring him to book for looting Virginia. The Company, however, made one point against him—and against itself as well.

Argall had exceeded his authority in condemning Captain Edward Brewster to death by court martial. No officer in Virginia had ever had the right to render judgment by court martial, for none of the charters had vested the Company or its representatives with any such powers—which was some solace to Brewster, but little to the scores who had been summarily hanged, shot, burned, broken on the wheel, or chained to trees to starve by Gates, La Warr, and Dale.

Now came grave news about the notorious *Treasurer*. Yeardley had confirmed the adventurers' worst fears, reporting that Argall had sent the ship "to rob the King of Spain's subjects in the West Indies, by direction of my Lord of Warwick." [3] Under its charter the Company was obliged to keep the Privy Council informed of all things that might become matters of State, and the piratical course of the *Treasurer* was certainly one of these, Sandys and the Royal Council of Virginia agreed, especially as the Spanish ambassador was loudly complaining. Taking extraordinary pains to shield all concerned, even Argall, "considering how deeply this might concern my Lord of Warwick, not only to the the loss of of his ship and goods, . . . but be of far more dangerous consequence to his person and estate," they managed the case so discreetly that it was "dismissed without prejudice to any, and so rested very quiett."

But like all else in the Virginia business, it did not rest quiet very long. Another letter came from Yeardley, more disturbing than the first, to report that an armed Dutch frigate, commanded by an English captain and manned by an English crew, had put in shortly after the adjournment of the Assembly. Having been on the prowl with the *Treasurer*, she had been sent ahead to learn how things stood in Virginia, whether Argall was still in command or not. On board, she had a number of slaves captured or stolen in the West Indies. Learning that Argall had fled, her captain quickly put to sea, having meantime sold to Governor Yeardley, Cape Merchant Peirsey, and others for corn and tobacco twenty "Negars"—with two Negresses among them—adding a new and major strain to the First Families of Virginia.

Shortly, also carrying stolen Negro slaves, the *Treasurer* put in under the command of Captain Daniel Elfrith, an old hand at "slie" courses. Warily anchoring at Point Comfort, he sent word to the Governor "to know his pleasure." Yeardley ordered him to come up to Jamestown so that he might seize his ship, as ordered. But without awaiting Yeardley's reply, not liking his "cold entertainment," Elfrith weighed anchor and put to sea, making for Bermuda, warning those at Point Comfort that unless they got some cannon mounted, "the Colonie would be quite undone—and that, ere long—, for undoubtedly the Spanyard would be here the next Spring" to take revenge for the injuries he had suffered.

This warning caused great alarm, not only at Jamestown but in London. Sandys and the Royal Council decided that the Company's innocence in the matter had to be quite clearly established, for the tough crew of the *Treasurer*, "dangerous-tongued fellows," were growling that they had been cheated of their share of the spoils, threatening that if not paid their "utmost penny of wages, they would go to the Spanish ambassador and tell all."

To protect the Company's interests, Sandys and the Council felt impelled to inform the Privy Council of Yeardley's second letter, as the Warwick-Argall faction complained, "and so put upon my Lord of Warwick suddenly a confiscation of his ships and goods." Again, the matter was hushed up, and all of those involved agreed to take communion together "in confirmation of their mutual accord."

But hard feelings remained and opened a breach that was never closed. Warwick and Argall now joined forces with Sir Thomas Smythe and Alderman Johnson, their recent enemies, in an effort to unseat Sandys and break his party's control of the Company, hatching their plot at Smythe's great house in Philpot Lane, the Company's former headquarters, with the King attending.

In May, 1620, when the Company met to elect officers for the year, a stranger walked in, announcing that he had a message from the King. It was his Majesty's pleasure that the adventurers should choose one of the following as Treasurer—"Sir Thomas Smythe, Sir Thomas Roe, Mr. Alderman Johnson, or Mr. Maurice Abbott, and noe other"!

Resenting this intervention, jealous of their rights and privileges, the adventurers listened in silence and then went on with their regular business. That completed, Sandys left the Chair and the meeting with the remark that they should now proceed to elect officers "according to the message lately receaved from his Majestie."

The adventurers found themselves "at an exceedinge pinch." If they did as commanded, they would suffer a "great breach into their Privilege of Free Election, graunted to them by his Majestie's Letters Patent." If they ignored the message, there would be trouble, for James, always spiteful and unscrupulous, had many ways to work his will.

To escape this painful dilemma, the Company violated a provision of its charter and postponed the election to the next quarter court, appointing a committee of notables to talk with the King. Led by the Earl of Southampton, they were to persuade him that he had been "much misinformed about the managing of their business this last year."

Sandys let it be known that he would gladly continue as Treasurer. He had accomplished more in one year with £8,000 ($400,-000), he declared, than Smythe had in twelve years with ten times that amount, as shown by their respective accounts, "if yet his be an account." He was being opposed only because he had done his duty—first, in refusing to abet Smythe and Johnson in courses which had led "to the dishartning of all Adventurers & the perpetuall keeping down of the Plantation"; second, because he would not tolerate the schemes of Warwick and his friends "for the enriching of themselves, or some of them, by meanes so unlawful as to the enhazarding of the destruction & utter extirpation of the Colonie."

But the King was not interested, raving and ranting in his habitual manner, telling Southampton and his committee that the Company had become the "seminary of a seditious Parliament," that Sandys was his greatest enemy, and that he could hardly think well of anyone who was his friend.

"Choose the Devil if you will," he exclaimed, "but not Sir Edwin Sandys!"

At the next quarter court, Southampton reported that his Majesty had "most gratiously condiscended" to allow the Company a free choice in selecting a Treasurer, that the messenger previously sent had misinterpreted his instructions, according to James. But the King had qualified this freedom of choice, saying that he would be pleased if the Company were to select "such a one as might, at all times and occasions, have free access unto his royall person."

As one of the great nobles of the realm, a member of the Privy Council, the Earl of Southampton obviously qualified. After "some final pause" he agreed to stand as Treasurer and when no other candidates came forward, the Company declared him elected unanimously.

Though Sandys had been unseated, the Smythe-Warwick factions would have been better advised to let well enough alone. The new Treasurer brought great personal prestige and politieal influence to the office, and he stood squarely behind Sandys, who exercised as much power as ever and was now shielded by the Southampton name.

As had been arranged at the Earl's request, Sir Edwin and his "honest & carefull" deputy, John Ferrar, continued to manage the affairs of the Company. It was they who shaped policy and directed operations, to the mounting fury of their opponents and to the growing concern of many friends, who kept cautioning them against being too much in a hurry, praising their zeal but advising them to temper it with some discretion.

XVII

The Rolls

*. . . I pray, Sir, give me tyme both to
provide meanes, and to build and settle,
before you lay on Load.*

—SIR GEORGE YEARDLEY

VIRGINIA needed so many things, and the Company had so
little money to provide them. Some new manner of proceeding, some new method of finance, had to be devised.

Pondering the matter, Sandys and Ferrar had an ingenious and
what seemed to be a happy idea, one that would enable them to
carry out all of their ambitious projects at once. They would set
up a separate "roll" for each.

Under their plan, the adventurers did not have to approve
of all the projects. If one seemed likely, they could invest in that
by signing the "roll" and signifying the amount they were willing
to risk. All profits—and losses—were to be shared by the sub-
scribers, and it should be said for Sandys and Ferrar that they
did not restrict or dictate their choice, offering them any number
of ways of losing money.

Rolls were set up to accomplish all kinds of things—to build
shipyards—to operate a fishing fleet in New England and Newfoundland waters—to establish a fur trade—to obtain "improved
silke-worme seede" from Spain and other countries—to obtain
French silkmasters from Languedoc—to obtain more French

vignerons—to obtain German carpenters and millwrights—to obtain skilled glass-makers from Venice—to obtain experienced furnace hands and iron workers from the Midlands.

Other rolls were established to provide the colony with food, clothes, livestock, tools, and "choyce Maids," who might make the planters "more settled & less moveable, who, by defect thereof . . . , stay there but to get something and then return for England, which will breed a dissolution and so an overthrow of the Plantation." There was not one woman to thirty men in the colony and, as a later governor observed, "*populus virorum* is of no long duration anywhere."

The first of these maids, "younge & uncorrupt," were soon dispatched. Where or how they were obtained is not clear, but the assembling of this fair merchandise had caused panic in many quarters. The Privy Council ordered the arrest of a messenger of the Court who had been going about pretending that he had a royal commission "to press maidens to be sent to Virginia and the Bermudas," creating "such a terrour to the poor maidens," the Privy Council was informed, "that forty have fled from one parish to obscure places and their parents do not know what has become of them."

Another, a clerk later hanged as a coin-clipper and counterfeiter, had been using his commission "to take up rich yeomen's daughters, or drive them to compound, to serve his Majestie for breeders in Virginia."

No matter how obtained, many of these maids were doubtless "younge & uncorrupt," but a number, it appears, came from the infamous Bridewell and other jails.

More and more people were recruited in spite of Yeardley's warnings, repeated by many others, that what Virginia needed was "rather a few able sufficient men, well provided, than great multitudes." Most of those sent out in 1619 had perished. As Sandys and Ferrar planned to dump even more upon Yeardley without warning, they decided to send him a present "for his better incoragement." Sir George certainly needed something to comfort him as ship after crowded ship came in "freighted more with ignorance than any other merchandise," though the *Jonathan* and *London Merchant* had brought many maids to make the men "feel at home in Virginia."

These maids should be allowed to choose their mates "according to the law of nature," said the Company, but within reason. They were not to marry indentured servants, but only such freemen as could pay for their passage and had the means to support them. Until married, they were to work as domestics and thus earn their keep.

Any planter desiring a bit of this fluffy merchandise had to pay 120 pounds of tobacco—soon raised to 150 pounds, as the demand was so great. And it had to be in good tobacco, only the best leaf, and not such "stuffe" as had been given for the Duty boys. At 3s. a pound, that much tobacco represented $1,000 or more, perhaps not an extravagant price to pay—though in not quite so obvious and forthright a manner, many men have paid more—for "yonge, handsome, and honestly educated mayds." They seem to have given general satisfaction, though some buyers had complaints to make, especially about the "widdowes" in the cargo.[1]

In 1620, a thousand people were shipped to Virginia. More than that number died at sea or along the James during the year. In spite of repeated warnings since Smith's day, most of the ships had arrived during the summer, "a most unfitt season," and their passengers came in "very weake and sick, some Crasey and taynted ashore," there to fall under the "great heate of weather." But they died more "of disease of their mind than of their body," declared one of the Council, "by having the countrey's victualls overpraised to them in England."

Why had such a multitude been sent without warning? Yeardley protested to Sandys. "Had not your zealous desires overhasted you, I should have been able to have done much better than now I can. . . . I protest before God I run myselfe out of all the provision of Corne I have for the feeding of these people." Though Ferrar claimed to have sent provisions for six months, the supplies on the ships would not last ten weeks.

"Mr. Ferrar is my worthye and loving friend, but herein I must blame him for casting up so shorte an allowance. Also for clothes, they come very shorte."

And why, Yeardley exclaimed, was he sent so many worthless people? There were few of any skill among them—not a carpenter except those sent to build the iron works, "and never a boatwright but that silly fellow who is dead." How could he build without "good and skillfull workemen"?

The Company should not run "into so great matters in speedy and hasty sending so many people over hither and undertaking so great workes before you have acquainted me, and have trewly bin informed by me of the state of the Plantation." After all, it was little more than a year since he had taken over the colony from Argall, who had left it in such ruinous condition.

"I have done what I can doe, and will doe still, to my utmost power," Yeardley assured Sandys. "But I pray, Sir, give me tyme both to provide meanes, and to build and settle, before you lay on Load."

Ignoring all this, Sandys and Ferrar prepared to send out even more people the next year. As the price of grain was high in England, those coming over would largely have to depend upon what Virginia could provide, they warned Yeardley. Let him be sure to plant plenty of corn!

Another batch of waifs off the London streets was obtained from the Lord Mayor for sale in the colony. More "mayds" were shipped, including an "extraordinary choyce lot" on the *Warwick*, for this desirable merchandise, it had been found, enjoyed a quick turnover. Many more servants were dispatched to labor in the iron works under the direction of John Berkeley, "held to be very sufficient that way." Still more servants were signed up to assist the French *vignerons* who had been struggling for years to establish a winery at Kecoughtan. The wild grape grew abundantly but did not lend itself to intensive cultivation.

Far from concentrating upon a few projects and bringing them to some perfection before starting others, Sandys and Ferrar embarked upon any number at once. Many apprentices and four skilled glass-makers from Venice were sent out with Captain William Norton to build a furnace to produce "round Glasse, drinckinge Glasse, and Beads." This was regarded as a most hopeful project, and £500 ($25,000) had been subscribed, "seeing that the comoditie of Beads is like to prove the verie Coyne of that Countrey."

Other men were dispatched to erect a salt works that was to provide the base of a prosperous fishing industry in local waters and along the New England coast. Though it had made a large haul, a recent fishing venture had cost the adventurers £1,800 ($90,000) for want of salt to preserve the catch. But many laughed at what the Company now proposed—boiling sea water in kettles.

He could make more salt in a day using "ye heate of ye sunne after ye manner used in France, Spaine, and Italy," said John Pory, than could be produced "in a year by that toylesome and erroneous way of boyling sea water into salt in kettles."

Without consulting anyone in the colony, Sandys and Ferrar obtained from Hamburg and shipped out some German carpenters to erect sawmills driven by water power. But in the low-lying tidewater, traced by sluggish estuaries, they could not find "any fitt water for their turne."

Envying the Dutch the profitable fur trade they had established in the rivers to the north, a trade said to be worth £10,000 ($500,-000) a year, the Company dispatched a ship to obtain a share of that trade and, if necessary, challenge Dutch control of the Hudson, on the ground that it lay within the original Virginia grant. Yeardley was to supply the ship with corn, cannon, and "fitt men" to strengthen the crew—and without excuse or delay, lest the vessel reach the Hudson "either too weake or too late."

Much money was spent to procure "improved silke-worme seed" from Spain and to hire eight French silkmasters to tend the worms and instruct the colonists in the mysteries of their delicate nurture and culture. This was a project dear to the heart of the King, who may have inspired it, for James, among his many fancies and foibles, had a passion for silk and loathed tobacco. In his *Counterblaste to Tobacco* (1604), he had expressed his utter aversion and now felt even more strongly that smoking was a "custom loathsome to the eye, hateful to the nose, harmful to the brain, dangerous to the lungs," and that its black stinking fumes nearest resembled the "horrible Stygian smoke of the pit that is bottomless."

The planters, the King informed the Company, should be forced to devote themselves to something more than tobacco, "which, besides much unnecessary expense, brings with it many disorders and inconveniences." They would do far better if they turned to that "rich and solid Commodity of silk," he opined, promising some worms from the royal silk farm he had established at Oatland, where Windsor Castle now stands.

The Company agreed, informing the planters of his Majesty's pleasure, sending them copies of a treatise on the art of making silk, and wine, and how "to set Olives, Oranges, Lemons, Pomegranates, Almonds, and many other fruits, &c." Only those colonists who had planted mulberry trees and built "fitt houses for the Silkwormes" were to be allowed the high privilege of buying any. And in payment for them, "no whitt of tobacco" would be accepted. This virtually precluded sale, even if there had been any interested buyers. But that problem was not posed, for the worms "miscarried" on the long ocean voyage.

All of the projects miscarried for one reason or another, but chiefly through want of foresight. Failing to find any "fitt water for their turne," the German millwrights were unhappy and clamoring to go home, being quite "disheartened with their entertainment." A glass furnace had been built, but the sand would not run. The French *vignerons* were finding it as difficult as ever to make any large quantity of potable wine from the wild grape. Even less salt than Pory had predicted came from the Company's boiling kettles. After long search, a site for the iron works had been found at a remote spot near the Falls, along the banks of Falling Creek. But little had been accomplished, for most of the skilled iron men had died, including John Berkeley, the director and chief engineer of the project. Work was everywhere at a standstill.

What could the adventurers expect under the circumstances? asked their trusted agent, Captain Thomas Nuce, who had recently arrived to take charge of all Company business, establishing himself with a large number of servants at Kecoughtan—or Elizabeth City, as it was renamed at this time.*

For one thing, the Company always promised more than it was able to perform, which created a deep sense of grievance and caused many fatal hardships. It promised wages and salaries, which were not paid. It promised good seed, cattle, clothes, plows, and various tools, which were not sent. It promised ample supplies, but these invariably came in "exceeding shorte," said Nuce, "which is not my complaint alone."

Second, nothing could ever be effected by the present manner of proceeding. Before embarking upon so heavy and important a task as establishing an iron works, why had the adventurers not given it some study? Why had they not sent over an experienced man to explore possibilities and make "sure of some abundant Iron mine and fit places to worke it in"? A year devoted to that would have been well spent. As it was, more than two years and a great deal of money had been almost wholly wasted.

And so with the business of building a water-powered sawmill. Why had those in the colony not been consulted about this? Even if the millwrights found some "fitt water for their turne," what then? As they were so few, who was to help them build the sawmill? Sandys and Farrar had suggested taking the tenants off the Company lands to assist. But how could the tenants "doe that and look after their livelihood"? Nuce pointedly asked. If they were taken off their fields and lost their crops, they would starve. Nor could any help be expected of the independent planters, as those at home naively hoped. The planters had their own concerns and would contribute no labor to the project since, "as they say, the benefitt thereof goes to ye Company."

The proposed silk business was equally ill conceived. The silkworm might possibly thrive in Virginia, said Nuce, but would the adventurers tell him why the planters should be interested since they could not hope to make a profit with the price of raw silk set at 2s. 6d. a pound? That price would not begin to pay the

* For Princess Elizabeth, later Queen of Bohemia, ancestress of Britain's present ruling House of Hanover, alias Windsor.

cost of tending the silkworms, even if it were possible to hire men for the purpose—which it was not, "for the time of their attendance falls out to be just at such a season as we are busiest about our Corne, so that no man but he who means to starve, will once look after them."

Because he could not write "pleasing things," Nuce addressed his letter not to the Company, but privately to Sandys, painting a scene of misfortune and woe. Many men, mostly servants, had died for want of "good foode, but chiefly of good Lodging, . . . if the conceit [thought] of their 7 years' servitude did not help them on, which course, I am of opinion, you should doe well to alter." Virginia desperately needed good seeds and many more cattle, "both for the plough and the payle," for almost all lived on nothing but bread and water and "such manner of meat as they make of their maize, which I would to God I could say they had in any reasonable plenty." In their fight against famine, three out of four men had to be employed in the cornfields, "which, if you consider, you will not wonder that so great workes as you expect to be done, have so slowe progress."

Virginia always had bad luck with her more able and sensible leaders. Things might have gone rather differently but for the untimely deaths of Gosnold, Scrivener, and Sir George Somers, to cite a few. Wise and humane, Captain Nuce might have brought some order out of the present chaos, for he was trusted both at home and in the colony, but he now went to a premature grave, and most of his men with him, as the mortality rate rose to a new height.[2]

Altogether, more than 1,500 people were sent to Virginia in 1621. During the year, almost 1,200 died on the ships or in the colony—newcomers, for the most part. As a rule, only one in five of these survived a year, usually dying within a month or two of arrival, especially if they came in the summertime, as many did because of the Company's stubborn folly.

During the past three years, since the winter of 1618, some 4,000 people had been recruited and sent to Virginia. But the population was little more than it had been in Argall's time, for more than 3,200 had perished at sea or in the colony during this tragic period. No war or epidemic in history, not even the Black Plague, took a higher proportionate toll. No wonder Virginia was known to many, and avoided, as a "slaughterhouse."

Still undaunted, Sandys and Ferrar pushed ahead. The planters could work a speedy cure of everything if they would "take into spetiall regard and estimation ye service of Almightie God and the observance of his Divine laws . . . according to the usuall forme and discipline of the Church of England." And let them send no more criticisms and complaints of the Company, said Sandys and Ferrar, who had plenty of complaints of their own to make.

Why had nothing been done in the Argall business? or in establishing a fur trade? or in getting the salt works under way? The delay in all things, especially in putting the iron workers and the Hamburg millwrights to work, "is with much indignation here resented," the planters were informed. What was wanted from them was "substance, . . . not letters, excuses, and promises."

If so many were sick, why did they not build, as so often instructed, some guest houses or hospitals? Dale had reported one under way ten years before, but none had yet been built. This could easily have been done "if half so much care and time had been taken to do it as hath beene spent in giving reasons to the contrary." It was a gross libel and a "strange error of judgment" to say, as some had, that guest houses provided only a "more regulated kind of killing of men."

Let those at Jamestown do something about the frequent complaints that certain men were engrossing the market, that they were buying up all corn and other goods for resale "to the poore people at excessive rates." Such oppression and grinding of the poor should be severely punished, and nothing would be "more pleasing unto us," they said, "than the exemplarie punishment of such Monsters as devour their brethren by this wicked and barbarous course, especially if such wickedness should be exercised by men in place of authority."

Also, the planters should know that they would no longer receive 3s. a pound for "their darling Tobacco." When it came to be sold, it never brought anything near that price. Henceforth, the Company would accept only the best leaf, and no more rolls filled with "base and rotten stuff" that should have been burned in the first place. If the next shipment of tobacco from the colony were not better than the last, it would not "vent at all."

And who were those wretches along the James who said, as they passed off their worthless stuff, "Anything is good enough for the Marchant!"

Let "that wicked phrase and conceit be rooted out of the mouths and harts of the Planters"!

What "monstrous ingratitude!" the adventurers exclaimed, threatening to cut off supplies. To think that they had spent £100,-000 ($5,000,000) without getting back a penny, and this was their reward—"evill and disgracefull words for our zeale!"

This had to stop, obviously.

"We expect a generall redress," they proclaimed, though they had nothing more helpful to suggest than a law to suppress "gaming and, above all, that odious vice of drunkeness," as well as "ryott in apparrel & otherwise." With the exception of the officers, no one was to wear any silk until it was of his own growth and manufacture.

The planters should leave tobacco and find "better employment." Let them grow corn and get on with commodities—iron, wine, silk, salt, glass, tar, soap ashes, and "Oyle of Wallnuts."

Massacre

*. . . not to perceive anything in so open and generall
a conspiracie, but to be made in part instruments of
contriving it and almost guiltie of the destruction by
a blindfold and stupid entertaininge of it . . .*

—THE VIRGINIA COMPANY

*T*HE LOSS of so many lives in Virginia and the miscarriage of
all projects there did not unseat the new management of
the Company. Southampton was again chosen as Treasurer, and
Sandys continued as the actual director of affairs. That both of
them were soon placed under house arrest for daring to raise
their voices in Parliament against that "grievance of grievances,"
the Marquess of Buckingham, the King's corrupt and arrogant
favorite, did not aid the Company's already strained relations
with the Crown.

As Yeardley was still clamoring to be relieved as Governor,
claiming that his office had already cost him £800 ($40,000), the
Company acceded to his request. For their part, the adventurers
had not been too pleased with him. Though the fault was certainly
not his, little had been accomplished during his administration.
He had done nothing about Argall and his accomplices, not recovering any of their loot, not even a cow. Besides, as he always
quite frankly admitted, Sir George was less interested in the public business than his private concerns. Even when there was little
or no tobacco for Company vessels, he usually managed to ship

large quantities to his agent in Holland and encouraged others to establish profitable private trades.

Profits from such trade were so large, it was said, that some planters were now making "£2,000 or £3,000 ($150,000) yearly that were not worth that many pence when they went," which could only be done, according to Captain Smith, "by oppressing the commonalty there or deceiving the generality here, or both." In any case, little could be expected of a governor who did not wish to be in command and was impatient to get on with his own business.

As his successor, the Company chose young Sir Francis Wyatt, finding him acceptable "in respect of his parentage, good education, integritie of life, and faire fortunes, being his father's eldest sonne, as also for his sufficiencie otherwise." But his chief distinction seems to have been that he was a Sandys in-law, having married Sir Edwin's niece. With its usual extravagance in some respects, though never in providing the ships with food, livestock, and tools as requested, the Company granted Wyatt £200 ($10,-000) to provide for his voyage, allowed him free transportation for his large household of twenty persons—domestics, for the most part—and had the flagship thoroughly cleansed and refitted "to accomodate Sir Frauncis and some other Gentlemen the better."

A whole new staff was appointed to assist Wyatt. Dr. John Pott, later a governor, was made Physician General, bringing with him "two Chirurgions, . . . a Chest of Phisicke and Chirurgery," and an apothecary, Joseph Fitch, who had been allowed only £10 ($500) for medicines. A new Vice-Admiral was strictly enjoined "to prevent the frauds and abuses of masters of Shipps and Mariners in detaining goods sent to the Planters and in sellinge their goods at excessive rates."

A new Secretary-Recorder was named, Christopher Davison. Though he appears to have remained remarkably sober, not once calling upon his friends to bail him out of some bibulous escapade, genial John Pory had not performed his duties "to the contentment of the Company." For one thing, he had been caught in clandestine correspondence with Warwick and Argall. For another, though he denied being his "owne carver" in the matter of salary, he had been charging the planters "intolerable" fees for recording land titles and performing other routine services.

Two new posts had been created. The colonists had complained that wine-makers, silk-makers, and salt-makers had been sent them, but never a surveyor, so that they could not properly lay out their lands, either public or private. William Claiborne, later a man of prominence, become the first Surveyor General, at a salary of £30 ($1,500) a year, plus a house rent-free and £20 for instruments and books. His fees for private surveys were not to exceed 6s. ($15) a day.

Accepting the suggestion made by the Assembly, the Company created the post of Treasurer in Virginia, attaching to the office 1,500 acres and fifty servants to work them. In addition to collecting rents and the many debts owed the Company, the Treasurer had the task of forwarding the iron works and other projects, and generally stimulating production by introducing some order into the Company's tangled affairs in Virginia, a task obviously requiring some experience in business and some special knowledge and skills.

But this difficult post was given to a poet, George Sandys, Sir Edwin's youngest brother, who was granted £150 ($7,500) for his voyage and free transportation for twenty persons. A man of some distinction in his day, George Sandys had already published his translation of five books of Ovid and on his passage, "amongst the roreing of the seas, the rustling of the Shrowdes, and Clamour of Saylers," he translated two more, continuing his work at Jamestown where he was usually to be found in his study, a friend reported, and doing nicely with his verse.*

Coming the short northern route with nine vessels, Wyatt's fleet arrived at Jamestown late in 1621, not having lost a man along the way. But the ships came in with their supplies so "badly conditioned"—what a nightmarish theme in the Virginia records! —that the "Hogs would not eat the Corne they brought, which

* Sandys had his "own chambers, . . . the fairest in Virginia," at the house of Captain William Pierce, commander of Jamestown, whose daughter Jane had become the third Mrs. John Rolfe.

was a great cause of their sickness and mortality," for the colony was again on very short rations. George Sandys fell critically ill, and many died.

But Wyatt was not too discouraged by this or by the state of the colonists, most of whom were in rags, with the planters indignantly protesting that the ships had brought nothing "wherewith to cover their servants' nakedness." The new governor, in his youth and inexperience, was quite confident that he could soon correct whatever was amiss.

Summoning the Assembly, he took drastic steps, as ordered at home, to restrain the "immoderate plantinge" of tobacco, persuading the Assembly to decree that, per worker, no one should set more than a thousand plants, and that these should be stripped down to nine leaves each. Thus, it was estimated, a planter would harvest about a hundredweight per worker.*

More encouraging than all else was the general peace that had reigned along the James for some years now, disturbed by only a minor incident or two. More confident of their own strength, feeling secure in view of the friendliness of the Indians, the planters felt "no more feare nor danger of their power or treachery," spreading out from the older settlements to establish new plantations in the wilderness. As Virginia had no roads and few trails, many of these plantations were quite isolated, being wholly dependent upon slow and uncertain travel by boat along wandering creeks. But this, except for its inconvenience, caused no concern at the moment.

In the settlements from the Falls to Point Comfort, the Indians frequented the planters' houses almost as if members of the family. Many braves had been taught the use of firearms and sent into the woods to hunt game by planters who wished to devote their time and their servants' wholly to planting tobacco.

Though it had long been forbidden to teach the Indians to "shoot our guns, on pain of death to learner & teacher," this decree was ignored, and it worried others than Captain John Smith

* If the tobacco sold at 3*s.* a pound, this represented a gross of £15 a year per worker—i.e., indentured servant. But as much tobacco sold for less, the average gross probably did not exceed £10 ($500) a year.

that the Indians were practicing arms while "our men practised little but the Spade, . . . rooting in the ground about Tobacco, like Swine." But this, too, was of no concern at the moment.

It now seemed, at last, that some progress might be made in converting the Indians. As directed by the King five years before when he was so impressed with Pocahontas' "godly graces," almost £2,000 ($100,000) had been collected by the bishops for building some churches and schools "for ye education of ye children of those Barbarians in Virginia." Observing that half of this had been raised within his diocese, the Lord Bishop of London in a sermon at St. Paul's publicly remarked his pride that so much had been drawn "from the breasts of this City" to suckle infant Virginia, which he had named, he said, "the little sister that hath no breasts." *

For its part, the Company had set aside 10,000 acres at Henrico as the College Lands. When the Smythe-Johnson faction and others protested that nothing so forward as a college should be undertaken until those in Virginia had "procured wherewithal to subsist," Sandys agreed that construction should not begin at once. Rather, servants should be sent over to open up and develop the tract, the profits from which would soon provide ample funds not only for building but maintaining the college.

Not only a college but a school was planned to prepare children in Virginia, both Indian and English, for the higher learning. An anonymous donor, who signed himself "Dust & Ashes," had pledged £500 ($25,000) for the purpose.† Additional sums had come from a remote and quite unexpected source. The men on three East India ships, homeward bound after a perilous voyage, had decided on rounding the Cape of Good Hope to make a thanksgiving offering and were persuaded by a chaplain on board, the Reverend Patrick Copland, a friend of Deputy Treasurer Ferrar, to contribute their offering to the spread of Christian teaching in Virginia.

---

* The good Bishop cannot have seen the "little sister" on the Virginia "cote."

† "Dust & Ashes," it transpired, was a prominent adventurer, Gabriel Barbour, manager of the lotteries.

From this and another East India voyage, almost £140 ($7,000) had been contributed, and the Company decided to combine this with the pledge of "Dust & Ashes" to build a "free schoole" at Charles City, where it set aside 1,000 acres for the grounds and maintenance of what was to be known as the East India School.[1]

Meantime, "by faire meanes," the planters should obtain a number of Indian children, who were to be brought up in their families and taught the "first elements of Literature, so to be fitted for the Colledge intended for them." But the Indians were very loath to part with their children, even to have them taught "true religion and a civil course of life."

A member of the King's privy chamber, Captain George Thorpe, "a most sufficient Gent., vertuous & wyse," had been placed in charge of the school business, being the deputy in charge of college lands. Almost alone of those who professed religious aims, this "Angell from Heaven" not only preached but practiced Christianity among the Indians in the hope of winning them to the faith. Only one convert had been made in almost fifteen years —Pocahontas.

Though genuinely devout, Thorpe was somewhat naive in his views, declaring that Virginia had suffered so many disasters "because God is displeased with us that we doe not, as we ought to doe, take his service with us by our serious endeavors to convert the Heathen that live round about us and are daily conversant amongst us." The colonists, for the most part, gave them "nothing but maledictions and bitter execrations, being thereunto falsely carried with a violent misperswasion (grown upon them, I know not how) that these pore people have done unto us all the wrongs and injuries that the malice of the Devill or man can afford."

Indeed, "if there be wronge on any side," said Thorpe, "it is on ours, who are not so charitable to them as Christians ought to be, they being (especially the better sorte of them) of a peaceable & vertuous disposition." If the chiefs were given a few gifts, "something in the matter of apparell & household stuffe," that would be a "good entrance into their affections." It would be well, too, if the Company made a public declaration of its "love and hartie affection" toward the Indians, "to be sent hither and published, thereby to molifie the minds of our people."

Though the Indians showed a marked disinterest in being converted, or in having their children prepared for the East India School or the college at Henrico, Thorpe felt that they could be won over and went to great lengths in his desire to gain their confidence and friendship. Any and all who mistreated them were severely punished.

The Indians had always disliked and distrusted the English dogs, especially the great mastiffs, which were savage and quick to attack strangers. When the Indians complained of the dogs at Henrico, Thorpe had many of the animals shot, to the fury of their masters, and would have gelded the rest "to make them more mild, might he have had his will." One dog was hanged for his offenses, it was said. But this was probably a bit of malice, for many had no use for Thorpe's philosophy and still less for his practice.

The Indians, too, were probably puzzled, and after their dealings with Smith, Martin, Archer, Ratcliffe, West, Percy, Gates, La Warr, Dale, and Argall, they must have had many a powwow on the strange ways of this paleface.

Many in the colony shared the view of one of the parsons, the Reverend Jonas Stockden, that the Indians could never be converted until all of their chiefs and especially their medicine men had been cornered and killed. It was all very well to talk of converting them by "faire meanes," he said, but when he and others questioned them about the Godhead, the Trinity, or the Holy Ghost, they got nothing but "derision and ridiculous answers."

Nor was there any point in trying to win them with gifts, for they just devoured them, "and so they would the givers if they could." This was no way "to draw them to goodness." But if Mars and Minerva went hand in hand, they would "effect more in an hour than these verball Mercurians in their lives," he said, "and till their Priests and Ancients have their throats cut, there is no hope to conversion." [2]

With the pulpit expounding such views, Thorpe had reason to be worried about relations with the Indians, who were still strong enough to strike the colony a powerful and even a fatal blow. Their answers to questions about the Trinity and their untutored attempts to expound such awful mysteries as the Holy Ghost may have been ridiculous enough, but they seemed disposed to keep the peace.

Convinced that with tact and patience he could win his goal, Thorpe began to woo the bold and crafty Opechancano, chief of the Powhatan Confederacy for more than three years now. Thorpe had a "fair house after the English fashion" built for the chief, and the latter was delighted with it, especially with the door, passing in and out and "locking and unlocking it a hundred times a day," finding no device in the world more wonderful. Opechancano gave him every reason to believe that he might soon be converted, "for he willinglye Acknowledged that theirs is nott the right waye, desiring to be instructed in ours."

Wyatt, too, had been encouraged by the chief. Soon after his arrival, Sir Francis had visited him to present a brass plate engraved with the terms of the league of peace and friendship negotiated in Yeardley's time. Nailing the plate to a great oak tree, Opechancano had proclaimed that the peace would outlive the oak and last forever.

Reporting this and other "hopefull" things in his first letter home, Wyatt seems rather to have stretched himself, for his good news, the adventurers informed him, "bredd such abundance of joy" that it could not be contained among themselves but had to be declared in a "publique thanksgiving unto God Allmightie."

It was now clear, they said, that God's wrath against the planters was "at last appeased," and the latter would now go on successfully in all things—iron works, wine works, salt works, and especially silk works, for his Majesty, "above all things, requires from us a proofe of silke, sharply reprooving the neglect thereof."

In their jubilation, the adventurers arranged a public service in Bow Church and invited all of their friends to hear a thanksgiving sermon by the Reverend Patrick Copland, whose zeal for Virginia had recently been honored with his appointment as rector of the nonexistent college at Henrico.

In his sermon, entitled "Virginia's God be Thanked," Copland painted a pretty picture of the "Happie Successes of the Affayres in Virginia this last Year." He quite agreed with the adventurers that the wicked and impious colonists had succeeded at last in turning away the wrath of God, and that the Lord now had better things in store for Virginia. Naturally pleased, the adventurers decided to print the sermon and distribute it widely to assure even the most skeptical that all was now well in Virginia.

In view of the Company's experience with previous publications on the "Happie Successes" of the colony, some of the adventurers may have feared that something dreadful was bound to happen. It had—even before Copland spoke, and the bad news was on the way.

Biding his time, Opechancano had taken a terrible revenge for all the injuries and indignities suffered by his people. Though the Indians had committed numerous outrages, they excused or conveniently forgot these as they planned retribution and struck out against those who were slowly crowding them out of their homeland.

Not long after the nailing of the brass plate to the oak tree, a strange incident had occurred to cause general apprehension. It involved one of Opechancano's more decorative braves, a member of his war council, long known to the English as Jack of the Feathers, for he used to come into the field, said George Percy, "all covered with feathers and Swans' wings fastened unto his Showlders, as thowghe he meante to flye."

Always trustworthy, this brave had been asked by one Morgan, a planter, to accompany him on a trading expedition among the Indians. He soon returned to report that Morgan had been slain by hostile Indians—possibly the Monacan. But Morgan's young servants were skeptical, suspecting that Jack of the Feathers was implicated, for he was wearing their master's cap. If he had been implicated, as the shrewd and able brave pointed out, he would not have returned to the plantation, least of all wearing Morgan's cap.

But the servants insisted upon taking him to Jamestown to

answer before the authorities there. When Jack of the Feathers resisted, they shot him, placed him in a boat, and started down the river. Along the way he died, allegedly making two strange requests before he expired. First, he wished to be buried among the English. Second, the Indians should never be told that he had been "slaine with a bullet," for his people accounted him their "chief Captaine and immortal from any hurt that could be done him by the English."

Whether the simple-minded servants so reported or not, the Jamestown authorities made this their story to explain their attempt to keep the fact and manner of his death a secret, but the Indians were not deceived.

When Opechancano learned of the death of Jack of the Feathers, he "much grieved and repined," so much so that Wyatt anxiously sent a messenger to find out how things stood. To Jamestown's relief, the messenger returned with the chief's assurance that he "held the peace so firme, the sky should fall before he dissolved it."

Everything seemed quiet and peaceful as before. The Indians were "friendly fed at their tables, and lodged in their bed chambers." They guided the planters "with much kindness through the woods, and one Browne that lived among them to learn their language, they sent home to his Master." More of them than ever frequented the settlements and early in 1622, with the approach of spring, it was noted that they were doing a great deal of traveling back and forth across the James, borrowing the planters' boats for the purpose.

As on other days, so on Good Friday morning, March 22, they came unarmed into the planters' houses with "Deere, Turkies, Fish, Fruits, and other provisions to sell—yea, in some places sat downe to breakfast with our people."

Suddenly, at the stroke of eight, they jumped up, wherever they were, and all along the James the blood of the English began to flow under the flash of knives and the roar of guns as the planters' own weapons were seized and turned upon them and their families. So sudden was the attack that "few or none discerned the weapon or blow that brought them to destruction."

The Indians killed many more in the fields, "well knowing in what places and quarters each of our men were, in regard of their familiaritie with us for the effecting of that great master-peece of worke, their conversion."

Seeing the "hell-hounds" approach, one of Captain Thorpe's men took to his heels, shouting a warning to his master "to look to himself." But Thorpe, "out of his good meaning, was so void of suspition and full of confidence that they had slaine him before he could or would beleeve they would hurt him." Most of his men perished, and the College with them—not to be resurrected for almost a century.

The Indians attacked the iron foundry along Falling Creek. At a cost of more than £4,000 ($200,000), the works had finally produced an iron bar, a shovel, and a pair of tongs. Killing the master of the mill and all his men, the Indians fired the buildings after tossing the machinery into the creek—which was the end of the iron business.*

Of the larger settlements, Jamestown alone escaped unscathed, thanks to a providential warning given the midnight before by a converted Indian youth, who revealed the plot to Captain Richard Pace, a planter living opposite Jamestown. Hastily securing his house, Pace rowed across the river before daylight to give the alarm, which threw Jamestown into a panic. Neighboring plantations were warned in time for some of their people to escape. Finding Jamestown on guard, the Indians made a few sallies and then withdrew, as they did wherever they encountered any resistance, even with "spades, axes, and brickbats."

On the day of the massacre, Yeardley sailed up to Flowerdieu Hundred to see how his plantation there had fared and what men or goods might be rescued. He found many dead and recovered only a sow, an injured calf, "some poulterie from the roust of one Taylor's howse," a chest containing "very ill-conditioned" tobacco, and some trumpery of "litle or no valew." Setting fire to houses and barns, the Indians had "carried away all other things," leav-

* Virginians were nothing if not persistent, returning to the iron business a century later with as little success.

ing the countryside a shambles with the contents of chests and barrels strewn all about the fields.

Altogether, according to the first count, the Indians slaughtered on this day 347 men, women, and children—and there is reason to believe that the death toll was much higher. The victims included six members of the Council, and one may have been that re-nowned lover, Powhatan's son-in-law, John Rolfe, who died at this time or soon after.

But for the providential warning that saved Jamestown, all would probably have perished—if not on this gruesome Good Friday, then not long after, as Opechancano had planned in work-ing out his well-kept secret. If Jamestown and its people had been destroyed, the scattered survivors in the colony would have had no place of refuge and could easily have been overwhelmed one by one. The Indians lost not a man in executing Opechancano's diabolically brilliant coup which missed complete success by just a hair.

As it was, Virginia's life again hung in the balance. With the Indians picking off stragglers and keeping everybody at "wit's end," several weeks passed before Wyatt and the Council decided to abandon outlying plantations and concentrate survivors in a few larger settlements, principally in Jamestown.

Unwilling to lose everything they had built "with much time, charge, and labour," a few bolder spirits defied this order—no-tably, "Mistresse Proctor, a proper, civill, modest Gentlewoman." But she was finally forced to bring away her family and servants when the authorities threatened to "fire her house themselves, as the Salvages did when they were gone." But the authorities failed to budge Captain Daniel Gookin from Newport News, where he remained with thirty-five men and boys, or Samuel Jordan from Beggar's Bush, "where he fortified and lived in despight of the enemy." [3]

Devastating in itself, the massacre brought a host of troubles in its train. There was no shelter for most of those crowded to-gether in the few remaining settlements. In narrow and unsanitary quarters, familiar and unfamiliar epidemics broke out. Men dared not "step out of doors either for woode or water." Almost all livestock had been slaughtered or driven off. A large part of their supplies had been lost. They could till only a few neighboring acres, and they hesitated to plant corn even here, fearing that when it was grown, the Indians would use it for ambush. Besides, so many men had to be kept "watching and warding, night and day," that few could be used for any other purpose.

As the colony could not long continue in this fashion, Wyatt and the Council seriously considered the possibility of abandoning Jamestown, sending Yeardley and a "number of the greatest Gallants in the Land" to the Eastern Shore, to Accomac, to see if they could obtain from the friendly Indians there a suitable site for a new chief settlement.

Having a large new plantation there, Yeardley stayed six weeks, bringing back a little corn. "But as he adventured for him-selfe, he accordingly enjoyed the benefit," selling it to those who could afford to buy at 10*s.* ($25) a bushel. Several small magazine ships arrived with supplies, which were quickly snatched up, though these "caused few but the Chieftaines to be little better for them."

Though it was rightly deemed a "very uncertaine and hazardous course," many parties were sent out to obtain what corn they could from the Indians—by trade if possible, "by force if necessary"—and their indiscriminate marauding and senseless violence only made matters worse.

Under a typical commission, Yeardley marched off "to make warr, kill, spoile, and take by force, or otherwise, whatsoever boote [booty] of Corne or anything else he can attaine unto." Yeardley and other captains made spoil enough, announcing that they had killed Opechancano, "it beinge impossible that he should escape, ye designe beinge Chieflie upon his person." But they returned with little or no "boote" to relieve hunger along the James. Aroused after several months of quiet, the Indians struck back and killed scores.

Informing London of their "lamentable Afflictions" and desperate needs, Wyatt and the Council asked for a large immediate shipment of supplies "to feede soe many mouthes as are here, two thirds partes wherof are women, children, & unserviceable people, since there was never more cause to feare the miserable ruine of ye Plantation by a relapse into an extreame famine than at this tyme." They needed sufficient supplies, "very good and well Chosen," to support the colony for a whole year, for they had no hope of any harvest.

If the sorrowing and worried planters expected any substantial aid from the Company, or even a bit of sympathy, their hopes were sadly misplaced.

Copland's fulsome sermon was just off the press, and the adventurers were busily circulating this welcome reassurance of Virginia's now certain success when, like a bolt from the blue, came word of the "fatall blow of the Massaker." This shattering news fell among them like a bombshell, leaving them speechless for a moment.

Then their gorge rose. Feeling that they had been imposed upon again, that they had been meanly cheated, that the colonists had carelessly and almost deliberately let them down just when their hopes were highest, the adventurers let their wrath explode in a scorching letter, drafted by Nicholas Ferrar, a prim, pious, and always cocksure young man who had recently succeeded his brother John as Deputy Treasurer.

Now in his late twenties, Nicholas Ferrar subsequently entered the Church and won some renown from his extreme devotions and his addiction to pious observances, being known to some as the "Protestant Saint Nicholas," and to others as the "useless enthusiast." At Little Gidding, in Huntingdonshire, he founded an Arminian Nunnery and there had services conducted continuously, twenty-four hours a day. Nor did he show any want of zeal, though a marked lack of charity and pity, as he now dashed off a letter to let those in Virginia know just what he thought of them. What fools they were!

"To fall by the hands of men so contemptible; to be surprised by treacherie in a time of knowne danger; . . . to be secure in an occasion of so great suspition and jealousie as was [Jack of the Feathers'] death; not to perceive anything in so open and generall a conspiracie, but to be made in part instruments of contriving it and almost guiltie of the destruction by a blindfold and stupid entertaininge of it, which the least wisdom or courage sufficed to prevent, even on the point of execution"—it was unbelievable, it was shameful, "more miserable than death itself!"

No matter what dangers or hardships they faced, there should be no thought of abandoning the colony. That would be a "Sinne against the dead, . . . a horrible Cryme even against God himself, to whom this great work is principally consecrated."

It was bad enough as it was. That the iron works, Henrico, the College lands, Charles City, Martin's Hundred, and other settlements had been abandoned, was a "thing not only of discontent, but of evill fame." To reoccupy them immediately was an "absolute necessity," particularly the College lands, which were "not only a publique but a sacred bussines." Special care should be taken of the iron works until the Company could "againe renue that bussines so many times unfortunately attempted."

Let there be no more talk of abandoning Jamestown. Though the Company had repeatedly urged this, as recently as Argall's time, Sandys and Ferrar would not now hear of it. The change could only be "for the worst—nay, to the utter overthrow not only of all our labours & charges past, but to the frustrating of our intentions and hopes and the expectation of his Majestie and the whole state."

The Company also reversed itself on its order that new plantations should be settled at least ten miles apart, now commanding that steps be taken against "inordinate straggling." The scattered planters should come together and build, "if not handsome Townes, yet compact and orderly villages"—a naive and wholly verbal solution of a presently dangerous problem arising from the dispersive forces inherent in the plantation system.

What did the colonists mean by asking for supplies? They knew very well, or should, that the treasury was empty, "utterly exhausted." It was their own fault if they now faced famine. That would teach them to grow more corn, be more provident, and not trust their lives "to the uncertaintie of one harvest."

Above all, the colonists should get on with "staple commodities, . . . the want whereof hath been the truest objection against ye succeedinge of the Plantation." Let them learn, once and for all, that the "improving of the Companie's revenues and the recoverie of its debtes is of those things without which neither we nor you can subsist." The Company would tolerate no more "unanswerable neglect." If the planters did not quickly mend their ways, they would be "cleane left & abandoned from any supplies hereafter."

The colonists had only themselves to blame for their miseries, which had been brought upon them by their notorious "neglect of the Devine worship" and their even more notorious sins. Here, too, there had to be immediate amendment—in particular, "a speedie redresse of those two enormous excesses of apparell and drinking, the crie whereof cannot but have gone up to Heaven, . . . to the detestation of all good mindes, the scorne of others, and our extreame griefe and shame."

Massacre or not, let them get busy and provide plenty of "victuall," for the Company intended to send over "hundreds of people."

XIX

Confusion

*Swoondes, I could teare myself to see what
weather-beaten Crowes we are . . .*

—CAPTAIN WILLIAM CAPPS

*A*s with all bad news from Virginia, the Company attempted
to keep the massacre a secret, but it was soon known all over
England. Reaching for its usual crutch in times of adversity, the
Company turned to the printing press and issued *A Declaration of
the State of the Colony and Affaires in Virginia,* hastily written by
Edward Waterhouse, one of the adventurers, who observed that
the "late unhappie accident" was certain to be "misreported"—as
it certainly was, and by him above all.

Virginia, as "generally knowne to all," was a wonderful land,
being "naturally rich and exceedingly well-watered, very temperate and healthfull to the inhabitants." Its cattle were larger
than those at home, and its horses "more beautifull and fuller of
courage." It had fine timber for all purposes, the best iron in the
world, and other mines "of the best and most desired mettals." It
would soon be producing as good wines as France and Spain, more
and better silk than Italy and Persia.

Above all, it would soon be enjoying a "most rich trade to
Cathay, China, Japan, and those other of the East Indies," for the
planters had assurance at last that the South Sea lay nearby, "not

above a hundred and fifty miles from the head of the Falls." [1]

While some attributed the massacre to the Devil, Waterhouse ascribed it to God, for it was really a blessing in disguise. Who could be so shallow of understanding "as not to perceive that this must needs be for the good of the Plantation afterwards, and the losse of this bloode to make the body more healthfull?"

The Indians could be enslaved and put to work "in mynes and the like." All of their lands would be taken from them to provide "more ample and faire choice of fruitfull habitations." Now was the time to invest before Virginia began to bloom like a rose and all choice habitations were taken up.

As good as its word, the Company shipped out large numbers of people very scantily supplied. The reported crisis in Virginia was taken so lightly by Sir Edwin Sandys that he allowed his niece, Lady Margaret Wyatt, to depart; she sailed on the *Abigail* with her numerous train, several hundred other passengers, and much foul beer supplied by a member of the Company, one Duppa.

As the colonists had requested arms and ammunition, saying that two out of three able-bodied men could not take the field in want of these, some antiquated weapons had been obtained from the Tower of London—heavy suits of chain and plate armor, iron casques, battle-axes, and similar things. Relics of the days of Richard III, the arms were genuine antiques, "altogether unfit and of no use in modern service," said the Company, "but very serviceable against that naked people." And how the Indians must have laughed if the colonists were so foolish, as seems unlikely, to stagger out to meet them in their clanging coats of mail, each whirling a battle-axe and hoping that some bemused Indian would stray within its ambit.

The voyage of the *Abigail* was as wretched and disastrous as any. "There never came Shipp so full to Virginia as ours," complained Lady Wyatt. "I had not so much as my Cabin free to my-selfe." The stench of the foul beer was overpowering, even on deck, and the vessel was "so pestered with people & goodes, . . . so full of infection," she exclaimed, putting the blame upon the two Ferrars, "that, after a while, we saw little but throwing folks overboard."

Nine months after the massacre, the *Abigail* arrived at James-town late in 1622, having lost half of her passengers along the way, bringing in the antiquated arms, a greyhound and some "hott waters" for George Sandys, very few supplies, and a "pestilent fever . . . never knowne before in Virginia," brought ashore by those who had been "poisoned with stinkinge beer, all falling sicke & many dyinge, everywhere dispersing the contagion."

Hang "that villaine Duppa," cried George Sandys, and for the love of God "send us some *ships with provisions!*"

And why, exclaimed Sandys, had the Company hired such a strange purser, "a man without or out of wits"? The stores on the *Abigail* had been few enough, and he had lost most of them "by throwing them upon the shore scarce above the high water mark," without informing anyone or setting a guard to watch them.

Shortly, another Company ship, long given up as lost, came in after a troubled voyage, the *Margaret and John,* "in great distresse for provision" and carrying more pestilence—apparently the plague or something like it, for scores were suddenly stricken, dying "like sheep with the rots, and rotted above ground."

Altogether, some five hundred people had perished in the year since the massacre—"more than was by it slayn," as one remarked, "and now at this time a great many sick, with no hopes of life."

And those that "incourage men to come out by vaine hopes of plenty," said another, "are the chiefe causers of their deaths." There was much talk in England of the deer, fish, and fowl to be had in Virginia, but these, "I can assure you, your pore servants have not had, since their comming into the Contrey, so much as the sent [scent]." In want of supplies from home, they considered themselves fortunate if their masters could provide them with their ration of a quart of meal a day.

But if the ships came in with little else, they always brought a plethora of instructions from home, and how Wyatt and the Council must have squirmed as they read these and Nicholas Ferrar's letter. They had certainly not expected the Company to add insult to injury by all but charging them with contriving the massacre. As to "excess of apparrel," if that remark had come from any but friends, they said, they would have taken it as a "floute of our povertie and nakedness."

Wyatt and the Council were not to think of abandoning the colony, which they had not. They were not to remove from Jamestown to the Eastern Shore, which they had already decided against, though George Sandys strenuously protested, arguing that the Eastern Shore far surpassed Jamestown in "fertilitie, convenience, all sorts of provisions, and strength both against the Native and forreiner." And as they chose to have a look at it, he indignantly remarked, "this is that treason against God and man for which we deserve to be hanged!"

Wyatt and the Council should be vigilant, maintain strict discipline, and see that all went to church. They should reoccupy all of the abandoned plantations, which they reluctantly agreed to do against their better judgment. At the same time, they should root the Indians out of the land.

"Let them have a perpetuall warre, without peace or truce." But the young should be saved, for their "bodies may by labour and service become profitable and their mindes, not overgrowne with evill Customes, be reduced to civilitie and afterwardes to Christianity."

Above all, they should plant more corn, get on with commodities, pay the debts due on the "Duty boyes," and collect good tobacco for the "Glass, Furr, Mayds, and Shipwright rolls."

As if the planters did not have enough to do, they were commanded to undertake an ambitious new project at great cost to themselves—lest they should "grow too rich," as George Sandys acidly remarked. The master of the *Abigail*, "boisterous" Captain Each, had contracted to build a fort at the mouth of the river, for the Company in its wisdom had decided, without consulting anyone in the colony, that Virginia had far less to fear from the Indians than from the Spanish. It was therefore necessary, *"above all things,"* to secure the river from suddaine invasion of Shipping."

Promised 64,000 pounds of tobacco, to be paid by the planters,* Captain Each had undertaken to lay his ship near Blunt Point

* At an average price of 2s. a pound, this represented £6,400 ($320,000).

and erect upon the oyster banks there "a blockhouse that should forbid the passage of any ship higher up the river." If he required help, the adventurers blandly suggested that he should call upon the free planters to contribute their aid.

Nothing could have been more preposterous, as Wyatt, George Sandys, and all protested. First, there were not 64,000 pounds of tobacco in the colony. Second, they had no authority to commandeer the services of the independent or "particular" planters, as the Company suggested. Third, there were not sufficient skilled men for the task. Fourth, even if there were, a fort could not possibly be built upon the oyster banks. These were flooded at high tide and rested upon a thin crust which easily gave way and did not provide a solid bottom for many fathoms.

"To save his credit," Captain Each soon died, and that was the end of this business, though the Virginia authorities made a gesture or two about building a fort on other ground where it would not immediately sink out of sight.

Twenty-five men had been sent out to build ships, both for fishing and general trade. As Sir Edwin Sandys regarded this as "ye best projecte for ye Countrey & most profitable for ye adventures," £2,000 ($100,000) had been subscribed for the purpose. But nothing was accomplished, for the master of the yard and all the skilled shipwrights soon died in the "generall decay."

Nor did things go better in other respects. Some Spanish silkworms, "held generally to be the verie best," had arrived, "well hatched & very hopefull." But these, too, had died. Little was produced by the wine works or the salt works. The German millwrights were still seeking some "fitt water to serve their turne."

As little success attended the glass works, which had been placed in charge of a Captain Norton, "a valiant industrious Gentleman adorned with many good qualities besides Physicke and Chirurgery." A glass house had no sooner been built than a tempest blew it down. The walls were put up again and a furnace was constructed, which, as soon as "ye fire was put in, flew in peeces." Then came the massacre to interrupt operations for months, and now death claimed Captain Norton and most of his servants, forcing George Sandys to take charge.

Claiming that the sand would not run, the Venetian glass-makers were restless and rebellious—"a more damned crew hell never vomited," declared Sandys, undertaking to find them some sand that would run. But the Italians were determined to return home, and one of them took a crowbar and smashed the furnace, which was the end of that "chargeable" business.

Nothing caused more resentment than the Company's command that a great amount of sassafras should be provided as freight for the *Abigail*. Seeing no other way to do this, Wyatt and the Council decreed that all in the colony, freemen as well as indentured servants, should cut and contribute sixty-six pounds each, on pain of forfeiting ten pounds ($75) of tobacco. This was actually a tax, a forced levy, and the planters resented it as an invasion of their rights and privileges under the Great Charter. Most of them declined to cut sassafras for the benefit of the Company, preferring to pay the fine. But the penalty was merely nominal, for the authorities found it impossible to collect the fines.

This imposition and others soon led to a memorable pronouncement, one echoed more and more frequently in all the colonies as time went on. Speaking through their Burgesses, the planters proposed and had the Assembly declare that the "Governor shall not lay any taxes or impositions upon the colony, their lands, or commodities other way than by the authority of the General Assembly, to be levied and employed as the said Assembly shall appoint." The Company should cut its own sassafras. It was not to order the colonists to pay 64,000 pounds of tobacco to build a fort on the oyster banks.

"*I would to God,*" wrote George Sandys in caustic criticism of his brother Sir Edwin and young Nicholas Ferrar, "*that some one of judgment and integritie, whom you trusted, might be sent over to give you a true information of our proceedings and the state of this countrye.*"

It was impossible to carry out their instructions, most of which were "inconvenient, for, to say the truth, they knowe nothing of Virginia, nor will believe anie thing from us that is not answerable to their former conceptions." They thought everything done as soon as conceived, "how unfeasable soever." When it was not done, they blamed the colonists. Rather, the fault was theirs, "but such is the disposition of those who glorie in their wisdomes that they will rather justify and proceed in their errours than suffer a supposed disgrace by reforming them."

Wyatt was equally critical, particularly of the practice of sending out large companies of people "without anie provision" or only "furnished by halves." Nor could he see any hope in many ill-digested projects all undertaken at once. "I often wish little Mr. Ferrar here," he wrote, "that, to his zeale, he would add knowledge of this Contrey."

As a case in point, Wyatt ridiculed the Company's talk of an "Army of 500 to issue out upon the Indians in all parts, and afterwards a runninge Army of 150 to vex them in all places." As the Company had also ordered that every fifth man should be commandeered to work on the fort, this "would leave some twenty men to guard forty plantations," said Wyatt, "halfe a man to each, counting any that were tolerable shott for a man. . . . Yet we are blamed if things be not executed just as they project." [2]

Wyatt could not keep a large army in the field against the Indians for an obvious reason. Men had to grow corn or starve. Though as eager as the Company to root the Indians out of the land, the planters found that this was easier said than done. They could get "neither fayre war nor good quarter," for the Indians would not stand and fight in conventional order, the caitiffs. Rather, they struck "like the violent lightning" and were gone as soon as perceived, so that they were "nott suddenlie to be destroyed with the sword by reason of their nymblenesse of foote and the advantage of the woods."

It might help, Jamestown decided, if some Indian allies were enlisted to join the fight. With this in mind and hoping to buy corn, Captain Isaac Madison went with a large party to visit the Potomac, always a friendly tribe, now ruled by that genial rascal Japazaws, who had betrayed Pocahontas. Negotiations went well until Madison, making impossible demands, flew into a rage and shot up the village, killing more than forty men, women, and children.

Seizing Japazaws and his sons as hostages to protect the retreat to the ships, Madison promised the prisoners their release as soon as his men were safely on board. Instead, he held them and brought them to Jamestown. Alarmed by this witless business, Wyatt and the Council sharply censured Madison. Immediately released, Japazaws was sent home with profuse apologies and many gifts both for himself and his people. But the powerful and always helpful Potomac had been alienated.

This occasioned another slaughter which took many lives, including that of Captain Henry Spelman, long a friend of the tribe, having lived with it for some years. As the colony's needs became more desperate, Spelman offered to obtain corn from the Potomac, presuming upon his ancient friendship with them. He and his men sailed up the Potomac and came ashore at the mouth of the Anacostia River, in what is now Washington, D. C.

Indians immediately attacked his vessels, seized the shallop and chopped it to pieces, and almost captured the *Tiger,* which had only four sailors and a few others on board. At the same time there was a great hullabaloo ashore. Seing a "man's head thrown down the banke," the men on the *Tiger* "whiffed up sayles" and fled, leaving Spelman and some thirty more to their fate, evidently a swift and terrible one, though nothing was ever certainly known.

"We ourselves have taught them how to be treacherous by our false dealings with the poore king of Patomeche that had alwayes been faythfull to the English," declared one of the old planters. "Spelman's death is a just revenge, . . . [but] it is a great loss to us, for that Captain was the best linguist of the Indian tongue in this Countrye."

Even worse treacheries and barbarities followed, for the colonists now sent to the Potomac "in culler to conclude a peace" a party carrying a butt of poisoned wine, prepared by a member of the Council, Dr. Pott, the Physician General.

After "many fayned speeches," a peace was negotiated, and it remained only to ratify this by drinking a health or two in sack. "So Capten Tucker began and our interpreter tasted before the Kinge would take it, but not of the same," and soon the chief, his sons, and all of his great men were dead drunk, literally. "How manye we cannot wryte of," a member of the party reported, "but it is thought some two hundred were poysoned."

On their way home after this outrage, Tucker and his men killed fifty more, cut off their heads, and brought some of these back to Jamestown, being persuaded that all of this would be a "great desmayinge to the bloodye infidelles." It dismayed others, too, and Pott was removed from his seat on the Council at the demand of the Earl of Warwick.

The Spelman disaster had struck the colony a double blow. Not only had it lost its best interpreter and thirty of its ablest soldiers, but it had been counting on Spelman's knowing ways with the Indians to provide some relief. When the *Tiger* returned empty, with only bad news and not a grain of corn, the hearts of all sank.

"God forgive me," exclaimed one, "I think the late massacre killed all our Countrie. Besides them they killed, they burst the hearts of all the rest." The Indians had won because the planters spent all of their time on tobacco, "rootinge in the earth like hogs," venturing their "lyves for smoke, like a Companie of Sheep-beaters. . . . Swoondes, I could teare myself to see what weather-beaten Crowes we are to suffer the heathen Kennell of dogges to indent with us in this order."

There was, it seemed, only one hope—the *Sea Flower,* which the Company had announced was on the way with large supplies. Unless this magazine ship soon arrived, there would "hardly be found a preservative against famine." Masters were saying that if aid did not come quickly, they would have to free their servants and turn them loose to feed on "barkes of trees and mouldes of the ground," as one of the latter cried out, young Richard Frethorne, in an anguished letter home, pleading with his parents to take him "out of this Egipt."

Apparently something of a scapegrace, as were so many in Virginia, young Frethorne had been indentured to the Company, living at Jamestown with the gunsmith there, one Jackson, who much marveled, the boy told his parents, "that you would send me a servant to the Companie. He saith I had beene better knockt on the head, and indeede so I find it now to my great griefe and miserie . . . I never felt the want of father and mother till now. But now, dear frends, full well I knowe and rue it although it were too late before I knew it."

Rescue him, he pleaded. If they would or could not, let them send food and clothes and "spice, or sugar, or strong waters, without the which one cannot lyve here." He had eaten more in a day at home than in a week at Jamestown. "You have given more than my day's allowance to a beggar at the doore." He had to work hard, "both earlie and late, for a mess of water gruell and a mouthfull of bread and beefe." If the *Sea Flower* did not come soon, he would starve.

Already, half of those who had arrived with him just a few months before were dead, and on every side people cried out, day and night, "Oh, that they were in England without their limbes, . . . yea, though they begged from door to door." Let his parents take pity on him. Their answer, he said, would mean "life or death" to him.

"Oh! that you did see my daily and hourly sighs, groans, tears, and thumps I afford mine own breast. . . . I thought no head had been able to hold so much water as hath and doth daily flow from mine eyes."

Before the answer came, the unhappy lad was dead, as were many more, for the *Sea Flower* had not arrived—and it never would, having gone to the bottom some months before. Apparently inexhaustible, Virginia's bad luck had not yet run out.

Coming by way of Bermuda, the *Sea Flower* had stopped there, and while she was at anchor, "summ in the Gunroome a-drinckeinge Tobaco by neclygense of ther fyer Blue uppe the Shyppe," which sank with many dead and all of the supplies for Virginia.

XX

Dissolution

*And consequently, . . . by exercising this
liberty, they may in the end carry away all
the King's subjects into a foreign land.*

—THE KING'S BENCH

VIRGINIA's many tragedies did nothing to improve the tempers
of the adventurers, provoking more strident quarrels and a
bitter struggle for power which soon wrecked the Company.

Ironically, however, it was not Virginia's many failures which
caused the final rupture, but her one successful enterprise—the
growing of tobacco. Whatever flags the quarreling factions flew at
various times, the conflict centered on the tobacco trade, with any
number of powerful and greedy men, from the King down, eager
to squeeze every penny they could out of that trade.

Again the King sought to influence the control of the Company
in behalf of the Smythe and Warwick factions. In May, 1622,
when the adventurers met to elect officers for the year, James
sent them two lists of names, with five on each. Though it was
not his desire "to infringe their libertie of free election," he said,
"yet it would be pleasing unto him if they made choice for
Treasurer and Deputy of one each from the following lists."

Two were chosen from the first list to run against Southampton,
who was overwhelmingly re-elected. The two chosen from the
second list were roundly beaten by Nicholas Ferrar. When in-

formed of this, James "flung himself away in a furious passion," growling that merchants were "fittest for the government of that plantation" because of their business abilities and their skill "in raising staple commodities"—as shown, he said, by the progress and prosperity achieved under Sir Thomas Smythe's administration! Now, "only tobacco was followed," which was true enough, and it was becoming a large and lucrative trade.

The King had recently prohibited the planting of tobacco in England or Wales. It was well known "what dislike we have ever had of the use of tobacco as tending to a general and new corruption of men's bodies and manners," he said. But if tobacco had to be used, it should be imported and not be planted "within this realm to abuse and misemploy the soil of this fruitful Kingdom." As Virginia and the Bermudas had the "proper and natural" climate for growing the weed and received "much comfort" from shipping it to England, they should be allowed to do so. Besides, this tended "to the increase of our Customs."

But the King now issued another proclamation limiting tobacco imports to 55,000 pounds a year. At the same time, he granted a monopoly for its import and sale to a group of Virginia adventurers headed by Sir Thomas Roe, one of the Smythe faction and an influential courtier. It was this Stuart penchant for granting oppressive monopolies—usually to worthless and corrupt favorites—that contributed so much to the rising discontent that would flame to revolution under Charles.

As Virginia and Bermuda, each of them, were now producing more than 55,000 pounds of tobacco a year, this meant that their market was cut in half, which shocked and concerned adventurers and planters alike, and there was a sharp outcry from Jamestown.

To tell what agonies they had suffered from hunger alone would be too "horrible to reporte to your sacred eares," exclaimed the planters in a petition to the King. Having overcome their difficulties "in some sorte," they were again to be reduced to misery "by the sinister practize of principall persons of our Companie at home, who, pretending your Majestie's profitt but intending their owne more, have gone about to blow us up at once with a proclamation which they have procured from your Majestie (as we hope, upon some false grounds) prohibiting our Importation of tobacco, the only Commodity which we have had hitherto meanes to rayse towards the aparelling of our Bodyes and other needfull supplements. . . . We must all here perish. . . ."

They begged the King "either to revoke that Proclamation and restore us to our ancient liberty or otherwise to send for us all home, and not suffer the Heathen to triumph over us and to saye, Where is now your God?"

In their dilemma, the Virginia and Bermuda adventurers agreed that all tobacco for England should come from Bermuda. Virginia tobacco would be shipped to Holland where a market for it had been established by the initiative of Yeardley and others. But the Privy Council soon made this arrangement unprofitable by ordering ships from Virginia, as the law required, to put into an English port and pay his Majesty's custom duties before proceeding to foreign parts.

Designed to increase the revenues of the Crown, a new plan was offered by the Lord Treasurer, the crafty Lionel Cranfield, who proposed that the Virginia and Bermuda companies should have a seven-year monopoly on the importation of tobacco, paying the Crown £20,000 ($1,000,000) a year for the privilege. Though some hesitated to swallow this "gilded pill," the proposal seemed to offer a way out of many difficulties, and both companies accepted it in principle after much discussion.

As the tobacco monopoly would entail wide operations on a day-to-day basis, the adventurers decided to conduct it as a separate enterprise with a considerable staff of its own, to consist of a director, a treasurer, two cashiers, bookkeepers, and others at a cost of £2,000 ($100,000) a year.

Many grumbled about the size and expense of the staff. Then a roar went up when it was announced that the director would be Sir Edwin Sandys, at a salary of £500 ($25,000) a year. The treasurer was to be his friend John Ferrar, at £400 ($20,000) a year—and this at a time, as more than one exclaimed, when there was not £100 to relieve the urgent needs of those in Virginia.

There was no need of a director, the Smythe and Warwick men howled. As for the treasurer, a salary of £100 was quite sufficient.

In addition, Sandys and Ferrar were the least likely men to make a success of the business. Under their administration, Virginia had suffered disaster after disaster, and the Company was now bankrupt. They had killed thousands by sending over multitudes before the colony was "provided with able and fitt persons to direct, or with convenient lodgings and provisions to receive, relieve, and mayntayne them." Both they and their agents at Jamestown were "men of contemplation and discourse, & not of action or experience in government."

With charges and counter-charges flying thick and fast, the Company's meetings became "cockpits rather than courts." The members of the contending factions became so embittered against one another, as a neutral observed, "that they seldom meet upon the Exchange, or in the streets, but they brable and quarrel." * The Earl of Warwick and Lord Cavendish had words after a Company meeting, "the lie passed and repassed," and the rumor ran that they were off to the Continent to fight a duel.

Annoyed by these "brablements," the King "invited" the adventurers to leave their verbal differences and get on with the "business of plantation." Foolishly ignoring this command, Sandys and Nicholas Ferrar struck back at their critics, expelling one of the more violent, rushing through the press *A Declaration of the Present State of Virginia, comparatively with what had been done in former times.*

This tract, like all Company publications, presented a quite distorted view of events in Virginia. All had been misery under Sir Thomas Smythe, it declared, which was true. But under new management the colony was enjoying peace and great prosperity. Alderman Johnson framed a reply to prove just the opposite, *A Declaration of the Prosperous State of the Colony during Sir Thomas Smythe's tyme of Government.* Very few had perished during those years, and they were "people, for the most part, of the meanest Ranke." The colonists had enjoyed plenty of everything—which must have come with some surprise to the few sur-

* The strife extended into the Somers Island Company. At this time, Sir Thomas Smythe was unseated as Treasurer, being succeeded by a member of the Sandys-Southampton party, Lord Cavendish, later Earl of Devonshire.

vivors of the Starving Time and any number of subsequent disasters. Above all, Virginia had been blessed with "worthie and expert Commanders"—like La Warr, perhaps, or Argall.

A more devastating attack came from an unexpected quarter—*The Unmasked Face of our Colony in Virginia, as it was in the Winter of the Yeare 1622,* written by one of Warwick's men, a governor of Bermuda, Captain Nathaniel Butler, who had paid the colony a brief and cursory visit.

Virginia was in a confused and miserable state, he declared, which could scarcely be denied, for it was just struggling to its feet after the massacre. All of its ills, however, were attributed to Sandys' maladministration. Unless matters were speedily reformed by "some divine and supreame hand," Virginia would cease to be a colony and be known only as a "slaughter house, and so justly become both odious to ourselves and contemptible to the world."

Sandys and his friends had been particularly ill-advised to make the quarrels within the Company a public matter by issuing their *Declaration,* which published to the world the delinquencies of Smythe, Warwick, Argall, and others. Feeling themselves seriously injured, the latter appealed to the King, who was very angry at what he termed these "scandalous imputations against men of note" set forth "by some distempered spirits," being so very angry that he placed Sandys, Lord Cavendish, Nicholas Ferrar, and his brother John under house arrest for weeks.

Also very unwisely, Sandys and Ferrar revived a case which had been buried by common consent three years before—the piracies of the *Treasurer.* To show his stand in the matter, and his contempt for those who were still vainly trying to bring Argall to book, the King now dubbed him Sir Samuel, increasing the cool and scornful arrogance of that always brash young man.

At the suggestion of Smythe and Warwick, the King appointed a commission of seven members to investigate Virginia affairs from the beginning, but especially the present state of the colony. At the same time, the Privy Council ended the dispute about "the Salleries" by disapproving of the tobacco monopoly proposed by the Lord Treasurer, which meant that more than a year had been spent in fruitless controversy. Shortly after, when the Company met in the spring of 1623 to elect officers, the King commanded the adventurers not to proceed. They should postpone the election until his pleasure was "further made known unto the Company." Consequently, Southampton continued as Treasurer, with Nicholas Ferrar as Deputy, until the end.

The new commissioners demanded the books of the Company and while digging into these, were deluged with specious pleas by the contending parties, each painting a fanciful picture of its virtues and achievements. Virginia had been very happy under the "mild & discreet" management of Sir Thomas Smythe. No, Virginia had never been happy until the Company came under new management.

This latter thesis burst like a bubble when the *Abigail* came in with scores of highly critical letters from Wyatt, George Sandys, and others. Making a "map of the Colonie's miseries," these were far more devastating than Butler's "unmasking" or the partisan diatribes of the Smythe-Warwick faction, and they fell into the hands of the commissioners, who received and opened all letters from Virginia.

As the planters and their servants were again starving, the Privy Council commanded that relief be sent them, "for relieved they must be, and that presently—and for this time, by the aid of the Company here." All stockholders were to be assessed, and no foolishness or excuses.

Again interfering, the King ordered that Company meetings were to be attended only by those who had placed men on their lands in Virginia or engaged themselves to do so by the next ships. All other adventurers presuming to attend meetings were to be "proceeded against as factious and seditious persons." This had been suggested by Warwick's kinsman, Sir Nathaniel Rich, chief conniver of the opposition, which always found itself heavily outvoted. Sandys packed the meetings with his friends, Rich and others protested, and the proceedings were "Democratical and tumultuous, and therefore fit to be altered and reduced to the hands of some few persons."

But the King had to beat a hasty retreat several weeks later when the Company suspended its meetings until it learned just what his Majesty had in mind. That was plain enough, but as the order grievously impaired the rights and privileges of all adventurers, James limpingly explained that it was aimed only at those "unduely and without certaine right admitted."

Rich had also proposed a devious device to shield Argall, Warwick, Smythe, and others from attack. No complaint against any individual adventurer should be brought in the courts or before the commissioners in the name of the Company. As complaints in the latter's name could not be brought until they had been "openly debated and resolved," that course tended "only to defamation and to raise more contention."

It was so ordered, but here, too, the "silly monarch" had to beat a retreat, admitting that the Company necessarily had the right to use its name in bringing suits and making complaints. Sandys and Ferrar thereupon asked the commissioners to examine Argall on his looting, Smythe on his accounts, and Butler on his *Unmasking of Virginia,* which had done more harm, they declared, than the massacre.

But the commissioners were not interested, being engaged in drawing up a new frame of government for both the Company and the colony, as ordered by the King. Knowing what was expected of them, they decided that the original plan of government had worked best—that is, as it had been in the days of "garboile" and down through the Starving Time. If it had remained unchanged, "much better effects would have been produced than had been by the alteration thereof into so popular a course, . . . which had caused much contention and confusion."

The King should nominate the Royal Council for Virginia, and the governor and the members of the Council at Jamestown. This was what James wished to hear, for he was determined, "out of his great wisdom and depth of judgment, to resume the government and to reduce that popular form so as to make it agree with the monarchical form which was held in the rest of his Royall Monarchie."

With this resolved, the Privy Council commanded Ferrar to call a meeting of the Company immediately to see if the adventurers were content to surrender their former patents and "accept a new Charter, . . . and to return the Answer with all expedition to this Board," for the King wished to proceed without delay.

Meeting a week later, with more than a hundred attending, the Company "seemed greatly amazed at the Proposition, so as no man spake therunto for a longe time."

As nine out of ten were opposed, the adventurers informed the Privy Council that the Company under its charter could not decide so weighty a matter till its next quarter court, about a month hence. Besides, the planters and each of the adventurers, more than a thousand in all, would have to be consulted.

Finding this merely "dilatory," as it was, the Privy Council peremptorily ordered the Company to meet the following Monday and "deliver a cleare, direct, and finall Aunsweare."

At that meeting, with more than 130 adventurers present, the motion to surrender their charter and accept a new one was supported by only nine—among them, Sir Samuel Argall and cantankerous Captain John Martin, who had not returned to Virginia since his delegates from Martin's Brandon had been expelled from the Assembly almost five years before.

Upon the adventurers' refusal to surrender, the King's Bench served Ferrar with a writ of Quo Warranto, the tenor of which was to inquire—as if nobody knew—"by what authority they claime to be a Companie and to have and use those liberties and privileges" granted to them by their patents.

A sub-commission had been appointed to report on affairs at Jamestown. Two of its members were planters—Abraham Piersey, the former Cape Merchant, and Captain Samuel Mathews, later a man of great prominence. The other two were Captain John Harvey, later a governor, and amiable John Pory, again in need of employment. Harvey and Pory arrived late in February, 1624, to find the Assembly in session, "the first fruites whereof were most bitter invectives in the highest pitche of spleen and detraction against the twelve yeares' government of Sir Thomas Smythe, and in answer to Mr. Alderman Johnson and Captain Butler."

Quickly dismissing Butler as ignorant and malicious, the Assembly turned to the fictions of Alderman Johnson. While he and Smythe had governed them, declared the planters in their *Tragical Relation,* they had lived "in great want and misery under the most severe and crewell lawes," mercilessly executed by hanging, burning, shooting, breaking men upon the wheel, and chaining them to trees to die in the slow agonies of starvation. They were reduced to eating "Dogges, Catts, ratts, Snakes, Toadstooles, horse hides, and what not, . . . and indeede so miserable was their estate that the happyest day that ever some of them hoped to see was when the Indyans had killed a mare, they wishinge whilst she was a-boylinge that Sir Thomas Smythe were uppon her backe in the fire."

Rather than live again under the government of such men as Smythe, Johnson, and Argall, they wished the King would send over commissioners, they said, "with authoritie to hang us."

Surprised and shocked when Pory and Harvey informed them of the contemplated change in the frame of government, which included no provision for an elected House of Burgesses, they immediately drew up petitions to the King and the Privy Council.

It was their humble desire, they said, that the "Governors that are sent over may not have *absolute authority.* We desire that the Governor may be restrayned, as formerly, to the consent of his *Counsell.* . . . But, *above all,* we humbly intreat your Lordships that we may retaine the *Libertie of our Generall Assemblie,* than which nothing can more conduce to our satisfaction or the publique utilitie."

When the commissioners demanded to know whether or not they would submit to the "King's princely pleasure" in surrendering the old patent and accepting a new one, the members of the Assembly unanimously replied that they would answer at the proper time, being sure that "his Majestie's intention of changing the government hath proceeded from much misinformation," which would be corrected after he had received their "more faithful declarations."

Resenting their presence and their mission, Jamestown treated the commissioners with scant courtesy and consideration, challenging their authority on every occasion. Not trusting Pory and

Harvey—and with cause, it transpired, for both were secret agents of the Earl of Warwick—, the Assembly kept its proceedings secret. To make sure that its petitions to the King and the Privy Council reached their proper destination and were not tampered with along the way, Vice-Admiral John Pountis was sent to England to deliver them in person.

But the Assembly might have spared itself all of this expense and trouble, for Pory sailed a few days later carrying a copy of all of its proceedings, obtained by bribing Edward Sharpless, the clerk of the Council. It was his hope and Harvey's that the pilfered papers could be delivered to Sir Nathaniel Rich before Vice-Admiral Pountis arrived so that steps might be taken to counteract any influence the Assembly's petitions might have.

Quickly discovering Pory's "duble dealinge," rightly suspecting "some Synister intention of forestalling our counsells," the authorities at Jamestown took out their rage on poor Sharpless. For betraying their "Secrecye," they sentenced him "to stand in the Pillory and there to have his Ears nailed to it and cut off." Relenting a bit, they sliced off only part of one ear, but double-dealing James was infuriated, denouncing this as a bloody and barbarous act.

Vice-Admiral Pountis never reached England, dying within sight of its shores, and the Assembly's petitions and other papers fell into the hands of the opposition. But they had come too late, in any case, for events had moved rapidly to a climax.

Aware of their weakness in this contest with the Crown, the adventurers had turned to the Parliament for support, presenting a petition in which they denounced Sir Nathaniel Rich as an "active ill instrument" and attributed their recent woes to the shifty Lord Treasurer, Lionel Cranfield, who had been made Earl of Middlesex and was now under impeachment.* It was he who had

* In the midst of all their troubles, Sandys and Ferrar had the pleasure of being named by the House of Commons, of which they were members, to draw up a petition to the King against Cranfield's notorious bribery and extortion. As a consequence, he was deprived of office, fined £50,000, and committed to the Tower of London.

led them into the trap of the tobacco contract "out of his private and most unjuste ends."

If speedy remedies were not applied, Virginia would die, and as they were unable to be "their own physicians without higher assistance, . . . they now presented to the present Parliament this child of the Kingdom, exposed as in the wilderness to extreme danger and, as it were, fainting and labouring for life."

As the business appeared to be "very foul," the House agreed "to have it ripped up," appointing a committee to hear the case. But the next day the King told the members of the House "not to trouble themselves." Consideration of the Company's petition would only "further increase Schisme and Faction." He and the Privy Council had the Virginia question well in hand, and the House should proceed to "more great and weighty occasions." Greeting this with general silence, the Commons agreed to drop the case, "but not without soft muttering that any other business, in the same way, might be taken out of the hands of the Parliament."

There was nothing more to do. The fight was lost. The last appeal had been blocked. On June 16, 1624, the Lord Chief Justice handed down a pronouncement on the Quo Warranto proceedings, declaring the Virginia charter null and void.

The bewigged King's Bench had accepted the Attorney General's plea that the charter was, "in general, an unlimited vast patent." Its "main inconvenience" was that the Company could "carry away and transport to Virginia as many of the King's loving subjects as were desirous to go thither. And consequently, . . . by exercising this liberty, they may in the end carry away all the King's subjects into a foreign land."

And then where would James be! The niceties of the well-trained legal mind are always wonderful to behold.

A few days later, as ordered, Nicholas Ferrar surrendered all of the Company's books and records to the Privy Council.[1] And thus the Company "broke," as Captain John Smith declared in his *Generall Historie* published at just this time, "not making any account, nor giving any satisfaction to the Lords, Planters, Adventurers, or any." [2]

XXI

Resurrection

*Corn is so plentiful . . . that 5,000 bushels have
been exported for the relief of New England.*

—SIR JOHN HARVEY

BY REMOVING its heavy hand and inept control, by allowing the
colony more freedom of decision than it had yet known, the
dissolution of the Company, united with the turn of events at
home, proved to be the salvation of Virginia.

The planters, however, had no reason to foresee this, preferring known to unknown evils, rightly being apprehensive about
what might now happen under the King, especially in view of
the men he had chosen to advise him.

To a royal commission established "for settling a government in
Virginia," James named some members of the Privy Council, one
being Captain John Martin's brother-in-law, a man of great power
and influence, Sir Julius Caesar, Master of the Rolls. The "others"
included a number of familiar and odious names—Sir Samuel
Argall, Sir Thomas Smythe, Alderman Johnson, Captain Nathaniel
Butler, Sir Nathaniel Rich, and John Pory, who had been twice
caught in "duble dealing."

It was quite like old times as they gathered once a week at
Smythe's great house in Philpot Lane, the Company's former
headquarters, to discuss the destiny of the colony. In one of their

first acts, they forbade the departure of any ship for Virginia until they had decided what government Jamestown should have, "lest the report of the dissolution of the former government might breed a confusion there."

This decree, if carried out, would have been fatal, for the commission never made up its mind and Virginia needed supplies. Consequently, while the question of government was being debated, the King allowed ships to depart and temporarily continued in office Governor Wyatt and most of the Council, though he deposed a few members and substituted others, naming perhaps the most unpopular man in the colony, a vain and violent bully, Captain John Harvey, one of the unwelcome commission sent out to investigate affairs at Jamestown.

Another of the new members was the equally unpopular and always irksome Captain John Martin, who, after causing endless trouble and commotion, had finally agreed to accept a new and proper patent for his lands at Martin's Brandon. He had returned to Virginia armed with an order from the Privy Council, doubtless obtained through his brother-in-law Caesar, that the authorities at Jamestown should show him "more than ordinarie respect" and help him rebuild his "ruinated Plantation." But Martin was full of venomous complaints about what the authorities failed to do for him.

Finding him as insufferable as he had been "from his first entrance into the land," his colleagues soon removed him from the Council and denounced him as a "man of a prostituted conscyence, a sower of disentione and seditione, one from whose false accusations no innocencye can be safe, disobedient to Government, and a person exceedinge dangerous to the state and Colonie." And with this final malediction, the curtain falls on the last resident member of the original Council, who died a few years later, presumably at Martin's Brandon, though the time and circumstances of his death are not known.

Others had died whose passing was certainly not lamented in the colony—for one, Sir Thomas Smythe, in the autumn of 1625. Earlier in that year, still pondering what to do with Virginia now that he had taken it into his "princely care," the King was carried off by a "tertian ague," whatever that might be, and the passing of the "wisest fool in Christendom" was really a godsend.

With his death, the authority of his proclamations and commissions ceased, leaving Virginia affairs where they had stood when the Quo Warranto decision was handed down, abruptly ending the deliberations of the scheming group that had been meeting at Sir Thomas Smythe's.

Not sharing his father's violent personal antipathies, free of many of his prejudices, Charles I approached Virginia with an open mind, even calling in Sandys and his friends to consult them, asking their opinion on the "best forme of government to be made for Virginia" and how to frame a tobacco contract that would at once provide a large revenue for the Crown and still "not be grievous unto the Plantation." The Sandys group had nothing more instructive or constructive to suggest than the re-establishment of the Company, with themselves in control.

But Charles would have none of this. He was resolved, he said, to establish "one uniforme course of government in and through our whole Monarchie." To that end, Virginia should immediately depend upon him and "not be commyted to anie Companie or Corporation, to whom it maie be proper to trust matters of trade or commerce, but cannot be fit or safe to communicate the ordering of State affaires, be they of never so mean consequence."

By proclamation, Virginia became a royal colony, directly dependent upon the Crown, being the special responsibility of a committee of the Privy Council.* But so far as the form of government in Virginia was concerned, this change at the top made little difference.

As before, the governor and the Council and all chief officers were appointed in London and paid from there, now by the Crown instead of the Company, and Charles continued Sir Francis Wyatt and all other incumbents in office. Though the proclamation did

---

* This arrangement continued until 1634, when responsibility passed to a new board of twelve members, the Commissioners for Plantations, an institution which developed into that great nuisance of later years, the Lords of Trade.

not provide for it, the General Assembly continued to meet in an informal fashion for several years, until 1627, when Charles restored it with all of its former powers.

While the King and his ministers interfered from time to time, they had so "many other urgent occasions" in trying to stem the rising tide of rebellion at home that they had little time for Virginia, leaving the colony more and more to its own devices, which was a great blessing.

In addition to the Company's demise, the year 1624 brought another sharp and significant turn for the colony. For the first time, Virginia planted sufficient for her needs and reaped a "plentifull harvest of Corne." Though serious shortages would occur now and again, the dread specter of famine had been laid at last, thanks to the distractions at home which had kept those in London from sending over "multitudes of people ill-provided." Those who had survived the recent calamitous years were now well "seasoned," and the death rate fell sharply.

Though now able to stand on her own feet, Virginia was far from robust, as the 1625 census revealed. Of the many thousands of people sent out, only 1,200 remained, and these needed tools, cattle, and other livestock. Only three of those who had arrived on the first ships were still alive and in the colony, and all had come up in the world.

Aged eighteen at the time of his arrival, listed as a laborer, John Dods was now living at Charles City with his wife Jane, having 50 acres at Jamestown and 150 acres across the river. William Garret, who had come as a bricklayer, owned 200 acres up the James. Another laborer, John Laydon, who had founded the First Family of Virginia, was living with his wife Ann and four daughters at Elizabeth City.

Indentured servants constituted more than a third of the population, numbering almost five hundred, and their numbers would increase with the years, for, as Pory had observed, the "principall wealth consisteth in servants." Of the bond slaves who raised the tobacco that made their masters rich, ten were held by Captain

Ralph Hamor,* while George Sandys had seventeen of his own and seventeen more on the Treasurer's lands, including "Mr. Vincencio, the Italian," who in a rage had taken a crowbar to the glass furnace.

The number of Negroes had not increased since the embarrassing business with the *Treasurer* and her Dutch consort six years before. Twenty in all—thirteen men, six women, and one child—, they were probably held as slaves, though slavery was not formally recognized by law till some years later.[1] Yeardley and Captain Abraham Peirsey, who as officers of the colony had removed the stolen Negroes from the Dutch ship, still retained most of them. Yeardley had eight, and Peirsey four, while one Angelo, "a woman from the *Treasurer*," probably employed as a domestic, belonged to George Sandys' host at Jamestown, Captain William Pierce, one of the old planters.

Sandys had a high opinion of his host, now lieutenant in command of Jamestown. Pierce "refused no labour nor sticks at any expense that may advantage the publique," he said, being "expert in the Countrie . . . and of a capacity that is not to be expected in a man of his breeding, nor will be overborne (which Sir George Yardlie knowes) by the bigg lookes of his betters." As for Sandys, though he had not been a conspicuous success as general manager of the Company's affairs and supervisor of its many projects, he had at least accomplished something, completing his translation of Ovid.†

Forced to withdraw under the pressure of repeated attacks, Indians were now seldom seen along the James, and the plantations began to spread outward again. Within three years, by 1628, the population doubled, approximating 2,500, and the people, for the most part, were "well housed . . . and well stored with cattle, as likewise with goates and swine in abundance, and great store of poultrie." They had "plentie" of bread, made of both

* Nevertheless, Hamor was so poor that he was "reduced to shiftes," according to George Sandys. If so, what of the great majority of planters who had no servants?

† The great John Dryden liked the work, considering Sandys the "best versifier of his age," and Alexander Pope found Sandys' poetry "excellent."

corn and wheat. They brewed "good ale, both strong and small," and distilled quantities of corn liquor, the hottest of "hot waters," so that few drank any water. Though the "plentie" was exaggerated, for many were still desperately poor, life in Virginia gradually became more comfortable, at least for a few, affording some of the amenities and even the luxuries of life. Returning to visit England after an absence of almost twenty years, the wife of Captain Pierce, "an honest and industrious woman," the mother of Rolfe's third wife, declared that out of her Jamestown garden of three or four acres she could "keepe a better house in Virginia than here in London for £300 or £400 [$20,000] a year, yet went thither with little or nothing."

A Jamestown merchant who died at this time bequeathed to his friends a number of interesting items—5,000 pounds of nails, six pounds of soap, white and blue starch, a thousand pins, twenty needles, threads of many colors, buttons, a gilded mirror, a jar of oil, a weeding hoe, a rundlet of ink, six quires of letter paper, a bushel of salt, a pound of pepper, a pound of ginger, a pair of silk stockings, a firkin of butter, two pounds of candles, a pair of red slippers, sheets, towels, napkins, tablecloths, a sea-green scarf edged with gold lace, a cross cloth of wrought gold, four gallons of vinegar, a black beaver hat with a gold band, a black camlet doublet, a "Polander" fur cap, a pewter candlestick, and a pewter *pot de chambre.*

Still, in the eyes of those used to the English scene, Virginia was as "uncouth" as Pory had found it. There was no tavern or public house, no church of any permanence or grandeur, and no town of any size—only two scraggly hamlets, Jamestown and Elizabeth City, each with a few short streets lined with not more than a score of nondescript wooden houses. Though it now had two breweries, Jamestown had no public building to provide offices for the governor and his staff or a meeting place for the Assembly, which continued to sit wherever it could, usually in private houses.[2]

As before, and as continued for centuries, tobacco was the planters' chief concern. When the Crown, like the Company, tried to divert them, the planters persisted, saying that they had to subsist on tobacco "for awhile, until, by degrees, they fell upon more stable commodities, as upon slate, fishe, hemp for cordage, flaxe for linnen, and other things." There was now little talk of iron, wine, glass, salt, silk, gold, and the discovery of the South Sea, though this last illusion was not yet dead, persisting for decades.

In 1625, Yeardley had been sent to England to protest against the tobacco monopoly established by James. Surprised to discover Charles on the throne, he found the new monarch vaguely sympathetic but accomplished little, returning to Virginia late in 1626, inciting the planters to renewed pleas against the tobacco monopoly. They should not be allowed to fall into the hands of "avaricious and cruel men," they said, "whose exorbitant and wide consciences" intended only the "ruin of the plantation for the profit and gain of themselves."

Deliberating this, Charles came to his "final resolution touching all sorts of tobacco." None should be grown in England, none should be imported from Spain, and none should be brought from Virginia or Bermuda without a special license. As Virginia was "wholly built upon smoke," a quite unsound foundation, the planters would be well advised "to apply themselves to solid commodities."

Still, if Virginia persisted in growing tobacco, he had a proposition to make, said Charles, taking this occasion to authorize the election of Burgesses and a meeting of the General Assembly, thinking that this might make his "bargain" more acceptable. Meeting for the first time under the new order, the Assembly boldly and summarily rejected the King's plan, offering drastically different proposals of its own. This angered Charles, but he did not abolish the Assembly, as many had feared in view of the increasingly arbitrary and violent temper of the times.

As Sir Francis Wyatt had asked to be relieved of his post, the King appointed Sir George Yeardley to succeed him, stipulating that the governorship should next go to Captain John Harvey and then to Captain Francis West, that old "runnygate" and general nuisance, who had laid out a large plantation up the river at the Falls. As it embraced Powhatan's Tower—Smith's Nonesuch—he chose to name it West Tower, or Westower, later the renowned Westover, for generations the seat of the Byrd family.

Yeardley had been in office only a year when he died, late in 1627, fighting the tobacco battle to the last. Though some dismissed him as "that worthie statesman for his own profit," he had been, as the Council declared, "a main pillar of this our building & thereby a support to the whole body."

Probably the richest man in the colony, a grizzled veteran of almost sixty, Yeardley had risen by his own efforts, without the special favors bestowed upon his self-styled "betters." Whatever his faults, he was sincerely devoted to Virginia, having chosen to make it his home, being the first and almost the last of the colonial governors to do so. The rest, for the most part, were merely placemen, interested only in what they could make out of Virginia. A planter himself, he always spoke the planters' view, which did not ingratiate him with the authorities in London, whether of the Company or of the Crown.

As Harvey was in England, Francis West became governor and did little but marry Yeardley's widow, now in her early forties. Upon her death a year later, West resigned and went to England to spend some time there, as he had done so often before. Returning to Virginia in 1630, he dropped from sight and died a few years later, presumably in the colony, though the circumstances of his passing are not known, which is no loss.

If West did little as governor, his successor did even less—Dr. John Pott, who had arrived with Wyatt in 1621 to become Physician General of the colony and a member of the Council. And what a "pittifull Councellor" he was, exclaimed George Sandys. The Doctor had been recommended to the Company as "a Mr. of Artes, well practised in Chirurgerie and physique, and expert allso in distillinge of waters." He was not only an expert in distilling "strong waters," but a glutton in guzzling them, according to Sandys, who declared that he consorted "too much with his inferiours, who hung upon him while his good liquor lasted," and later took up with one Captain Whitaker, "a man of no good example." Though restored two years later, Pott had been removed from the Council in 1624 for his part in poisoning several hundred Indians after the Spelman disaster.

The Doctor had been governor only a year when he was again

in trouble, with the arrival of Harvey to succeed him. The latter denounced him for pardoning a confessed murderer and arrested him as a cattle thief. Pott had a large plantation named Harrope, where the town of Williamsburg now stands, and while not a professional rustler, it would seem, he had there more animals than he could legally account for. In the first trial by jury to be held in the colony, he was convicted of stealing cattle, a felony punishable by death. But this was too much even for "rough" Harvey, and the tosspot Doctor was finally pardoned, largely because he was the "only physician in the colony skilled in epidemical diseases," many of which were then raging.

Though it may stretch credibility, and a strong case can be argued for others, Harvey was certainly as bad as, and probably worse than, any of the long line of incompetents and rascals that London foisted upon the colony for almost two centuries. As previously ordered by the King, the governorship had fallen to Harvey upon Yeardley's death, but he chose to spend the next two years at home trying to persuade Charles to increase his powers as governor and especially his salary, which was £1,000 ($50,000) a year. Failing in that, he procured himself a knighthood and now returned as Sir John, as vain and violent as ever, even more arrogant than he had been as a visiting commissioner six years before, making a great display of his authority, never stirring abroad without his company of "halberdeers."

To him, as to so many in his position, Virginia was merely a road to fortune, and Harvey tramped it hungrily, bestowing upon himself and his favorites great tracts of land, selling various rights and privileges for his own profit, extracting every possible penny from the planters in the form of fees and fines. At the same time, he kept imploring the King to raise his salary. He "might as well be called the host, as the governor, of Virginia," he complained, saying that if "relief" did not come soon, it would break not only his purse, but his heart.

By his commission, Harvey could act only in accordance with the majority decision of the Council, but he pursued an arbitrary and high-handed course from the start. Always "choleric and impatient," he angrily brushed aside all opposition, proclaiming himself a sub-king, a viceroy with virtually sovereign powers, arousing more and more discontent among the planters.

Even so, Virginia continued its slow growth. Within six years, by 1634, its population had again doubled, approximating 5,000. Twenty settlements were now sending Burgesses to the Assembly, twice as many as in 1619. In addition to those along the James and on the Eastern Shore, plantations had begun to creep up the York River, reaching as far as Cheskiack—or Cheesecake, as it came to be called.

The rising demand for labor in the tobacco fields had brought in a few more Negroes, but most of the newcomers were indentured servants. Hundreds of these were children, "gathered up in divers places," while many others had been procured from the poorhouses and jails.

While there was still occasional talk of more ambitious and illusory projects, like discovering the South Sea, the planters wisely concentrated their attention upon their corn and tobacco fields. In 1634, a novel and welcome departure, they grew enough corn not only to feed themselves and 1,200 new arrivals, but to provide an export surplus, shipping 5,000 bushels to New England, to the Puritans in Massachusetts who had settled around Boston Bay.

Suddenly, as Harvey boastfully exclaimed, Virginia had become the "granary of all his Majestie's northern colonies."

This was a more than usually extravagant boast, for the Pilgrims and the Puritans had quickly taken hold and succeeded in feeding themselves almost from the start.

Still, Virginia had come a long way since those dismal days, ten years before, when the Company had been staggering to its doom, issuing nonsensical directives to the last.

XXII

Intruders

A pox on Maryland!
—CAPTAIN SAMUEL MATHEWS

A MONUMENT to the durability of human life, Virginia had
finally achieved after almost thirty years a degree of
strength and security that seemed to promise relative ease and
quiet. It was a pleasant prospect, though a fleeting one, for a
host of intruders now descended upon the colony—Dutch, English, and Swedish—bringing more "infelicities, which, though they
seem ever at the height, yet new addition arises by some unfortunate accident. And behold now, tumults and broyles, wrongs and
oppressions, perpetrated with a high hand."

By royal patent, Virginia extended two hundred miles north
from Point Comfort, approximately to where Philadelphia now
stands. Consequently, the colony claimed all of the territory around
the great bay that had come to be known as the Delaware, named
for Virginia's first and last Captain General, the "painefull" La
Warr, who certainly did not deserve such a memorial.

As Virginia made no effort to settle this territory, the Dutch
entered the Delaware, or the South River, as they called it, and
built Fort Nassau, in what is now Gloucester, New Jersey, just
below Philadelphia. While the colony resented this, it did not

have the power to expel the Dutch, who, after a time, abandoned the settlement. Seizing this opportunity to assert its claim, Virginia sent men to reoccupy the fort. But the Dutch quickly returned, carried the Virginians to Manhattan, and shipped them home with a warning not to go there again, which they did not.

Three years later, in 1638, Swedes and Finns "crept" into the Delaware under an arrangement with the Dutch, as Jamestown complained. But the settlements were not disturbed, for the planters were having troubles enough with intrusion nearer home, right on their doorstep.

It infuriated them that these most troublesome "interlopers" were English, recruited to carry out a scheme hatched by the first Lord Baltimore, born George Calvert, the son of a rather humble Yorkshire family. A supple and subtle courtier, he had risen rapidly in the favor of King James. None went to greater lengths than Calvert in pandering to the King's prejudices and peculiar tastes. None took higher ground than he in defending James' absolutist doctrines, for which he was knighted in 1617 and made principal Secretary of State, virtually the prime minister, two years later.

In 1625, Calvert announced his conversion to the Roman faith, which compelled him to resign, for he could not take the Oath of Supremacy. But James consoled him by making him an Irish peer, Baron of Baltimore, granting him a large estate in County Longford.

Meantime, always eager to enlarge his fortune, Calvert had obtained a large grant from James and in 1623 sent colonists to establish a settlement at Avalon, on the southeastern shore of Newfoundland. In 1628, Baltimore came out with a large company, intending to stay, but life on the cold North Atlantic proved to be too much for him. He decided to abandon Avalon to fishermen and "other rough fellows able to encounter storms and bad weather," informing King Charles that he was tempted "to leave all proceedings in plantations" and return to his "former quiet."

But as he wished to spend his remaining days expanding his Majesty's dominions in the New World, he could think of nothing better than to take some of his company to Virginia, "where, if your Majesty will please to grant me a precinct of land with such privilege as the King, your father, my gracious Majesty, was pleased to grant me, I shall endeavour to the utmost of my power to deserve it."

Disapproving of this for many reasons, Charles commanded Baltimore to return home, saying that men of his quality and breeding were "fitted for other employment than the forming of plantations, which commonly have rugged and laborious beginnings and require much greater meanes in managing them than usually the power of one private subject can reach unto."

But without awaiting the King's reply, Baltimore sailed with a large part of his company to Virginia, arriving late in 1629, to the surprise of all and the acute embarrassment of the governor, poor Dr. Pott, who did not know what to do with the newcomers. His Lordship casually announced, as if it were a matter of right, that he intended to establish a colony nearby, "to the Southward."

Pott and the Council feared to get into the bad graces of a Lord so obviously favored by both James and Charles. Yet they feared to be remiss in those duties so insistently required by both monarchs. They therefore asked Baltimore and his company to take the Oath of Supremacy, which he and all of those who made "profession of the Romishe religion" refused to do, offering to take a much modified oath instead.

Consequently, Baltimore and his "Romishe" were ordered to leave, for, as Pott and the Council hesitantly explained to the King, they could not imagine that "soe much latitude was left for us to decline from the prescribed forms so strictly enforced, and so well justified and defended by the pen of our late Soveraigne Lord, King James, of happy memory."

They had always enjoyed "freedom of religion," they said, never having suffered any Papists "to settle their abode amongst us, the continuance whereof we most humblie implore your most sacred Majestie." *

* Freedom of religion, and of speech and opinion, has usually been of this kind. There is always "freedom" for the expression of those opinions—religious, social, political, economic, and moral—which have not been proscribed. All else is "heresy," or "subversion."

Returning home in high dudgeon, Baltimore persuaded the King that he should be rewarded for his trials at Avalon and his summary treatment in Virginia. As he had nothing else at hand, Charles carved out a large piece of Virginia and gave it to Calvert as a lord proprietorship, with extraordinary rights and privileges. In gratitude, the latter named it Maryland for the Queen, born Henrietta Maria of France, patron of the Catholics in the realm. Though the patent stipulated that the official church should be the Church of England, this did not preclude practice of the Roman rite.

Within his domain, the Lord Proprietor was virtually a sovereign, being responsible only to the King. His acts were not subject to review by the Privy Council. He could appoint all officers, levy taxes, coin money, and even grant titles of nobility. For this, he paid a tribute of two arrows a year, though the Crown had reserved for itself a fifth of all precious metals found.

But the first Lord Baltimore did not live to enjoy his proprietorship, which passed to his son Cecilius, an even more supple courtier and subtle schemer. The latter recruited some three hundred colonists, most of whom were Anglicans. Tended by two Jesuits, Catholics constituted only a fourth of the company which embarked on the *Ark* and the *Dove* under the command of Leonard Calvert, one of Baltimore's younger brothers.

Early in 1634, having come the long southern route and lost many people along the way,* the ships entered the Chesapeake and dropped anchor off Point Comfort, with all on board "full of fear lest the English inhabitants, to whom our plantation is very objectionable, should plot some evil against us."

Most Virginians would have been happy to sink the ships, but the King had sent a letter asking Governor Harvey to aid the newcomers and provide them with anything they might need. Always anxious to curry royal favor, Harvey eagerly complied and assigned an old planter, Captain Henry Fleet, "a man very much

* In the West Indies, they stopped at the small island of Montserrat, which, they said, was "inhabited by Irishmen . . . expelled by the English of Virginia on account of their profession of the Catholic faith." There is no record of such expulsions, though they may well have occurred.

beloved by the savages and acquainted with their language and settlements," to assist the Marylanders.

Guiding them up the Chesapeake, he led them into the mouth of the Potomac, where, on the north bank, Calvert bought a large tract from the local Indians and began to build a town, naming it St. Mary's, for the Virgin Mary. It was, it seemed to them, "a place for settlement such that Europe cannot show a better for agreeableness of situation." But St. Mary's, like Jamestown, was ultimately abandoned and nothing remains of the old town today.

Harvey continued to aid the Marylanders, sending them cattle and tools, winning the thanks of the King—though not the salary increase he hoped for. But however pleasing to the King and to the Calverts, his calculated generosity was regarded as treachery, even treason, by the Virginia planters. They disliked having a rival so near, particularly one tolerating the Roman faith which most of them abhorred and feared. That such a settlement had been established on lands snatched from them heightened their anger and sense of grievance.

If the King could cavalierly dispose of one part of Virginia, he could give away any other part, if the fancy struck him—which, as events proved, was not an idle fear. The coup of the Baltimores was "hint enough to other Courtiers . . . to find something of the same kind to make Money of." The Maryland question brought relations between Harvey and the planters to the breaking point.

"I have almost all against me in whatever I propose, especially if it concerns Maryland," the Governor complained, "and the proceedings of the Council do so embolden others that, notwithstanding the obligations of Christianitie and his Majestie's commands to be assisting to them in their first beginning, many are so averse as that they crye . . . they would rather knock their Cattell on the heads than sell them to Maryland."

He denounced an old planter and a member of the Council as the "patron of this disorder"—Captain Samuel Mathews, who, when informed of the King's "request," threw his hat to the ground and stamped on it in fury, crying,

"A pox on Maryland!"

Opposition ever threw Harvey into a foaming rage, and he now began to revile the Council in open court, taking a cudgel to one of them, Richard Stephens, and knocking out his teeth.* As "his Majestie's substitute," he had the power, he declared, "to dispose of all matters."

When some publicly questioned this, protesting that he should rule with the consent of the Council as his commission required, he had these "malcontents" seized. Declaring that he would shoot them for mutiny, he ordered a court martial. When the Council objected, he turned on them "with a frowning countenance" and asked:

"What do you think they deserve that have gone about to persuade the People from their obedience to his Majesty's substitute?" Why had a petition been drawn up against him?

Because of his refusal to transmit to the King the planters' letters of complaint, replied George Menefie.

"Do you say so?"

"Yes."

"Then I arrest you on suspicion of treason," shouted Harvey.

"And we the like to you, Sir," said Captain John Utie, as the members of the Council closed in on the purple-faced Governor who had rushed at Menefie and given him a thump, cursing and raining blows on every side till Captain Mathews pinned his arms to his side.

"There is no harm intended against you," Mathews assured him. "Sit down in your chair and listen to the complaints of the colonists."

The colonists had no just complaints, no real grievances, he growled, refusing any cooperation, scorning a suggestion that a meeting of the General Assembly be called so that he might hear the voice of the planters speaking through their Burgesses. "The Assemblies, being composed of rude, ignorant, and ill-conditioned people, were more lykelye to effect mutinye than good lawes and orders, especially whilst the Counsell gave them such examples."

* Stephens' wife evidently approved of this. In any case, she did not hold it against Harvey, whom she quickly married after her husband's death.

Finally, an agreement was reached that he would call the Assembly and the Council would support him so long as he ruled by the terms of his commission. While the Burgesses were being elected, Harvey fled from Jamestown "unto the Mills," to the house of one William Brocas, "a great traveler," whose wife was "generally suspected to have more familiarity with him than befitted a modest woman." From this pleasant retreat, he sent many threatening letters to the Council by his creature, Richard Kemp, Secretary of the colony. It was quite evident that Harvey did not intend to reform.

On May 5, 1635, the Assembly met with Captain Mathews and his friends in full control. Several insulting letters designed to intimidate the "rude, ignorant, and ill-conditioned" Burgesses came from Harvey, who appeared a few days later and met a reception that left him quite breathless with surprise.

"Sir," said Captain Mathews when the Governor had taken his place, "the people's fury is up against you, and to appease it is beyond our power unless you please to goe for England, there to answer their complaints."

Just then, at a signal given by Dr. Pott, who waved a handkerchief from an upper window, a company of forty musketeers marched up and surrounded the meeting chamber, led by the commander at Jamestown, Captain William Pierce. It was a dramatic and significant moment. For the first time in our history, the colonists were up in arms against a royal governor, the direct representative of the Crown.

Both Harvey and Kemp turned pale, as well they might, not knowing just what to expect. As resistance was futile, Harvey acceded to the Assembly's demand, asking only to be allowed to name the deputy to govern in his absence. Though he now spoke "very mildly," the Council refused this and chose one of its members to be acting governor, Captain John West, "an ancient inhabitant, a very honest Gentleman of noble family," another of the late La Warr's brothers.

While Harvey was waiting to sail, tension and bitterness were heightened by an event which many had feared—an armed clash with the Marylanders, involving one of the Virginia Council,

William Claiborne, who had arrived with Wyatt in 1621 to be Surveyor General. He had since become a rich and far-ranging Indian trader, dealing largely in furs, having his main post high up the Chesapeake, on Kent Island,* which commanded the route up the Susquehanna into the interior of the country, where the French and the Dutch were plying a very profitable fur trade.

Kent had been settled for some time and since 1632 had been sending Burgesses to the Virginia Assembly. But Leonard Calvert now claimed it for Maryland, declaring that it lay within the Baltimore grant, which it did. Naturally, Claiborne protested, refusing to surrender it, objecting so violently that Harvey removed him as Secretary of the colony.

Seeking corn and peltry, the crew of Claiborne's ship, the *Long Tayle*, now clashed with Calvert's men along the Eastern Shore, which cost the lives of five, three being Virginians. A few weeks later, a Maryland force attacked another group of Claiborne's men, capturing four of his Kent Island company, including the agent in charge, who was tried for piracy and sentenced to be hanged. This sentence was not carried out as a truce had been proclaimed, but bitterly hostile feelings remained.

Still crying "mutiny," threatening dire reprisals against his enemies in Virginia, causing the arrest of those sent back to testify against him, Harvey arrived in London to find the King not so sympathetic. With England drifting toward revolution, Charles had problems enough of his own.

Still, the "thrusting out" of Harvey could not be condoned. It was an affront both to him personally and to the authority of the Crown. Bumptious Sir John had to resume his post in Virginia, if only for a day, as it was the royal prerogative to appoint and remove governors.

Harvey soon sailed on the *Black George*, a prize ship, evidently a captured African slaver, which was carrying a hundred passengers, "more than twenty being Gentlemen of qualitie." Leaking badly, the ship had to turn back, inspiring more whines from

* Lying almost opposite the point where the Marylanders later built Annapolis.

Harvey, who pleaded with the King for a proper vessel and "some speedy supply . . . in compassion for my great losses." But Charles had other things to think of, letting the huffing and puffing Governor cool his heels for many months.

Arriving at length with "some few of his company," Harvey made himself as insufferable as ever, alienating even his friends and eventually the King, who in 1639 sent out a new governor. Sir John would now have been very happy to "goe for England," but he was restrained, for sharp measures had been taken against him to recover some of the loot he had gathered.

"I am so narrowly watched that I have scarce time of privacy to write," he moaned. "My estate has been torn from me. My return to England has been denied, notwithstanding my many bodily infirmities, which are beyond the skill of the Colony."

In time, he was allowed to depart, full of self-pity, loudly bewailing his unfortunate lot, for he had failed even as a depredator, having been far less successful in this than Argall and many another Virginia viceroy.

For some obscure reason, as the Sandys' clan was anti-royalist, the King chose Sir Francis Wyatt as the new governor. After an absence of thirteen years, Wyatt found Virginia with three times as many people and in a far more prosperous state than he had left it. But he did little to improve matters, for he was chiefly interested, it appears, in some devious maneuvers to revive the old Company.

Some years before, in 1631, Charles had appointed a commission "to consider how the plantation now standeth . . . and what commodity may be raised in those parts." It had been heavily weighted with members of the Company, and of the Sandys' party in particular—Wyatt, Nicholas Ferrar, John Ferrar, the Earl of Dorset, Gabriel ("Dust & Ashes") Barbour, and George Sandys, who returned from Virginia about this time. His brother, Sir Edwin, would doubtless have been a member but for his death two years earlier.

Reverting to an old theme, the commission recommended that the Company should be restored—with almost sovereign powers, as before. As the planters were vehemently opposed, the King did nothing about this. But the question continued to be agitated by a few interested men, and in 1639 the Assembly made George Sandys its agent in London with the explicit duty of thwarting any attempt to revive the Company and of keeping Jamestown informed of the machinations of those trying to achieve this.

But Sandys, it transpired, was a machinator himself. Quite contrary to his instructions, he drafted and presented to the House of Commons, in the name of the planters, a petition asking for the restoration of the Company with all of its original rights but one— the Crown, as it had been doing since 1624, should appoint the Governor.

Virginia rose as one man against this. Summarily discharged for "exceeding his authority," Sandys retired to Kent and died there two years later, in 1644, "a very aged man, . . . having a youthful soul in a decayed body." He had lived his last years with his niece, Lady Margaret, the widow of Sir Francis Wyatt.

Removed from command at Jamestown, Wyatt had returned home in 1642, dying soon after. Neither of his administrations had been distinguished by any noteworthy achievement or any particular ability on his part. But Wyatt deserves to be remembered for one thing. In the confused period after the dissolution of the Company, when no provision had been made for an Assembly, he chose to keep the principles and procedures of popular representation alive, calling in the planters' delegates to discuss general matters, issuing decrees in the name of the "Governor, Councell, and Collony of Virginia assembled together."

Anxious to bury intrigue in behalf of the Company once and for all, the planters informed the King in a long petition that they were now happily "naturalized under a monarchical and not a popular or tumultuary Government." They wished to remain so, for they remembered only too well the "intolerable sufferings, illegal proceedings, and barbarous treatment under the said Company's sway."

The Company, if restored, would manage and monopolize all trade, which would be wholly under the "control and direction of their Quarter Courts, held at so great a distance from us that it is not probable, or possible, for them to be acquainted with the accidental circumstances of the Colony so as to form proper rules and regulations for our trade." That could be much better done by the Assembly, which was "acquainted with the clime and accidents thereof." Instead of free trade, they would have to bring their produce "to the Magazine of the Company, there to exchange it for unprofitable and useless wares," as they had done before.

They now enjoyed the right to trial by jury in all cases, criminal and civil, instead of brutal and capricious martial law. They could write home if and as they pleased. They could present their grievances to the King "upon all occasions, . . . which so much distinguisheth our happiness from that of former times when private letters to friends were rarely admitted a passage."

Above all, the restoration of the Company would upset property rights and land titles, and the planters begged to be excused if they declined "to depart with what, next to our lives, nearest concerns us (which are our estates, the livelihood of ourselves, our wives, and children), to the courtesy and will of such taskmasters, from whom we have already experienced so much oppression."

Virginia felt so strongly about this that the Assembly undertook a revision of the laws to remove every vestige of the Company's authority. Among other things, it released the "publick tenants from their servitudes, who, like one sort of villains [serfs] anciently in England, were regardant to the land appropriated by the Company . . . for the support of the Governor and other officers of State." Anyone aiding or abetting those seeking "to reduce this Colony to a Company or Corporation" should be regarded as a public enemy and forfeit his entire estate.

Though caught in an avalanche of events that would eventually carry him to the executioner's block, Charles took time to assure the worried planters that he had not the "least intention to consent to the introduction of any Company over that colony."

This, as much as anything, brought Virginia to the side of the Crown in the Great Rebellion which had already begun and would soon triumph as Oliver Cromwell and his Roundheads routed the Cavaliers.

XXIII

Sir William Berkeley

A subject and a sovereign are clean different things.

—CHARLES I

*E*NGLAND had been seething with discontent for many years
now, provoked by the increasingly arbitrary rule of the
Stuarts. Demands for reform in both Church and State grew
louder and louder. More and more objected to being taxed without
the consent of their representatives in the House of Commons.
Quite as many objected to Archbishop Laud's attempts to make
the Anglican Church more Roman in ritual and doctrine.

Under Calvinist influence a number became Presbyterians and
suffered prosecution and persecution on that account, for the law
commanded the strictest conformity and was ruthlessly enforced
by the bishops. A larger number had joined the reformist left wing
of the Anglican church, becoming Puritans, who had been so
named not because of their moral code but for their theological
doctrine. They objected to the elaborate apparatus and ceremonials
of the Church, wishing to strip away the externals of belief and restore the originally simple Christian faith to its "ancient purity,"
as set forth in Holy Writ. Nothing was "lawfull" unless war-
ranted by Scripture. All else was "human invention."

And where in the Holy Book, they asked, did one find anything

283

about an archbishop, or an archdeacon, or a prebend, or the use of the surplice, or indulgences, or dispensations, or making the sign of the cross at baptism, or most of the matters laid down in the Book of Common Prayer? As these "human inventions" were to be abolished, it is no wonder that the higher clergy found the Puritans "peevish and forward," harrying them throughout the realm.

For eleven years, Charles ruled without a Parliament, having as little use or respect for "that noise" as Archbishop Laud. But in 1640, he had to capitulate, for he was unable to raise by forced loans or other exactions the funds he desperately needed to conduct the war precipitated by his stubborn resolve to impose Laud's high Anglicanism upon the stiff-necked Scots, who had established a Presbyterian kirk of their own.

Calling his first Parliament since 1629, Charles quickly dismissed it when the House insisted upon talking of grievances before granting any money. But six months later he had to call another, the historic Long Parliament that soon brought him to his knees and eventually to the grave.

Forced to give way, Charles cravenly and disgracefully sacrificed his chief advisor, the Earl of Strafford. Archbishop Laud was committed to the Tower and later executed. Parliament abolished all extra-legal courts—in particular, those two sharp engines of oppression, the awful Star Chamber and the equally fearsome Court of High Commission.

Amid these distractions, the King had to choose someone to succeed Wyatt as governor at Jamestown, a relatively unimportant matter. But Charles made a good choice—both for himself and for the colony, in the beginning at least—naming a rich and personable young blade in his early thirties, an ardent royalist, Sir William Berkeley, son of one of the original Virginia patentees.

Though narrow in his interests and a man of no particular distinction, Berkeley had purpose, energy, courage, and a fund of common sense, which he used to good advantage in his earlier years, though his sagacity vanished as he grew older. Above all, he had a genuine and abiding interest in the colony, as his life demonstrated, for he chose to devote the rest of it to Virginia, residing there for almost thirty-five years—until shipped back to

London in disgrace for having provoked a great rebellion, as his royal master had done, and in much the same manner.

Early in 1642, soon after his arrival, Berkeley learned that the conflict at home had passed from the halls of debate to the battle-field, that Charles had raised the royal standard at Nottingham, calling upon all loyal subjects to rally round and help smash the forces of Parliament. Berkeley marched under that banner all of his years, shaping his course as it rose and fell.

That the planters, in general, were royalist in sympathy pleased him, and he did his best to aid them, seriously considering their problems, joining them in their persistent efforts to obtain better prices for their tobacco. The planters, for their part, liked and respected him, finding him courteous, generous, and honest. He immediately won the good will of all by nullifying many of the fraudulent and unjust grants that had been made by Harvey.

When the fortunes of war cut off his salary, the members of the Assembly unanimously agreed to pay it, imposing a poll tax of 2*s.* ($5.00) for the purpose. They gave him a house and two acres at Jamestown as a "free and voluntary gift in consideration of many worthy favours manifested toward the Colony." When the poll tax proved to be "insupportable for the poorer sorte," Berkeley suggested a fairer levy, which added to his popularity.

Other measures brought general satisfaction, especially one aimed at doctors and lawyers, who were—too many of them— seeking "inordinate lucre." Doctors in particular were charging such exorbitant fees that masters allowed their sick servants to die rather than "fall into the hands of griping and avaricious men." Old planters who had arrived before 1616 were freed from military service and from paying any taxes but those for the support of the local ministers. Those who had fled from England to escape their debts were not to be prosecuted in the colony. If fugitive debtors could be prosecuted by their English creditors, said the Assembly, "it might hazard the deserting of a great part of the country."

Becoming a planter himself, Berkeley established himself at Green Spring, a few miles above Jamestown, where he built a large brick house and planted a huge orchard. He also began to grow grapes, but nothing came of this, for "as he was full of projects, so he was always very fickle and set them upon foot only to shew us what might be done, and . . . so never minded to bring them to perfection."

The leader in the "thrusting out" of Harvey, "worthy" Captain Mathews, had one of the better plantations, at Blunt Point, above Newport News, where he had a fine house and "all things answerable to it"—great fields of tobacco, wheat, barley, hemp, and flax; weavers to work the flax into cloth; a tannery which kept eight shoemakers busy; barns filled with cattle; a dairy and a slaughterhouse; and forty Negro servants, whom he brought "up to Trades in his house." Altogether, he lived "bravely," being honored as a "true lover of Virginia."

Within ten years, since 1634, the population had again doubled, exceeding 10,000, and the colony was well stocked with thousands of cattle and sheep, several hundred horses, and "innumerable swine and poultry." It had four windmills and five water-powered mills for grinding corn, but no sawmill as yet. There were six breweries, though most people brewed their own beer, "strong and good." Many made wine for themselves, while others were making cider and perry from their orchards, or "excellent good Metheglin," a heady ferment made from honey.

Food was rather plentiful and not too expensive for those who had to buy. One could enjoy beef and pork at 4*d*. ($.80) a pound, butter at 8*d*. a pound, and a good stewing hen at 1*s*. ($2.50). Corn could be had at 10*s*. ($25) a barrel and imported English beer at 4*s*. ($10) a gallon.

A Dutch merchant who had visited Jamestown before came again to spend the winter in 1643, noting much improvement in the people's manner of life. He had a pleasant and even a rather gay time with the planters, who were still given, he observed, to dicing, carding, and losing their "servants by gambling." While the Virginians were a hospitable people, they were, in his opinion, a bit too sharp in business.

"You must look out when you trade with them," he observed, "or you will get struck in the tail, for if they can deceive anyone, they account it a Roman action. They say in their language, 'He played him an English trick.' "

The war at home did not affect the colony for several years. But in the spring of 1644 there was a clash in the James, which brought down upon Virginia a stunning blow in a quite unexpected and yet familiar manner. A Bristol ship flying the royal standard was attacked by two larger London vessels flying the Parliament flag, under the supreme command of the new Lord High Admiral, that old schemer, the Earl of Warwick, long a Puritan in his religious views. Outgunned, the Bristol ship managed to escape with little damage and only one man killed—a planter who was on board buying supplies.

Alarmed by this and the King's declining fortunes, Berkeley decreed that Good Friday should be a day of fasting and prayers for the speedy triumph of the royalist cause. There were prayers on that day, and much fasting, but not as intended.

Twenty-two years before, on a Good Friday morning, the Indians had come into the settlements and many were eating breakfast with the planters when they suddenly turned on their hosts and killed hundreds.

This time the blow fell a day earlier, on Holy Thursday morning, before daybreak, when the Indians struck with astonishing force and fury all along the settlements, again achieving complete surprise—which would seem to argue something either about them or the colonists. More were killed than in the first massacre, with reports of the dead running from three to more than five hundred, while the Indians apparently lost not a man.

Though his death had been confidently announced many times, the great Opechancano was very much alive. Once more, he had completely outwitted the colonists, though his "flesh was all macerated, his sinews slackened, and his eyelids had become so heavy that he could not see but as they were lifted up by his servants."

As determined as ever to retain the lands of his people, the old chief had been biding his time, awaiting an opportunity for a final stroke. The clash of the ships in the James had flashed the signal for which he had been waiting. With his enemies at one another's throats, "now was his time, or never, to roote out the English."

And he might have succeeded "if God had not abated the courage of the Salvages," for he planned, after the massacre, to keep the colony in a constant state of alarm, slaughter its cattle, and destroy all crops. But to the surprise of the terrified planters, who expected Virginia to be "utterly deserted and ruinated," the Indians did not press their advantage. After a few daring raids, they "retyred themselves many miles distant from the colony, which little space of time gave the English an opportunity to gather themselves together, call an Assembly, secure their Cattell, and thinke upon some way to defend themselves."

After a long pursuit, Berkeley succeeded two years later in surprising and capturing "old King Ope Chankino," now so aged that he had to be carried about in a litter.* Brought to Jamestown, he remained brave and proud to the last, accepting his captivity as part of the fortunes of war, objecting only to the crowds of the curious that were let in to see him, telling Berkeley that if their roles had been reversed, he would "not meanly have exposed him as a show to the people."

Otherwise treating his prisoner with kindness and respect, Berkeley talked of sending the chief to England, "hoping to get a reputation by presenting his Majestie with a Royal captive." Besides, this "ancient Prince" might be used to combat ill reports of the Virginia climate by showing the "healthiness and long life of the natives of the country." But Berkeley's design was defeated by one of Opechancano's guards who "basely shot him through the back." [1]

Other Indian troubles would plague the colony and create a tremendous uproar, but this ended the long and bloody conflict with the once powerful Powhatan Confederacy, fought with such revolting savagery and treachery on both sides. Opechancano's successor agreed to withdraw all of his people from the territory be-

---

* Some reported him to be almost a hundred years old, which is not unlikely. If he were Powhatan's junior by a few years, as is probable, he would have been in his middle nineties at this time.

low the Falls on both the James and the York, and to do their hunting elsewhere.

For greater security, the Assembly now belatedly ordered the building of forts at the falls on all of the principal rivers. That on the James, in what is now Richmond, was commanded by Colonel William Byrd, the first of that name in Virginia, who conducted a profitable trade with the Indians to the south and southwest. Fort James on the Chickahominy was assigned to Pocahontas' son, Lieutenant Thomas Rolfe, now a man in his thirties, who had returned to Virginia after more than twenty years in England and in 1641 asked permission to go into the Indian country to visit his aunt "Cleopatra."

The rise of Puritan power in England, which constituted the core of opposition to the King, brought new problems. Virginia was seriously split, for the first time, on religious matters, though there had been Puritan influences in the colony from the start, as manifested by the many strict laws about religious observances and keeping the Sabbath and by numberless edicts against swearing, playing cards, dicing, "excess in apparel," and other more innocent vices.

The first minister at Henrico, Alexander Whitaker, son of an eminent Puritan scholar and divine, had belonged to that school, and the formidable and ferocious Marshal, Sir Thomas Dale, apparently was inclined that way, for Whitaker pronounced him a "Godly" man, a term never lightly used by the Puritans, who bestowed it only upon those who had seen the "light."

The Yeardley family had Puritan leanings, it would seem, perhaps due to the Governor's wife, Temperance, who had come from Norfolkshire, long a center of religious dissent. In any case, the Yeardleys' sons, Argall and Francis, became Puritans and staunch Parliament men.

But the center of Puritanism lay along the Nansemond, in one of the "particular" plantations, founded in 1621 by John Bennett, a rich merchant of London. As the bishops under James and Charles demanded stricter and stricter conformity, Bennett and his associates sent out an increasing number of people who objected to some of the tenets and rites of the Anglican Church.

As early as 1631, the Assembly had taken notice of Puritanism, proscribing all "innovations in religion," warning that worship had to be by the Anglican rite.[2] At the same time, echoing a frequent Puritan complaint, it spoke out against the type of worldly and wine-bibbing parson so familiar at home, declaring that such would not be tolerated in the colony.

"Ministers shall not give themselves to excesse in drinking or riott, spending their tyme idellye by day or night playing at dice, cards, or any other unlawfull game," the Assembly decreed. "But at all tymes convenient, they shall heare and reade somewhat of the Holy Scripture, or shall occupie themselves with some honest study or exercise, always doing the things which shall appertayne to honesty, and endeavour to profit the Church of God, always showing in mynd that they ought to excell all others in puritie of life. . . ."

Too many of the clergy "paddled in factions and state matters," a good Anglican remarked, being "such as wore black coats and could gabble in a pulpit, roar in a tavern, exact from their parishes, and rather by their dissoluteness destroy than feed their flock."

In spite of the law, Puritan practices were winked at, and there were many among the more respectable and othodox who lamented that John Winthrop had led his large Puritan company to Massachusetts and not to more southerly parts, in or near Virginia. In 1631, Harvey had sent a member of the Council to invite them and all other heretics in New England who disliked the "coldness of ye climate or barrenness of ye soil" to come to Virginia, offering them lands along the Delaware. But the Pilgrims at Plymouth and the Puritans in the Massachusetts Bay Colony were not tempted.

By 1641, the Puritan parish along the Nansemond had grown so populous that it was divided into three parishes. These immediately asked Boston for "three able ministers," which signified that the congregations had decided to break with the Anglican church and follow the "Congregational way," as it came to be called—a way laid out by the Pilgrims and adopted by the Massachusetts Puritans, who had arrived as rebellious Anglicans and were soon converted by the "Saincts" at Plymouth, now being "Saincts" themselves.

Three "Godly" ministers were sent by way of Long Island and, having suffered shipwreck in passing through Hell Gate, at the upper end of Manhattan, finally reached Virginia early in 1643, to find that Berkeley had succeeded the complaisant Wyatt, who was perhaps a Puritan himself, for most of the Sandys family and in-laws embraced that view.

While Berkeley was not devout and had no religious views as such, summing up his philosophy by saying that ministers should pray often and preach less, he nevertheless hated Puritanism and all that it stood for, especially as a political and moral force. He had been ordered to "suffer no invasion in matters of religion," which he was not disposed to do in any case. Ministers should conform to the doctrines and rituals of the Church of England, he decreed, and were "not otherwise to be admitted to teach or preach, publicly or privately." Whether clerical or lay, all non-conformists, if commanded to leave by the governor and Council, were "to depart the colony with all convenience."

The New England pastors found "loving and liberal entertainment" along the Nansemond, where they preached in private houses to many whose "hearts seemed to be much inflamed with an earnest desire after the Gospel." But not wishing to go on preaching against Berkeley's orders, the three pastors soon sailed for Boston, taking with them a notable convert, young Daniel Gookin, who later made a name for himself in Massachusetts and throughout New England as a man of affairs and an eloquent advocate of the Indians' cause.

Opechancano's braves struck soon after, and some interpreted the massacre as divine punishment for the sin of harboring "heretics." But Governor Winthrop of Massachusetts ascribed it to God's wrath for the sin of expelling the New England pastors— a view now suddenly and disconcertingly adopted by Berkeley's close friend and private chaplain, Thomas Harrison, who had led the hue and cry against the Puritans. Renouncing the Anglican church, Harrison went down to the Nansemond where he preached to large congregations in spite of Berkeley's fulminations until he was driven out four years later, fleeing to Boston.

Eager to obtain as many people as possible for his huge proprietorship, not practicing religious conformity himself, being a Catholic as his father had been, Lord Baltimore let it be known after the expulsion of Harrison that Maryland would welcome the persecuted Puritans of Virginia. Upon the death of his brother Leonard, he made another politic move, choosing a planter from the Eastern Shore, Captain William Stone, as governor. A liberal Anglican himself, Stone was enjoined not to disturb anyone because of religious beliefs.

Going further, Baltimore drafted his celebrated Toleration Act, which the Maryland Assembly adopted on April 21, 1649. As a toleration act, it left much to be desired. It was for Christians only. It did not establish the complete religious freedom which Roger Williams had proclaimed in Rhode Island some years before. It was less liberal than the laws in force at home, passed by the Long Parliament after overthrowing the Church of England in 1645. Yet it marked a significant step forward, granting far more latitude than was then allowed in Jamestown, Plymouth, or Boston.

Anyone blaspheming against God, or denying that "our Saviour Jesus Christ" was the son of God, or denying the Holy Trinity, or the Holy Ghost, or the "Godhead" of any of these, or the "unity of the Godhead," was to be executed and have his estate confiscated. Anyone using "reproachfull" words about the Virgin Mary, or the holy apostles, or the Evangelists, should pay £5 ($250).

But no person "professing to believe in Jesus Christ shall from henceforth bee any waies troubled, molested, or discountenanced for or in respect to his or her religion." And no one should call another a religious name "in a reproachfull manner"—as "heretick, Scismatick, Idolator, Puritan, Independent, Prespiterian, popish priest . . ."—upon pain of paying 10s. ($25).

Whatever Baltimore's motives, no matter how much self-interest was involved, this was an enlightened step and it brought Maryland, as he had hoped, many people—hundreds from Virginia, which lost almost a tenth of its population to its rival.

More than a thousand from the Puritan settlements along the

Nansemond and from the Eastern Shore, another Puritan center, moved up the Chesapeake, led by their ruling elders, William Durand and Richard Bennett, later a governor of Virginia. They settled along a sluggish river which they called the Severn, naming their community Providence, out of which grew Annapolis, one of the most charming of our old towns. These Virginia Puritans repaid Baltimore's hospitality by soon seizing control of Maryland and passing a new "toleration" act, denying liberty of conscience to those favoring "popery, prelacy, or licentiousness of opinion," decreeing that no Roman Catholic could vote or hold office.[3]

The conflict in Maryland reflected events at home. After much devious winding and many futile dodges, the King had been forced to give in. His armies had been smashed—by Oliver Cromwell and his Ironsides at Marston Moor in 1644, with a great slaughter of Cavaliers,* whom "God had made," said Cromwell, "as stubble before our swords." The New Model army had completed the rout at Naseby the next year.

Virtually a prisoner of Parliament, having learned nothing from adversity, Charles clung to his high doctrine and low practices, indulging in duplicity to the last—"playing the game," he called it. He secretly contrived to have the Scots invade England in his behalf, an invasion hurled back in great disorder. He now secretly tried to persuade the Irish to invade the realm and reduce his people to obedience—a "more prodigious treason" could scarcely be imagined, said Cromwell, and it cost the King his head.

Now firmly in control, Cromwell and his Independents purged the Long Parliament of appeasers, expelling those Presbyterians disposed to compromise with the King. Proclaiming that the "people, under God, are the original of all just power," they appointed a court to try the King for high treason. When the House

---

* As is generally known, the King's men contemptuously dubbed their enemies the Roundheads because so many of the Parliamentary supporters were apprentices and humble people who wore their hair cropped short. What is not so generally known is that the latter just as contemptuously dubbed their opponents the Cavaliers, using the term as one of reproach and opprobrium, signifying a freebooter, a swagman, a soldier of fortune, a man of no industry, skill, or trade, a decorative parasite.

of Lords objected to this, they abolished that House as "useless and dangerous." England was now a Commonwealth, stripped of feudal trimmings in Church and State.

On January 30, 1649, Charles I went to the block in the palace yard at Whitehall, calm and courageous, a nobler figure in his death than in his life, but stubborn and unyielding to the end. He had worked as much as anyone for the liberty and freedom of the people, he declared as he stepped to his doom, "but I must tell you that their liberty and freedom consist in having government. . . . It is not their having a share in the government. That is nothing appertaining unto them. A subject and a sovereign are clean different things."

XXIV

Under the Commonwealth

> *. . . do but follow me. I will either
> lead you to victory or . . .*
>
> —SIR WILLIAM BERKELEY

VIRGINIA gasped when it learned of the King's execution.
Berkeley was horrified, as was the Assembly, pronouncing it
treason to justify the proceedings of Parliament, to question
Charles II's right to succeed to the throne, or to propose any
change in the officers or frame of government at Jamestown. Dire
punishment awaited any who should "go about by unreverent or
scandalous words or language to blast the memory and honour of
the late most pious King (deserving of altars and monuments in
the hearts of all good men)."

As Berkeley declared, though with some exaggeration, "Virginia
was whole for the monarchie and the last country belonging to
England that submitted to obedience to the Commonwealth." Refusing to recognize the latter, the Governor had his commission
renewed by the King's son, subsequently Charles II, who had fled
to the Continent.

The first of the fugitive Cavaliers soon began to arrive, having
been "industriously" invited by Berkeley, who offered them all the
advantages of Virginia as a "place of security . . . where they
might live plentifully," especially if they could afford to bring
servants.

One of the first groups to come, led by Colonel Henry Norwood, "nearly related" to Berkeley, had suffered a typically Virginian voyage which must have given them pause and led many to wonder if they had been wise in leaving home. During a long and storm-tossed voyage, death claimed many, and then food and water ran out. Unable to work his way into the Chesapeake against strong head winds, the captain of the ship landed a score of them on what he took to be the Maryland coast.

But he had left them, as they soon learned with a great shock, on an island, where they were marooned without supplies and unable to find anything but a few oysters to sustain them. A woman died, and they ate her, as Norwood suggested. Four more died, and they were consumed. Aften ten days of this, some Indians crossed from the mainland and were not too friendly until someone in the party happened to utter a magic word—"werowance," which he chanced to remember from reading Captain John Smith's books.

Rescued and guided by the Indians, Norwood and his remaining friends were taken to the Eastern Shore, where they were wined and dined for more than a week by Argall Yeardley, "a Gentleman of good name," though he was a Puritan and a Parliament man. Crossing the Chesapeake, they learned that some friends lately come from England were "feasting and carousing" at Captain Ralph Wormeley's. Journeying there, they enjoyed "very good cheer" before they went on to Jamestown to be warmly welcomed by Berkeley, "who showed great respect to all the royal party who made that colony their refuge. His house and purse were open to all that were so qualifyed."

Norwood was invited to stay at Green Spring, and good care was taken of his particular friends. To one of them, a Major Richard Fox, who had fled without a penny, Berkeley showed a "generosity that was like himself." To another, Major Francis Morison, Norwood's chief aide, he was "more than kind." He not only gave him command of the fort at Jamestown, "which was profitable to him whilst it held under the King, but did advance him after to the government of the country [as acting governor], wherein he got a competent estate," the aim of every colonial governor almost without exception. Berkeley gave the profitable treasuryship of the colony to his kinsman Norwood, but the latter was so misguided that he soon returned home, where he spent four years in the Tower of London.

Colonial affairs had been placed in the hands of a new board of commissioners under the Earl of Warwick. As Virginia, Maryland, and the Barbadoes had not declared for the Commonwealth, the commissioners forbade all intercourse with these colonies and ordered foreign ships to stay away, hoping in this manner to bring about their submission without a show or use of arms. This measure hurt Virginia, for merchants increased the price of their goods and, in want of buyers, the price of tobacco fell sharply.

Worse, in 1650, Parliament passed a restrictive Navigation Act, the first of many that were to harass the colonies down to the Revolution. Under this, all goods sent to and from the colonies were to be carried in English or colonial ships, and the captain and the majority of the crew had to be English. The act was not strictly enforced. But in theory at least, it closed the ports of Virginia to the Dutch who had been doing most of the trading and shipping there for some years now, since the outbreak of the civil war, and Berkeley uttered a loud protest, adding a bold defiance of all Commonwealth authority.

The rebels at home, he told the Assembly, might have thought of something to "strengthen us to beare those heavy chains they are making for us, though it were but an assurance that we shall eat the bread for which our owne oxen plow and with our owne sweat we reape."

But no, the planters were to be "their Worships' slaves, bought with their money and, by consequence, ought not to buy or sell but with those they shall authorize with a few trifles to cozen us of all . . ."

Virginians would be craven slaves if they allowed themselves to be "shaken with these paper bullets, and those, on my life," he declared, "are the heaviest they either can or will send against us."

As England groaned with misery, Virginians had every reason to be happy with things as they were. What more could they wish or ask for?

Was it liberty? The sun did not shine on a people more free from all oppression.

Was it peace? The Indians had at last been subdued. Was it wealth? The lives of hundreds demonstrated what a little industry and thrift could do. Was it security to enjoy that wealth?

"Without blushing, I will speak it," said Berkeley. "I am confident there lives not that person can accuse me of attempting the least act against any man's property."

The planters had nothing to fear but the "Londoners who would faine bring us to the same poverty wherein the Dutch found and relieved us, would take away the liberty of our conscience and tongues, and our right of giving and selling our goods to whom we please," he declared.

"But, Gentlemen, by the Grace of God, we will not so tamely part with our King and all these blessings we enjoy under him. And if they oppose us, do but follow me. I will either lead you to victory or lose a life which I cannot more gloriously sacrifice than for my loyalty and your security."

The Commonwealth had decided, after long consideration, that Virginia, Maryland, and the Barbadoes had to be brought to heel, appointing four commissioners for the purpose. The latter were given wide discretion in granting indemnities and pardons, but they were commanded to see that all in the recalcitrant colonies swore to be "true and faithful to the Commonwealth of England as it is now established without King or House of Lords." They were to see that all writs ran "in the name of the Keepers of the Liberty of England, by authority of Parliament."

Three of the commissioners were old Virginia planters—William Claiborne, who still had his eye on Kent Island; Richard Bennett, a leader of the Puritan exodus to Maryland; and Thomas Stegg, a rich merchant of London, who had vast interests in the colony, having served as Speaker of the first Assembly called by Berkeley.

Embarking on the *John* and a Dutch frigate, they sailed with a large fleet of armed ships carrying more than six hundred men— most of them Scottish prisoners of war, whom the planters had "desired" and been granted upon their assurance "to give them

Christian usage." Two years previously, after Cromwell's capture of Drogheda, hundreds of Irish had been shipped to Virginia and other colonies desiring them.

The commissioners quickly persuaded the Barbadoes to submit and appeared at Jamestown in March, 1652, to the spluttering rage of Berkeley. The latter talked loudly of resistance, encouraged in this by the "malignants," as the Cavaliers were known to many—"by those same unhappy Gentlemen," the commissioners observed, "that helped ruine themselves and their King," and now would ruin Virginia.

But a number of planters favored the Commonwealth. Still more had no desire to fight a losing battle in an already lost cause, a view made quite plain through their Burgesses. Consequently, the Assembly offered to capitulate if the submission of Virginia were accepted as a "voluntary act" and not as the result of conquest.

The commissioners readily agreed, offering generous terms of settlement, and the transfer of power was quietly and quickly effected. After all his brave talk, Berkeley did nothing but hurry a messenger to Charles II to explain his failure to hold Virginia or even make a fight for it, saying that he was "defenceless." This was true, but his failure to make even a show of resistance was never forgiven.

A general amnesty was proclaimed. As Berkeley desired to remain in the colony, he was allowed to do so, retiring to Green Spring.* If he and his friends wished, they might continue to pray for the King and sing his praises for a year, but only in their families or at private gatherings. A year's grace was also allowed Anglican parsons, the Book of Common Prayer, and any who refused to take the new oath of allegiance.

Under the capitulation agreement, subsequently ratified by Parliament, the Assembly acquired new and much broader powers. Though the right had been asserted before, it was now officially decreed that the colony was to be "free of all taxes, customes, and

* As a contemporary historian, the great Clarendon, remarked: Berkeley "was suffered to remain there as a private man upon his own plantation, which was a better subsistence than he could have found anywhere else."

impositions whatsoever," except those levied with the consent of the Assembly. As the "representatives of the people," the House of Burgesses acquired the right to elect all general officers—the county commissioners, the thirteen members of the Council, and even the governor.

To succeed Berkeley, the Burgesses chose one of the commissioners, Richard Bennett; and as Secretary, another of the commissioners, William Claiborne. Among others elected to the Council were Argall Yeardley and two of the leaders in the "thrusting out" of Harvey, "gallant" Captain Mathews and Captain John West, formerly a governor. All of these had been in high command before and were familiar figures in Jamestown, so that they represented no new or alien influence.

For the planters, life went on much as usual, with no marked change except in the churches. The suppression of Anglicanism aroused no resistance or commotion, for Virginians, however devout, did not bring much passion to any particular credo.

As four out of five parishes were without services, the Assembly offered a bonus of £20 ($1,000) to anyone who would bring over a minister. It also decreed that ministers, together with their families and six servants, were not to pay taxes so that they might better "attend both publick commands and their private cares."

Some "Godly" ministers were attracted by this, but most visitors of any piety had a low opinion of the Virginia clergy. A few were "religious and laborious," but there were many—the majority— "whose wicked and profane lives caused the worship of God not only to be slighted, but to be little less than abhorred." Most of them had come "out of some aims and ends of their own," being such as were "ashamed or afraid" to live any longer in England. And their parishioners were not much better, such visitors remarked, being "those wicked and ungodly wretches heretofore planted there."

The planters failed to provide for the maintenance of ministers. When they undertook to do so, they fobbed off on the poor pastor all of their worst tobacco. They should be made to pay their best tobacco, "and with Cask; otherwise, experience hath shewed that a Minister's livelyhood there will be very uncertain."

Nor were the planters eager to build churches. Those they did put up were a shame and a disgrace. "Why will not all the Christians of a parish bestow as much cost in building the house of their great God as one particular Christian among them bestows upon his own house?"

There was a lack of "Christian neighborhood, . . . and Civil Conference and Commerce," and an "almost general want of schools" for the education of their children. The latter were naturally "beautiful and comely persons, and generally of more ingenious Spirits than those in England." But in want of training, they were "unserviceable for any great employments, either in Church or State."

The planters should be forced to live in towns, the only fit place for Christians to reside. This could be done by establishing a market town in every county and forbidding the sale of goods elsewhere. Those with servants should then be ordered "to build themselves houses in the Towns nearest to them, and to inhabit them." They should then "take care that, upon Saturday afternoon (when, by the custome of Virginia, servants are freed from their ordinary labour), their servants (except one or two left by turns to secure their plantations) may repair to their houses in the towns and there remain with their Masters until the publick worship and service of the Lord's Day be ended."

As it was, service was so neglected on the Lord's Day that "some of the Heathen have complained that it is the worst of the seven for them," because the servants of nearby plantations, "being left at liberty, oft spend that day in visiting the Indian towns, to the disquiet of the Heathen and certainly to the great Scandall of the Christian religion." The planters' neglect of religion was the "prime cause of their long languishing improsperous condition, for it puts them under the Curse of God."

Whether this was the reason or not, trade was languishing in Virginia, with many complaining that there was "no profit to be had there." The price of tobacco kept falling, and renewed attempts were made to encourage the production of other things than "that contemptible, beggarly, Indian weed." A sizable bonus was offered to anyone who exported flax, hemp, or hops worth

£200, or 200 pounds of wound silk, or English wheat worth £500, or "two tunne of wine raised out of a vineyard in this Colonie," or almost anything at all but tobacco. But the bonus, ironically enough, was to be paid in tobacco—10,000 pounds.

Two Armenian silkmasters had been brought over by Edward Digges, who became governor in 1655, succeeding Bennett. After many losses and with great toil, he was winding enough silk to make £7 or £8 ($400) a year. But there now came, a voice from the past, an ecstatic tract from England, *The Reformed Virginian Silk Worm*, dedicated to the "beloved Planters" and written in almost breathless excitement by Virginia, daughter of John Ferrar, the Company's former Deputy.

She had discovered, she said, "a thing scarce credible, because not heretofore thought of"—silkworms could be raised on trees, in the open, and did not require special houses. Could anything be more auspicious for Virginia?

None could deny that the silk business was the best of all trades "in regard of its great and certain gain in so small a time." A man and a boy could tend sufficient worms to yield a profit of £60 ($3,000) a year. As the colony had innumerable wild mulberry trees, nothing was wanting "to make Virginia rival Peru for wealth." The planters could now give up their tobacco, which was but "smoak and vapour," and turn to this "reall-royall-solid-rich-staple Commodity."

Any child could learn the business, and it was a "most fit recreation for Ladies." Altogether, it just fitted the planters' needs, "not requiring strength of Body, of Wit, of Purse."

Besides, it would offer "most proper imployment for the lazie Indians." If offered 5s. for all the silk they collected, they would set about it briskly, which would give some hope at last of civilizing and converting them.

The colony's happiness would thus be raised in every way "to the height of blisse," Virginia concluded in boundless rapture. "And so, Lord, prosper this work in their hands. Lord, prosper their handywork. Good luck I wish you all in the name of the Lord. *Amen, Amen, Amen.*" Virginia added a cautionary postscript.

"*Memorandum,* that you take notice that the Birds will eat up the Silkwormes on the trees. . . . If all else fails, a boy may be set to affright them all away with some noise. . . ."

Again, events at home shook the colony. After five years as Lord Protector, the great Oliver Cromwell died, being succeeded by his son Richard. The latter was ineffectual and as the power of the Roundheads was obviously declining, Richard resigned after less than a year in office, in May, 1659. A few months later, the governor at Jamestown died, "worthy" Captain Samuel Mathews.

In this anomalous situation, with England having no ruler and Virginia no governor, the Assembly moved cautiously. Meeting early in 1660, it declared itself, for the time being, "the Supreme power of the government," and its members approached Berkeley to ask if he would resume command. Subscribing himself as their "most Humble and Affectionate friend and Servant," he suggested that they choose someone with "more vigorous qualities to manage and support your affaires," and one with more dexterity in untying those knots which he could "neither unloose nor breake amongst the Council."

When pressed, Berkeley agreed to serve if the Council, solidly composed of Commonwealth men, would concur in his election. They expressed their approval, and after eight years of retirement Berkeley again assumed office at the call of the Burgesses, who laid down three conditions for his return. He was to call the Assembly at least every two years. He could not dissolve the Assembly without the consent of the Burgesses. His choice of Secretary of the colony had to be approved by the Assembly. All of this seemed to assure a continuance of representative and responsive government.

Berkeley's election was a personal triumph. It did not represent a victory for the royalist cause, still less for Stuart absolutism. Many prominent Puritans and Commonwealth men were placed in office at the same time—William Claiborne, as Secretary, and Theodore Bland, related to the Bennetts, as Speaker of the Assembly that had laid down the conditions of Berkeley's return.

But Sir William was grateful for the confidence placed in him, raising no objections to his "rebel" colleagues or to the limitations imposed by the Burgesses.

"You have given me a treasure," he told them, "but in vaine excepte you helpe me to carry it to some place of safetie. You have raised a high expectation of me, but you must instruct and prompt me how to satisfye it. You have laid high honours on me, but except you helpe to support me under them, they will sink me into disgrace."

Berkeley could command a noble eloquence on occasion, and these were wise words that he would have done well to remember, for they would have guided him away from many troubles and the final explosion that brought him to his grave in disgrace.

About six months later, Virginia learned of the landing and coronation of Charles II. At Berkeley's order, the news was proclaimed in every county, where many brimming toasts were drunk to the sound of drums and trumpets, the rattle of small arms, and the boom of cannon. Sir William later paid out of the public treasury large sums for the celebration of this occasion—for gunpowder, trumpeteers, a sermon, salvoes of "great gunnes, and 211 gallons of cider"—hard, no doubt.

Still, Berkeley was uneasy about his position, wondering whether he should have accepted office from the Burgesses in view of the Crown's assertion that it was the royal prerogative to appoint and remove governors. He was worried also by his meek surrender to the Commonwealth. Throwing himself at the feet of Charles II as his "most Humble, most Dutifull, Loyall, & Obedient Subject, Servant, and Creature," he protested that he had not been "guilty of weakness" in giving up Virginia, that he had merely leaped "over the fold" to save his Majesty's flock. Of this, he said he could offer a thousand proofs, "besides the Awful Reverence I ever had of your Sacred Majestie."

The Assembly was even more abject, for none surpassed Virginia's servility in approaching the Throne. By accepting the rule of the Commonwealth, it had been an accomplice of "that execrable power that so bloodily massacred the late King, Charles the First, of ever blessed and glorious memory." To expiate that sin, it had decreed that the day of his execution should be "annually solemnized with fasting and prayers," and that May 29, the birthday of Charles II and also the day of his coronation, should be forever celebrated as a "holy day."

Virginians were only too happy to carry out the King's injunction to "forget animosities begotten by the late distracted and unsettled times, and affectionately unite so that former differences be buried in oblivion." The shift to the Restoration was made as quietly and quickly as that to the Commonwealth eight years before, and with little change except in the churches.

Again, all services were to be conducted "according to the profession of the Church of England." Pending the time when the Merry Monarch expressed his "pious thoughts" on the matter, the Anglican liturgy should be "thoroughly read" every Sunday, the Assembly decreed, and every church should be adorned with the proper "ornaments"—a great Bible, a Book of Common Prayer, "a communion cloath and napkin, a pulpit and cushion."

Even those planters most sympathetic toward the Commonwealth felt that a change for the better might occur under the new regime. In repealing the decrees of the Long Parliament and of Lord Protector Cromwell, Charles II would surely rescind the navigation laws that had so depressed the price of tobacco. To plead the planters' cause and make his own personal obeisance to the King, Berkeley was only too happy to go to England, where he wrote and published a *Discourse* on Virginia, designed to explain its problems, stir up interest in the colony, and defend his course of action.

If the navigation act profited the majority in the realm or the Crown, the planters would not mind, he said. But as it did not, Virginia could not help "but resent that 40,000 people should be impoverished to enrich little more than forty merchants, who, being the only buyers of our Tobacco, give us what they please for it and, after it is here, sell it how they please," thus commanding the planters' labor and reducing them to virtual slavery.

To the criticism that Virginia depended entirely upon tobacco, Berkeley replied that the fault was largely Lord Baltimore's. Whenever laws were passed "for the erecting of Staple Commodities and setting a stop to the unlimited planting of Tobacco," they could not be enforced, for the people fled to Maryland where

Lord Baltimore, always eager for settlers, allowed them to plant as much tobacco as they pleased.

Besides, there was a "great scarcity of good men—that is, of able Workemen," which was Virginia's chief want. The colony was sent "only such servants as have been brought up to no Art or Trade," only such as the pangs of hunger or the fear of jail had driven from England, or the wilder and more improvident sons of "better" families.

Still, said Berkeley, Rome had been built by such as these, and some of the riffraff in Virginia had become "sober and thrifty."

But the colony desperately needed "men of manufacture," skilled artisans, and only decent wages could induce such men to leave home and "hazard (as they style it) their lives." As the planters could not offer such wages, the King should add a penny to the duty of tobacco and contribute this to Virginia, which would enable the colony to pay all public charges, "build mills for Iron and Planks, procure us on good salaries able men for Silk, Cordage, Mines, and Flax," as well as for "lead, pitch, tar, masts, timber for ships of the greatest magnitude, and wood for potashes." Within seven years, said Berkeley, Virginia would be shipping annually "as much silk into England as now costs the nation £200,000 [$10,000,000] at least."

Then the planters would not have to fix their hopes upon "that vicious weed of Tobacco," which had brought them to such an extremity that they could not "subsist with or without it." The price of it had fallen so low that it did not even provide them with coarse clothing. All that could be said for it was that it brought the Crown more revenue than anything else from the New World.

To Berkeley, London provided a welcome change from the rusticity of life at Jamestown and Green Spring. He liked the bustle and excitement of the city, which, after long years of turmoil and Puritan gloom, was gay and boisterous again, with the Merry Monarch setting the pace with his revels. The taverns were roaring, the theaters were open once more, crowded to capacity, and Berkeley had the pleasure of attending a performance of his own play, *The Lost Lady,* a tragi-comedy written and produced in 1638 before his departure for Virginia.

Samuel Pepys went to see the play, too, but had a miserable time of it. Being in one of his thrifty moods, which took such curious turns and so often got him into trouble, he bought a 1s. seat in the pit. But observing some clerks from his office sitting above him in the half-crown seats, he fretted throughout the performance lest they spy him in the mob down below. Somewhat impressed, however, he came to see the play again, bought himself a seat in a respectable part of the house, and this time, he acknowledged, "it pleased me more."

Enjoying himself in London after his long absence, Berkeley informed Charles of his intention of waiting upon his "royall person one half year." But as his expenses were high and he needed money, he asked to be allowed to bring in, customs free, a ship of tobacco, "hoping your Majesty, God's vice-regent, will imitate your great exemplar, God, and reward good intentions."

But he little knew his royal master, who cavalierly and almost insultingly dismissed him.

"Sir William Berkeley shall have a ship of tobacco of 300 tons, customs free, when he shall send or bring over a ship of the same burthen laden with silk, hemp, flax, pitch, and potashes, the produce and growth of Virginia," replied the King, ordering Berkeley to "repair speedily" to Jamestown.

XXV

Restoration

*It is an undoubted truth that the riches of all
plantations consist in the well-peopling of them.*

—MAJOR FRANCIS MORISON

*A*FTER more than a year's absence, Berkeley returned to Jamestown late in 1662, a disappointed and embittered man. For
his loyalty to the loyalist cause, for his services to the King, he
had been snubbed. He had received no mark of distinction from
Charles who was strewing honors and rewards about with such a
lavish hand.

Unhappily, Sir William turned his rancor and resentment
upon the colony. As the King would not advance him and his
fortunes, he would enrich himself and the planters would pay.
Formerly so just and honest, he turned the government into an
oppressive engine for private gain, multiplying fees and fines, making a jobbery of all offices. Determined to do as he pleased, eaten
up by avarice, he became increasingly arbitrary in his acts and
testy in manner, flying into a rage at the slightest criticism or
opposition.

"Age and misfortunes have withered my hopes," he observed
a few years later, adding in an obvious reference to himself,
"Ambition commonly leaves sober old age, but covetousness doth
not."

Besides, Berkeley now had a divided loyalty, being a partner in a vast proprietorship to the south, christened Carolina in honor of the King (Carolus Rex). The grant had been obtained through the influence of Sir William's older brother, Lord John Berkeley, who stood close to the Throne, having shared Charles's exile as tutor to his younger brother, the Duke of York, the future James II of evil fame.

The English title to the territory was based upon a purchase made by Francis Yeardley and others under the Commonwealth. Having joined the Puritan exodus to Maryland, Yeardley left that colony in 1654 and moved below Virginia, where he and his friends bought from the Indians for £300 "three great rivers and all such others as they should like southerly."

Eyeing this, Lord Berkeley and his associates, "excited by a laudable and pious zeal for the propagation of the Gospel," as proprietors always were, sought and obtained a patent granting them lordly rights over a huge tract extending from Virginia to the St. Mathias River in Florida. Sir William was to exercise immediate supervision, appointing as its first governor an able Scotsman, William Drummond, whom he later hanged in Virginia.

Not only had Berkeley returned a changed man, but he brought the depressing news that the King, far from rescinding the Commonwealth's navigation acts, intended to enforce them more strictly and even extend them. No goods should be bought from foreign vessels. No staples should be shipped anywhere but to England. No one in the colonies should set himself up in business as a merchant or a factor. Goods transported from colony to colony were to pay the same customs duties as if shipped to England. It heightened the planters' sense of grievance that the "disaffected" New England colonies evaded these laws while "loyal" Virginia obeyed and suffered.

Of better omen, Berkeley brought back the King's pardon for all who had embraced the Commonwealth cause. There were to be no punishments or reprisals. Former political differences were to be buried and forgotten. Also, no one was "to be molested or disquieted in the exercise of his Religion, so he be content with the quiet and peaceable enjoying of it, not giving therein any offence or scandall to the Government." *

Whatever his faults, Charles II was not a bigot and it was his wish, he said, "to give all possible encouragement to persons of different persuasions of Religion to transport themselves thither with their stock."

But the Assembly did not believe in such latitude, immediately passing drastic laws against those who, "out of the new-fangled conceits of their own hereticall inventions, refuse to have their children baptized," and against Quakers, "praters of nonsense," many of whom received thirty-two stripes "with a nine-corded whip, three knots in a cord."

If no Quakers were hanged here as in Massachusetts, it was "not owing to the moderation of the church, or the spirit of the legislature," as Thomas Jefferson later remarked. It was entirely a matter of circumstance—no Quakers chose to violate the Virginia law that prescribed the death penalty for any "notorious heretic" daring to return to the colony after being twice expelled.

Other "praters of nonsense" came under the displeasure of the Assembly—"babling women," who got their husbands into fist-fights, law suits, and other troubles. Gossips were to be punished "with ducking," and if the scandal were too great, a second and third ducking. But the "babling" remained incessant—as it was in the beginning, is now, and ever shall be—and for calling her neighbor a "hoare," one Jane Butler was not only ducked but "drawen over the Creeke at the starne of a boate," and on the following Sunday, "between the first and second lesson," she had to acknowledge her fault before the congregation and ask for prayers of forgiveness.

After more than fifty years, Virginia did not yet have a public building in which the Assembly might meet, the court sit, and the governor and his staff have offices. Shocked by this, the King commanded that Jamestown should be graced with a state house. Berkeley should also build some substantial towns, as had been

---

* The governor, however, was to worship according to the Anglican rite and recommend it to all, "so farre as it may consist with peace and quiet of our said Colonie."

done by "their neighbors of New England who have in a few years raised that Colony to breed wealth, reputation, and security." Planters should be forced to live in these towns and stop their straggling.

Ignoring the command about the capitol, the Assembly prohibited any more wooden buildings in Jamestown and ordered the construction there of thirty brick houses, to be built "in a square or such other forme" as Berkeley might decide. Each was to be forty feet long and twenty feet wide, with a steep roof of slate or tile.

As Jamestown wanted skilled workers, the counties were ordered to "press" carpenters, bricklayers, and other artisans to do the work. After many trials, a few brick houses were completed, but at great cost, as the Council complained, for "our poor assaye of building four or five houses lost us hundreds of people"—in large part, skilled workers, the best in the colony, who fled to Maryland to escape being pressed.

As before, Maryland remained a sharp thorn in the side of her "dear sister," Virginia. Attempts had been made to reach an agreement with her to restrict the planting of tobacco—primarily, to curtail the supply and thus enhance its price; incidentally, to stimulate the production of silk, hemp, flax, masts, and other "more staple commodities," which the Crown, following the Company, had so long desired. But Lord Baltimore and shipowners in the tobacco trade blocked this, and Virginia was unable to do anything alone. Whenever one colony tried to improve the tobacco market by prohibiting the "trash of that commodity," the other poured into England all that it could grow, "both good and bad, without distinction."

In 1663, representatives of Virginia, Maryland, and Carolina reached an agreement, but the Maryland Assembly rejected it. Virginia then petitioned the Crown to forbid the shipment of tobacco for a year. The price of tobacco had fallen so low, the planters complained, that they were running into debt at the rate of £50,000 ($2,500,000) a year.*

---

* Virginia was shipping 50,000 hogsheads of tobacco a year, worth £3 each, or £150,000 in all. But as yearly imports totaled £200,000, the colony had a very high trade deficit.

Again, Lord Baltimore blocked action, saying that the small planter lived on a slender margin and could not afford to hold his crop. If any lived poorly in Virginia, it was "not from the low price of tobacco," he declared, "but from their own sloth, ill husbandry, and purposely spending their cropps in Brandewine and other liquors, it being evident and known that such as are industrious were not destitute."

Maryland's system of taxation also caused complaint along the James. Revenue in Virginia was raised entirely by poll tax—"all paying equal," as one of the Council explained, so that a man with ten acres paid as much as one with ten thousand. Maryland, on the other hand, taxed by the acre and offered "good land free from all Incombrances" to any who would come.

"By this meanes, we yearly lose considerable numbers of people, and by it have fewer hands to act anything for our advantage, or for the advance of his Majestie's service, and fewer persons to pay for it," protested the colony's agent in London, Major Francis Morison, urging that steps be taken "to make the neighbourhood of Maryland less prejudiciall to us."

And what was as "infinitely ruinous" and should be stopped, Maryland granted "tolleration to all sorts of sects, which, by their neighbourhood (a river only severing us), infect our people and by that drawes them from us, or spreads their venom amongst us."

Still, said Morison, he could not help admiring Baltimore for "his prudent management that never omitts to improve the least occasion to his advantage. . . . It is his Lordship's interest to gett people to him, as it is ours to fix them with us, for it is an undoubted truth that the riches of all plantations consist in the well-peopling of them."

Twice as populous as when the Commonwealth was proclaimed, Virginia now had some 40,000 people, of whom 2,000 were Negro slaves, a marked increase since 1649 when there were only 300. Though the importation and sale of captured Negroes did not become a major business until the next century, slavery had been encouraged by the incorporation in 1662 of the Royal African Company, of which the Duke of York was head and the King a principal stockholder. Berkeley and succeeding governors received strict instructions to be vigilant about the Royal African's business interests in Virginia.

In most years, about 1,500 newcomers arrived—chiefly "Christian servants." Formerly, not one in five of these had survived their first year. While new plantations were still unhealthy until "thoroughly cleared of wood," the death rate had dropped sharply since the country had been opened up.

Of the indentured servants, most were English, Berkeley reported, though there were a few Scottish and fewer Irish. To some, they seemed the "very scum and offscouring" of society, "vagrants or condemned persons, or such others as by the looseness and viciousness of their lives" could no longer live at home. This was true in part, for the authorities at home transported an increasing number of felons from the jails and lewd women from the Bridewell and other houses of correction, charged with prostitution or walking the streets "after ten at night."

The Council became so concerned about the peace of the colony, fearing that it would be "endangered by the great numbers of fellows and other desperate villains sent hither from the several prisons in England," that in 1670 it forbade anyone to "bring in and land any jail-birds or such others who, for notorious offences, deserved to dye in England." Not only did these constitute a present danger, but they gave Virginia the reputation of being a "place only fitt to receive such base and lewd persons."

Many of these "villains" were not villainous at all, as their lives proved. Some of them, indeed, brought enlightenment to the colony. As true of many planters' sons, George Washington "had no other education than reading, writing, and accounts," which were taught him "by a convict servant whom his father had bought as a schoolmaster."

But the immigrants, in the main, were simply poor unfortunates transported at the expense of the planters or brought in for sale by the shipmasters. Most of them had come voluntarily as indentured servants, having agreed to serve their masters without pay for a number of years, from four to seven. They brought the planters a double benefit—not only their slave labor, but a "head right" to fifty acres for every person so transported.

But a growing number—men, women, and children—had not come voluntarily, having been kidnaped by "Spirits," who plied a profitable twofold trade in supplying all but the New England colonies with white servile labor. Those pursued by the law or in other difficulties sought hiding with them and were secreted away. But their chief business was to kidnap the young, the inexperienced, and the friendless, who were lured into taverns and there seized to be sold in Virginia as "servants or slaves" to those who bid the most for them—"a practice proper for Spirits, namely Spirits of the Devill."

Most of the newcomers were put to work in the tobacco fields which continued to expand in spite of the vagaries of that trade and the dangers of a one-crop economy. Aware of those dangers, recognizing the need of "improving all means of raysing and promoting manufactures amonge ourselves," the Assembly had flax seed imported from England. It ordered every county to set up a loom within two years and provide a skilled weaver at public expense. It offered larger premiums—paid in tobacco—to encourage the production of silk, hemp, pitch, turpentine, and tar, among other things.

Silk seemed the "most hopeful commodity," and the planters sent the King three hundred pounds of it as a present, "being the first fruits of their labours in that kind." Berkeley informed Charles that, with his "gracious permission," he would come to England that year and "goe into France to procure skillful men" for that great work. Once this were done, Virginia would "noe longer depend wholly upon tobacco, to the ruine of the colony and decay of your Majestie's customs." The King thanked Berkeley for the silk, saying that it would be "wrought up for ye use of Our owne person," but did not invite him to England.

Already low, tobacco prices again fell and taxes went up after June, 1665, when the King informed Berkeley of his intention of declaring war on the Dutch and ordered him to prepare for hostilities. A rumor that Admiral De Ruyter was approaching with a large fleet threw Virginia into a panic, and Berkeley hastily wrote home for cannon and armed frigates. Levying a heavy tax for the purpose, he began building a fort at Jamestown.

Informed of this, the King ordered the fort to be built at Point Comfort, which entailed extra expense and more taxes. As Berkeley and the Council much preferred Jamestown, where the inhabitants would be a "sufficient garrison to defend it, without public charge," Secretary Thomas Ludwell spoke not only for them but for all the planters in expressing the wish "that the Governor and the Council, who must necessarily have the most experience of what may be most advantageous to the colony, might have something referred to their judgement."

The forts left much to be desired. Because of general poverty, little had been spent on them, as Secretary Ludwell apologized to London. The average planter grew 1,200 pounds of tobacco a year. At a ha'penny a pound, the prevailing price, his crop brought him £2 8s. ($120) a year.

"When all taxes are deducted from this amount, a very little will remain to a poor man who hath perhaps a wife and children to cloath and other necessarys to buy—truly soe much too little," said Ludwell, "that I can attribute to nothing but the great mercy of God their loyalty to the King and their affections to the Governor . . . that keeps them from mutiny and confusion."

Belatedly, two years after the request, some cannon arrived and were lying in the *Elizabeth*, a man-of-war dispatched to guard the colony. A few days after her arrival, while the captain was on shore banqueting with his mistress, three Dutch warships sailed in, sank the *Elizabeth* with all the cannon, destroyed seven merchant vessels, and captured thirteen more. Many other ships carrying Virginia tobacco were captured on the high seas by Dutch privateers, to the great loss of the planters.

The Dutch war disrupted trade for some time. With planters complaining that they had more tobacco than could be carried away in three years, discontent began to rise rapidly, but Berkeley chose to ignore it, every day becoming more arbitrary, crotchety, and vindictive, savagely striking at anyone who opposed him, at anyone with ideas.

Thank God, he exclaimed, there were no free schools in Virginia, "nor printing, and I hope we shall not have them these hundred years. For learning has brought heresy and disobedience and sects into the world, and printing has divulged them. God keep us from both!"

As he grew more manic, his friend, Secretary Thomas Ludwell, informed his brother, Lord John Berkeley, that his condition was "very sad." Even his kinsman, Colonel Henry Norwood, treasurer of the colony, remarked the damage done by the "Governor's passion, age, and weakness," attributing the general restlessness in Virginia to this and to "extreme and grievous taxes."

Already unpopular, Berkeley became an object of ridicule and a butt of obscene jokes when, in 1670, at the age of sixty-four, he married a woman half his age, Frances Culpeper, widow of Samuel Stephens, governor of Carolina. "Vigorous and energetic," quite as acquisitive as her doddering husband, Frances encouraged Sir William in his "covetous Fole-age."

In their exasperation, the planters had nowhere to turn, for the Assembly had become a mockery of representative government, a screen for privilege and plunder. The Council had been captured by wealthy planters and merchants who quite frankly had no regard for anything but their own interests. The Burgesses were quite as bad, having become the Governor's creatures. Saying that "men were more valuable in any calling in proportion to their experience," Berkeley kept the same Burgesses in office year after year by the device of proroguing instead of adjourning the Assembly. There had been no elections since 1660.

Thus secure in office, the Burgesses neglected public affairs, conducting their business in taverns, doing little but vote themselves handsome salaries, soon enlarging these to include the travel and maintenance of a man servant and two horses for each of them during the sessions. As the Assembly did nothing, some counties decided to send only one Burgess to save expense. But the Burgesses, finding this an ill example, promptly ordered them to send two, as prescribed, "for the better service of the publique."

Once more the King irresponsibly declared war, once more Virginia was totally unprepared, once more Dutch ships swept into the Chesapeake in 1673 and sank eleven vessels loaded with tobacco, capturing many more on the high seas, paralyzing trade. But the heaviest blow came directly from the King, one that aroused all in Virginia.

Many years before, while an exile on the Continent, Charles had rewarded some of his favorites by granting them a large proprietorship in Virginia, all of the territory between the Rappahannock and the Potomac, the Northern Neck so called. But as it was impossible under the Commonwealth for his favorites to take possession and as Charles said nothing about it, Virginia was ignorant of this until the Restoration, when the King blandly announced that he had given away almost a third of the colony.

Virginia so loudly objected to this cavalier disposal of its territory and the Assembly so tenaciously obstructed that the King in time withdrew the grant, only to turn around and give away all of the colony! Were there no document to show this, the whole business would be incredible.

In 1673, for a period of thirty-one years, Charles granted to Lord Culpeper and other worthless courtiers "all the dominion of land and water called Virginia." They were given almost sovereign rights and powers. They could create manors and manorial courts, grant lands and question former titles, appoint sheriffs, surveyors, and other minor officers. They were to enjoy all church patronage, naming the ministers. All quitrents and escheats were to go into their pockets.

The Northern Neck grant had been bad enough, though it immediately affected the interests of only a few. But this new patent immediately and vitally touched the interests of all. It threatened their liberty and their property at once, and the planters raised such an outcry that the proprietors hesitated to act.

Again the poor groaned as new taxes were raised to send three agents to London to try to have the patent revoked. They failed in this but succeeded in buying off Culpeper and his associates. They agreed not to exercise any of their rights except that of receiving quitrents and escheats if they were paid a penny ha'penny on every pound of tobacco exported,* which constituted a new tax on the planters.

Anxious not to be carved up again, Virginia petitioned the King for a charter defining its limits and rights. Charles agreed in principle, and the three agents remained in England several years conducting negotiations on the matter. They drafted a charter which promised ample protection.

The colonists should be authorized to form a corporation to buy the Northern Neck from Culpeper and his band of leeches. No more land should be granted by the Crown without the consent of the governor and the Council. Acts of the Assembly should be valid unless vetoed by the King within two years. All chief officers should continue to reside in the colony, and not in London. Above all, "no manner of imposition or taxes shall be laid or imposed upon the inhabitants and proprietors there but by the common consent of the Governor, Council, and Burgesses, as hath hitherto been used."

When objection was raised to this last article, the agents replied that it contained what they conceived "to be the right of Virginians, as well as all other Englishmen, which is not to be taxed but by their consent, expressed by their representatives."

The Council for Foreign Plantations accepted and recommended the substance of these proposals which, with a few changes, were incorporated in a final draft. The charter was ready for the Great Seal when word came of an uprising in Virginia, and the charter business collapsed, never to be revived.

---

* At the expense of the consumer, they got three times more out of a pound of tobacco than the poor planter did. It was nice work to be a Lord in those days.

XXVI

Marches and Counter-Marches

*That old fool has hanged more men in that
naked country than I did for the murder of
my father.*

—CHARLES II

VIRGINIANS later recalled that in 1675, arousing uneasy speculation in the minds of all, there had appeared "three prodi-
gies"—a large comet flaring in the heavens every evening for a
week, a great flight of pigeons covering the entire sky such as had
not been seen since the Indian massacre of 1644, and huge swarms
of flies "rising out of spigot holes in the earth" and devouring the
trees—all regarded as "ominous presages."

Discontent continued to rise and was brought to a head, curiously,
by one of Berkeley's better and more enlightened policies. As
peace had been established with the Indians, he sought to preserve
it by removing causes of friction and complaint. He prohibited the
enslavement of the Indians, which had been practiced by kidnaping
adults or buying their children. He protected their lands against
squatters. As the manner was usually by force or fraud, no one
was to acquire Indian lands in any manner without the consent of
the governor and Council. Friendly Indians were given badges
that served as passports so that they might freely move about.
Nor were these merely paper laws. Berkeley punished many for
violating them, even some very powerful planters.

Evidently as much to control the whites as the Indians, a line of forts was built along the frontier to the west and north, a project which occasioned much criticism and ill will. Heavy taxes had been levied for the purpose, but the forts were a disgrace. Berkeley's cronies had obtained profitable contracts to build them, spending as little as possible on construction, pocketing the rest.

Provoked by outrages on both sides, skirmishes along the frontier had become more frequent, and many were clamoring for war against the Indians. Instead, hoping to keep the forces apart and at peace, Berkeley now forbade any trade or intercourse with the Indians. But he seized this opportunity, it was charged, to enter the rich Indian fur trade himself and monopolize it for the profit of himself and his little circle of toadies.

A minor quarrel along the Potomac set in train an unfortunate series of events that rapidly precipitated a crisis. Some of the Potomac, of the Doeg tribe, claiming to have been cheated by a local planter, one Mathews, drove off a few of his swine and cattle. Going in pursuit, Mathews and neighboring planters caught and shot some of the Indians. In retaliation, the Doeg returned to Mathews', killed a half dozen there, and then fled across the Potomac into Maryland, which was having Indian troubles of its own.

Pressed by the powerful Seneca, their hostile cousins, the Susquehannock were being forced from their homelands at the head of the Chesapeake. Fleeing south, they pushed their way into Maryland, having frequent brushes with the uneasy planters as they marched down to the Potomac and joined forces there with their friends, the Piscataway. Though hostile to the Marylanders, both tribes—the Susquehannock especially—had always been and were still very friendly toward Virginia, a friendship which accident and treachery now broke at the cost of hundreds of planters' lives.

Determined to punish the fleeing Doeg, a Virginia force crossed the Potomac under the command of Captain Giles Brent and Captain George Mason, both of whom had been heavily fined for their previous dealings with the Indians. Brent's force tracked down the Doeg and scattered them, killing the chief and ten more.

But Mason lost his way and followed the wrong track. Coming upon an Indian village, not stopping to discover whose it might be, he and his men opened fire and had killed a number before Mason shouted:

"For God's sake, shoot no more! These are our friends, the Susquehannock."

Angry and suspicious, the Susquehannock and their allies moved a little distance up the Potomac, remaining on the Maryland side, and built a strong encampment there. Not liking these unbidden guests, Maryland sent a force of a thousand men against them. Laying siege to the encampment, finding themselves "too weake to do the worke themselves," they asked Virginia to aid them with an equal force, a request "too soon granted," and a thousand men marched into Maryland under the command of Colonel John Washington, great-grandfather of the great George.

When the Virginia forces arrived, the Susquehannock sent six of their chieftains under a flag of truce to ask the "reason for this hostile appearance." Showing their badges to prove that they were friendly, they declared that they had no hostile intentions against anyone even though the Marylanders had harried them. But the leaders of the joint forces scorned them and their assurances.

"Why keep them any longer?" exclaimed Colonel Washington. "Let us knock them on the head"—which was done.

Denouncing this treachery as "barbarous and inhuman," Maryland cashiered its leaders, disbarring them forever from any position of public trust. Virginia did nothing though Berkeley was outraged, protesting that if they had killed his grandfather and grandmother, his father and mother, and all of his friends, "yet if they had come in peace, they ought to have gone in peace." Both colonies offered reparations, but the Susquehannock had been alienated. To all proposals for a truce, they replied,

"Where are our six cockarouses?"

As the Indians could not hunt deer, they took to hunting the besiegers' horses and with such skill that those who came "on horseback began to feare they should be compeld to trot home on foot—and glad if they escaped so, too, for these beleagured blades made so many sallies and the beseigers kept such neglegent gards that there was few days passed without some remarkable mis-chiefe."

After six weeks, having inflicted heavy losses upon colonial forces, the Susquehannock slipped through the lines one night, crossed the Potomac, and swept down through Virginia to the upper James, refraining from burning houses or destroying crops but killing sixty people, ten for every one of their slain chieftains.

They then sent a "Remonstrance" to Berkeley, "demanding what it was moved him to take arms against them, his professed friends, in behalf of the Marylanders, their avowed enemies." Not only had their chieftains been knocked on the head, but Virginia had countenanced the fact, for which reason they had taken their revenge by killing ten times more of the English, for their chief-tains were "persons of quality" while their victims were "of in-ferior Rank." If they were given satisfaction for the injuries they had suffered, they would renew their league of friendship. "Other-ways, they would prosecute the war to the last man."

Having a bear by the tail through its own want of wit, Virginia would have done well to let go. But the offer of peace was rejected "as being contrary to the honour of the English," and the Sus-quehannock soon killed three hundred more as the outlying plant-ers cried plaintively for some help and protection.

An experienced Cavalier soldier long in the country, Sir Henry Chicheley, had been ordered to recruit a large force and take the field against the Indians. But just as he was ready to march, Berke-ley canceled his commission and disbanded his troops, perhaps fearing that friendly Indians would suffer more than the Susque-hannock in any campaign. Nothing was done to aid those along the frontier except to order the building of more forts, "a great grievance, juggle, and cheat, . . . a design of the grandees to en-gross all of the tobacco into their own hands."

The forts provided small protection against the Indians, who "quickly found out where the mouse traps were sett, and for what purpose, and so resolved to keep out of the way," as a disgusted planter remarked. "It rent the hearts of many that they should be compeld to work all day—nay, all the year—to reward those mole-catchers at the forts (nobody knew for what), and at night could not find a place of safety to lie downe in to rest their weary bones for fear they should be shattered all to pieces by the Indians."

In alarm and desperation, the planters on the upper south side of the James began "to beat up drums for volunteers" to go against the Indians and "so continued sundry dayes." Several hundred assembled near Charles City, including the chief military officer on the Southside, Colonel William Byrd, commander of the fort at the Falls.

These irate men were soon joined by a young planter from the Curles, a newcomer, Nathaniel Bacon, who had arrived about two years before. Not yet thirty, the son of a wealthy squire of Suffolk, he was "gay, extravagant, and headstrong." It was later said that, having squandered his inheritance at home, he had repaired to the colony to retrieve his fortune and was therefore only too eager to fish in the "troubled waters of popular discontents." This was evidently false, for he had arrived with £1,800 ($90,000), an appointment to a seat on the Council, and already had two large plantations with many servants—one in the Curles, the other near the Falls. It is more probable that he had been induced to come by his "oppulent" cousin and namesake, a rich bachelor in his fifties, Colonel Nathaniel Bacon, also a member of the Council, whose heir he expected to be.

The planters gathered on the Southside sent two men to ask Berkeley for an order permitting them to march against the Indians, saying that if it were not received "by a certaine day, they would proceed, commission or no commission."

As this was obviously dangerous, Colonel Byrd and other more conservative leaders raised no objections at all—indeed, were probably pleased—when young Bacon stepped forward and was proclaimed General Bacon. Eagerly accepting this "commission from the people's affection," he recruited more volunteers, writing their names in a ring so as not to reveal who signed first, giving them "brandy to wind up the charm."

Denouncing the men on the Southside as "fools and loggerheads," Berkeley commanded them to disband, proclaiming that any who proceeded without a commission would be hanged as rebels, "whereupon those of estates obeyed." Less than sixty of some three hundred chose to follow Bacon, who had sworn to march against the Indians if but twenty would "adventure the servis with him."

With a shock of black hair, slender, and "indifferent tall," Bacon had endeared himself to many as a "man of quality and merit, brave and eloquent." He had been chosen by the people "not so much for what he had yet done . . . as for what they expected he would doe to deserve their devotion." He had all the endowments "which constitute a compleate man (as to intrinsecalls)— wisdom to apprehend and discretion to chuse."

Others, however, found him "of an ominous, pensive, melancholy aspect; of a pestilent and prevalent logical discourse tending to atheism in most companies; of a most imperious and dangerous hidden pride of heart, despising the wisest of his neighbours for their ignorance; and very ambitious and arrogant."

Like that other proud and "imperious" young man during his brief stay in the colony, Captain John Smith, Bacon aroused sharp partisanship, into which one need not go. Bacon's acts, like Smith's, speak for themselves, and certainly they were always rash.

Instead of keeping his men along the James to protect the troubled settlements, he led them far off to the south, almost two hundred miles, to the seat of the friendly Occaneechee, "commodious for trade and the mart for all Indians for at least 500 miles." Along the way, he found some Susquehannock and attacked them, killing thirty women and children. As he had marched with few provisions, he demanded supplies of the Occaneechee, which the latter refused, saying they had none to sell—least of all, to give away. Feigning friendship, Bacon and his men gained entrance to the town, which they then burned after great slaughter.

Coming up the James with a small force and finding Bacon gone, Berkeley denounced the "young, inexperienced, rash, and inconsiderate General" and his "rude, dissolute, and tumultuous" followers. Depriving Bacon of his seat on the Council, he proclaimed him a rebel, to be hanged on sight.

If "to plead the cause of the oppressed," declared Bacon, always given to histrionics, "if after the loss of a great part of his Majesty's colony . . . freely with our lives and estates to endeavour to save the remainder be treason, Lord Almighty judge and let the guilty die."

Though many disapproved of Bacon's precise course, he had become the standard bearer of all those who found life under Berkeley increasingly intolerable. No other had stepped forward, and his audacity provided a hope for all of the discontented who now became so vocal and threatening that the old Governor, now in his seventies, was forced to give way.

On May 29, 1676, still protesting that nothing was amiss, Berkeley issued a call for the election of new Burgesses, the first in sixteen years. At the same time, he issued a "Declaration and Remonstrance," a campaign document to be read in every county.

He was "as uncorrupt and diligent as ever Governor was," he declared. "I doe not know of anything relative to this Country wherein I have acted unjustly, corruptly, or negligently in distributing equall Justice to all men & taking all possible care to preserve their properties & defend them from barbarous enimies." Reverting to an old theme, he declaimed his readiness to "dye in defence of my King, his laws & subjects, which I will cheerfully doe, though I alone doe it."

When the sheriff of Henrico County stood up to read this "Declaration," Bacon snatched it from his hands, and the voters "unanimously" returned him as a Burgess.* Coming down in a sloop with forty armed men to present his credentials, Berkeley turned cannon on him. Retreating up the river, Bacon came ashore and crept into Jamestown after dark to consult with two of his friends and chief supporters, both men of influence in the colony, respected by almost all.

One of these, William Drummond, "a sober Scotch gentleman of good repute," had been the first governor of Carolina, appointed by Berkeley acting for the proprietors. After a quarrel, Berkeley had dismissed him and the two men had long been at swords' points.

---

* This was quite illegal, for Bacon had been proclaimed an outlaw. If that proclamation was invalid, then he was still a member of the Council and therefore not entitled to sit as a Burgess.

The other was an interesting but a rather blurred and enigmatic figure, Richard Lawrence, a "thinking man," who "formerly was of Oxford University and for wit, learning, and sobriety was equalled there by few." He shared the general dislike of the "forwardness, avarice, and French despotick methods" of Berkeley, at whose hands he had suffered himself.

"Honest, affable, and without blemish in his conversation and dealings," Lawrence had more frequent opportunities than most to make known his views. At Jamestown, he had married a wealthy widow who kept a large tavern there, "unto which resorted those of the best quality and such others as business called to the town." As he was even-tempered and a man of parts, his conversation was "coveted by persons of all ranks, so that, being subtile and having these advantages, he might with lesse difficulty discover men's inclinations and instill his notions where he found these would be imbibed with greatest satisfaction."

Returning to his sloop after seeing Lawrence and Drummond, Bacon was chased and captured by the *Adam and Eve,* and brought to Jamestown, expecting the worst. But Berkeley was politic, receiving him with surprising civility.

"Mr. Bacon," he asked, "have you forgotten how to be a Gentleman?"

"No, may it please your Honour."

"Then, I'll take your parole."

While on parole, Bacon took shelter with his "oppulent" cousin, the elder Nathaniel Bacon, who persuaded him to make his peace with Berkeley while he could, drafting a public apology for that purpose.

"If there be joy in the presence of the angels over a sinner that repenteth, there is joy now," said Berkeley, rising in the Assembly a few days later. "Call Mr. Bacon."

Going down on one knee, reading a signed confession acknowledging his "miscarriages and unwarrantable practices," Bacon promised his obedience and offered his entire estate as security for his "good and quiet behavior for one whole year from this date, and do promise and oblige myself to continue my said duty and allegiance at all times afterward."

"God forgive you, I forgive you! God forgive you, I forgive you!" said Berkeley, repeating this a third time.

"And all that were with him," added a member of the Council. "Yea, and all that were with him."

Upon the unanimous recommendation of its members, Bacon was restored to his seat on the Council and awarded £70 for the damage done to his sloop by the *Adam and Eve*.

With the incident apparently closed, the Assembly turned to the grievances of the planters. Berkeley, however, wished it "to medle with nothing until the Indian business was dispacht," warning it against "two rogues," Lawrence and Drummond, "both dwelling at Jamestown and who were not at the Piscataway seige."

The Assembly declared war on the Indians, authorized a force of a thousand men, named Bacon as "general and commander-in-chief," and again turned to the planters' grievances, passing "Bacon's Laws," though he probably had little to do with them. As remarked by a member of the Burgesses, one T. M., a Baconite but an objective observer, Bacon was "too young, too much a stranger there, and of a disposition too precipitate to manage things . . . had not thoughtfull Mr. Lawrence been at the bottom." [1]

Correcting many notorious abuses, the Assembly decreed that no man was to hold more than one public office at once, that officials should charge only the prescribed fees, that sheriff and under-sheriffs should serve only a year, that all public accounts should be inspected and audited. The act of 1662 limiting the franchise to householders was repealed, which restored to all freemen the right to vote. [2]

Now the scene quickly changes and takes on an air of *opéra bouffe* as the actors fly about orating on every occasion, charging up and down the stage with passionate fury, changing roles and changing back for no apparent reason. While the individual lines and actions are clear enough, the scene as a whole often fails to make much sense.

With everything quiet, Bacon suddenly fled Jamestown and returned to the Curles, ostensibly because his wife was sick, actually because he thought himself in danger. He had grown suspicious of Berkeley's delay in issuing the commission he had promised. Raising many hundred soldiers, he marched on Jamestown to demand his commission from Berkeley, who had been recruiting men to oppose him. After much bluster by the Governor, Bacon marched in unopposed and drew up his troops on the green facing the state house.

When the Assembly gathered for its daily session, Bacon approached the state house "with a file of fusileers on either hand." Berkeley and the members of the Council came out to meet him, and from a window the Burgesses saw the Governor "open his breast and Bacon strutting betwixt his two files of men, with his left arm on Kenbow [akimbo], flinging his right arm every way, both like men distracted; and if, in this moment of fury, that enraged multitude had faln upon the Governor and the Councill, we of the Assembly expected the same immediate fate."

"Here," shouted Berkeley, baring his breast, "shoot me! Fore God, a fair mark! Shoot!"

Bacon demanded the commission that had been promised, declaring that "now we will have it before we go." As Berkeley and the Council withdrew to consider this, Bacon walked after them "with outrageous postures of his head, arms, body, and leggs, often tossing his hand from his sword to his hat." Getting no immediate reply, he lost all reason.

"Damn my bloud," he swore, "I'll kill Governor, Councill, Assembly, and all, and then I'll sheath my sword in my own heart's bloud!"

Entering the House of Burgesses, Bacon asked them to give him a commission. But they protested that it was not in their "province or power nor of any other save the King's vice-regent, the governor." After a long "harangue on preserving our lives from the Indians, inspecting the publick revenues, the exorbitant taxes, and redressing the grievances and calamities of the deplorable country," Bacon withdrew, only to come back immediately with a detachment of soldiers who pointed their guns "at a window of the Assembly chamber, filled with faces," and kept repeating in a menacing way,

"We *will* have it! We *will* have it!"

One of the frightened Burgesses, taking out his handkerchief, waved it from the window and shouted,

"You *shall* have it! You *shall* have it! You *shall* have it!"

That "pacifick handkercher" saved the Burgesses, according to T. M., who was one of those at the window "filled with faces," for in his "paroxism of phrentick fury" Bacon had ordered that when he gave the signal by drawing his sword, his soldiers were "to fire and slay us, so near was the massacre of us all that very minute."

In a day or two, Berkeley issued a commission at the urging of the Burgesses and the Council. With differences settled, the Assembly adjourned after a tumultuous month. Now feeling safe, Bacon marched up-country against the Indians. Pleased that they had done so well, the new Burgesses returned home "little expecting to hear of more intestine broils."

Bacon was no sooner well away than Berkeley, hurriedly writing the King for troops, fled from Jamestown to Gloucester, on the lower north bank of the York, "a place the best replenished for men, arms, and affection of any county in Virginia." Calling out the militia, ostensibly to fight the Indians, he again proclaimed Bacon a rebel—which "unhappy accident," as royal commissioners later termed it, made the Indian war recoil into a civil war.

Leaving them angry and bewildered, the news of Berkeley's action put Bacon and his men "shrewdly to their Trumps, believing that a few such deales or shuffles . . . might quickly ring both cards and game out of his hands." Turning back, Bacon marched his troops down-country to meet Berkeley and the Gloucester men. Unwilling to fight Bacon, the latter abandoned Berkeley, who fled, stopping to strip Fort Henry of all arms and ammunition for his own use.

Gathering his forces at Middle Plantation, where Williamsburg now stands, Bacon issued a proclamation detailing Berkeley's crimes and inviting "all the prime Gentlemen in those parts to give him a meeting in his quarters." Issued in the name of the "Commons of Virginia," the proclamation listed all but four of the Council as Berkeley's "wicked & pernicious" confederates and abettors, and ordered them to surrender within four days on pain of being proclaimed "trayters to the people" and having their estates confiscated.

In answer to the proclamation, a "grate convention of people" met at Middle Plantation, where Bacon denounced Berkeley's "doting and irregular actings." Declaring that those who went out to fight should have the full support of the planters, he offered an "Ingagement for the people (of what quallety soever, excepting servants)."

Under this "Ingagement," or oath, all should pledge their lives and estates to prosecute the Indian war. None objected to this. Second, they should take all necessary measures against Berkeley to prevent him from blocking or weakening the campaign. Some hesitated about this formal challenge to the Governor's authority. But the last article in this "bugbeare," as many called it, caused serious apprehension—they should be prepared to resist any troops that might be sent from England until the King and the Parliament had an opportunity to hear the colony's case against Berkeley.

To defy the now senile Governor was one thing. To battle the King's troops was another, and there was long and sharp debate on this, "pro and con," from noon till midnight.

At this hour, the gunner of Fort Henry rushed in to implore aid, saying that the Indians had attacked in Gloucester and that many had fled to the fort for protection, which it could not provide unless speedily furnished with arms and ammunition.

This startled everybody, and Bacon inquired how it was that the "most considerablest fortress in the Countrey" could be threatened by the Indians.

Because, said the gunner, Berkeley had removed all of the arms the day before and then sailed away, presumably for home, as he had not since been reported.

Not knowing "what construction to put upon this," especially in view of Berkeley's recent erratic conduct, many of those otherwise well disposed toward him began to have doubts. As a result, Bacon's oath became "more smooth and glib to be swallowed, even by those who had the greatest repugnancy against it." Issuing a call for the Assembly to meet a few weeks later, the convention adjourned and Bacon again marched up-country.

In leaving Gloucester, Berkeley had not gone home. He had crossed to the Eastern Shore, to Accomac, where he began recruiting a large force by promising his followers the estates of the rebels. Knowing that Jamestown was lightly held, he sailed there and demanded its surrender, promising a pardon to all but Drummond and Lawrence.

Only a few people lived in the town, just a dozen families in all, "getting their living by keeping of ordinaries at extraordinary rates." Most of them found Berkeley's offer acceptable, but others, fearing some "after-claps of revenge," moved out, "everyone shifting for himselfe with no ordinary fear, in the gratest haste possible." Lawrence hurriedly abandoned his house "with all his welth and a faire cupbord of plate entire standing, which fell into the Governor's hands the next morning."

By a swift march, before the news of his approach reached Berkeley, Bacon appeared at Jamestown with 150 men and "in a trice blocks up the Governour in the towne, to the generall astonishment of the whole countrey," building earthworks across the sandy neck joining the peninsula to the mainland.

Having a thousand men, Berkeley sent against him most of his "Accomackians, who, like scholers going to school, went out with hevie harts but returned home with light heels." The Governor was "extremely disgusted" and a few days later shipped himself, his soldiers, and all of the inhabitants of the town and their goods, and so to Accomac again, leaving Bacon to enter Jamestown at his pleasure, which he did the next morning.

Before nightfall, Jamestown was in ruins. Saying that Berkeley and his "rogues should harbour no more there," Bacon and his "Cabinett Councell . . . in the most barbarous manner converts the whole towne into flames, cinders, and ashes, not so much as sparing the church, . . . the first that ever was in Virginia."

Lawrence and Drummond led the arson squads, taking a torch to their own houses, the best in Jamestown. From the descriptions of this "Flagrant and Flagitious Act," one gets the impression of a mighty holocaust, with flames leaping from street to street consuming all in their path. It was flagitious enough, but the loss was seventeen or eighteen houses, some of them unoccupied and falling down, all there were in the town which straggled a mile or less along the riverside.

Going to Green Spring, Bacon feasted his men at Berkeley's expense for two or three days and then proceeded to Gloucester County, where the people had shown no desire to take the "Ingagement" proposed at Middle Plantation. The Gloucester men asked "to be indulged in the benefitt of Neutralitie," but as Bacon refused, they soon signed the oath.

When word came that Captain Giles Brent was marching from the Potomac with a large force to attack them, Bacon's men were eager to meet them and marched off "with showtes and acclamations," leaving behind all of their impedimenta, everything but their "oathes and wenches." After several days, they turned back, having been joined by most of the men from the Potomac, who had abandoned Brent and left him to shift for himself. This brought all of Virginia west of the Chesapeake under the rebels' banner.

Bacon now "thought it not amiss, but worth his labour, to go and see how the Accomackians were doing," which put Berkeley and those with him in great terror. They were safe enough, however, for Bacon, "sick of a flux," unexpectedly died in October, 1676, just six months after he had so suddenly flashed on the horizon, snatched away by what many planters not unfriendly to him regarded as an "admirable and ever-to-be-cellibrated Providence."

While they admired Bacon's courage and his skill and dash in the field, they distrusted his judgment. Expecting English troops to land any day now, they had no desire to cross swords with the Crown. Virginians would do that one day, when they were stronger and the issue was rightly posed. Their quarrel at the moment, however, was not with the King, but with Berkeley. The Middle Plantation "Ingagement," at which so many stuck and which Bacon so vehemently demanded, had been a great mistake and compromised their cause.

Bacon's body was spirited away so that his bones could never be "exposed on a gibbet, as was purposed." Weighted with stones by Lawrence, his coffin was probably consigned to the waters of the York.

Command passed to a newcomer, Colonel Ingram, "a milke-sop," and the forces arrayed against Berkeley began to disintegrate rapidly. When he heard of Bacon's death, the Governor, "shut up in the Ark" for some time, sent out a "winged messenger to see if, happily, the Delluge was any whit abated," dispatching Major Robert Beverley with several armed ships. Proceeding to Glou-cester, Beverley's party captured twenty men under Colonel Hans-ford, "a valiant stout man and a most resolved rebel," who, car-ried to Accomac, had the "ill luck to be the first Virginian born that dyed upon a paire of Gallows." Other raids netted more prisoners to be hanged, for the Governor had developed Marshal Dale's passion for the "rope dance."

Venturing forth himself at length, Berkeley met the *Concord* coming in from England, commanded by a Captain Grantham, who announced that English troops were on the way. As the Captain was acquainted with Ingram, who had come to the colony on his ship, he suggested that he should go to see the new rebel leader. Disposed to talk terms, which were accepted, Ingram agreed that he and his men would surrender if all were pardoned except those on Berkeley's proscribed list, headed by the names of Drummond and Lawrence, "the chiefe Incendiarys."

But the Baconians, still holding a number of strongholds, hesi-tated to lay down their arms, fearing savage reprisals, as well they might. Convinced that "smoothe words" would accomplish more than "rough deeds," Grantham decided to entice them "as the Devill courted Eve, though to a better purpose, with never-to-be-performed promises."

Those who had taken the field against the Indians should be allowed to retain their arms. Any who wished to return home should be paid for their services in accordance with the schedule laid down by the last Assembly. Any servants who had fought against the Indians and acquitted themselves well were to be im-mediately freed from their indentures at the cost of the colony, which would give their masters a "valluable satisfaction for every servant so set free."

Seduced by this, many laid down their arms. Freemen among them were imprisoned and fined by Berkeley. Servants were sent back to serve out their indentures. Those not taken in by soft words did far better for themselves—notably those at Green Spring. Under the command of a Captain Drew, a miller by profession, they made themselves so strong that they had peace on their own terms, which points a political moral.

The man whom Berkeley regarded as the "originall cause of the whole rebellion," his former friend, "sober" William Drummond, was captured in the Chickahominy Swamp and dragged before the Governor.

"Mr. Drummond, you are very welcome," said Berkeley, mocking him with an elaborate show of courtesy, making him a low bow. "I am more glad to see you than any man in Virginia. Mr. Drummond, you shall be hanged in half an hour."

"What your Honour pleases," said Drummond, walking quietly to his death a few hours later.

Knowing they were doomed, Lawrence fled with four others, marching away toward the west in "snow ancle deep," and as they were never heard of again, it was presumed that they "cast themselves into the branch of some river rather than be treated like Drummond." Many left the colony, going to Maryland and Carolina, even to New England.

More were executed than had been killed in the entire civil war, and Berkeley "would have hanged half the country," had it not been for the arrival early in 1677 of three royal commissioners— a former governor of Virginia, Major Francis Morison, one of Berkeley's fast friends and long the colony's agent in London; Sir John Berry, in command of a regiment of battle-scarred veterans sent to suppress the rebellion; and Herbert Jeffreys, named by the King to succeed Berkeley, who had asked to be relieved.

Charles had ordered the commissioners to look into all matters in Virginia, hear the planters, study their complaints, and make recommendations. They had also brought a royal proclamation granting a pardon to all who voluntarily laid down their arms, with one exception—Bacon should be hanged.

But Berkeley would have none of this. He resented the presence and the questions of the commissioners, challenging their authority at every turn, refusing to surrender his post to Jeffreys, declining to help them in finding quarters for their troops, asking if they thought he could "do impossibilities."

Instead of the King's proclamation, he issued one of his own adding new names to the list of those he had proscribed—about forty in all. Though hostilities had ceased two months before, he continued to govern by martial law, becoming very angry when the commissioners objected to his practice of seizing and selling the estates of the proscribed before they had been tried and convicted—a source of plunder that enriched not only him but Major Robert Beverley and other favorites.

Because of their constant quarrels and as Berkeley was now quite deaf, as well as senile, the commissioners suggested that all discussion should be conducted in writing, for "loud and fierce" speaking would make it impossible to keep their conversations private and would "sound angrily" in the ears of the people. But the Governor preferred to go on shouting.

Calling for new elections, Berkeley summoned the Assembly to meet at Green Spring late in February, 1677. Packed with violent and rapacious men thirsting for revenge on the rebels, the new Assembly repealed all of the laws passed by the previous Assembly, some members of which had been executed, "persons of honest reputations and handsome estates."

Each county had been asked by the commissioners for a frank and specific statement of the people's complaints and grievances, to which the Assembly took strong exception. When Gloucester raised questions about the poll tax and how it was spent, the Assembly denounced this as "scandalous" and ordered the "authors of the complaint to be sent for and punished." Though the colony was in great distress, the Burgesses took this occasion to vote themselves an increase in salary, dismissing the objections to this as "mere clamour." There was nothing wrong in Virginia, they said, except that the "precipitate giddy multitude" had chosen to follow Bacon and was still infected with his malign ideas.

But the Assembly and the commissioners agreed on one thing —the hangings should stop. Berkeley violently disagreed, hanging another man the day this joint recommendation was made, and executing seven more a few days later.

Even his friend Morison was highly critical, joining his fellow commissioners in reporting that the only disturbance to the peace of the colony was Berkeley's presence there and the "fierceness of those who call themselves the loyal party, which are not many. Their rapacious insolence exasperates the other party, . . . which, indeed, is little less than the whole country."

Thoroughly annoyed, Charles peremptorily ordered Berkeley to turn the government over to Jeffreys and come at once to England, instructing Jeffreys to ship him home by force if necessary. Berkeley was informed by his Majesty's principal Secretary that only his "long services and the loyalty of himself and family have kept the King from resolutions." Why had the Governor "delayed, if not refused, obedience to the King's orders?" asked the Secretary.

"The King himself is not a little surprised, as well as troubled, to find a person, who has been so loyal, fall in such errours as to affront the King's proclamation by putting out one of his own. . . . The King hath very little hope that the people of Virginia shall be brought to a right sense of duty to obey their governors when the governors themselves will not obey the King."

A few months later, thirty-five years after his first arrival, his "angry voice and Berklean look" faded, plaintively likening his sufferings to those of Jesus Christ, the old Governor departed, the bright promise of his youth gone, thrown away with his own hand, but still hoping to see Charles and explain his way back into royal favor. The King refused to see him, sharply snubbing him, and even hastened his death, which occurred a few months later, by exclaiming:

"That old fool has hanged more men in that naked country than I did for the murder of my father."

". . . which shuts up this tragedy."

XXVII

Grandees, Imported and Domestic

Souls? Damn your souls! Make tobacco!
—ATTORNEY GENERAL SEYMOUR

WITH the raging Berkeley out of the way, Governor Jeffreys
and the royal commissioners did their best to restore peace
within Virginia and along its frontiers, quickly succeeding in one
respect at least.

During the fighting provoked by the drive of the Susquehannock through Virginia to join tribes to the south, friendly Indians
had suffered at the hands of the terrorized and infuriated planters
as Berkeley had feared. Bacon had gone out of his way to attack
the Pamunkey, loyal and useful allies since Opechancano's death,
and the Pamunkey struck back.

A month after Berkeley's departure in April, 1677, a lasting
peace was made with the "Queen" of the Pamunkey and the chieftains of ten subordinate tribes. Proud old Powhatan and dedicated
Opechancano must have spent some unhappy days in the Happy
Hunting Ground when they learned that the Queen had signed
away all the rights and territories of the once formidable Powhatan
Confederacy. Acknowledging the sovereignty of the English King,
she and her chieftains agreed to pay an annual quitrent of a few
arrows and beaver pelts for the King's generosity in allowing them

to retain some small part of their ancestral homelands. The tracts assigned to the Pamunkey, the Mattaponi, and the Chickahominy at this time are still occupied by a few of their descendants who scratch out a meager existence on their small barren reservations as wards of the State.

It was far more difficult to restore peace and quiet in Virginia. Confident that Sir William would soon be in command again, the Berkeley faction ignored the commissioners and insulted them, led in this by the secretary of the colony, Philip Ludwell, and by the clerk of the Assembly, Robert Beverley, who had been commander-in-chief of Berkeley's chicken-hearted forces.

Openly disregarding the King's order for an amnesty and a pardon for all but Bacon, the Berkeleyites relentlessly pursued the rebels with a hungry eye on their estates. They brought many heavy damage suits against them, being determined to recover by any means at all whatever losses they had suffered during the uprising. When Jeffreys put a stop to this in the spirit of the King's proclamation, Ludwell publicly denounced him as a "hateful little fellow in a periwig" and a worse rebel than Bacon, exclaiming that he "broke the country's laws, which Bacon never did."

Suspending Ludwell, Beverley, and other "turbulent mutinous spirits" from office, Jeffreys called for a new election of Burgesses. The Assembly that met at Middle Plantation late in 1677 was more conciliatory, decreeing heavy fines for those who went on calling others "traitors, rebels, rogues, and such like," for this destroyed the "former estate of love and friendship desired by all good people."

Traduced and defied to the last by the small Berkeley faction, which was not prepared to surrender, Governor Jeffreys died a year later. He was succeeded by Sir Henry Chicheley, a Cavalier who had done very well for himself since his arrival almost thirty years before as a destitute refugee, having married the widow of a wealthy planter, the beginning of so many careers in Virginia.

Now old and feeble, Chicheley was not disposed to make trouble for himself, pursuing a sober and moderate course until relieved in the spring of 1680 by his superior, Lord Culpeper, who still retained the almost sovereign rights over Virginia and the North-

ern Neck proprietorship which Charles II had given him years
before. More recently, in 1678, he had been made governor of
the colony for life.

As his Lordship was related to the rapacious and vindictive
Lady Berkeley, *née* Frances Culpeper, now the wife of "fiery"
Philip Ludwell, the Berkeley faction again hoped for a day of
revenge and plunder. But Culpeper had his own ideas. He was
only interested in his pocket and in filling it full as quickly as possible so that he might return to London to resume his gay life
there.

As instructed by the King, Culpeper proposed an act of general pardon and indemnity. As his Majesty "hath forgott it himselfe," he declared, "he doth expect this to be the last time of
your remembering the late Rebellion, and he shall looke upon
them to be ill men that rubb the sore by using any future re-
proaches. . . ."

Acceding to this, though with reservations, the Assembly listened with marked distaste to other proposals nominally made by
the King but doubtless suggested by Culpeper as Lord Proprietor.
The governor's salary—that is, his own—should be increased from
£1,000 to £2,000 ($100,000) a year, to be paid from an export
tax of 2*s*. on every hogshead of tobacco. Though formally an order
from the King, the Assembly refused to agree without amendments.

"If this continues," Culpeper warned, "it will make the exercise
of Assemblies wholly impracticable, if not impossible."

If the "exercise" had been made impossible, his Lordship would
have been pleased, for he had come with the intention of clipping
the wings of the Assembly, as its members were startled to learn.

Henceforth, Culpeper announced, the Assembly was to meet
not at the call of the resident governor, as formerly, but only at
the order of the Crown. Furthermore, the Burgesses were to initi-
ate no legislation. All bills were to be drafted by the governor and
the Council, submitted to London for approval, and then returned
to the Assembly for approval or rejection.

As this made local self-government a mockery, a sham, the Assembly unanimously and so vigorously protested, warning of seri-

ous trouble, that the "King's" proposals were kept secret and later withdrawn.

Finding Jamestown dull and his duties tiresome, Culpeper put his servants, soldiers, gold plate, and furniture on board the *Betty* after three months in the colony and sailed for home. He left affairs in the hands of Chicheley, who soon found himself in a most uncomfortable position, made doubly difficult because his friends had placed him there.

Again, revolt was brewing—which may be one reason why the Lord Proprietor was so eager to be off. The price of tobacco had fallen so low that all were groaning. "The low price of tobacco staggers the imagination," as Culpeper had remarked, "and the continuance of it will be the speedy and fatal ruin of this noble Colony." As there was "vast poverty and infinite necessity" on every hand, discontent was rapidly rising not only here but in Maryland. Lord Baltimore anxiously observed that the people in Virginia were "as ripe and ready for another Rebellion as ever they were . . . [and] if his Majestie please not to send some loyall active person to command under Sir Henry Chicheley (who is now superannuated) very speedily, the government in Virginia will be in danger."

Though directed not to do so, Chicheley felt compelled to summon an Assembly in 1681 to consider a grave problem raised by the soldiers sent out to quell Bacon's Rebellion five years before. These troops were still in the colony, and the Crown now refused to pay them any longer. If they took to foraging, there might be a serious clash. But the Burgesses refused to discuss this unless they could also discuss measures for suspending the planting of tobacco for at least a year, as the large planters were demanding.

"If care be not taken for a cessation," said one of them, a member of the Council, "we must all go a-plundering."

Chicheley, though a large planter himself, would not agree to "cessation," fearing the wrath of the Crown if its large revenues from tobacco were cut off. He abruptly dissolved the Assembly, the members of which—both of the Council and the Burgesses— returned home in an angry mood to report how they had been blocked at Jamestown in their efforts to better the planters' lot.

The Tobacco Rebellion began early in 1682 on the north bank of the York, in Gloucester County, and soon spread to other parts. Led by Robert Beverley, a determined advocate of "law and order" in Berkeley's time, large planters destroyed their own tobacco crops and then organized bands of servants and others to go from plantation to plantation to pull up or cut down young plants, destroying a large part of the crop. This worked great hardship upon small planters who could not afford to lose their tobacco, needing it to buy clothes and other necessaries.

Forced to send troops against the rioters, Chicheley arrested many, including his friend Robert Beverley, who was imprisoned on the Eastern Shore to prevent a rescue by his powerful friends. Privately in sympathy with the plant-cutters, Chicheley soon proclaimed a general pardon on the ground that the rebels were "unimportant people."

At report of the Tobacco Rebellion, the King sharply ordered Culpeper to return to his post, which he had left without Charles's permission. On his arrival, he revoked Chicheley's general pardon and brought many to trial for their lives, digging up an ancient statute that any lawlessness which decreased the customs duties was treason. Six of the plant-cutters were hanged—but not Beverley, who had carefully concealed his tracks and was a man of influence and wealth through Berkeley's favor.

Culpeper had been authorized to suspend the planting of tobacco if that seemed desirable. But as this would decrease the Crown's revenue, and his own as well, he chose rather to stimulate production, reporting to London that he had "soe encouraged the planting of tobacco that . . . there will bee a greater Cropp by far than ever grew since its seating," which should yield the customs "£50,000 more than ever heretofore in any one year." He realized, he said, that this would reduce Virginia to the "utmost exigencies again," but if there were any more plant-cutting, he knew the cure for that!

More bored than ever with Jamestown, his Lordship remained only a short time, departing after three months, a happy event that brought unexpected blessings. Angered by his second return home without permission, the King deposed Culpeper as governor and canceled his proprietary rights in the colony. But he allowed him to retain his grant to the Northern Neck, a huge tract of 5,000,000 acres which he had done nothing to deserve and nothing to develop—a property that, by descent, became the Fairfax Tract upon which, as a young surveyor, George Washington found his first employment.

But welcome as it was, Culpeper's summary dismissal did not immediately improve matters, for an even worse governor was inflicted upon the colony—Lord Howard of Effingham, a hungry placeman, who spent four years trying to reduce Virginia to utter subservience. He forbade the operation of any printing press without the King's consent. He complained that the planters cheated him by paying taxes in tobacco and not in coin, of which they had little or none. Contrary to specific enactments and "established usage," he vetoed acts of the Assembly by proclamation.

More alarming, he designed a new official seal and charged extortionate fees for stamping it on wills, deeds, and all legal papers, saying that this was usual in other parts of the empire. The Burgesses protested "in all humility" that they did not know what was usual in the rest of the empire, but of this they were sure—Virginians had the rights of Englishmen and "noe payment by ye name of any fee, Duty, or other Imposition can or may be demanded, levied, or raised upon us but by and with our own Consent," echoing a principle first asserted in 1623, officially recognized under the Commonwealth, and insistently reiterated down to the day of Independence.

If Virginians were restive and discontented, the English were ready for revolt. In 1688, they rose in the "Glorious Revolution" to drive out the last of the insufferably arrogant and arbitrary Stuarts, James II, who had succeeded his brother Charles three years before. Prince William of Orange and his wife Mary, oldest of James II's daughters, were invited to the throne and accepted the famed Bill of Rights, framed by the Commons and the Lords "for the vindicating and asserting their ancient Rights and Liberties," most of which, in adapted form, appear in our Federal and state constitutions.

The Bill of Rights strengthened the struggle for civil liberties in all the colonies. In particular, Virginia could thank William and Mary for removing the heavy and sticky hand of Lord Howard of Effingham, though they allowed him to retain the governorship and half the salary of the office, which gave him a sinecure of £1,000 ($50,000) a year.*

As Effingham's deputy, their Majesties chose Francis Nicholson, formerly in command of New York, from which he had recently fled after almost precipitating revolution. Now more circumspect and conciliatory, Nicholson decided to learn something about Virginia for himself, making an extended tour of the colony. He repeated this year after year, inviting the people to speak out on their problems and grievances, being on occasion so indulgent that he "suffered the Mob to come into the Room where he was entertaining company at dinner and was much diverted with their scrambling amongst themselves and taking all Victualls off from the table before him."

In 1698, for the third time, fire destroyed Jamestown. With only a few protesting, Nicholson seized this opportunity to move the capital elsewhere. As a consequence, Jamestown was not rebuilt, soon becoming a heap of "bricks and rubbish, with three or four inhabited houses." By 1893, when the Association for the Preservation of Virginia Antiquities acquired some twenty acres here, it had reverted to wilderness, as forbidding as the day Newport brought in the first ships and moored them to the trees along the bank.

Bought by the Federal Government and the State in 1933, the site is now a pleasant and much-frequented memorial park—so restful and pleasant indeed that there is not an echo of the "disgustfull" brawls and appalling tragedies that occurred here as the town rang to the curses and screams of the dying. Of old Jamestown, nothing remains but some foundations, part of an early brick church, and a few weather-worn gravestones—among them, that of proud and covetous Lady Berkeley. Though she died the wife

* This arrangement continued to the eve of the Revolution. The governorship had become a juicy political plum to be given to royal favorites. The governors remained at home and each year received £1,000, later £1,200, for doing nothing. Virginia was ruled by deputies till 1768.

of Philip Ludwell, she was buried "Lady Berkeley," doubtless as she peremptorily commanded.

Partly because a small college had been established there and its buildings might be used till a new state house was erected, the capital was moved to Middle Plantation, now renamed Williamsburg in honor of the King.

After the Indian massacre in 1622, which destroyed the college project at Henrico, the authorities had done nothing about schools, but a few had been established by private means. In 1634, Benjamin Syms left 200 acres, a fine house, forty cows, "and other accomodations" to found a free school in Elizabeth City—or Hampton, as it is now known. Another free school was founded there in 1659 by Thomas Eaton, a surgeon. The Syms school, the first free school in the colonies, and the Eaton school were later merged, becoming the Syms-Eaton Academy, today a part of the Hampton public school system. Scattered about, there were a few parish schools—seven or eight at most—each with a handful of restless scholars.

The very rich occasionally sent their sons to school in England. As for the rest, except for the children of prosperous planters who could afford to hire a tutor or pay the local minister to give instruction, there was almost no opportunity for schooling, and most Virginians remained untaught except in crafts and trades.

The idea of a college was revived by a hotheaded but able Scotsman, the Reverend James Blair, who had been named by the Bishop of London as commissary, or superintendent of church affairs in the colony.* Blair proposed a "Grammar School to teach Latin and Greek, a Philosophy School for Philosophy and Mathematics, and a Divinity School for the Oriental Languages and Divinity," to be known as the College of William and Mary.

Supported by Nicholson, Blair journeyed to London to interest their Majesties, who seemed to be much flattered, granting the college 20,000 acres of land, the receipt of certain taxes, and a sum of £2,000 ($100,000). When directed to draw up a charter, Attor-

---

* All of the English colonies in America were part of the diocese of London. But the New England colonies had never paid the Bishop any heed, going their own "Congregational way."

ney General Seymour found this liberality excessive, misdirected, and ill-timed. England was at war and badly needed money, he protested, saying that he could see no need for a college in Virginia. The college would train ministers of the Gospel, Blair replied, and whatever anyone might think, the people in Virginia had souls to be saved.

"Souls!" exclaimed the Attorney General. "Damn your souls! Make tobacco!"

Chartered in 1693, granted the right to send a Burgess to the Assembly, the college opened in temporary quarters a few years later with a staff of three—Blair as president, at a salary of £150 ($7,500) a year; Mungo Inglis as "writing master," at £30 ($1,500) a year; and one Mullikin as usher, at £25 a year. Teachers' salaries appear to have been as ridiculously small then as now, and the overworked Inglis soon twitted Blair with taking so much of the payroll, saying that if he were not so greedy, the staff might consist of six as planned.

Still standing and in use, the college's beautiful main building, "modeled" by Sir Christopher Wren but "adapted to the nature of the country by the Gentlemen there," was near enough to completion in 1699 to receive the Assembly, which continued to meet in its great hall until a new capitol was built, a substantial structure of brick.

Gutted by fire in 1705, the college buildings were not fully restored until 1723 for want of funds and public interest. One of the professors, the Reverend Hugh Jones, rector at Jamestown, described it at this time as a "college without a chapel, without a scholarship, and without a statute [i.e., without the right to grant degrees]; a library without books, comparatively speaking, . . . and a Burgess without electors."

William and Mary began as nothing more than a boarding school at the preparatory level for richer planters' sons. Their extravagance and escapades sorely tried the patience of Blair, who suffered their indifference and deviltries for fifty years. But many distinguished Virginians studied here, including Thomas Jefferson, though he did not think much of it in his day.

Entering in 1760 for advanced study, Jefferson found the college "filled . . . with children"—that is, with beginners in Latin, Greek, and other subjects. Study was on a rudimentary plane. Students were treated like children, often being flogged. Jefferson objected especially to the religiosity into which instruction had been cast by Blair, the charter, and various endowments, remarking that the college was "just well enough endowed to draw out the miserable existence to which a miserable constitution has doomed it."

Like other young bloods, Jefferson had a gay time at "Devilsburg," as he often referred to Williamsburg in his student days. And yet, though formal instruction in the college did not help much, he succeeded in obtaining as fine an education as anyone could desire. By chance and his own abilities, he found it in a brilliant small group that included two professors of the college— William Small, an Englishman of wit and wide learning, who later returned home to become the "great Dr. Small of Birmingham"; and a self-educated Virginian, George Wythe, not yet forty but already a leading lawyer, a profound scholar who trained not only Jefferson but John Marshall, James Monroe, and Henry Clay in the law.

Though not yet twenty, Jefferson was taken up by Small and Wythe, who introduced him into the small circle that dined at least once a week with the governor, Francis Fauquier—"the ablest man who had ever filled that office," said Jefferson in later years. An accomplished man of the world, a scholar and a fellow of the Royal Society, son of a rich banker, Fauquier had ruined himself at the gambling tables in London and, at fifty-four, accepted the relatively modest post of command in Virginia, where he spent his remaining years.

At their frequent dinners in the Governor's Mansion, or Palace as it was called, these men with a few carefully chosen and discreet guests ranged the universe in their talk, freely and boldly exploring every avenue that seemed to beckon even if it led into territory posted as dangerous—such as the powers and rights of Parliament. Did Parliament have the right to command the colonies in all things? And should there be an established church? What about revealed religion? Was slavery defensible on any ground? As the Madeira flowed, they talked law, institutions, constitutions, economic theory, taxation, finance, philosophy, matters of faith, history, literature, agriculture, wines, women, architecture, breeding of horses, and music, for which Fauquier and Jefferson both had a passion.

Wythe had already developed the doctrine that the colonies and the mother country were united only by their common allegiance to the Crown—now the accepted doctrine of the British Commonwealth. Parliament therefore did not have the right to intervene in Virginia's internal affairs, especially in matters of taxation. Both Wythe and Jefferson were already convinced that slavery was an evil that had to go.

Intellectually, culturally, politically, Virginia was growing up. There was a stir in the air, and Williamsburg would soon resound to angry voices in "bloody debate."

But in 1760, when Jefferson came to the college, Williamsburg was just a small sleepy country town except during the "season" when the Assembly was in session. At that time it was filled with people "hurrying back and forwards from the Capitoll to the taverns, and at night Carousing and Drinking in one chamber, and box and Dice in another," which commonly went on till morning. Trailing a retinue of servants, many rich planters and their families came to attend balls, routs, fairs, cock fights, horse races, and the theater, the first of which opened in 1716 for the "performance of Comedies, Drolls, and other kinds of stage plays."

Not long after, Williamsburg had a printing press and in 1736— no doubt with the ghost of old Sir William Berkeley moaning and predicting dire disaster—the *Virginia Gazette* began publication with a subsidy from the Burgesses.

As seen during the Williamsburg "season," life in Virginia was gay and brilliant. But however glittering on top, it was a society far from sound below. A shift had occurred in the economy and the character of the colony. Few had made great fortunes during the first century. Now there were scores of "Grandees," the wealth of all based upon vast land holdings and "shoals" of Negro slaves.

Up to 1700, Virginia had been, in the main, a land of sturdy small farmers who worked their fields with their own hands and with only such aid as their families could give them. But slavery ruined these small independent planters, for they could not compete with the mass production of slave-grown tobacco. The "common people make the best," Governor Gooch reported in 1731, for the tobacco from the great plantations "frequently proves very mean stuff. . . . Yet the rich man's trash will always damp the market and spoil the poor man's good tobacco which has been carefully managed."

With prices depressed by the "rich man's trash," the "common people" found their small holdings unprofitable. Many emigrated to other colonies, some took employment as overseers on the large plantations, a few became small slave-owners, but most sank into misery and shiftlessness, becoming the "poor whites," without resources and indisposed to work because Negro slavery had cast a stigma upon labor.

Growth in the number of slaves had been slow during the early years. In Berkeley's day, they constituted a very small part of the working force, numbering not more than one in twenty of the population. After the turn of the century, however, their numbers grew so rapidly that by 1750 two out of every five Virginians were Negroes. The colony repeatedly tried to restrict the importation of slaves, in part from fear of a slave insurrection, but the Crown had an interest in the slave traffic and overrode the colony's objections.[1]

Though their character and working habits were often abused by those who sat at ease and did no labor, it was the "careless" Negro slave and the "indolent" white servant who built the great plantations of eighteenth-century Virginia. They brought the planter a double benefit. They grew the tobacco that built the fine house on the hill overlooking one of the great rivers. In addition, the planter received for each of them that he brought in a "headright" to fifty acres of land.

Most of the land, often in huge blocks, was patented by headright, though large grants were occasionally made for other reasons. In 1679, on his promise to settle 250 people on the spot to guard the frontier, the first William Byrd, already possessed of many great tracts and a large fortune, was granted eighteen square miles at the Falls on the James—a very profitable venture, for in 1733 his son laid out here the foundations of Richmond.

Many large estates were legitimately acquired, but many were not. Land-grabbers grossly abused the head-right system, obtaining immense tracts by chicanery and fraud. Lists of transported persons were padded. Certificates of transportation were used over and over. County clerks and especially the clerks in the Secretary's office, "a constant mint of these rights," carried on a brisk under-the-counter business in the sale of head-rights, which could "be purchased at very easy rates"—for as little as 1s. ($2.50) each, which was considerably cheaper than paying £5 ($250) to bring in a man.

On one occasion, Secretary Philip Ludwell brought in forty servants, which entitled him to 2,000 acres. With his own hand he added a cipher and wrote himself a patent for 20,000 acres. Though this was well known, nothing was done about it, for Ludwell was powerful and a dangerous man to cross.

There were frequent frauds in laying out grants through the "knavery of surveyors," who frequently ran no lines at all, merely describing the properties by a few natural bounds, always making "sure to allow large measure so that the persons for whom they surveyed might enjoy larger tracts of land than they were to pay quitrents for"—two or three times larger, or even ten times as much.

Trickery was used in evading the regulations for "planting and seating." The holder of a head-right had three years within which to build a house, put livestock on the land, clear an acre of ground, and plant it, on pain of forfeiting his grant if he failed to do so. The land-grabbing gentry, which included most of the "better" families, would cut down twenty or thirty trees, build a hut, turn a few hogs loose in the woods, plant a row or two of corn, have this certified as "planting and seating," and then not come near the tract for years, holding it for speculation or future use.

The annual quitrent of 2s. ($5.00) for every hundred acres was not burdensome on lands in production. But when paid on vast tracts of idle and undeveloped land, it became a rather heavy drain. In the 1630's, with the aim of speeding settlement, Charles I had remitted the payment of quitrents on lands along the frontier. But this was revoked by Charles II, who declared that remission had retarded settlement, for many had "abused that grace and taken occasion thereby to take and create title to themselves of such quantities of land which they never intend to or in truth can occupy and cultivate, but thereby only keep out others who would plant and manure the same."

But the Grandees, who monopolized the principal offices, knew their way around and found many ways to avoid paying quitrents on their huge idle tracts. They "concealed" hundreds of thousands of acres. No surveyor who valued his job reported the true acreage of the unoccupied lands held by the members of the Council, the Burgesses, or other larger planters. Nor did the sheriffs dare to hale them into court and challenge their rolls, being so overawed by the "richer sort of inhabitants, some holding forty, fifty, or sixty thousand acres, . . . that they take their accounts as they themselves would have them."

By 1700, most good and accessible land had been taken up, though relatively little was in use. Concerned about this, the authorities in London suggested that future patents should be limited to 500 acres and that anyone so minded should be permitted to plant "on any vacant piece of land," whether patented or not. He should be allowed a hundred acres and as many more for every indentured servant he brought in within three years. The Board of Trade and Plantations asked Nicholson to take appropriate action after discussing this with the Council and the Burgesses.

"If the Governor ever laid the scheme before them," as a distinguished Virginia scholar has remarked, "it is certain that the Council, so far from telling him how to put it into force, advised him to report back that it was unwise and impracticable." [2]

As auditor in 1703, William Byrd found "very great abuses" in the rent rolls, and at the Crown's direction Nicholson was foolhardy enough to try to correct this. Singling out Major Lawrence Smith, a member of the Council, he brought suit against him in the General Court for £80 ($4,000) due on quitrents. As the General Court consisted of members of the Council, all of whom were land-grabbing and evading taxes, Nicholson might as well have asked them to pass sentence on themselves. Warned to mind his own business, he compromised the suit and the abuses continued.

Nicholson succeeded, however, in preventing fraud and chicanery in the patenting of lands in the new Blackwater section below the James. Outraged by such a dangerous innovation, the Council turned on him and drove him from office, with the Grandees showering maledictions upon him.

A decade later, Governor Alexander Spotswood found himself similarly unpopular when he proposed the confiscation of lands on which quitrents remained unpaid for more than three years. William Byrd and the younger Philip Ludwell proposed, instead, that the Assembly petition the King to abolish such rents. When Spotswood opposed this as unwise, they pilloried him as a public enemy. Thwarted by the Grandees, Spotswood joined them. When he learned that he was to be relieved as governor, he granted 60,000 acres to three men whom he had placed under bond to deed the land to him as soon as he was out of office.

Adopting Virginia as home, which few governors did, Spotswood retired to Germanna where he lived in lordly style in his "enchanted Castle," with its terraced gardens, its marble fountain, its living room "elegantly set off with Pier Glasses," the whole graced with a "brace of tame Deer [that] ran familiarly through the House." Though his successor protested Spotswood's grant, he was allowed to keep it.

But none of the engrossers had the tireless energy and sharp appetite of Robert Carter, an agent for the Northern Neck proprietors. In one year alone—1724—he granted patents to himself, his sons, and his grandsons for almost 87,000 acres. At his death he owned more than 300,000 acres, having meantime given tens of thousands more to members of his family and to his many relations, near and distant. The proprietors tolerated this graft because "King" Carter virtually ruled the Council and jealously guarded the proprietors' interests there, succeeding in having their boundaries pushed far to the west into the rich Shenandoah Valley.

With their vast holdings and legions of slaves, no wonder the Grandees lived in baronial splendor. But "near these rich plantations, in which the Negro alone is unhappy," as a French traveler observed, "are often found miserable huts inhabited by whites whose wan faces and ragged garments give testimony to their poverty. . . . The indolence and dissipation of the middling and lower classes of white inhabitants in Virginia is such as to give pain to every reflecting mind."

By 1730, Virginia had become a land of extremes, with no middle group between slaves and slave-owners. It was a most undemocratic society, rigidly stratified, static, and unprogressive, being content to follow the familiar routines of its one-crop economy. There was little in it, apparently, to stimulate the creative activities of the mind, to set the wheels of thought turning, to refine the sensibilities of the heart. It seemed a most unlikely seed-bed for great leaders, revolutionary thinkers, and passionate democrats.

Yet from this society there now came as brilliant a generation or two of leaders as any society or comparable area ever produced —George Washington, Thomas Jefferson, Patrick Henry, Richard Henry Lee, George Mason, James Madison, John Marshall, and James Monroe, to name a few.

XXVIII

Independence

Sound doctrine and unanswerable reasons!
—GEORGE WASHINGTON

FOR MORE than a century, Virginians manifested an astonishing want of curiosity about what lay to the west in the farther reaches of the colony. In the beginning there had been much talk of marching over the mountains to the South Sea. But after Newport's fiasco with his "five-peeced" boat, nothing was done about westward "discoveries" for years. As late as 1700, little was known of the country beyond the Fall Line.[1] Settlement was still confined to the tidewater, but pressure for expansion was growing as the good land was taken up.

At length, in 1716, with great fanfare that has become the subject of much romantic nonsense, Governor Spotswood led a gentlemanly troop of fifty—his "Knights of the Golden Horseshoe"—over the Blue Ridge and down into the beautiful Shenandoah Valley, part of the great Valley of Virginia that stretches south from the Potomac for hundreds of miles. Though Grandees got their hands on large parts of this, the Shenandoah and other valleys began to fill up with German and Scotch-Irish families, former redemptioners, largely from Pennsylvania.* Previously, a

* Redemptioners were indentured servants of a particular kind. The length of their indentures varied greatly, depending upon the amounts advanced to

353

thousand or more spirited Huguenots, fleeing religious persecution, had settled along the upper James.

Hard-working and thrifty, stubborn and self-reliant, these groups, together with a scattering of English Quakers and Welsh Baptists, brought a new spirit into the colony. Dissenters in religion, they were dissenters in politics as well, having ideas of their own, not being disposed to follow the lead of Tidewater lords. Their weight in affairs steadily grew until, in the days of 1776, the power of these independent backwoods farmers became decisive.

With the Shenandoah Valley opened up, Virginians began to look beyond the Alleghenies to the broad valley of the Ohio, which the colony claimed under its 1609 charter. With George Washington and his older half-brother as members, a Virginia and Maryland group organized the Ohio Company in 1749 and obtained a patent to 500,000 acres along the river.

But the French also claimed that territory and began to build a line of forts from Lake Erie to New Orleans. Rejecting such pretensions, Governor Dinwiddie sent a messenger to warn the French to keep out of the Ohio country, entrusting the mission to young George Washington, already an adjutant of the Virginia militia though just turned twenty-one. The French laughed at the warning and told Washington that it was their "absolute Design to take possession of the Ohio and, by God, they would do it!"

To forestall this, Dinwiddie sent a small party to begin construction of a fort where the rivers Monongahela and Allegheny join to form the Ohio, ordering several companies of militia to follow under Colonel Joshua Fry, with Washington as his aide. While on the march, they learned that the French had captured the advance party, taken over their work and completed it as Fort Duquesne.

Leading the vanguard, Washington advanced to Great Meadows, about forty miles from Fort Duquesne, where he built a weak redoubt. When scouts reported a small French reconnaissance party

them to pay their transportation and other costs. All of them had some means of their own, though needing a subsidy to make the voyage. The Germans were of the same stock as the industrious and frugal "Pennsylvania Dutch."

in the vicinity, Washington surprised it, attacking at night, killing the commander and nine others, taking more than twenty prisoners. The shot fired here, without parley or warning, was truly the shot heard round the world, bringing on a great war, a mighty shift of empire, and the American Revolution.

Young and inexperienced, evidencing none of the balance and sound judgment that marked his later years, Washington had acted very rashly, for the vastly superior forces at Fort Duquesne now came down upon him. Aware of his danger, he retreated to Fort Necessity, at Great Meadows. But after a short siege, having suffered heavy losses, Washington had to capitulate, quickly accepting the generous terms offered by the French. He and his men were allowed to depart with their arms and with their colors flying, but this was not an auspicious start for one of the world's most distinguished military and political careers.

The fighting that began here on the remote Virginia frontier, known in America as the French and Indian War, developed into a great armed conflict, the Seven Years' War, fought in many lands almost all around the globe. By 1763, when peace came, Britain had established herself as the world's strongest power. She had driven the French from India, she had gained control of the seas, she had acquired Canada and undisputed possession of the territory west to the Mississippi, except for the town of New Orleans.

Delighted to have the French removed, eager to exploit western lands, the colonists received a rude shock when the King proclaimed that the country beyond the Alleghenies was closed to settlement. But as this decree was thought to be merely temporary, it aroused far less complaint and resentment than Britain's decision that the colonies should contribute something to the support of empire. With huge new territories to defend, Britain did not propose to bear the entire cost, especially as she had emerged from the Seven Years' War with a greatly enlarged national debt. To the growls of the dominant gentry, this had brought higher taxes at home, and it seemed only fair that the colonies should pay at least part of the cost of their defense.

Besides, the structure of empire obviously needed mending.

Built in a haphazard fashion, it should be remodeled and strengthened. Colonial policy should be uniform, with more central direction and control from London. As the colonies soon learned, the
happy days of "salutary neglect" were over. They were to be
fitted into a new imperial pattern.

Britain first tightened enforcement of the hated Navigation Acts
and trade laws, for all of the seaports—including Norfolk,
founded at the mouth of the Chesapeake in 1705 and now Virginia's largest town—thrived on a profitable smuggling business,
to the detriment of the Exchequer. Seizures and searches for
contraband under writs of assistance created much ill feeling,
particularly in Boston and Newport. The northern colonies were
highly incensed when Parliament passed the Sugar Act, which
struck at the foundation of New England's unsavory triangular
trade—rum to Africa to buy slaves, who were sold in the West
Indies for molasses, which was brought back to make more rum
to buy more slaves, *ad nauseam*.

While merrily evading the law, the colonies had never challenged Parliament's right to make laws for the regulation of
trade, even when this involved the imposition of customs duties.
These duties constituted a tax, true enough, but it was an indirect
tax, an "external" tax, part of the regulatory machinery and
not designed primarily to raise revenue.

The colonies, however, had never admitted Parliament's right
to tax them directly, and it was this right which Parliament chose
to assert in 1765 by passing the "infamous" Stamp Act, requiring
stamps on all commercial papers, legal documents, newspapers,
and other publications.

"It is highly reasonable the colonies should contribute something toward the charge of protecting themselves and in aid of the
great expense Great Britain has put herself to on their account,"
said George Grenville, head of the ministry. "No tax appears
to me so easy and equitable as a stamp duty. . . . If the colonists
think of any other mode of taxation more convenient to them
and make any proposition of equal efficacy with the stamp duty, I
will give it all due consideration."

Not objecting to stamps as such, the colonies could think of nothing "more convenient" than a few mild protests against direct taxes in general. The Stamp Act had passed Parliament with little trouble, and it appeared that it would be accepted by the colonies in the same way. There were only a few feeble out-cries until the Virginia Assembly met in the spring of 1765.

Dominated by the more conservative, the Burgesses began mildly enough. In petitions to the Crown and the Commons, they opposed the tax as a "long & hasty stride." But they wished to avoid the "least Disposition to any sort of Rudeness," they in-sisted—to the disgust and growing impatience of a new member from one of the western counties, young Patrick Henry, who had already made something of a name for himself as a people's advocate in the "Parsons' Cause," during which he had denounced the King as a "tyrant."

Biding his time to strike, waiting till the end of the session when most members had gone home,* Henry found his oppor-tunity when the Burgesses decided to give further thought to the Stamp Act, reopening discussion on May 29, 1765, which was Henry's twenty-ninth birthday—and how he celebrated it to his everlasting honor and renown!

With only two of his colleagues knowing what he intended, Henry got the floor, made a few placatory general remarks, took out of his pocket a flyleaf torn from an old law book, *Coke on Lyttleton*, and began to read from what he had written there.

"Resolved, That the first adventurers and settlers . . . brought with them . . . all the privileges, franchises, and immunities that have at any time been held, enjoyed, and possessed by the people of Great Britain.

"Resolved," that "these privileges, franchises, and immunities have been confirmed" by two royal charters.

"Resolved, That the taxation of the people by themselves or by persons chosen by themselves . . . is the distinguishing char-acteristic of British freedom . . .

"Resolved," that Virginians "have uninterruptedly enjoyed the right of being thus governed by their own Assemblies in the article of their taxes and internal policy . . ."

* Only 39 of 116 Burgesses were present.

All of this was good Virginia doctrine. But older and more conservative members were beginning to get restive, not liking the drift of this argument, protesting that more or less the same ground had been covered in the petitions which the Burgesses had already adopted and sent to London. Until replies from these were received, nothing more should be done. But Henry's first four resolutions finally passed, though by the scantiest of margins.

"Resolved, therefore, That the General Assembly of this colony have the only and sole exclusive right and power to lay taxes and impositions upon the inhabitants of this colony . . ."

While the Randolphs, Carters, Blands, and other Grandees in the House agreed with the substance of this, they disliked this resolution in its context and still more for its blunt tone. But in spite of their opposition, it passed by a majority of one.

"By God, I would have given a hundred guineas for a single vote," exclaimed Peyton Randolph. But he and his friends had yet to hear the worst.

"Resolved, That . . . the inhabitants of this colony are not bound to yield obedience to any law or ordinance whatever designed to impose any taxation whatsoever upon them other than the laws and ordinances of the General Assembly aforesaid;

"Resolved," that anyone maintaining the contrary "by speaking or writing . . . shall be deemed an enemy to his Majestie's colony."

These last resolutions were too much, and the Burgesses rejected them, even reversing their vote on the previous resolution after Colonel Peter Randolph, a member of the Council, had searched the Assembly's journals "to find a precedent for expunging a vote of the House."

Standing in the doorway, young Thomas Jefferson,* still a student at Williamsburg, attentively followed the "most bloody" debate as Henry defended his resolutions with passion and eloquence, speaking "as Homer wrote," exclaiming at one point:

"Tarquin and Caesar had each his Brutus; Charles the First, his Cromwell; and George the Third—"

* Closely related to the Randolphs, his mother being one.

"Treason!" cried the chairman.

"Treason! Treason!" shouted many more.

"—and George the Third," Henry quietly resumed, "may profit by their example. If this be treason, make the most of it!"

Though only four of his seven resolutions were finally adopted, a surprising and momentous victory had been won by Henry and what Governor Fauquier called the "Young, hot, and Giddy" members of the House. Most of these came from the western counties, though the "Giddy" included some Tidewater Grandees —notably, Richard Henry Lee, descended from Colonel Richard Lee, one of the early Cavaliers. The Lees had established themselves on a large plantation along the Potomac, living in splendor at Stratford Hall, later the birthplace of General Robert E. Lee. Though one himself, Richard Henry Lee did not believe in the rule of "aristocratical" men or domination of the "opulent," stepping forward as one of the most advanced and ardent democrats of his day.

Objecting to the Virginia Resolutions as "rash heat," Fauquier promptly dissolved the Assembly, but the damage had been done. Published in the *Virginia Gazette,* the resolutions were carried to all the colonies, where they were reprinted in full, creating the impression that all seven had been adopted. Overnight, Henry became the idol of the people everywhere, the "noble Patriot," our first American hero.

"I own myself a democrat," said Henry in later years, and down to his death he held the faith and warm affections of the people, especially of those in Virginia where his name always worked magic. As Washington observed, he had only to say, "Let this be Law, and it is Law." Virginians showered honors upon him, many of which he refused, though he never shirked a task that needed doing.

Massachusetts had suggested a meeting of the colonies to consider the Stamp Act. But this proposal was very coolly received until the publication of Henry's resolutions, which became the "signal for a general outcry." Here was the tocsin for which many had been waiting. As Governor Hutchinson of Massachusetts complained, nothing extravagant had appeared in the newspapers "till an account was received of the Virginia Resolves." If the oldest and traditionally the most loyal of the colonies took the lead, why should others hesitate to follow?

Because Governor Fauquier blocked the way, Virginia was not represented at the Stamp Act Congress that met in New York in October, 1765. But the nine colonies represented knew that they spoke for Virginia when they denied Parliament's right to tax them directly and recommended a boycott of British goods.

It had been Grenville's idea that the tax might be made more palatable if collected by American stamp masters, at a salary of £300 a year. But this was a mistake, arousing great popular indignation. "Foreigners" could be expected to show no scruples, but the people found it shameful and intolerable that some of their "Fellow Slaves" would undertake the dirty job of fastening the iron chains of bondage upon them. With Sons of Liberty on their heels, stamp masters were soon fleeing for their lives, up back alleys in the towns and along unfrequented lanes in the countryside.[2]

Somewhat surprised by all this clamor about a few stamps,* not a little alarmed by the boycott which had markedly reduced British trade, Parliament repealed the Stamp Act early in 1766. But at the same time it restated its right to legislate for the colonies "in all cases whatsoever." So long as this right remained theoretic, the colonists did not mind, and quiet was restored.

The repeal of the stamp tax relieved all Virginians. Williamsburg celebrated with a "ball and elegant entertainment at the Capitoll," and the Assembly talked of erecting a statue to "good" King George. Until Tom Paine and George himself smashed the myth ten years later, the colonists looked upon the King as their friend, who was being misled by his "wicked" ministers and their dupes in Parliament. He had only to rid himself of these "Master Devils" and the colonists would quickly and happily return to humble obedience.

After a year of no alarms, not content to let well enough

* The British people had long paid stamp duties, and the Stamp Act aroused no clamor in other British colonies—Canada, Nova Scotia, East Florida, Bermuda, and the British West Indies.

alone, the brilliant but irresponsible Charles Townshend thought that he had hit upon a neat trick to confound the colonial logicians. He would lay a tax upon glass, lead, paper, pigments and tea, to be collected in the form of customs duties, similar to the duties that the colonies had long been paying on various other goods. If the stupid colonists wished to draw a silly distinction between internal and external taxes, he did not care, so long as they contributed something to the royal treasury.

But these duties were not external taxes in the usual sense, as the Massachusetts General Court was the first to point out, dispatching a circular letter to arouse all the colonies. The duties were not for the regulation of trade. They were primarily designed to raise revenue, as Townshend frankly admitted, and therefore clearly "unconstitutional."

Virginia agreed and seconded Massachusetts by sending out a circular of its own to expose this flank attack on the colonies' liberties, urge a renewal of the boycott, and defend the right of the colonies to act together in matters of common concern—a right which had been challenged.

When Governor Botetourt dissolved the Assembly for this, the Burgesses repaired in a body to the Raleigh Tavern, which is still standing and doing business on the Duke of Gloucester Street in old Williamsburg. Here they signed an "Association," or agreement, that no slaves, wine, tea, or British manufactures should be imported until the Townshend duties were repealed. Drafted by George Mason, another of those who were at once exalted Grandees and advanced democrats, the agreement was presented to the meeting and sponsored by George Washington, who had come to the opinion that "no man should scruple or hesitate a moment to use a-ms in defense of so valuable a blessing" as the "liberty which we have derived from our ancestors, . . . on which all the good and evil of life depends."

Protests from all the colonies poured into London, and the pinch of the boycott again forced Parliament to retreat. Early in 1770, all of the Townshend duties were repealed except that on tea, which was kept merely as a matter of principle, a standing assertion of Parliament's right to tax the colonies if it pleased.

Unfortunately, the day of repeal was the day of the Boston Massacre. Not responsible for their presence in town and under orders to do their duty, poor British soldiers found life very hard in Boston, where they were insulted on every hand, pelted with stones and snowballs. Exasperated, they fired into a threatening crowd and killed four, creating pandemonium, an occasion which Samuel Adams seized to "persuade" Governor Hutchinson to remove the troops from town to Castle William in the harbor—another retreat that did not pass unnoticed in the colonies.

Two years later, Rhode Islanders captured and burned the revenue cutter *Gaspee*, catching her when she ran aground. Britain ordered the *Gaspee* rioters sent home for trial and passed an act for the transportation of similar offenders, a decree that aroused Jefferson and many others. If a poor man were shipped to London on some specious charge by a customshouse officer or an irritable royal governor, what chance would he have of a fair trial there—far from home, without money, friends, or witnesses?

Inviting Patrick Henry, Richard Henry Lee, George Mason, and several more to meet at the Raleigh Tavern, Jefferson presented the danger. Probably at the suggestion of Richard Henry Lee, who had been talking about the idea since 1768, the group decided that the situation required a regular system of intercolonial communication, proposing that the Burgesses should establish a "Standing Committee of Correspondence and Inquiry."

This seemed innocuous enough, and the House adopted the suggestion unanimously, choosing Jefferson, Henry, and Lee to serve on the committee of ten. As urged by Virginia, six other colonies soon had their official standing committees to keep information, plans, and suggestions constantly flowing. Previously, in 1772, Samuel Adams had organized a network of non-official committees throughout Massachusetts.

Here was the machinery of revolution, the nucleus for expanding organization, the training school of those who would soon take power, furnishing the villages and the capitals alike with leadership. Little wonder that frantic Tories described the committee system as the "foulest, subtlest, and most venomous serpent ever issued from the egg of Sedition."

It remained for Lord North, in one of his sleepier moments, to light the fuse that set off the explosion. The great East India Company, which Sir Thomas Smythe had helped to found along with the Virginia Company so long ago, had millions of pounds of unsold tea on its hands and needed money. North gave it the American market, granting it various immunities and tax refunds so that it could undersell colonial merchants who had bought their stock legitimately or smuggled it from Holland.

Notorious for its rapacity and vicious exploitation, the East India Company, it seemed, was about to wrap its tentacles around another victim. If it could establish a virtual monopoly in tea by having its "consignees" sell directly to the consumer, throwing colonial merchants out of business, what would prevent it from establishing a monopoly in the sale of spices, silk, wine, china, and other things?

But this menace, real as it was, directly touched the interests of only a few. The cheapness of East India tea would probably have tempted the colonists to buy it, to the ruin of many local merchants. But the tea never got in. The tax on tea still stood, and the many Committees of Correspondence took up the cry that the tax should not be paid. Sons of Liberty were soon forcing "consignees" to resign or take to their heels with all of the desperate speed of the stamp masters before them.

In Boston, led by Sam Adams and the Sons of Liberty, a town meeting demanded that the tea ships leave the harbor. When this was refused, the "Mohawks" struck and dumped into the harbor £18,000 of cargo in Boston's famous Tea Party. Other colonies had their tea parties. At Annapolis, the *Peggy Stewart* went up in flames with her East India cargo on board.

Dumbfounded by this, aware at last of the danger, declaring that it was no longer a question of taxation but whether Britain possessed any authority over the "haughty American Republicans," Parliament passed severe retaliatory measures by overwhelming majorities.

Not wishing to stir up general resentment and resistance, Lord North singled out Boston for punishment, convinced that none would come to her assistance. He would bring the "Boston mutineers" to heel by starving them into submission. He closed the port of Boston to all shipping until the tea was paid for and the town gave some satisfactory evidence of reform.

Going further, North revoked the Massachusetts charter, gave the governor new authoritarian powers, ordered that town meetings were to be held only when approved by the governor, and directed that rioters should be sent to England for trial. He named General Thomas Gage, British commander-in-chief in America, as governor and sent him four regiments, which, so Gage judged, would be "sufficient to prevent any disturbance." Even retiring Governor Hutchinson was shocked by the severity of this for what had been, after all, only a minor riot, a malicious frolic, in which no person had been hurt.

Among many others, Benjamin Franklin advised Boston to pay for the tea and make obeisance. But Sam Adams and his men were now in control and would have none of that, dispatching Paul Revere to New York and Philadelphia to obtain aid, writing all the colonies to persuade them that the struggle at Boston was their own. The replies to this letter brought surprising support, for, as George Washington observed, why should Americans "supinely sit and see one province after another fall a prey to despotism"?

Boston proposed a Solemn League and Covenant for the suspension of all trade with Britain, both imports and exports, until the Port Act was repealed. But many found this too radical, still believing that there was room for negotiation, that a moderate course might yet bring about a reconciliation. Distrusting "mobbish Boston," more conservative New York proposed a continental congress, a suggestion seconded by Philadelphia. In such an assembly the hotheaded Bostonians would have to keep in step if they wished others to march with them.

When news of British action against Boston reached Virginia in May, 1774, Jefferson called Henry, Lee, and four or five others to take council. Though a freethinker himself, Jefferson suggested a day of fasting, humiliation, and prayer—this was in the Puritan tradition, though Jefferson and his friends kept that fact to themselves—and persuaded pious and church-going Robert Carter

Nicholas to present it to the Burgesses. Who could object to prayer? Accordingly, the House proclaimed that June 1st, when the blockade of Boston was to begin, should be observed as a fast day throughout the colony.

The governor, Lord Dunmore, a bumbler and a dolthead, fell into the trap, damning the resolution, dissolving the Burgesses, who had "all agreed," said Jefferson, "to go home and see that preachers were provided in our counties and notice given to our people, . . . who came together in great multitudes, wondering what it meant," having their curiosity satisfied and learning other things as well.

But before breaking up, the Burgesses met at the Raleigh Tavern with Peyton Randolph, their Speaker, in the chair. Son of Sir John Randolph, the only native Virginian ever to be knighted, Peyton Randolph was one of those who had opposed Henry's resolutions nine years before, but he had since stepped forward.* He now joined the great majority at the Raleigh, who took their stand solidly with Massachusetts, praising Boston's resistance, promising assistance, endorsing the Solemn League and Covenant.

Unaware of New York's recent proposal, the Burgesses suggested a continental congress, urging that one should be held every year. At the same time, they issued a call for a convention to meet at Williamsburg on August 1st, to be composed of delegates chosen by popular election in the counties. By these "wise, spirited, and seasonable proceedings," as Connecticut called them, or by what the Crown preferred to call the "extraordinary conduct of the Burgesses," Virginia encouraged the fainthearted and rallied the hesitant colonies to unite in defense of hard-pressed Massachusetts.

Meeting in defiance of the governor, the Williamsburg convention, the first such assembly since Bacon's day a century before, endorsed the proposed continental congress, named seven dele-

---

* Peyton's brother John took the Loyalist side and left Virginia for England in 1775. But his son, Edmund Randolph, remained to play a secondary but important part in the Revolution, being one of Washington's aides in 1775, in time becoming the first Attorney General of the United States and the second Secretary of State, succeeding Jefferson in 1794.

gates, ordered the suspension of all trade with Britain, and pledged supplies and aid to Boston.

"I will raise one thousand men," declared Colonel George Washington in a thundering speech, "subsist them at my own expense, and march myself at their head for the relief of Boston."

Nothing could have been better calculated to bury all hopes of peace than the Quebec Act which Parliament now saw fit to pass, granting religious toleration to the French Catholics in Canada. Toleration is always admirable in itself. But as many at the time pointed out, Britain might have applied the noble principle nearer home—to the harried Catholics in Ireland. The Quebec Act was a politic and strategic move—and it worked—to detach Canada from the rebellious Protestant colonies and preserve it as a military base in the event of hostilities. Quite as bad, the act extended the boundaries of Quebec south to the Ohio River, arbitrarily stripping Massachusetts, Connecticut, and Virginia of their western lands.

In the historic First Continental Congress that met at Carpenters' Hall in Philadelphia on September 5, 1774, Virginia had seven delegates—George Washington, Patrick Henry, Richard Henry Lee, Peyton Randolph, Richard Bland, Benjamin Harrison, and Edmund Pendleton. The Congress chose Randolph as president. When no one seemed disposed to take the floor, Patrick Henry rose and made the opening address, a stirring call for united action.

"The distinctions between Virginians, Pennsylvanians, New Yorkers, and New Englanders are no more," he concluded. "I am not a Virginian, but an American."

All in the Congress knew that they had taken their lives in their hands, and many doubtless shared the doubts of the great John Adams. Leaving Boston with his cousin, Sam Adams, that "hellhound of Sedition," John noted in his diary:

"There is one ugly reflection. Brutus and Cassius were conquered and slain. Hampden died in the field, Sidney on the scaffold, Harrington in jail, &c. This is cold comfort."

Wishing reconciliation and not revolution, led by the skillful John Dickinson of Pennsylvania, the moderates had control of the

Congress.* Bracing themselves to withstand and beat down the extreme proposals they expected from the "wild men" of Massachusetts, they were caught quite off balance when the high talk and bold proposals came from an entirely different quarter, from the wealthy, respectable, and ordinarily sedate gentlemen who represented the southern colonies.

Christopher Gadsden of South Carolina urged an immediate attack upon the British in Boston before their troops could be reinforced. Richard Henry Lee proposed a total boycott and wrote a rousing memorial to the "inhabitants of the British colonies." Patrick Henry declared that the empire was already dissolved, leaving the colonies in a "state of nature," so that they were free to make what decisions they pleased.

"There are some fine fellows come from Virginia," a Pennsylvanian observed, "but they are very high. The Bostonians are mere milk-sops to them."

But the Bostonians were not half as soppy as they seemed. Warned not to proceed too fast, they were content to remain quietly in the background. Though saying nothing publicly, their leaders had reached conclusions that would have shocked the Congress and sent most of its members running for cover.

"I expect no redress," John Adams confided to Patrick Henry, "but, on the contrary, increased resentment and double vengeance. We must fight!"

"By God, I am of your opinion," exclaimed Henry, the only man in the Congress who agreed with him, said Adams.

Led by Richard Henry Lee and Patrick Henry, "the Cicero and the other the Demosthenes of the age," aided by the quiet incessant work of George Washington—who seldom spoke but was, in Henry's opinion, "a man of more solid judgment and information than any man on that floor"—, the Congress voted to support Massachusetts' resistance to the "Intolerable Acts." It banned all trade with Britain and all consumption of British goods, a decree to be enforced by committees of "safety and inspection" to be

* The delegates, John Adams recorded, were "one third Tories, another Whigs, and the rest Mongrels."

elected by the people. Merchants were suspected, rightly, of having sabotaged previous boycotts.

At the same time, the members of the Congress adopted Dickinson's petition humbly begging their "Most Gracious Sovereign" to redress their injuries by turning out of office those "designing and dangerous men" who were bringing all to confusion. The Congress went out of its way to disclaim any thought of independence. The colonies had no other wish than to return to the ways of the "Old Empire," to the days of "salutary neglect" before 1763.

But on neither side was there any disposition to give way. The British ministry declined to bend before the rising storm. The colonies began to drill their militias, recruit volunteers, and collect arms—to the grave public and private concern of royal governors, none of whom had any sizable forces except General Gage at Boston.

With tension rising, another Virginia convention assembled at Richmond in March, 1775. Taking command as he always did in such assemblies, supported by Jefferson and Lee, Patrick Henry declared and the convention agreed that Virginia should be put "in a posture of defense," immediately, for there was not an hour to lose.

"*There is no longer any room for hope,*" Henry exclaimed. "If we wish to be free—if we mean to preserve inviolate those inestimable privileges for which we have been so long contending—if we mean not basely to abandon the noble struggle in which we have been so long engaged . . . —we must fight!—I repeat it, sir, we must fight!! An appeal to arms and to the God of hosts is all that is left to us! . . .

"They tell us, sir, that we are weak—unable to cope with so formidable an adversary. But when shall we be stronger? Will it be the next week, or the next year? Will it be when we are totally disarmed, and when a British guard shall be stationed in every house? Shall we gather strength by irresolution and inaction? Shall we acquire the means of effectual resistance by lying supinely upon our backs and hugging the delusive phantom of Hope, until our enemies shall have bound us hand and foot? . . . There is no retreat, but in submission and slavery! Our chains are forged, their clanking may be heard on the plains of Boston! The war is inevitable—and let it come! I repeat, sir, let it come!!

"It is in vain, sir, to extenuate the matter. Gentlemen may cry peace, peace—but there is no peace. The war is actually begun. The next gale that sweeps from the north will bring to our ears the clash of resounding arms. Our brethren are already in the field. Why stand we here idle? What is it that gentlemen wish? What would they have? Is life so dear, or peace so sweet, as to be purchased at the price of chains and slavery? Forbid it, Almighty God! I know not what course others may take; but as for me, give me liberty, or give me death."

As Jefferson remarked at this time, Henry "left us all far behind."

Alarmed by the proceedings at Richmond, fearing a raid on military stores, Lord Dunmore removed most of the powder from the magazine at Williamsburg, placing it on board an armed schooner anchored in the James. Militiamen and volunteers marched in force on Williamsburg, led by Patrick Henry, who sent forward a demand that the powder be restored.

Dunmore huffed and puffed, threatening to free the slaves and burn Williamsburg to the ground if any violence were offered. Finally, he agreed to pay £320 for the powder, twice what it was worth. As soon as Henry withdrew his troops, his Lordship pronounced him an outlaw, as Berkeley had outlawed Bacon under circumstances somewhat similar. Like Berkeley, too, Dunmore soon turned tail and fled, taking safe quarters on a man-of-war in the Chesapeake. As nothing could induce him to come ashore, the Burgesses named a Committee of Safety to act in his place.

The day before the removal of the powder, which almost provoked a shooting argument, a clash had occurred to the north, as Henry had predicted. On the night of April 18-19, 1775, General Gage marched his troops out of Boston hoping to surprise the town of Concord, seize military supplies hidden there, and arrest John Adams and John Hancock, reportedly in the neighborhood. But William Dawes and Paul Revere, the pony express of the Revolution and a fine silversmith, had anticipated the British, who at dawn came upon the minutemen of Lexington drawn up on the Green. The firing that began here continued all day as the British fought their way back to Boston with heavy loss from the sharp-shooting of "embattled farmers" who doggedly held on their flanks, sniping from behind rock walls and trees.

This was war, as the Second Continental Congress recognized when it met at Philadelphia a few weeks later, again with Peyton Randolph in the chair. After Lexington, minutemen from all parts of Massachusetts had swarmed to Boston, 18,000 strong, all eager to fight, but wanting supplies and organization. Other colonies were recruiting forces. All of these needed support. Above all, a top command was required to plan, guide, and coordinate action.

As John Dickinson and many more still hoped for peace and reconciliation, the Congress did not close the door on that possi-bility. Adopting Dickinson's "olive branch" petition,* it resolved at the same time that the "colonies be immediately put into a state of defence," taking over the Massachusetts forces as the first unit of a Continental Army, to be directed by a single com-mander-in-chief.

But who should be the commander was a touchy question. The colonies were all jealous of one another, quick to assert their prerogatives and prejudices. Would the troops of one colony obey a commander who came from another? It seemed doubtful if the commander came from Massachusetts.

John Adams, as usual, had anticipated events and already picked his man. He had watched him very carefully in the Con-gress, observing, in the words of another, that he was always "cool, like a Bishop at his prayers." He had talked to other dele-gates about him and was now convinced that he was the one man the Massachusetts troops would obey, and probably the only man that all of the colonies would follow.

Colonel George Washington was Adams' nomination, a choice which the Congress unanimously approved. Departing immedi-ately for Massachusetts, drawing up his horse under an elm in Brattle Square, Cambridge, the new general—just turned forty-

* London denounced it as an "insult and mockery."

three—drew his sword in sight of cheering troops and took command of the Continental Army that he would lead through terrible years to final victory at Yorktown.

Though hostilities had begun, the mention of independence was still taboo. It was a "Hobgoblin of so frightful Mien that it would throw a delicate Person into Fits to look it in the Face," in Adams' phrase. But it became clear early in 1776 that separation was not far off, especially after Tom Paine had blasted "Good King George," who had recently done himself a bad turn by denouncing his "loving" subjects as "traitors" deserving of the rope.

It was nonsense, ran Paine's *Common Sense* argument, to talk of going back to 1763, to the days of the "Old Empire." The colonies had to go forward and they would, but they had to have a goal. What could fire and unite them? Only one thing. The colonists had to have something worth fighting for—independence!

"Sound doctrine and unanswerable reasons!" Washington declared.

Britain had no sizable forces in the colonies except at Boston, and Washington now chased out General Gage and his soldiery and their Loyalist allies, who sailed away to Halifax. Lord Dunmore was still in the Chesapeake with a few small ships, bombarding towns, making occasional raids on the countryside, but he was not a threat, only a nuisance.

Early in 1776, Massachusetts informed her agents in Philadelphia that she would follow a move toward independence. In April, North Carolina instructed her delegates that they might concur in separation. Meeting at Williamsburg in May, a Virginia convention took action far beyond any measures yet taken elsewhere. It instructed its delegates in the Continental Congress not merely to support but propose independence. It declared the bonds with Britain "totally dissolved," adopted a Declaration of Rights and a constitution drafted largely by George Mason, proclaimed itself the free and independent Commonwealth of Virginia, and elected Patrick Henry as its first governor.

"Resolved," spoke Richard Henry Lee in the Continental Congress on June 7, carrying out his instructions, "that these united

Colonies are and of right ought to be free and independent States. . . ."

As the delegations of New York, New Jersey, Pennsylvania, Delaware, and South Carolina had no instructions on this question, the vote was postponed. Meantime, a proclamation of independence should be drafted, a task that fell to one of the younger members, Thomas Jefferson. Though only thirty-three, he was an old hand at drawing documents.

Secluding himself in his lodgings on Market Street, in the house of a brickmaker of German descent, Jefferson spent days writing, revising, and polishing, and then recasting the whole again, for he wished to make the document, he said, "an expression of the American mind"—and express that mind he did in one of the great declarations of the ages.

"I know only," said Jefferson in later years, "that I turned to neither book nor pamphlet while writing it. I did not consider it as any part of my charge to invent new ideas altogether, and to offer any sentiment which had never been expressed before."

When he had finished, he showed his paper to John Adams and Benjamin Franklin, who suggested a few slight changes, and on July 2nd the draft came before the Congress.

"When in the course of human events it becomes necessary for one people to dissolve the political bonds which have connected them with another," it began and went on, "We hold these truths to be self-evident: that all men are created equal; that they are endowed by their Creator with certain inalienable rights; that among these are life, liberty, and the pursuit of happiness. That, to secure these rights, governments are instituted among men, deriving their just powers from the consent of the governed; that, whenever any form of government becomes destructive of these ends, it is the right of the people to alter or abolish it, and to institute new government, laying its foundation on such principles, and organizing its powers in such form, as to them shall seem most likely to effect their safety and happiness . . ."

Shades of Marshal Dale, Sir John Harvey, and Sir William Berkeley!

This was not merely independence, this was revolution! And

attacks came from many sides, for the Congress was sharply divided. Some were afraid of the consequences. Others could not bear the thought of separation, the wrench of breaking old and familiar ties. John Dickinson led a determined rearguard action by the reconciliationists.

From whatever quarter the attacks came, John Adams rose and hurled them back, being the "main pillar of debate," as gratefully acknowledged by Jefferson, who hated to speak and almost never did, having the distinction of being probably the only great politician and statesman who did not like to hear himself talk.

For several days the debate raged, with most delegations split. Finally, on July 4th, the issue came to a vote, and the Declaration of Independence was adopted.*

No cheers echoed through Carpenters' Hall, for this was grim business. There were no parades, no firing of guns, no shouting and dancing in the streets. Not till July 8th was the Declaration publicly read, to a small, solemn, and doubtless worried crowd gathered in State House Yard, Philadelphia. All had good cause to worry, for on July 3rd Lord Howe had appeared off New York with a large force. But they had cause to rejoice, too.

Quietly, out of the travail of Virginia and all the colonies, a new nation, a new order, had been born.

* New York did not vote and did not formally join the new United States until July 15th.

Notes

Notes

Chapter I

1. Though England had long envied Spain her gold, silver, and other loot from the New World, she did little to gain herself a share of this treasure until 1576, when Sir Humphrey Gilbert published a *Discourse* that proved, to his satisfaction at least, that there existed a "passage by the Northwest to Cathay and the East Indies."

With this assurance, Captain Martin Frobisher dashed off in a "wild search for the northern El Dorado" and the "certain" passage to the elusive South Sea.

Two years later, in 1578, Gilbert sailed with a sizable fleet and brought back from Labrador some "black earth" that seemed to be gold. Hurriedly, a group of adventurers was organized, the Company of Cathay, for the discovery of the South Sea and the colonization of any "heathen lands not actually possessed of any Christian prince or people."

Sailing again in 1583 in five ships, Gilbert took out a large company that included "minerall men and refiners." Infection broke out in the fleet, many died, two of the vessels foundered, and nothing was accomplished. On the voyage home, two more vessels were lost, including the tiny *Squirrel* (10 tons), with Sir Humphrey on board.

Gilbert's patent to the unoccupied "heathen lands" in America passed into the hands of his renowned half-brother, Sir Walter Raleigh, who in 1585 sent out seven ships under his "noble and gallant" cousin, Sir Richard Grenville. Making his way into a large sound in what is now North Carolina, Grenville put more than a hundred settlers ashore on a small island in what had been named Virginia, for the Virgin Queen, Elizabeth.

A year on lonely Roanoke Island was quite enough for the colonists, who hitch-hiked a ride home with Sir Francis Drake on his return from a marauding expedition in the Caribbean.

The following year, in 1587, Raleigh sent out a larger expedition of almost 150 persons, including seventeen women and nine children, to found on Roanoke Island the "Citie of Ralegh in Virginia." As supplies soon ran short, Governor John White, a "skillful and ingenious Painter," sailed for England to obtain provisions. Raleigh dispatched two ships with supply, but these "betook themselves wholly to hunt after pillage upon the Spanish coast, . . . a common corruption of the time," and returned home without having been anywhere near Virginia.

The attack of the Spanish Armada now intervened to prevent, or at least to excuse, the sending of aid to those stranded at Roanoke. But there was no excuse for the long delay that ensued after the shattering defeat of the Armada. Three years passed before Governor White set sail, arriving at Roanoke after a leisurely voyage to find the "Citie of Ralegh" deserted.

On a tree had been carved the letters C R O A . . . , in Roman capitals. Assuming this to be part of a prearranged signal, White supposed that it referred to Croatan Island (now Ocracoke) some miles down the coast, where he hoped to find the company that he had left in distress four years before—a company that included his daughter Eleanor, the wife of Ananias Dare, an assistant governor, and the mother of the celebrated Virginia Dare, the first English child born on our shores.

But the entire company had vanished, and no trace has ever been found of the Lost Colony. Its tragic fate remains a mystery to this day.

2. That the ships must have put to sea and then turned back has never been noted, so far as I know, and it seems the only reasonable inference from the record.

George Percy states quite plainly, and others bear him out, that on "Saturday, the twentieth of December in the yeere 1606, the fleet fell from London, and the fifth of January we anchored in the Downes."

From London to the Downs is some seventy miles by sea, and it certainly did not take the ships almost two and a half weeks to sail that distance. If it did, Newport should have been cashiered at the start, which might have been a good thing in view of his subsequent blunders and want of judgment.

3. The "Maria" in his name caused many to suspect Wingfield of being a Roman Catholic, which he was not, though his father had been. Descended from a long line of distinguished soldiers, he was the son of Thomas-Maria Wingfield, who had been so christened with Cardinal Pole and Queen ("Bloody") Mary as his god-parents.

Chapter II

1. Of the 104 or 105 survivors, Smith listed the names and "qualitie" of eighty-two. Fifty-four of these—or 65 per cent—appear as "Gents." But it is doubtful if this high proportion held for the original company of "six score." But the "Gents." apparently constituted at least half the company, which was quite enough.

Chapter III

1. To explain Wingfield's charge, Smith's more adulatory and misguided biographers have invented for him a "walking tour" through the Emerald Isle, for which there is no evidence whatever.

Chapter IV

1. According to Thomas Hariot's account, the first party at Roanoke astonished the Indians with their "magic," finding that their "Compasses, Perspective Glasses, Burning Glasses, Clocks, Books, Writing, Guns, and other Instruments and Inventions so exceeded their capacities and amazed them that they thought them to be the works of Gods rather than men—or, at least, that the Gods had taught the English how to make them. This caused them to give great credit to whatever they said concerning God and religion."

When traveling about, Hariot would "show them the Bible and explain the contents: that in that Book was taught the true and only God, his Omnipotence, the Doctrine of Salvation by Jesus Christ." But he had to explain that there was no magic in the physical book, but only in the doctrines it contained, "for they paid their kind of Adoration to the Book by handling, hugging, and kissing it, and by applying it to their Head and Breast and stroking it over the other parts of their Body."

Chapter V

1. Spain claimed Virginia as part of Florida, having attempted a small settlement in the Chesapeake area as early as 1526. Even before the King had signed the Virginia patent, the Spanish ambassador in London was complaining about this trespass, reporting to Madrid that the leader in the business was Lord Chief Justice Popham, "a very great Puritan," who explained that he was undertaking it "in order to drive out from here thieves and traitors, to be drowned in the sea."

But the real reason for the Virginia business, the ambassador informed Philip III, was to establish a base "for privateering and making attacks upon the merchant fleets of Your Majesty. . . . It appears clearly to me now that it is not their intention to plant colonies, but to send out pirates from there, since they do not take women, but only men. . . . It is very desirable Your Majesty should command that such a bad project be uprooted while it can be done so easily. . . ."

Chapter VI

1. In addition to his unprovoked attacks upon the Indians at Kecoughtan and along the Chickahominy, Smith fell upon the local Paspahegh for "meddling" with him, giving them "such an incounter as some he so hunted up and downe the Ile, some he so terrified with whipping, beating, and imprisonment" that they quickly came begging for peace. The Council "would gladly have wrangled with Captaine Smith for his cruelty, yet none was slaine to any man's knowledge." Such truculence, however, did not lead to friendly relations.

On one occasion, Smith had an encounter with the chief of the Paspahegh, Wowinchapuncka, "a most strong stout Salvage," who picked up Smith, a much smaller man, and "bore him into the river, to have drowned him. Long they struggled in the water." Finally, two of the "Polanders" ran to Smith's rescue and aided him in locking up the chief as a prisoner. This was the story Smith told in his *Proceedings*

(1612). But when he came to repeat it in his *Generall Historie* (1624), he dropped the Poles and single-handedly overpowered the huge chief.

2. Writing in 1707, Virginia's first native-born historian, Robert Beverley, a student and observer of Indian ways, recorded that it was their hospitable custom to entertain important visitors with feasts and dancing "till Bed time, when a Brace of young Beautiful Virgins are chosen to wait upon him that night for his particular refreshment. These Damsels are to Undress this happy Gentleman and as soon as he is in bed, they gently lay themselves down by him, one on one side of him, and the other on the other. They esteem it a breach of Hospitality not to submit to everything he desires of them, . . . and the Young Women are so far from suffering in their Reputation from this Civility that they are envyed for it by all the other Girls. . . . Their Women are generally beautiful, possessing an uncommon delicacy of Shape and Feature."

This was high praise from one of the richest and most cultivated planters of his day, a brother-in-law of the elegant William Byrd II.

Chapter VIII

1. "It is true," reads Smith's *Proceedings* (1612), that "she was the very Nonparell of the kingdome and, at most, not past thirteen or fourteen yeares of age. Very oft she came to the fort with what she could get for Captaine Smith who ever loved and used 'all the Countrie well. But her especially he ever much respected, and she so well requited it that when her father intended to have surprised him, she by stealth in the darke night came through the wild woods and told him of it. . . . If he would, he might have married her, or have done what he listed. . . . But her marriage could no way have intitled him by any right to the kingdome, nor was it ever suspected he had ever such a thought. . . ."

Chapter X

1. The Pilgrims and the Puritans held only three services a week: morning and afternoon on Sundays—or the Sabbath, as they insisted upon calling it—and one every Thursday, which was Lecture Day. Though very zealous, the stiff-necked "Saincts" would certainly have

rebelled if they had been required to attend fourteen services a week. Nor did they enforce attendance by anything remotely resembling martial law. The worst that could befall a sinner was to be excommunicated from the "sweet" company of the Saints.

Though the penal code of the Massachusetts Bay Colony was rather severe, that of Plymouth was simple and, for its day, remarkably humane. The Pilgrims limited capital offenses to seven—treason, murder, witchcraft, adultery, rape, sodomy, and arson—and actually took life for only one, murder, though there was the case of an unhappy youth executed for sodomy.

2. On his way down the coast, Argall had discovered a great bay just above the Chesapeake. The northern cape at its entrance he christened Cape LaWarre. The cape lost its name, but the bay became known as the Delaware, giving its name in turn to a great river and later to a colony that became one of our original states, thus preserving the memory of one who does not deserve to be remembered for any part he played on our shores.

3. Under the new charter, the Company was to hold weekly meetings, or courts, for the conduct of ordinary business. But no decision on matters of importance was valid until it had been passed by one of the Company's great Quarter Courts, which met four times a year—at Hilary, Easter, Trinity, and Michaelmas.

Chapter XI

1. The Company subsequently "rated" Captain Newport's person and services at thirty-two shares ($20,000), little more than half of Dale's. The Company declined to "rate" Smith at all, as the Captain complained, declaring that he had never received a penny or any recognition for his services, whereas the Company was giving to many others, including always troublesome Captain Martin, many shares of stock and thousands of acres of land "in reward."

2. Dale had first taken a company down to explore the Nansemond where Captain Martin had lost so many men and deserted a part of his force two years before. The Indians were still hostile, wounding several, including Martin, who was acting as guide. But the Indians did no great harm because the English were wearing iron helmets and

coats of mail which Dale had brought from London. The Indians were quite mystified, according to George Percy, when they "did not see our men fall as they had done in other conflicts."

Puzzled, the Indians fell "into their exorcismes, conjuracyons, and charmes, throwing fyer upp into the skyes, runninge up and down with Rattles, and making many dyabolicall gestures with many inigramantcke [?] Spells and incantaciones."

And with "very remarkable" effects, said Percy, for while the Marshal and "some of the better sorte" were sitting in an Indian house, "a fantasy possessed them that they imagined the Salvages were sett upon them, eache man takinge one another for an Indyan, and so did fall pell-mell one upon another, beatinge one another downe and breakinge one another's heades. . . . Mutche mischiefe might have bene donn but that itt pleased God the fantasy was taken away whereby they had been deluded and every man understood his errour."

The Indians may have been using some very powerful charms in "making medicine," but this mad brawl rather suggests the always potent spell of firewater.

If the Indians were superstitious, the English were no less so, being quite convinced that the Indians had dangerous "witches" among them.

Chapter XII

1. At this time, in 1612, there was published Captain Smith's *A Map of Virginia, with a Description of the Countrey, . . . whereunto is Annexed the Proceedings of those Colonies, since their first departure from England. . . .* The *Proceedings,* as I have referred to this work throughout, incorporated Smith's *True Relation* (1608), with additions, subtractions, and amendments, plus accounts of events "taken faithfully, as they were written, out of the writings of . . . other diligent observers" who had been or still were in Virginia. The *Proceedings* carried events down to the arrival of Gates with his fleet of six vessels.

2. About this time, the Spanish ambassador in London informed Madrid that Virginia had "lost much ground, as it was sustained by companies of merchants who were disappointed at finding no gold or silver mines nor the passage to the South Sea which they had hoped for. They now fix their eyes upon the colony in Bermuda, partly be-

cause of its fertility and being unoccupied by savages so that they will meet with no opposition."

A few months later, he added that as the adventurers were "weary of spending so much money without any hope of reaping a profit because the soil produces nothing, they now think of carrying all the people that are there to Bermuda or to Ireland by the coming spring."

Chapter XIII

1. When Spain claimed all of America on the basis of Columbus' voyages, asserting that Virginia lay within its domain, England vehemently denied this, declaring that vast regions could not be roped off by mere paper claims, insisting that title to particular territory could be established only by actual or token occupation and possession. Now the shoe was on the other foot, and the English were asserting paper claims against the French on the basis of the voyages by the two Cabots.

2. This, in any case, is what Hamor soon published in his *True Discourse of the Present State of Virginia* (1614).

Before this, if a report of the Spanish ambassador in London can be credited, opinion in Virginia had been growing that "some of them should marry the women of the savages of that country . . . there are already forty or fifty thus married and . . . a zealous minister of their sect was seriously wounded in many places because he reprehended them." This report came from a man who had just returned from Virginia and "who tells me the truth," said the ambassador. The latter was usually very well informed, but there is no corroborative evidence for the report.

The historian Beverley later deplored that there had not been intermarriage from the start. "Intermarriage had been indeed the method proposed very often by the Indians in the beginning, urging it frequently as a certain rule that the English were not their Friends if they refused it. And I can't but think," said Beverley, "that it would have been happy for that Country had they embraced this proposal. For the jealousie of the Indians, which I take to be the cause of most of the Rapines and Murders they committed, would by this means have been altogether prevented and consequently the abundance of blood that was shed on both sides would have been saved; the great extremities they were so often reduced to, by which so many died, would not have happened; the Colony, instead of all those losses of men on both sides, would have been encreasing in Children to its advantage; . . . and in all likelihood many, if not most, of the Indians would have been converted to Christianity by this kind method. . . ."

Later, after Independence, the great Patrick Henry proposed intermarriage as the solution of a troublesome problem. Distressed by the sad plight of the Indians, he suggested that marriage between them and the whites should be encouraged by payment of a bounty at the time of marriage and at the birth of each child. Such unions should be exempt from certain taxes, and free schools should be provided for their children. His bill to accomplish this passed its second reading in the Virginia legislature, but was allowed to drop when Henry left the chamber to become governor for the second time.

Chapter XIV

1. This letter to the Queen and the story it contained first became known in 1624, eight years later, when Smith incorporated the letter in his *Generall Historie*. Many have expressed great skepticism about the letter and the Pocahontas story, insinuating and even directly charging that both are fabrications.

This seems unlikely. It is easier to believe that Smith wrote such a letter than that he faked it, especially as the Queen and King James were still alive when the letter appeared. Smith would certainly have been called to task if he had dared publish a fictitious letter to the Queen. Smith's enemies, who were legion, fired many charges at him, but none questioned the authenticity of the letter.

It is likewise easier to believe than to disbelieve the Pocahontas story. When the *Generall Historie* appeared, George Percy wrote a blistering criticism of Smith's many distortions of fact. Percy had been at Jamestown all the time that Smith was there and wrote from first-hand knowledge. He found the *Generall Historie* full of romancing about what Smith had done and accomplished, but he did not question the Pocahontas story. Nor did any other at the time.

Though Smith lied frequently, as is obvious, it is my feeling that Smith did not make up incidents out of whole cloth, that there was a basis of fact in everything he related, however much he embroidered his theme.

2. "After a modest salutation," said Smith, Pocahontas "turned about, obscured her face, as not seeming well contented," remaining so for several hours before she spoke:

"You did promise Powhatan what was yours should be his, and he the like to you. You called him father, being in his land a stranger, and by the same reason so must I do you."

When Smith protested against this because she was a "King's daughter," Pocahontas went on:

"You were not afraid to come into my father's country and caused fear in him and all his people (but me), and fear you here I should call you father. I tell you then I will, and you shall call me child, and so I will be forever and ever your countryman.

"They did tell us always you were dead, and I knew no other till I came to Plymouth. Yet Powhatan did command Uttamatomakkin to seek you and know the truth, because your countrymen will lie much."

Tomakin had also been commanded by Powhatan to get Smith's aid in obtaining an audience with God and with the King.

"Concerning God," said Smith, "I told him the best I could," informing Tomakin that he had already seen the King. Tomakin had been at Court but refused to believe that snivelling James was actually the King. Assured of this by Smith, he replied "very sadly: You gave Powhatan a white dog, which Powhatan fed as himself. But your King gave me nothing, and I am better than your white dog."

3. Under Governor Daniel Tucker, who had been Cape Merchant at Jamestown during the Starving Time, Bermuda was very harshly governed, "imitating divers orders used in Virginia by Sir Thomas Dale." Tucker hanged a Frenchman for making "distasteful" speeches and "oft executed with a bastinado amongst the poorer sort." In despair, five men built a small boat and ran out to sea, miraculously succeeding in reaching Ireland.

Tucker erred in taking the Company seriously when it urged the growth of more corn and other produce. He saw to it that this was done and for his pains lost his job, being dismissed as one "fitter to be a gardiner than a Governour." The Company, he was informed, wanted "commodities" for shipment home.

Chapter XV

1. In 1621, the Reverend Buck—"a verie good preacher," said Rolfe —was still trying to collect on the promises the Company had made him when he sailed for Virginia twelve years before. He wanted the money promised him, he wrote to Sir Edwin Sandys, "or els some

servants at ye Companie's charg, . . . having a charg of children to provide for & but one boy to be an helper to me in my busines. How precious therfor a few servants would be to me, I leave to your wise consideration."

But months passed with no sign of money or servants.

"I have no acquayntance about London to solicit my sute to you," Buck plaintively wrote Sandys. "Let my cause plead for itself. . . . I have sent to you a Copi of ye agreements which ye Company made with me, but as yet I have had little performed to me. Yet I am content so that I might have that mony which I have allredy payd & left in ye hands of ye Company, which, were it layd out in men, with ye other monies in provisions, would be a good estate for me & ye reliefe of my wife & Children, . . . & I shall be therby ye better incoraged to goe forward in ye work of ye Lord. . . ."

Chapter XVI

1. So the Latin legend ran in Stow's *Survey of London* (1632). The engraver of Smith's map appears to have made a mistake in inscribing the final adjective as "quintum," to agree with *regnum* (kingdom) understood.

In 1702, the "quintum" was changed to "quintam," to agree with *coronam* (crown) understood.

When the English and Scottish crowns were united in 1707, the "quintam" was changed to "quartam." The Virginia "cote" remained so down to 1776.

2. Writing more than a century later, a native Virginian, the Reverend William Stith, observed in his *History of the First Discovery and Settlement of Virginia* (1747): "And I cannot but remark how early that Custom arose of transporting loose and dissolute Persons to Virginia as a Place of Punishment and Disgrace, which, although originally designed for the Advancement and Increase of the Colony, yet has certainly proved a great Prejudice and Hindrance to its growth. For it hath laid one of the finest Countries in British America under the unjust Scandal of being a mere Hell upon Earth, another Siberia, and only fit for the Reception of Malefactors and the vilest of People. So that few People—or at least, few large Bodies of People—have been induced willingly to transport themselves to such a Place, and our younger Sisters, the Northern Colonies, have accordingly profited

thereby. For this is one Cause that they have outstripped us so much in the Number of their Inhabitants and in the Goodness and Frequency of their Cities and Towns."

3. Warwick appears to have made a business of privateering and had just recently been in trouble with the Privy Council when the East India Company complained that several of its ships had been plundered by one of his captains. In 1618, Warwick had taken the lead in organizing a company known as the Adventurers of London Trading to Africa. Ostensibly, the company was "to trade for gold." Actually, it aimed at breaking into the profitable slave trade. The mission of the *Treasurer* was related to this.

Chapter XVII

1. "Women are necessary members for the Colonye," a Virginia planted agreed, but "poore men are never the nearer for them, they are so well sould." Women should be sent not merely to be wives but to perform some useful general work. They might take in washing and tend the sick, he suggested to the Company, for "your poore Tenantes that have nothing, dye miserablie through nastiness, & many departe the World in their owne dung for want of help in their sickness. Wherefore, for prevention, I could wish women might be sent over to serve the Company for that purpose for certayne yeares, whether they marry or no, for all that I can find that the multitude of women doe, is nothing but to devoure the food of the land, without dooing any daye's deed whereby any benefitt may arise either to ye Company or Countrey."

Vagrants and "mayds" were also being shipped to Bermuda at this time, being "of such bad condition," according to the governor, "that it seemed they had picked the Males out of Newgate and the Females from Bridewell." Still, he decided "to grant out the women to such as were so greedy for wives and would needs have them—for better, for worse."

Two Indian "mayds" who had been in Pocahontas' train were among those sent out to be married in Bermuda so that "after they were converted and had children," they might be sent to Virginia to "civilize" their kindred there. One of the girls, evidently a sister of Pocahontas, was soon married "to as fitt and agreeable an husband as the place afforded, and the weddinge feast kept in the Governour's newe house and at his charge," with a hundred guests attending.

2. "So long as Captaine Nuse had anything, we had part," wrote one of the Captain's men. "But now all being spent and the people forced to live upon Oysters and Crabs, they became so fainte no worke could be done. And where the law was, 'no worke, no meat,' now the case is altered to 'no meat, no worke.' Some small quantitie of milke and rice the Captaine had of his owne, and that he would distribute gratis as he saw occasion. I say gratis, for I know no place else but it was sold for ready payment. Those eares of corne that had escaped till August, though not ripe by reason of the late planting, the very Dogs did repaire to the corne fields to seeke them, as did the men till they were hanged.

"And this I protest before God is true that I have related, not to flatter Nuse, nor condemne any, but all the time I have lived in Virginia I have not seen nor heard that any Commander hath taken such continuall paines for the publike or done so little good for himselfe. . . .

"For my owne part, although I found neither mulberries planted, houses built, men nor victuall provided as the honourable Adventurers did promise me in England, yet at my owne charge, having made these preparations and the silke wormes ready to be covered, all was lost. . . ."

Chapter XVIII

1. Under the bequest of "Dust & Ashes," instruction was to be given a "convenient nomber of younge Indians . . . in the readinge and understandinge the principalls of Xtian religion." They were to be taken at the age of seven, or younger, and schooled till they were twelve. They were then to be "trayned and brought up in some lawfull Trade, with all humanitie and gentleness," till they were twenty-one, at which time they should "enjoye like liberties and priveledges with our native English in that place."

In his will, Nicholas Ferrar, father of the Deputy Treasurer, left £300 to be paid to the college when "there shall be ten young Salvages placed in it." Meantime, the interest on the money should be "distributed unto three discreet and godly young men in the Colony to bring up three wilde young Infidels in some good course of life."

Other gifts had been made—some books, and a "Communion Cupp with a Cover and case, a Trencher plate for the Bread, a Carpett of

Crimson Velvett, a Linnen Damaske table cloth," for use in the college chapel.

2. That great cosmographer of the day, the Reverend Richard Hakluyt, did not share this view but warned the Company that it might have to beat God into the heads and hearts of the Indians. "To handle them gently, while gentle courses may be found to serve, . . . will be without comparison the best," he observed. "But if gentle polishing will not serve, we shall not want hammerers and rough masons enow—I mean our old soldiers trained up in the Netherlands —to square and prepare them to our Preachers' hands."

3. Jordan died a year later, and there was a rush for the hand of his young wife, led by the Reverend Greville Pooley. Jordan had been in his grave only a day or two when Pooley sent Captain Isaac Madison to plead his suit. Cicely replied that she would as willingly take Pooley as any other. But as she was pregnant, she would not engage herself, she said, "until she was delivered."

But the amorous Reverend could not wait and came a few days later with Madison, telling her "he should contract himself unto her —and spake these words—'I, Grivell Pooley, take thee, Sysley, to my wedded wife, to have & to hold till death us do part and, thereto, I plight thee my troth.' Then (holding her by the hand) he spake these words: 'I, Sysley, take thee, Grivell, to my wedded husband, to have & to hold till death us do part.' "

Cicely said nothing, but they drank to each other and kissed. Then evincing some delicacy about her situation and condition, she asked "that it might not be revealed that she did so soon bestow her love after her husband's death." Pooley promised but was soon boasting of his conquest, very foolishly, for "Sysley" now engaged herself to William Ferrar, one of the Deputy Treasurer's younger brothers.

Enraged, Pooley brought suit for breach of promise. The case was too much for the authorities at Jamestown, who referred it to London, meantime issuing a proclamation against "certain women within this Colony [who] have, of late, contrary to the laws ecclesiastical of the realm of England, contracted themselves to two several men at one time, whereby much trouble doth grow between parties. . . ." Ministers were ordered to give notice that whoever "shall use any words or speech tending to the contract of marriage, though not right and legal, yet may so entangle and breed struggle in their consciences, shall for the third [!!!] offense undergo either corporal punishment, or the punishment by fine or otherwise, according to the guilt of the persons so offending."

The jilted Pooley soon found solace in a bride, it appears, but met a tragic death in 1629 when Indians attacked his house and "slew him, his wife, and all his family."

Chapter XIX

1. This "assurance" about the South Sea was based upon (a) a "China Boxe" shown to some by the chief of the Potomac, and (b) a paper proving the existence of a North West Passage, written by "that learned Mathematician, Mr. Henry Briggs," a member of the Company. Briggs had demonstrated, to his and Waterhouse's satisfaction at least, that the South Sea lay not more than a few hundred miles away, sharply criticizing those who, "giving too much credit to our usuall Globes and Maps, doe dream of a large Continent . . . westward."

2. According to John Smith, though there is no evidence of this in the detailed Company records, the adventurers had turned to him for advice after the massacre. Smith proposed that he be given a hundred soldiers and thirty sailors to be employed as a "running Army . . . to inforce the Salvages to leave their Country or bring them to that feare and subjection that every man should follow his businesse securely." After that were done, the army could be settled somewhere in the colony as a permanent garrison.

As a means of financing this, Smith suggested that the Crown might remit customs duties and that taxes should be laid in Virginia. For himself, he asked nothing, he said, "but what I can produce from the proper labour of the Salvages."

Many liked this proposal "exceedingly well," according to Smith, but the adventurers were so divided that he could "obtaine no answer but this: the charge would be too great, their stock was decayed, they did thinke the Planters should doe that of themselves if I could find meanes to effect it."

Chapter XX

1. The papers surrendered to the Privy Council have disappeared. Fortunately, many of them were copied and, after remarkable travels,

now lie in the Library of Congress, which has made them generally available by publishing them under the brilliant editorship of the late Susan Myra Kingsbury. For a fascinating account of the Company records and others that have been preserved, see the Introduction to Volume I of the *Records of the Virginia Company* (Washington, 1906).

2. According to Smith, though again there is no corroborative evidence, the Virginia commissioners turned to him for suggestions and advice, asking him seven questions.

The colony had not made headway, he replied, because of "idlenesse and carelessnesse," which, within six months of his departure, had destroyed everything he had accomplished. Only tobacco was grown because the Company declined to set a sufficient price on corn, so that all were forced to grow tobacco—which was true. The massacre had resulted from "want of marshal discipline" and from teaching the Indians the use of firearms, which had not occurred during his command in the colony.

All would have been well in Virginia if he had been given £20,000 ($1,000,000) to hire "good labourers and mechanicall men and have furnished them with cattle and all necessaries, and a hundred of them would have done more than a thousand of those that went, though Lord La Warr, Sir Ferdinando Waynman, Sir Thomas Gates, and Sir Thomas Dale were perswaded to the contrary. But when they tried, they confessed their errour."

The present remedy was to spend £5,000 ($250,000) to send out "Souldiers and all sorts of labourers, and necessaries for them." Nor were matters helped by the "multiplicity of opinions here and of Officers there," nor by those adventurers who were anxious to employ their ships, "having £6 ($300) for every passenger and £3 for every tun of goods," so that their ships were "so pestered as occasions much sicknesse, disease, and mortality, for though all the passengers die, they are sure of their fraight."

At this time, Smith published his *Generall Historie*, saying that he had been asked by the Company "to doe it," for which there is also no evidence. But that does not matter. Without Smith's writings, unreliable as they often are, the history of early Virginia would be bare indeed.

Smith had previously made what is probably his major contribution to the settlement of America, setting forth his important explorations of the northern Atlantic coast in *A Description of New England* (1616), which contained a remarkably accurate map of the region. The Pilgrims had studied it attentively and had it with them when they made their landfall at Cape Cod late in 1620.

Smith had suggested to the Pilgrims that he should be taken along to guide and advise them. But the Pilgrims were not interested, declaring that it was cheaper to buy his book and map than to hire him, with the result, said Smith, that their "humorous ignorances caused them for more than a year to endure a wonderful deal of misery with infinite patience, . . . thinking to find things better than I advised them."

But it is probably just as well for Smith that he did not go, for if he had carried on at Plymouth as he did at Jamestown, rashly going his own way, scorning all advice and criticism, his measure and his head would quickly have been taken by a hot-headed captain of equal mettle, one who would have been more than a match for him, Captain Myles Standish, commander-in-chief of the Pilgrim forces, another hard-bitten graduate of that "universitie of the warres," the Netherlands. The Pilgrims had "garboile" enough as it was.

Interested in Virginia and New England to the last, his offers of service ignored, Smith became poorer and poorer and more embittered. In 1630, the Earl of Kildare wrote that he had living with him a Captain Smith, "who, through unfortunate disasters in his Majesty's service, is a subject of pity." The next year, at the age of fifty-one, Smith died at the house of Sir Samuel Saltonstall in London and was buried nearby in St. Sepulchre Church, which stood "next to a fair and large inn, without Newgate, called the Saracen's Head," according to E. D. Neill, "and here Smith in the poverty of his last days may often have lounged, an appropriate place to tell the story of his taking three Turks' heads."

Chapter XXI

1. The first judicial support of slavery in Virginia, except as punishment for crime, was given in 1654. Curiously, the case involved a free Negro planter who sued to have a Negro servant returned to him, saying that "hee had ye Negro for his life," to which the Court agreed. For an informative and fascinating book on the subject, see *The Negro in Virginia* (New York, 1940), a work of the Virginia Writers' Project.

2. Speaking of Virginia as he knew it almost a century later, the historian Robert Beverley wrote: the "Liberty of taking up land, and the ambition each man had of being Lord of a vast though unimproved territory, together with the advantage of the many rivers which afforded a commodious road for shipping at every man's door, has made the country fall into such an unhappy settlement and course of trade that, to this day [1722], they have not any one place of cohabitation among them that may reasonably bear the name of a Town."

Chapter XXIII

1. "This King in Smith's history is called brother to Powhatan," wrote Robert Beverley, "but by the Indians he was not so esteemed. For they say he was a Prince of a Foreign Nation and came to them a great way from the South-West. And, by their accounts, we suppose him to have come from the Spanish Indians somewhere near Mexico, or the mines of St. Barbe."

Curiously, Hamor had long before reported that Powhatan was of "foreign" extraction, that his father had come from the West Indies, having been driven from there by the Spanish.

2. Puritanism had been strong in Bermuda from the start, through the influence of the Earl of Warwick, who had large holdings there. There was great objection to the Anglican rite and particularly to the Book of Common Prayer. Governor Butler worked out a compromise, introducing the liturgy used on the islands of Jersey and Guernsey, "being one and the very same with that of the French Protestants, those of the United Provinces [the Netherlands], and even Geneva itself." He translated the liturgy himself "out of a French Bible which he had brought over with him."

The Reverend Patrick Copland, who had done so much for the ill-fated college at Henrico, migrated to Bermuda in 1626. Early in 1643, Copland and his congregation left the Anglican Church and organized themselves as Independents in accordance with the Pilgrim and Massachusetts Puritan rite.

3. Virginia had never ceased protesting Lord Baltimore's grant and soon exerted considerable pressure in London to have Maryland returned and incorporated as part of the colony, to be governed from Jamestown. But with characteristic astuteness, the second Lord Balti-

more beat off this attack in spite of the fact that he was suspected by both of the contending parties at home.

Chapter XXVI

1. Of the contemporary narratives of Bacon's Rebellion, the best of them, in my opinion, is this one by T. M. (Thomas Mathew, probably), though it was written thirty years after the events. As a member of the House of Burgesses, he knew what was going on in front of the scenes and behind the scenes as well. A mild Baconite, he took a very objective view both of the rash young rebel and the irrational and senile Berkeley. He did not share Bacon's bitter and revengeful attitude toward the Indians though he had suffered much at their hands.

2. The writ for the election of the first House of Burgesses in 1619 stipulated that its members should be chosen by the "inhabitants," but this term should not be taken literally. Indentured servants and women were certainly not regarded as "inhabitants" in this sense. The franchise was limited to freemen. Under the Commonwealth, an Assembly had passed and then quickly repealed a law limiting the franchise to householders. In words quoted more than a century later by George Mason during the fight for Independence, the Assembly declared that it was "something hard and unagreeable to reason that any person should pay equal taxes and yet have no vote in elections."

The franchise was again limited under Berkeley when the Assembly decreed that only landowners and householders should "have a voice in the election of any Burgesses in this country, and that the election shall be at the Court House"—where the land titles could be consulted.

Though repealed during Bacon's Rebellion, this act was soon restored, and in 1733 the franchise was further restricted when the Assembly decreed that "no free negro, mulatto, or Indian whatsoever shall have any vote at the election of Burgesses or any other election whatsoever."

When this bill came before the Board of Trade and Plantations for review, the counsel of the Board urged that it be vetoed. "I cannot see why one freeman should be used worse than another merely on account of his complexion," he argued. "It cannot be right to strip all free persons of a black complexion from those rights which are so justly valuable to any freeman." But the Board allowed the bill to stand.

Chapter XXVII

1. Slavery dried up the stream of white indentured servants who during the later part of the seventeenth century had been coming at the rate of several thousand a year. But some unwelcome white servants were received—prisoners from British jails.

Before and after the dissolution of the Company, a relatively small number of convicts had been dumped into the colony at the order of the Crown, but Virginia succeeded in putting a stop to that in 1670.

In 1717, however, Parliament forced the colony to open its doors to those convicted of certain crimes. Formerly a discretionary matter, banishment was now written into the law as a regular mode of punishment. Down to the Revolution, which forced Britain to look elsewhere for a penal colony—Australia was chosen for the purpose—, some 20,000 convicts and loose women "from Bridewell, Turnbull Street, and such like places of education" were shipped to Virginia. There they were sold as servants under indentures of seven years for minor offenders and of fourteen years for those guilty of serious crimes.

"Thou art called our Mother Country," the *Virginia Gazette* protested in 1751. "But what Mother ever sent Thieves and Villains to accompany her children? . . . In what can Britain show a more Sovereign contempt for us than by emptying their jails into our settlements—unless they would likewise empty their Jakes on our tables!"

In his *Moll Flanders* (1722), Defoe had that celebrated trollop shipped to Virginia for her sins and trumperies.

2. For two excellent books on the Virginia land and labor system, see Thomas Jefferson Wertenbaker's *Planters of Colonial Virginia* (Princeton, 1922) and *The Old South* (New York, 1942).

Chapter XXVIII

1. A small party did a little exploring in 1643, and another in 1653, under William Claiborne. In 1668, Berkeley rode out with an expedition to find the South Sea but soon turned back, because "of rain." A German physician, John Lederer, explored the headwaters of the York in 1669 and the next year proceeded southwest into Carolina from the Falls on the James. In 1671, Berkeley sent four men "for ye finding out of the ebbing and flowing of ye waters behind the

mountains in order to make the discovery of the South Sea." This party penetrated to the Ohio River watershed. With that, exploration ceased for almost a half century, except on the part of trappers and Indian traders, who kept what they learned to themselves, having no desire to see the country settled.

2. A Virginia planter, Colonel Mercer, came back from London with a prized commission as stamp master in his pocket. Arriving in Williamsburg, he found himself hanging in effigy and his father writing in the *Virginia Gazette* against the stamp "tyranny." As the General Court was in session, the town was crowded. When some proposed taking the Colonel in hand, the stamp master ran to submit his resignation to Governor Fauquier, who refused to accept it. Taking another look at the angry crowd, Mercer solemnly promised that he would not use his commission and became a hero, being carried through the streets in a great demonstration. That night, with bells ringing and the town illuminated, Williamsburg enjoyed a "splendid" victory ball, drinking many toasts to the Colonel. But the "noble" stamp master was uneasy and went to London as soon as he could, "on business."

Selective Bibliography

Selective Bibliography

As the basic materials on colonial Virginia are voluminous and widely scattered, it is very difficult to draw up a list that might be of interest and use to a general reader who wished to do some exploration for himself.

For that purpose, there is no point in listing the *Calendar of State Papers, Colonial Series, America and West Indies, 1574-1733,* in forty volumes, or the *Journals of the Commissioners for Trade and Plantations, 1704-82,* in sixteen volumes, or the *Journals of the House of Burgesses, 1619-1776,* in thirteen volumes, or W. W. Hening's *Statutes at Large, 1619-1808,* in thirteen volumes.

Nor shall I list the many informative articles to be found in the *Virginia Historical Register,* the *Virginia Magazine of History and Biography, Tyler's Quarterly Historical and Genealogical Magazine,* or *William and Mary College Quarterly Historical Magazine.* All but the most recent of the articles in these can be run down by consulting E. G. Swem's *Virginia Historical Index,* 2 vols., 1934-6.

Fortunately, a few useful compilations of original materials have been made. For the earliest period, there are these:

1. *The Genesis of the United States,* by Alexander Brown (Boston, 1891). This is an invaluable reproduction of Virginia records from

the beginning to 1617—official and unofficial letters, instructions from London, reports from Jamestown, Spanish dispatches on the Virginia business, reproductions or abstracts of Company tracts, etc. It also contains a very useful appendix of "Brief Biographies" of the chief actors in the foundation of Virginia, both of those in London and Jamestown.

2. *Narratives of Early Virginia, 1606-1625,* by Lyon Gardiner Tyler (New York, 1907). This contains Smith's writings on Virginia, *Observations* by George Percy, La Warr's *Relation,* letters of Don Diego de Molina and Father Pierre Biard, the proceedings of the first Virginia Assembly in 1619, the "Virginia Planters' Answer to Captain Butler" (1623), the "Tragical Relation of the Virginia Assembly" (1624), and the "Discourse of the Old Company" (1625).

3. *Records of the Virginia Company,* by Susan Myra Kingsbury (Washington, 1906-1933). Vols. 1 and 2 contain the minutes of the meetings of the Virginia Company from April, 1619, to its dissolution in 1624. Vols. 3 and 4 contain invaluable letters, orders, memoranda, etc., from 1607 to 1624.

4. *Captain J. Smith's Works,* by Edward Arber (Birmingham, 1884), contains all of Smith's writings, plus George Percy's *Observations,* a "Discourse" by Edward-Maria Wingfield, a *Relation* of the first expedition up the James, a *Relation* by Henry Spelman, and some letters by Gabriel Archer, John Ratcliffe, and others on events during the colony's first years.

Unfortunately, such useful collections do not exist for the years after 1624. Nor is there any general history of colonial Virginia that is at once readable, informed, and perceptive. The best, in my opinion, is that of a British scholar, J. A. Doyle, *The English in America: Virginia, Maryland, and the Carolinas* (London, 1882). The single volume that tells the most and best gives the "feel" of Virginia, both early and late, is (American Guide Series) *Virginia, a Guide to the Old Dominion* (New York, 1940).

As for the rest, perhaps the following selective list of more available works may serve some purpose.

I. DOWN TO 1625

Brown, Alexander. *The First Republic in America.* Boston, 1898.

Craven, Wesley F. *The Dissolution of the Virginia Company.* New York, 1932.

Jourdan, Sylvestre. *A Discovery of the Barmudas, Otherwise called the Ile of Divels* (in Force's *Tracts*, vol. 3). London, 1610.

Lorant, Stefan. *The New World.* New York, 1946. A fine book on the Roanoke colony, reproducing original materials, including Governor White's paintings.

Neill, Edward D. *History of the Virginia Company of London.* Albany, N. Y., 1869.

Percy, George. *Observations* (in Arber and Tyler listed above).

———. "*Trewe Relacyon of the Procedeinges and Ocrentes of momente which have hapened in Virginia* (from Gates' shipwreck on Bermuda to Percy's departure in 1612; appears in *Tyler's Quarterly Historical and Genealogical Magazine,* April, 1922).

Stith, William. *The History of the First Discovery and Settlement of Virginia* [1606-1624]. Williamsburg, 1747.

Strachey, William. *The First Decade of the Historie of Travaile into Virginia Britannia.* London, 1612.

Virginia Company, publications of. (Many of these appear in full or in part in Alexander Brown's *Genesis*—see above.)

Wodenoth, Arthur. *A Short Collection of the Most Remarkable Passages from the original to the dissolution of the Virginia Company.* London, 1651.

II. FROM 1625 TO 1676

Alvord, Clarence W., and Lee Bidgood. *Travels in Virginia* [1650-1674]. Cleveland, 1912.

Berkeley, Sir William. *Discourse and View of Virginia.* London, 1662.

Ferrar, Virginia. *The Reformed Virginian Silk Worm.* London, 1655.

Gatford, Lionel. *Publick Good without Private Interest.* London, 1657.

Green, Robert. *Virginia's Cure, or an Advisive Narrative concerning Virginia* (in Force's *Tracts*, vol. 3). London, 1662.

Hammond, John. *Leah and Rachel, or the Two Fruitful Sisters, Virginia and Mary-land.* London, 1656.

Neill, Edward D. *Virginia Carolorum* [1625-1685]. Albany, N. Y., 1886.

Norwood, Colonel Henry. *A Voyage to Virginia* (in Force's *Tracts*, vol. 3). London, 1651.

Plantagenet, Beauchamp (Sir Edmund Plowden). *Description of the Province of New Albion* (in Force's *Tracts*, vol. 1). London, 1642.

Shrigley, Nathaniel. *True Relation of Virginia and Maryland.* London, 1669.

Virginia and Maryland, or the Lord Baltimore's Printed Case Uncased and Answered (in Force's *Tracts*, vol. 2). London, 1655.

Wodenoth, Richard. *A Perfect Description of Virginia.* London, 1649.

III. BACON'S REBELLION

Andrews, Charles M. *Narratives of the Insurrections, 1675-1690.* New York, 1915.

Anon. *A Narrative of the Indian and Civil Wars in Virginia in the Years 1675 and 1676* (in Force's *Tracts,* vol. 1).

Anon. *Strange News from Virginia, Being a full and true Account of the Life and Death of Nathaniel Bacon, Esquire.* London, 1677.

————. *More News from Virginia, 1677: A Further Account of Bacon's Rebellion.* Charlottesville, Va., 1943 (facsimile reprint).

Cotton, Mrs. Ann. *An Account of our Late Troubles in Virginia* (in Force's *Tracts,* vol. 1). Richmond, 1804.

T. M. *The Beginning, Progress, and Conclusion of Bacon's Rebellion* (in Force's *Tracts,* vol. 3). Richmond, 1804.

Wertenbaker, Thomas Jefferson. *Torchbearer of the Revolution.* Princeton, 1940.

IV. FROM 1676 TO 1776

Beatty, R. C. *William Byrd of Westover.* Boston, 1932.

Beverley, Robert. *The History and Present State of Virginia.* 2nd rev. ed. London, 1722.

Bland, Richard, *An Introduction into the Rights of the British Colonies.* Williamsburg, 1766.

Boucher, Jonathan. *A View of the Causes and Consequences of the American Revolution.* London, 1797.

Clayton, John. *A Letter to the Royal Society* (in Force's *Tracts,* vol. 2). London, 1688.

Conway, Moncure Daniel. *Barons of the Potomack and the Rappahannock.* New York, 1892.

Eckenrode, H. J. *The Revolution in Virginia.* New York, 1926.

Fithian, Philip Vickers. *Journal and Letters, 1767-1774.* 2 vols. Princeton, 1900-1934. An intimate description of the manner of life among the Grandees.

Hartwell, Henry, et al. *The Present State of Virginia and the College* (1697). London, 1727.

Jefferson, Papers of. vols. 1-2. Ed. by Julian P. Boyd, Princeton, 1950-51.

Jones, Hugh. *The Present State of Virginia.* London, 1724.

Lee, Edmund Jennings. *Lee of Virginia.* Philadelphia, 1895.

Lee, Richard Henry. *Letters of Richard Henry Lee, 1762-1794.* 2 vols. New York, 1914.

Malone, Dumas. *Jefferson, the Virginian.* New York, 1948.

Maury, Ann. *Memoirs of a Huguenot Family.* New York, 1872.

Nock, Albert Jay. *Jefferson.* New York, 1926.

Rowland, Kate Mason. *The Life of George Mason, 1725-1792.* 2 vols. New York, 1892.

Tyler, Lyon Gardiner. *Williamsburg, the Old Colonial Capital.* Richmond, 1907.

Wirt, William. *Sketches of the Life and Character of Patrick Henry.* Philadelphia, 1817.

V. GENERAL

Bruce, Philip Alexander. *Economic History of Virginia in the Seventeenth Century*. 2 vols. New York, 1896.

———. *History of Virginia* (vols. 1 and 2). New York, 1924.

———. *Institutional History of Virginia in the Seventeenth Century*. 2 vols. New York, 1910.

———. *Social Life of Virginia in the Seventeenth Century*. Lynchburg, Va., 1927.

Brydon, George Maclaren. *Virginia's Mother Church*. Richmond, Va., 1948.

Burk, John. *History of Virginia*. 4 vols. Petersburg, Va., 1804-16.

Craven, Wesley. *The Southern Colonies in the Seventeenth Century*. Baton Rouge, La., 1949.

Dorfman, Joseph. *The Economic Mind in American Civilization*. New York, 1946. Indispensable for anyone who would understand our colonial beginnings and what we have become.

Federal Writers' Project. *Maryland* (American Guide Series). New York, 1940.

———. *The Negro in Virginia*, New York, 1940. An invaluable and fascinating account of all aspects of Negro life in Virginia down to the present day.

Goodwin, Edward Lewis. *The Colonial Church in Virginia*. London, 1927.

Jefferson, Thomas. *Notes on the State of Virginia*. Paris, 1784.

Meade, William. *Old Churches, Ministers and Families of Virginia*. 2 vols. Philadelphia, 1931.

Miller, John C. *Origins of the American Revolution*. Boston, 1943.

Neill, Edward D. *English Colonization of America during the Seventeenth Century*. London, 1871.

———. *History of Education in Virginia during the Seventeenth Century*. Washington, 1867.

Robert, Joseph Clarke. *The Tobacco Kingdom*. Durham, N. C., 1938.

Smith, Abbott Emerson. *Colonists in Bondage: White Servitude and Convict Labor in America 1607-1776*. University of North Carolina Press, 1947.

Stanard, Mary Newton. *The Story or Virginia's First Century*. New York, 1928.

Umbreit, Kenneth. *Founding Fathers*. New York. 1941.

Wertenbaker, Thomas Jefferson. *Planters of Colonial Virginia*. Princeton, 1922.

———. *The Old South*. New York, 1942.

———. *Virginia under the Stuarts*. Princeton, 1914.

Wright, Louis B. *The First Gentlemen of Virginia*. New York, 1940.

Index

Index

South Virginia Company, 8

Southampton, Earl of, 124, 204, 213-14, 225, 251

Spain, 62, 92, 139-40, 184; reports on Virginia, 152-3, 380, 383-4; and Somers Island Company, 180; claim to Virginia, 380

Sparrow, 95

Spelman, Henry, 99; brings message from Powhatan, 109; sentenced to slavery, 192; food expedition to Potomac Indians, 248

Spence, William, 169

"Spirits," 314

Spotswood, Alexander, 351; expedition into Shenandoah Valley, 353

Stamp Act, 356-60; repealed, 360

Stamp Act Congress, 360

Standish, Myles, 393

Star, 134

Star Chamber, 284

Starving Time, 59, 107, 110-11, 114-15

Stegg, Thomas, 298

Stephens, Richard, 277

Stephens, Samuel, 316

Stith, William, 387-8

Stockden, John, 231

Stone, William, 292

Strafford, Earl of, 284

Studley, Thomas, 35, 37; death, 38

Stukley, Lewis, 177

Sugar Act, 356

Surveyor General, 227

Susquehanna River, 21

Susquehannock Indians, 65, 320-2

Swallow, 109-10

Syms, Benjamin, 344

Syms-Eaton Academy, 344

T

Taxation, 347, 356; in Maryland, 312; in Virginia, 246, 299, 315; in Virginia, under charter of 1676, 318; in Virginia, under Culpeper, 339; in Virginia, under Howard, 342; Stamp Act, 356-60

Tempest, The, 112

Third Supply, 87; leaves England, 94; conditions aboard ships, 94; first ships arrive at Jamestown, 95; "hurycano," 95; "wicked Impes," 96; departs Jamestown for England, 102; arrives in England, 105

Thorpe, George, 230-1; and Opechancano, 232

Tiger, 248-9

T. M., 327, 395; *see also* Bacon's Rebellion

Tobacco, 21, 177, 181, 205, 223-4, 249; Rolfe's experiments, 163; importance to colonists, 178, 191-2; James I on, 219-20; profits in, 225-6; planting prohibited in England and Wales, 252; importance in economy, 267-8; fall in price, 301, 311, 340; expansion of economy, 314; destroyed in Tobacco Rebellion, 341

Tobacco Rebellion, 341

Toleration Act, 292

Tomakin, 386

Tories, 362

Townshend Acts, 361

Tragical Relation, 259

Treasurer, 156-60, 211-12, 255, 388; under command of Rich, 184; *see also* Piracy

Treasurer in Virginia, 227

Trial, 146

Triumvirate, *see* Mutinies

True and Sincere Declaration, A, 106-7

True Declaration, A, 130, 135

True Discourse of the Present State of Virginia, 384

True Relation, A, 45, 63